Essential
Family
Favourites

Essential
Family
Favourites

Over 500 delicious step-by-step recipes

Love Food™ is an imprint of Parragon Books Ltd

Parragon
Queen Street House
4 Queen Street
Bath BA1 1HE, UK

Love Food™ and the accompanying heart device is a trade mark of
Parragon Books Ltd

ISBN 978-1-4075-0510-7

Design by Fiona Roberts
Cover artwork by Diana Birkett
Line illustrations by Victoria Mitchell
Editor: Fiona Biggs

Printed in China

Notes for the Reader

This book uses metric and imperial measurements. Follow the same
units of measurement throughout; do not mix metric and imperial. All spoon
measurements are level, unless otherwise stated: teaspoons are assumed to
be 5 ml, and tablespoons are assumed to be 15 ml. Unless otherwise stated,
milk is assumed to be whole, eggs and individual fruits such as bananas
are medium, and pepper is freshly ground black pepper.

Recipes using raw or very lightly cooked eggs should be avoided by
infants, the elderly, pregnant women, convalescents and anyone suffering
from an illness. Pregnant and breast-feeding women are advised to
avoid eating peanuts and peanut products.

Contents

* * *

Introduction

Whenever you flick through a magazine, listen to the radio or watch daytime television, you will be bombarded by the message that home-cooked food using fresh ingredients is both nutritious and tasty. However, the two things that the media fail to mention – and they are just as important – is that preparing family meals yourself is actually very easy to do and is immensely satisfying. It is also easy to see that home cooking is more economical than buying prepared or takeaway meals and, of course, the dishes contain no artificial additives.

Nevertheless, it is hard to juggle the various demands of work and family life and finding time to cook can be a real problem. It is sometimes difficult and time-consuming even to decide what to cook in the first place. This vast collection of superb recipes is the solution.

When inspiration deserts you, simply browse through the pages until a recipe catches your eye and tempts your appetite. There are so many delicious dishes to choose from that you are sure to find exactly the right one, whatever the occasion and time of year. From salads to stews and from pasta to desserts, there is something to suit all ages and tastes. It is simplicity itself to mix and match the recipes to create a special celebratory meal, select a filling one-pot dish for a midweek dinner, or find a speedy snack for a weekend lunch. There are comfort foods and familiar favourites as well as some new dishes that are destined to become popular additions to the family menu.

The usefulness of this essential cookbook extends far beyond the profusion of bright ideas and the huge number of meal options. Clear step-by-step instructions make the recipes easy to follow even if you are a

✳ ✳ ✳

complete beginner. Each stage of preparation and cooking is explained in a logical and straightforward way so that there are no nasty surprises halfway through and no confusion that might lead to disappointment.

As there are so many recipes to choose from they have been divided into five chapters to help you find exactly the one you want. **Starters & Snacks** includes a fabulous array of hot and cold dishes featuring a huge range of ingredients – vegetables, cheese, mushrooms, fish and shellfish, meat and poultry, and fruit. More substantial but still light dishes, such as fritters, omelettes, soufflés and tarts, make great snacks and easy lunches.

Soups & Salads will prove a revelation for anyone who thought making soup was a time-consuming chore. This chapter is packed with mouthwatering, yet easy-to-prepare recipes for light summer soups, winter warmers, tempting first courses and meal-in-a-bowl broths. The salads, inspired by recipes from around the world, will also be an eye-opener. There are side salads and light lunches and both cold and warm salads. Some are based on rice, pasta and grains, others on vegetables and fruit, and still more on cheese, fish, meat and poultry – without a limp lettuce leaf in sight.

Main Dishes is the chapter at the heart of the book, just as they are at the heart of family meals and, once again, the variety of recipes is enormous. Not only can you choose from an array of dishes based on poultry, meat, fish, seafood, beans and pulses, vegetables or cheese, but also from an inspiring assortment of flavours. Without leaving your kitchen you can travel the culinary globe with delicate Italian risotto, spicy Mexican chilli, warming French stew, crisp Chinese stir-fry and piquant Louisiana prawns.

A glance through **Vegetables & Accompaniments** will fill you with enthusiasm for clever ways to make sure your family eats plenty of healthy vegetables. Greens have never tasted so good, carrots so crisp or beans so beautiful. There's a host of delicious potato recipes to satisfy the heartiest appetite or you can ring the changes with rice and noodle dishes that range from the delicately perfumed to the fiercely fiery. This chapter also includes fabulous breads and rolls that are much easier to make than you think, plus dips, sauces and salsas to add that extra special touch to family meals.

Baking & Desserts is the chapter for those with a sweet tooth or who want a special treat for a celebration. Home baking is always rewarding and the recipes include quick-and-easy cakes, muffins and biscuits, as well as fabulous fruit and savoury breads and scones. If they're not already family favourites, they soon will be. Finally, there are hot and cold desserts for every occasion, from a refreshing fruit salad to home-made ice cream and from luscious cheesecake to melt-in-your-mouth pie.

✢ ✢ ✢

Preparation & Cooking Techniques

Do not be daunted by all the different food preparation and cooking techniques and descriptions used in this book. The range of definitions given here will be all you will need.

Baking This is the term used for cooking food in the oven by dry heat.

Baking blind This means baking pastry cases without a filling. The quiche tin or pie dish is lined with pastry and then lined with baking paper or foil, which is then weighed down with baking beans. The beans and paper are then removed and the pastry case cooked for a while longer to dry it thoroughly.

Basting The process of moistening meat, fish or poultry while roasting in the oven. The cooking juices are spooned over the food to keep it moist, to add flavour and to improve the appearance of the finished dish.

Beating This term refers to mixing food to make it lighter by incorporating air or to make the consistency smooth and remove any lumps.

Blanching This means immersing food in boiling water briefly and then into ice water. This may be done to remove the skins of tomatoes or nuts, for example, or to prepare vegetables for freezing. Blanching also helps to preserve the colour of vegetables.

Blending Blending means combining ingredients, usually with a spoon. Blending also refers to mixing soups and purées in a blender to reduce to a smooth liquid and remove any lumps.

Boiling This is cooking food in a liquid (water, stock or milk) at 100°C/212°F (known as boiling point).The main foods cooked in this way are eggs, vegetables, rice and pasta.

Braising A long, slow method of cooking used for cuts of meat and poultry that are too tough to roast.

Casseroling Another, more modern, name for braising, taken from the name of the cooking vessel – an ovenproof casserole dish with a tight-fitting lid.

Cutting Cutting is a basic technique used to prepare meat, fruit and vegetables. A good knife and a firm board are essential.

Chopping This is one step on from cutting. The food is divided into small pieces by more than one cut. Chopping can be done roughly or finely: roughly means pieces of about 1 cm/½ inch, whereas finely means much smaller pieces.

Dicing This is like chopping, but the pieces must be a regular cube-like shape as well as the same size.

Folding in The term used to describe how to incorporate flour into a cake mixture. It is a gentle movement, made with a metal spoon or a plastic spatula to cut through the mixture in a figure-of-eight movement.

* * *

Frying The process of cooking food in hot fat. There are three main ways to fry food: pan-frying or sautéing, shallow-fat frying and deep-fat frying. Frying gives the food an appetizing colour and a wonderful flavour.

Glazing A glaze is a finish given to pastry and bread before baking. It can be simply milk, or beaten egg or a water and sugar glaze.

Grating A grater is used to shred food into small particles. The two most common uses are for cheese and for citrus fruit peel.

Grilling A quick and easy method of cooking, which is also very healthy. The food is cooked by radiant heat, which means that the outside of the food is well cooked and browned while the inside remains moist.

Grinding Grinding means reducing foods, such as spices or nuts, to a powder.

Kneading This technique is used in breadmaking. The dough is kneaded to develop the gluten in the flour so that it will hold its shape when risen. The dough is pummelled until it is smooth and elastic.

Marinating This involves allowing food to soak in a marinade, which will tenderize it and add flavour. The food can be marinated for a few hours or a few days.

Mashing This usually refers to potatoes and other root vegetables. Cooked vegetables are mashed, using a fork, a potato masher, or an electric hand mixer. This makes them smooth and light.

Mincing This means chopping food, such as lean meat, very finely. It is best done with a hand or electric meat grinder.

Peeling This is the removal of any unwanted peel from fruit and vegetables using a knife or vegetable peeler.

Poaching A gentle method of cooking food in a liquid at simmering point. Poaching is suitable for small pieces of fish or meat, eggs and fruit.

Roasting This is a method of cooking food in the oven, like baking, but it is usually used for meat, poultry, fish and vegetables. Roasting often requires added fat to protect the food and moisten it while it is cooked at a relatively high temperature.

Rubbing in This is a method used in cake making where the fat is rubbed into the flour using the tips of the fingers, lifting the flour high out of the bowl to trap air in the mixture.

Sautéing This method is similar to frying, but sautéing usually means 'moving' the food at the same time.

Sifting This is the same as straining but refers to dry ingredients, for example sugar and flour, to remove lumps and to add air to the mixture.

Simmering A method of cooking in liquid, like boiling, but simmering is done at a lower temperature.

❋ ❋ ❋

Straining This is a method of rubbing cooked food through a sieve to form a purée. Straining can also refer to draining vegetables after cooking to remove the cooking water.

Steaming This technique involves cooking food in the steam of boiling water. It is a very healthy way of cooking.

Stir-frying Stir-frying means sautéing a variety of foods together at a high temperature in a wok or large frying pan. Make sure all the pieces are the same size so that they will cook evenly.

Whisking This is another method used to incorporate air, but it is usually used for a lighter mixture, for example egg whites or cream.

Useful Equipment

Before you begin to cook, you need to consider the utensils you will need. The correct equipment is a worthwhile investment as it will save you time and effort in the long term.

Baking trays A good, heavyweight baking tray is a must. It is not worth buying a cheap one because it will buckle in the oven and possibly spill the contents.

Bowls You will need a variety of sizes for different tasks. Small bowls are useful for placing prepared ingredients in prior to cooking and a large mixing bowl is essential when making bread and cakes.

Cake tins There are so many shapes and sizes of tin available, but perhaps the best starting point is a 20-cm/8-inch round cake tin. Always use the tin size specified in the recipe. In addition, a bun tin is useful for making small cakes, tarts and muffins.

Can openers Although many cans have ring pulls nowadays, a can opener is still an essential piece of equipment. Make sure the opener has good handles that are easy to grip, and a firm and smooth action.

Casseroles Casserole dishes are for braising or stewing food. A heavy casserole is better because it will enable you to start the cooking on top and then put it in the oven for a long, slow cook.

Chopping boards Chopping boards are available in a variety of materials, such as wood, polyethylene and glass. Use different boards for cooked and uncooked foods, particularly meats.

Colander This is necessary for draining cooked vegetables, pasta and anything that has been cooked in water and needs draining.

Frying pan A shallow, round pan used for frying and sautéing.

❊ ❊ ❊

Grater A grater is essential for grating items like cheese, lemon rind, bread and chocolate. They are available with different sized gratings: coarse, medium and fine.

Knives A good knife can be used to prepare ingredients. They come in all shapes and sizes and are made from different materials; do be prepared to spend in order to buy the best you can. A sharp knife is safer than a blunt one, so always make sure that the blade is sharpened regularly, using either a steel or simple pull-through sharpener. The most useful to have would be a small vegetable knife and a larger cook's knife.

Ladle You can buy ladles in various sizes. They are useful for serving soup and stews.

Lidded saucepans A set in small/medium/large should cover all your needs. Make sure the bases are solid and flat, the lids are well fitting, and the handles are comfortable and heat resistant.

Measuring jug This is important for liquid measurements when recipe quantities need to be exact. Measuring jugs may also be used for dry ingredients.

Measuring spoons In baking, where accuracy is important, these spoons can be a great help. They come in all shapes and sizes – usually ¼ teaspoon, ½ teaspoon, 1 teaspoon and 1 tablespoon sizes linked together – and can be made from metal or plastic.

Plastic and rubber spatulas These are used for mixing and folding in ingredients in a bowl when baking and can also be used to reach the bottom of a jug or blender to scrape out the last remnants of food.

Roasting tins These are necessary for roasting meat, poultry, game and vegetables. Make sure the tins are a good, solid weight and that they have deep sides to prevent too much splattering.

Scales For many recipes you can manage to do without scales by using measuring jugs and spoons. However, when you want to cook more precise recipes, such as baked items, then accuracy is important and you might like to consider some scales. There are many types around: from old fashioned balance scales with weights through to hi-tech electronic scales with digital displays.

Scissors These are a very versatile piece of equipment in the kitchen. They are wonderful for snipping herbs, cutting rinds off bacon and trimming meat.

Sieve This is sometimes necessary for draining finer ingredients such as rice. It is usually a good idea to keep a separate one for sifting dry ingredients such as flour and sugar.

Slotted spoon A very useful tool for removing larger items from liquids, such as boiled and poached eggs and whole vegetables.

Vegetable peeler This makes the job of peeling firm vegetables and fruit much quicker and more efficient.

❋ ❋ ❋

Wire cooling rack A wire rack is particularly useful if you intend to bake bread and cakes. A rack allows the steam to escape from the baked items and prevents them from becoming too soggy.

Wooden spoons These traditional utensils are invaluable in the kitchen. You need a selection of sizes and shapes – the ones with one squared edge are good because they reach into the corners of the saucepan.

Kitchen Hygiene

When preparing food, it is necessary to be absolutely rigorous about hygiene. Here are some basic rules.

Buying

- Always buy from a reputable source where you have confidence in their food handling techniques.
- Buy the freshest foods and the best quality possible.

Storing

- Keep food for as short a time as possible before cooking or serving, and make sure that it is stored at a safe temperature. A refrigerator should operate at below 5°C/41°F, so keep a thermometer in it and check it from time to time to be sure it is working satisfactorily. Adjust the thermostat when necessary.
- Cover all food with clingfilm in the refrigerator so that one food will not contaminate another.
Be especially aware of any meat products, which might leak on to other foods.
- Check 'use by' dates on packets of food before cooking.
- Thaw frozen food thoroughly. Thaw it overnight in the refrigerator rather than at room temperature.

Preparing

- Carefully wash any foods that need cleaning and dry well with kitchen paper.
- Wash your hands frequently when preparing food. Use a separate hand towel, not a tea towel.
- Keep counters clean and use a separate chopping board for raw meat, poultry and fish.
- Wash knives and other kitchen utensils in hot water and soap between each use.
- Keep tea towels clean and make sure that you change them often.
- Keep bins covered and empty them frequently, disinfecting regularly.

Cooking

- Make sure food is cooked thoroughly and serve it piping hot as soon as is practicable.
- When cooked food needs to be kept, make sure it is cooled quickly, covered and placed in the refrigerator as soon as possible.
- Only reheat food once; if it is not used up, throw it away.

Simple
starters & snacks

Melon with Strawberries

¼ honeydew melon
½ Charentais or
Cantaloupe melon
150 ml/5 fl oz rosé wine

2–3 tsp rose water
175 g/6 oz small strawberries,
washed and hulled
rose petals, to garnish

❊ Scoop out the seeds from both melons with a spoon. Then carefully remove the skin, taking care not to remove too much flesh.

❊ Cut the melon flesh into thin strips and place in a bowl. Pour over the wine and sufficient rose water to taste. Mix together gently, cover and leave to chill in the refrigerator for at least 2 hours.

❊ Halve the strawberries and carefully mix into the melon.

❊ Allow the melon and strawberries to stand at room temperature for about 15 minutes for the flavours to develop – if the melon is too cold, there will be little flavour.

❊ Arrange on individual serving plates and serve sprinkled with a few rose petals.

Italian Platter

125 g/4½ oz low-fat
mozzarella cheese, drained
60 g/2 oz lean Parma ham
400 g/14 oz canned artichoke
hearts, drained
4 ripe figs
1 small mango
few plain grissini, to serve

DRESSING
1 small orange
1 tbsp passata
1 tsp wholegrain mustard
4 tbsp low-fat natural yogurt
fresh basil leaves
salt and pepper

❊ Cut the cheese into 12 sticks, 6.5 cm/2½ inches long. Remove the fat from the ham and slice the meat into 12 strips. Carefully wrap a strip of ham around each stick of cheese and arrange neatly on a serving platter.

❊ Halve the artichoke hearts and cut the figs into quarters. Arrange them on the serving platter in groups.

❊ Peel the mango, then slice it down each side of the large, flat central stone. Slice the flesh into strips and arrange them so that they form a fan shape on the serving platter.

❊ To make the dressing, pare the rind from half of the orange using a vegetable peeler. Cut the rind into small strips and place them in a bowl. Extract the juice from the orange and add it to the bowl containing the rind.

❊ Add the passata, mustard, yogurt and seasoning to the bowl and mix together. Shred the basil leaves and mix them into the dressing.

❊ Spoon the dressing into a small dish and serve with the Italian Platter, accompanied with grissini.

Figs with Parma Ham

40 g/1½ oz rocket	1 tbsp fresh orange juice
4 fresh figs	1 tbsp clear honey
4 slices Parma ham	1 small red chilli
4 tbsp olive oil	

❉ Tear the rocket into more manageable pieces and arrange on 4 serving plates.

❉ Using a sharp knife, cut each of the figs into quarters and place them on top of the rocket leaves.

❉ Using a sharp knife, cut the Parma ham into strips and scatter over the rocket and figs.

❉ Place the oil, orange juice and honey in a screw-top jar. Shake the jar until the mixture emulsifies and forms a thick dressing. Transfer to a bowl.

❉ Using a sharp knife, dice the chilli. Add the chopped chilli to the dressing and mix well.

❉ Drizzle the dressing over the Parma ham, rocket and figs, tossing to mix well. Serve at once.

Preserved Meats

3 ripe tomatoes	6 slices bresaola
3 ripe figs	4 fresh basil leaves, chopped
1 small melon	olive oil
60 g/2 oz Italian salami, sliced thinly	90 g/3 oz marinated olives, stoned
4 thin slices mortadella	pepper, to serve
6 slices Parma ham	

❉ Slice the tomatoes thinly and cut the figs into quarters.

❉ Halve the melon, scoop out the seeds and cut the flesh into wedges.

❉ Arrange the meats on one half of a serving platter. Arrange the tomato slices in the centre and sprinkle with the basil leaves and oil.

❉ Cover the rest of the platter with the figs and melon and scatter the olives over the meats.

❉ Serve with a little extra olive oil to drizzle over the bresaola, and sprinkle with pepper.

Antipasto Mushrooms

225 g/8 oz tomatoes
3 tbsp olive oil
2 garlic cloves, finely chopped
1 tbsp finely chopped
fresh oregano
500 g/1 lb 2 oz ceps or
other mushrooms
salt and pepper
sprigs of fresh flat-leaf parsley,
to garnish

❖ Skin, deseed and chop the tomatoes. Heat 1 tablespoon of the oil in a saucepan, add the garlic and cook over a low heat for 1 minute, stirring constantly. Add the tomatoes and oregano and season to taste with salt and pepper. Continue to cook over a low heat, stirring frequently, for about 20 minutes or until pulpy and thickened.

❖ Meanwhile, thinly slice the mushrooms. Heat the remaining oil in a frying pan. Add the mushrooms and cook over a medium heat, stirring frequently, for about 5 minutes, or until tender. Stir the mushrooms into the tomato mixture and season with salt. Reduce the heat, cover and simmer for a further 10 minutes.

❖ Transfer the mushroom mixture to a bowl and set aside to cool. Serve the dish at room temperature, garnished with the parsley.

Dressed Celeriac

❄ **SERVES 4** ❄

225 ml/8 fl oz mayonnaise
2 tsp lemon juice
1 tbsp Dijon mustard
225 g/8 oz celeriac
1 shallot, grated

6 lettuce leaves
salt and pepper
snipped fresh chives,
to garnish

❄ Combine the mayonnaise, lemon juice and mustard in a large bowl and season to taste with salt and pepper. Peel and grate the celeriac into the mixture.

❄ Stir in the shallot and mix thoroughly, making sure the celeriac is well coated in the dressing.

❄ Line a salad bowl with the lettuce leaves and spoon the celeriac mixture into the centre. Sprinkle with the snipped chives and serve.

Marinated Fennel

❄ **SERVES 4** ❄

2 fennel bulbs
1 red pepper, deseeded
and cut into large dice
1 lime, cut into 8 wedges
crisp salad, to serve

MARINADE
2 tbsp lime juice
4 tbsp olive oil
2 garlic cloves, crushed
1 tsp wholegrain mustard
1 tbsp chopped thyme

❄ Cut off and reserve the fennel fronds for the garnish. Cut each of the bulbs into 8 pieces and place in a shallow dish. Add the red pepper and mix well.

❄ To make the marinade, combine the lime juice, olive oil, garlic, mustard and thyme. Pour the marinade over the fennel and red pepper and toss to coat thoroughly. Cover with clingfilm and set aside to marinate for 1 hour.

❄ Thread the fennel and pepper on to wooden skewers with the lime wedges. Cook the kebabs under a preheated medium grill, turning and basting frequently with the marinade, for about 10 minutes.

❄ Transfer the kebabs to serving plates, garnish with the reserved fennel fronds and serve immediately with the salad.

Dressed Artichoke Hearts

250 g/9 oz mixed salad leaves, such as lollo rosso, escarole and lamb's lettuce
6 tbsp lemon juice
4 globe artichokes
5 tbsp Calvados
1 shallot, very finely chopped

1 tbsp red wine vinegar
3 tbsp walnut oil
salt and pepper
55 g/2 oz shelled walnuts, chopped, and 1 tbsp finely chopped fresh parsley, to garnish

❊ Place the salad leaves in a bowl and set aside. Fill a bowl with cold water and add 2 tablespoons of the lemon juice. Prepare the artichokes one at a time. Twist off the artichoke stalk, cut the base flat and pull off all the dark outer leaves. Slice the artichoke in half horizontally and discard the top part. Trim around the base to remove the outer dark green layer and place in the acidulated water while you prepare the remainder.

❊ Bring a large saucepan of water to the boil, add the remaining lemon juice and cook the artichoke bases, covered, for 30–40 minutes or until tender. Drain, refresh under cold water and drain again. Pull off the remaining leaves and scoop out and discard the chokes. Set the artichoke hearts aside.

❊ Pour the Calvados into a small saucepan, add the shallot and a pinch of salt and bring to just below boiling point. Reduce the heat, carefully ignite the Calvados and continue to cook until the flames have died down. Stir in the vinegar and oil and cook, stirring constantly, for 1 minute. Remove the pan from the heat.

❊ Spoon half the dressing over the salad leaves and toss well to coat. Transfer the salad leaves to a serving platter and top with the artichoke hearts. Spoon the remaining dressing over the artichoke hearts, garnish with the walnuts and parsley and serve immediately.

Orange-Dressed Asparagus

thinly pared rind and juice of 2 oranges
350 g/12 oz asparagus, trimmed
1 tbsp lemon juice

1 spring onion, finely chopped
1 garlic clove, finely chopped
2 tbsp extra virgin olive oil
1 tbsp white wine vinegar

❊ Bring a small saucepan of water to the boil. Cut the orange rind into very thin strips, add to the pan, bring back to the boil and simmer for 1 minute. Drain, refresh under cold water and drain again.

❊ Bring water to the boil in an asparagus kettle or a deep saucepan. Add the asparagus and cook for 5 minutes or until crisp-tender. Drain, refresh under cold water and drain again. Pat dry with kitchen paper.

❊ Arrange the asparagus on a serving dish, cover and chill until required.

❊ To make the orange dressing, combine 5 tablespoons of the orange juice with the lemon juice, spring onion, garlic and orange rind. Set aside at room temperature for 15 minutes to allow the flavours to mingle. Whisk in the olive oil and vinegar.

❊ Pour the orange dressing over the chilled asparagus and serve immediately.

Filled Aubergines

225 g/8 oz dried penne
or other short pasta shapes
4 tbsp olive oil, plus extra
for brushing
2 aubergines
1 large onion, chopped
2 garlic cloves, crushed
400 g/14 oz canned chopped
tomatoes
2 tsp dried oregano
55 g/2 oz mozzarella cheese,
thinly sliced
25 g/1 oz Parmesan cheese,
freshly grated
5 tbsp dry breadcrumbs
salt and pepper
mixed salad leaves, to serve

❖ Bring a large saucepan of lightly salted water to the boil. Add the pasta and 1 tablespoon of the olive oil, bring back to the boil and cook for 8–10 minutes or until the pasta is just tender but still firm to the bite. Drain, return to the pan, cover and keep warm.

❖ Cut the aubergines in half lengthways and score around the inside with a sharp knife, being careful not to pierce the shells. Scoop out the flesh with a spoon. Brush the insides of the shells with olive oil. Chop the flesh and set aside.

❖ Heat the remaining oil in a frying pan. Fry the onion over a low heat for 5 minutes, until soft. Add the garlic and fry for 1 minute. Add the chopped aubergine flesh and fry, stirring frequently, for 5 minutes. Add the tomatoes and oregano and season to taste with salt and pepper. Bring to the boil and simmer for 10 minutes until thickened. Remove the pan from the heat and stir in the pasta.

❖ Brush a baking tray with oil and arrange the aubergine shells in a single layer. Divide half of the tomato and pasta mixture between them. Scatter over the slices of mozzarella, then pile the remaining tomato and pasta mixture on top. Mix the Parmesan cheese and breadcrumbs and sprinkle over the top, patting lightly into the mixture.

❖ Bake in a preheated oven, 200°C/400°F/Gas Mark 6, for about 25 minutes or until the topping is golden brown. Serve hot with the salad leaves.

Mushrooms with Spinach

❉ **SERVES 4** ❉

225 g/8 oz fresh baby spinach leaves
4 field mushrooms
3 tbsp olive oil
55 g/2 oz rindless bacon, finely diced
2 garlic cloves, crushed
55 g/2 oz fresh white or brown breadcrumbs
2 tbsp chopped fresh basil
salt and pepper

❉ Preheat the oven to 200°C/400°F/Gas Mark 6. Rinse the spinach and place in a saucepan with only the water clinging to the leaves. Cook for 2–3 minutes until wilted. Drain, squeezing out as much liquid as possible, and chop finely. Cut the stalks from the mushrooms and chop finely, reserving the whole cups.

❉ Heat 2 tablespoons of the oil in a frying pan. Add the mushroom cups, rounded side down, and fry for 1 minute. Remove from the frying pan and arrange, rounded side down, in a large baking dish.

❉ Add the chopped mushroom stalks, bacon and garlic to the frying pan and fry for 5 minutes. Stir in the spinach, breadcrumbs, basil and salt and pepper to taste. Mix well and divide the stuffing between the mushroom cups.

❉ Drizzle the remaining oil over the top and bake in the oven for 20 minutes, until crisp and golden.

Creamy Stuffed Mushrooms

❉ **SERVES 4** ❉

25 g/1 oz dried ceps
225 g/8 oz floury potatoes, diced
2 tbsp butter, melted
4 tbsp double cream
2 tbsp chopped fresh chives
8 large open-cup mushrooms
25 g/1 oz Emmenthal cheese, grated
150 ml/5 fl oz vegetable stock
salt and pepper
fresh chives, to garnish

❉ Place the dried ceps in a small bowl. Add sufficient boiling water to cover and set aside to soak for 20 minutes.

❉ Meanwhile, bring a medium saucepan of lightly salted water to the boil and cook the potatoes for 10 minutes until cooked through and tender. Drain them well and mash until smooth.

❉ Drain the soaked ceps and then chop them finely. Mix them into the mashed potato.

❉ Thoroughly blend the butter, cream and chives together and pour the mixture into the ceps and potato mixture, stirring well to combine. Season to taste with salt and pepper.

❉ Remove the stalks from the open-cup mushrooms. Chop the stalks and stir them into the potato mixture. Spoon the mixture into the open-cup mushrooms and sprinkle the grated cheese over the top.

❉ Arrange the filled mushrooms in a shallow ovenproof dish and pour the vegetable stock around them.

❉ Cover the dish and cook in a preheated oven, 220°C/425°F/Gas Mark 7, for 20 minutes. Remove the lid and cook for a further 5 minutes until the tops are golden.

❉ Garnish the mushrooms with fresh chives and serve at once.

Stuffed Tomatoes

❖ **SERVES 4** ❖

4 large, ripe beef tomatoes
1 tbsp oil
8 spring onions, chopped
1 red pepper, deseeded and
  cut into short strips
2 tbsp chopped fresh parsley

115 g/4 oz fresh bread
125 g/4$\frac{1}{2}$ oz mature Cheddar
  cheese
salt and pepper
bay leaves, to garnish

❖ Preheat the oven to 200°C/400°F/Gas Mark 6. Cut the tops off the tomatoes and, using a sharp knife and teaspoon, scoop out all the seeds. Discard any hard centres, then roughly chop the remaining flesh and place in a large bowl. Set the tomato shells aside until required.

❖ Heat the oil in a large frying pan. Add the spring onions and red pepper and fry for 3–4 minutes until soft. Add to the tomatoes in the bowl. Place the parsley, bread and cheese in a food processor and process until finely chopped. Add to the tomato mixture and season well with salt and pepper.

❖ Arrange the tomato shells in a roasting tin. Divide the stuffing between the shells. Cook for 12–15 minutes, or until the tomatoes have softened and collapsed and the stuffing has browned. Garnish with bay leaves and serve immediately.

Stuffed Courgettes

❖ **SERVES 4** ❖

8 medium courgettes
1 tbsp sesame or vegetable oil
1 garlic clove, crushed
2 shallots, finely chopped
1 small red chilli, deseeded
  and finely chopped
250 g/9 oz lean beef mince
1 tbsp fish sauce or
  mushroom ketchup
1 tbsp chopped fresh
  coriander or basil

2 tsp cornflour, blended with a
  little cold water
90 g/3 oz cooked long-grain
  rice
salt and pepper
sprigs of fresh coriander
  or basil and slices of carrot,
  to garnish

❖ Slice the courgettes in half horizontally and scoop out a channel down the middle, discarding all the seeds. Sprinkle with salt and set aside for 15 minutes.

❖ Heat the oil in a wok or frying pan and add the garlic, shallots and chilli. Stir-fry for 2 minutes until golden. Add the beef and stir-fry briskly for about 5 minutes. Stir in the fish sauce, the chopped coriander and the blended cornflour, and cook for 2 minutes, stirring until thickened. Season with salt and pepper, then remove from the heat.

❖ Rinse the courgettes in cold water and arrange them in a greased shallow ovenproof dish, cut side uppermost. Mix the cooked rice into the beef, then use this mixture to stuff the courgettes.

❖ Cover the courgettes with foil and bake in a preheated oven, 190°C/375°F/Gas Mark 5, for 20–25 minutes, removing the foil for the last 5 minutes of cooking time.

❖ Serve at once, garnished with the sprigs of coriander and the carrot slices.

Filled Cucumber Cups

1 cucumber
4 spring onions,
finely chopped
4 tbsp lime juice
2 small red chillies, deseeded
and finely chopped
3 tsp sugar
150 g/5^1/$_2$ oz ground roasted
peanuts
^{1}/$_4$ tsp salt
3 shallots, finely sliced and
deep-fried, to garnish

❈ Wash the cucumber thoroughly and pat dry with absorbent kitchen paper.

❈ To make the cucumber cups, cut the ends off the cucumber, and divide it into 3 equal lengths. Mark a line around the centre of each one as a guide.

❈ Make a zigzag cut all the way around the centre of each section, always pointing the knife towards the centre of the cucumber.

❈ Pull apart the two halves. Scoop out the centre of each cup with a melon baller or teaspoon, leaving a base on the bottom of each cup.

❈ Put the spring onions, lime juice, chillies, sugar, peanuts and salt in a bowl and mix well to combine.

❈ Divide the filling evenly between the 6 cucumber cups and arrange on a serving plate.

❈ Garnish the cucumber cups with the deep-fried shallots and serve.

Stuffed Onions

40 g/1½ oz raisins
6 onions
1 tbsp sunflower oil
1 garlic clove, finely chopped
450 g/1 lb spinach, thick stalks removed

125 ml/4 fl oz natural yogurt
25 g/1 oz pine kernels, toasted
pinch of freshly grated nutmeg
2 tbsp fresh wholemeal breadcrumbs
salt

❄ Place the raisins in a small bowl, cover with water and set aside. Meanwhile, cut a thin slice off the bases of the onions so that they stand level. Cut off a 1-cm/½-inch slice from the tops. Using a teaspoon or melon baller, carefully scoop out the onion flesh, leaving a shell 1 cm/½ inch thick. Set a steamer over a saucepan of boiling water and arrange the onion shells inside it. Cover tightly and steam for 10–15 minutes until tender. Remove from the heat and set aside.

❄ Finely chop the scooped-out onion flesh. Heat the oil in a heavy-based frying pan. Add the chopped onion and cook, stirring occasionally, for 5 minutes until soft. Stir in the garlic and cook for 2 minutes, then add the spinach. Cover and cook for 3 minutes until the spinach has wilted. Season with salt and cook, uncovered, stirring occasionally, for about 5 minutes until all the liquid has evaporated. Remove from the heat and set aside to cool.

❄ Drain the raisins and add them to the onion and spinach mixture with the yogurt, pine kernels and nutmeg. Drain the onion shells, then spoon the spinach stuffing into them. Spread the remaining stuffing over the base of an ovenproof dish and stand the stuffed onions on top. Sprinkle the onions with the breadcrumbs and bake in a preheated oven, 180°C/350°F/Gas Mark 4, for 25 minutes. Place the dish under a preheated grill for 3–4 minutes, until the breadcrumbs are crisp. Serve immediately.

Sweet & Sour Baby Onions

350 g/12 oz baby or pickling onions
2 tbsp olive oil
2 fresh bay leaves, torn into strips

thinly pared rind of 1 lemon
1 tbsp soft brown sugar
1 tbsp clear honey
4 tbsp red wine vinegar

❄ Soak the onions in a bowl of boiling water – this will make them easier to peel. Using a sharp knife, peel and halve the onions.

❄ Heat the oil in a large frying pan. Add the bay leaves and onions to the pan and cook over a medium–high heat for 5–6 minutes or until browned all over.

❄ Cut the lemon rind into thin matchsticks. Add to the frying pan with the sugar and honey. Cook for 2–3 minutes, stirring occasionally, until the onions are lightly caramelized.

❄ Add the vinegar to the frying pan, being careful because it will spit. Cook for about 5 minutes, stirring, or until the onions are tender and the liquid has all but disappeared.

❄ Transfer the onions to a serving dish and serve at once.

Rice & Tuna Peppers

60 g/2 oz wild rice
60 g/2 oz brown rice
4 assorted medium peppers
200 g/7 oz canned tuna
in brine, drained and flaked
325 g/11½ oz canned
sweetcorn kernels, with no
added sugar or salt, drained
100 g/3½ oz mature Cheddar
cheese, grated

1 bunch fresh basil leaves,
shredded
2 tbsp dry white breadcrumbs
1 tbsp freshly grated Parmesan
cheese
salt and pepper
fresh basil leaves,
to garnish
crisp salad leaves, to serve

❊ Place the wild rice and brown rice in different saucepans, cover with water and cook for about 15 minutes or according to the instructions on the packet. Drain the rice well.

❊ Meanwhile, preheat the grill to medium. Halve the peppers, remove the seeds and stalks and arrange the peppers under the grill, cut side down. Cook for 5 minutes, turn over and cook for a further 4–5 minutes.

❊ Transfer the cooked rice to a mixing bowl and add the tuna and sweetcorn. Gently fold in the grated cheese. Stir the basil leaves into the rice mixture and season with salt and pepper to taste.

❊ Divide the tuna and rice mixture into 8 equal portions. Pile each portion into each cooked pepper half. Mix together the breadcrumbs and Parmesan cheese and sprinkle over each pepper.

❊ Place the peppers back under the grill for 4–5 minutes until hot and golden-brown.

❊ Serve the peppers immediately, garnished with basil and accompanied by fresh, crisp salad leaves.

Avocado Margherita

1 small red onion, sliced
1 garlic clove, crushed
1 tbsp olive oil
2 small tomatoes
2 avocados, halved and stoned
4 fresh basil leaves,
torn into shreds

60 g/2 oz mozzarella cheese,
thinly sliced
salt and pepper
fresh basil leaves, to garnish
mixed salad leaves, to serve

❊ Place the onion, garlic and the olive oil in a bowl. Cover and cook in a microwave oven on HIGH power for 2 minutes.

❊ Meanwhile, skin the tomatoes by cutting a cross in the base of the tomatoes and placing them in a small bowl. Pour on boiling water and leave for about 45 seconds. Drain and then plunge into cold water. The skins will slide off without too much difficulty.

❊ Arrange the avocado halves on a plate with the narrow ends pointed towards the centre. Spoon the onions into the hollow of each half.

❊ Halve and slice the tomatoes. Divide the tomatoes, basil and thin slices of the mozzarella cheese between the avocado halves. Season to taste with salt and pepper.

❊ Cook on MEDIUM power for 5 minutes or until the avocados are heated through and the cheese has melted. Transfer the avocados to serving plates, garnish with basil leaves and serve with mixed salad leaves.

Avocado Cream Terrine

2 ripe avocados
4 tbsp cold water
2 tsp gelatine
1 tbsp lemon juice
4 tbsp low-fat mayonnaise
150 ml/5 fl oz natural yogurt
150 ml/5 fl oz single cream
salt and pepper
mixed salad leaves, to serve
cucumber slices and
nasturtium flowers,
to garnish

❉ Peel the avocados and remove and discard the stones. Put the flesh in a blender or food processor or a large bowl with the water, gelatine, lemon juice, mayonnaise, yogurt and cream. Season to taste with salt and pepper.

❉ Process for about 10–15 seconds or beat by hand, using a fork or whisk, until smooth.

❉ Transfer the mixture to a small, heavy-based saucepan and heat very gently, stirring constantly, until just beginning to boil.

❉ Pour the mixture into a 900-ml/1¹/2-pint terrine, non-stick loaf tin or plastic food storage box and smooth the surface. Allow the mixture to cool and set and then chill in the refrigerator for about 1¹/2–2 hours.

❉ Turn the terrine out of its container and cut into neat slices. Arrange a bed of salad leaves on 6 serving plates. Place a slice of avocado terrine on top and garnish with cucumber slices and nasturtium flowers.

Turkey & Vegetable Loaf

❖ **SERVES 6** ❖

1 medium onion, finely chopped	1 medium egg white, lightly beaten
1 garlic clove, crushed	2 courgettes, 1 medium, 1 large
900 g/2 lb lean turkey mince	2 medium tomatoes
1 tbsp fresh parsley, chopped	salt and pepper
1 tbsp fresh chives, chopped	tomato and herb sauce, to serve
1 tbsp fresh tarragon, chopped	

❖ Preheat the oven to 190°C/375°F/Gas Mark 5 and line a non-stick loaf tin with baking paper. Place the onion, garlic and turkey in a bowl, add the herbs and season well. Mix together with your hands, then add the egg white to bind.

❖ Press half of the turkey mixture into the base of the tin. Thinly slice the medium courgette and the tomatoes and arrange the slices over the meat. Top with the rest of the turkey and press down firmly.

❖ Cover with a layer of kitchen foil and place in a roasting tin. Pour in enough boiling water to come halfway up the sides of the loaf tin. Bake in the oven for 1–1¼ hours, removing the foil for the last 20 minutes of cooking. Test the loaf is cooked by inserting a skewer into the centre – the juices should run clear. The loaf will also shrink away from the sides of the tin.

❖ Meanwhile, trim the large courgette. Using a vegetable peeler or hand-held metal cheese slicer, cut the courgette into thin slices. Bring a saucepan of water to the boil and blanch the courgette ribbons for 1–2 minutes until just tender. Drain and keep warm.

❖ Remove the turkey loaf from the tin and transfer to a warm platter. Drape the courgette ribbons over the turkey loaf and serve with a tomato and herb sauce.

Spinach Cakes with Fennel

❖ **SERVES 4** ❖

450 g/1 lb fresh spinach	25 g/1 oz plain flour, mixed with 1 tsp dried thyme
250 g/9 oz ricotta cheese	75 g/2¾ oz butter
1 egg, beaten	2 garlic cloves, crushed
2 tsp fennel seeds, lightly crushed	salt and pepper
50 g/1¾ oz Parmesan cheese, finely grated	

❖ Wash the spinach and trim off any long stalks. Place in a saucepan, cover and cook for 4–5 minutes, or until wilted. You may need to do this in batches as the volume of spinach is quite large. Place in a colander and leave to drain and cool.

❖ Mash the ricotta and beat in the egg and the fennel seeds. Season with plenty of salt and pepper, then stir in the cheese.

❖ Squeeze as much excess water as possible from the spinach and finely chop the leaves. Stir the spinach into the cheese mixture.

❖ Taking about 1 tablespoon of the spinach and cheese mixture, shape it into a ball and flatten it slightly to form a patty. Gently roll in the seasoned flour. Continue this process until all of the mixture has been used up.

❖ Half fill a large frying pan with water and bring to the boil. Carefully add the patties and cook for 3–4 minutes, or until they rise to the surface. Remove with a slotted spoon.

❖ Melt the butter in a saucepan. Add the crushed garlic and cook for 2–3 minutes. Pour the garlic butter over the patties, season with pepper and serve at once.

Spinach Cheese Moulds

100 g/3¹/2 oz fresh spinach
leaves
300 g/10¹/2 oz skimmed milk
soft cheese
2 garlic cloves, crushed
fresh parsley, tarragon and chive
sprigs, finely chopped
salt and pepper

TO SERVE
mixed salad leaves
fresh herbs
warmed pitta bread

❖ Trim the stalks from the spinach leaves and rinse the leaves under cold running water. Pack the leaves into a saucepan while they are still wet, cover and cook over a medium heat for about 3–4 minutes until wilted – they will cook in the steam from the wet leaves (do not overcook). Drain well and pat dry with absorbent kitchen paper.

❖ Line the bases of 4 small pudding basins or individual ramekin dishes with baking paper. Line the basins or ramekins with the spinach leaves so that the leaves overhang the edges.

❖ Place the cheese in a bowl and add the garlic and herbs. Mix together thoroughly and season to taste.

❖ Spoon the cheese and herb mixture into the basins or ramekins and pull over the overlapping spinach to cover the cheese or lay extra leaves to cover the top. Place a greaseproof paper disc on top of each dish and weigh down with a 100-g/3¹/2-oz weight. Chill in the refrigerator for 1 hour.

❖ Remove the weights and peel off the greaseproof paper. Loosen the moulds gently by running a small palette knife around the edges of each dish and turn them out on to individual serving plates. Serve the moulds immediately with a mixture of salad leaves and fresh herbs, and warmed pitta bread.

Spinach Meatballs

125 g/4¹/2 oz pork
1 small egg
1-cm/¹/2-inch piece of root
ginger, chopped
1 small onion, finely chopped
1 tbsp boiling water
25 g/1 oz canned bamboo
shoots, drained, rinsed and
chopped
2 slices smoked ham, chopped
2 tsp cornflour

450 g/1 lb fresh spinach
2 tsp sesame seeds

SAUCE
150 ml/5 fl oz vegetable stock
¹/2 tsp cornflour
1 tsp cold water
1 tsp light soy sauce
¹/2 tsp sesame oil
1 tbsp chopped chives

❖ Mince the pork very finely in a food processor. Lightly beat the egg in a bowl and stir into the pork.

❖ Put the ginger and onion in a separate bowl, add the boiling water and leave to stand for 5 minutes. Drain and add to the pork mixture with the bamboo shoots, ham and cornflour. Mix thoroughly and roll into 12 balls.

❖ Wash the spinach and remove the stalks. Blanch in boiling water for 10 seconds, drain well then slice into very thin strips and mix with the sesame seeds. Roll the meatballs in the mixture to coat.

❖ Place the meatballs on a heatproof plate in the base of a steamer. Cover and steam for 8–10 minutes until cooked through and tender.

❖ Meanwhile, make the sauce. Put the stock in a saucepan and bring to the boil. Mix together the cornflour and water to a smooth paste and stir it into the stock. Stir in the soy sauce, sesame oil and chives. Transfer the cooked meatballs to a warmed plate and serve with the sauce.

Stuffed Chinese Leaves

8 large Chinese leaves
1/2 vegetable stock cube
55 g/2 oz long-grain rice
4 tbsp butter
1 bunch spring onions, trimmed and finely chopped
1 celery stick, finely chopped
125 g/41/2 oz button mushrooms, sliced
1 tsp Chinese five-spice powder
300 ml/10 fl oz passata
salt and pepper
fresh chives, to garnish

❖ Blanch the Chinese leaves in boiling water for 1 minute. Refresh under cold running water and drain well. Be careful not to tear them.

❖ Bring a large saucepan of water to the boil and stir in the stock cube. Add the rice, bring back to the boil and simmer for 10–12 minutes until just tender. Drain well and set aside until required.

❖ Meanwhile, melt the butter in a frying pan and fry the spring onions and celery over a low heat for 3–4 minutes until soft but not brown.

❖ Add the mushrooms to the frying pan and cook for a further 3–4 minutes, stirring frequently.

❖ Add the cooked rice to the pan with the five-spice powder. Season to taste with salt and pepper and stir well.

❖ Spread out the Chinese leaves on a work surface and divide the rice mixture between them. Roll each leaf into a neat parcel, tucking in the sides to enclose the stuffing. Place the stuffed leaves, seam side down, in a greased ovenproof dish. Pour the passata over them and cover with foil. Bake in a preheated oven, 190°C/375°F/Gas Mark 5, for 25–30 minutes.

❖ Garnish the stuffed Chinese leaves with fresh chives and serve immediately, straight from the dish.

Steamed Cabbage Rolls

❄ **SERVES 4** ❄

8 cabbage leaves, trimmed	1 egg, lightly beaten
225 g/8 oz skinless, boneless chicken	1 tbsp vegetable oil
	1 leek, sliced
175 g/6 oz peeled raw or cooked prawns	1 garlic clove, thinly sliced
	sliced fresh red chilli,
1 tsp cornflour	to garnish
1/2 tsp chilli powder	

❄ Blanch the cabbage for 2 minutes. Drain and pat dry with absorbent kitchen paper.

❄ Mince the chicken and prawns in a food processor. Place in a bowl with the cornflour, chilli powder and egg. Mix well to combine all the ingredients.

❄ Place 2 tablespoons of the chicken and prawn mixture towards one end of each cabbage leaf. Fold the sides of the cabbage leaf around the filling and roll up.

❄ Arrange the parcels, seam side down, in a single layer on a heatproof plate and cook in a steamer for 10 minutes.

❄ Meanwhile, sauté the leek and garlic in the oil for 1–2 minutes.

❄ Transfer the cabbage parcels to warmed individual serving plates and garnish with red chilli slices. Serve with the leek and garlic sauté.

Vegetable Spring Rolls

❄ **SERVES 4** ❄

225 g/8 oz carrots	1/2 tsp arrowroot
1 red pepper	2 tbsp chopped fresh coriander
1 tbsp sunflower oil, plus extra for frying	8 sheets filo pastry
	25 g/1 oz butter
75 g/2¾ oz beansprouts	2 tsp sesame oil
finely grated zest and juice of 1 lime	chilli dipping sauce and spring onion tassels (see page 66), to serve
1 red chilli, deseeded and very finely chopped	
1 tbsp soy sauce	

❄ Using a sharp knife, cut the carrots into thin sticks. Deseed the pepper and cut into thin slices.

❄ Heat the sunflower oil in a large preheated wok. Add the carrot, red pepper and beansprouts and cook, stirring, for 2 minutes, or until softened. Remove the wok from the heat and toss in the lime zest and juice and the chilli.

❄ Mix the soy sauce with the arrowroot. Stir the mixture into the wok, return to the heat and cook for 2 minutes or until the juices thicken.

❄ Add the coriander to the wok and mix well.

❄ Lay the sheets of filo pastry out on a board. Melt the butter and sesame oil and brush each sheet with the mixture.

❄ Spoon a little of the vegetable filling at the top of each sheet, fold over each long side and roll up.

❄ Add a little oil to the wok and cook the spring rolls in batches, for 2–3 minutes, or until crisp and golden.

❄ Transfer the spring rolls to a serving dish and serve hot with the chilli dipping sauce and the spring onion tassels.

Pancake Rolls

4 tsp vegetable oil
1–2 garlic cloves, crushed
225 g/8 oz pork mince
225 g/8 oz pak choi, shredded
4$\frac{1}{2}$ tsp light soy sauce
$\frac{1}{2}$ tsp sesame oil
8 x 25-cm/10-inch spring roll
  wrappers,
  thawed, if frozen
oil, for deep-frying

CHILLI SAUCE
60 g/2 oz caster sugar
50 ml/2 fl oz rice vinegar
2 tbsp water
2 red chillies, finely chopped

❋ Heat the oil in a preheated wok. Add the garlic and stir-fry for 30 seconds. Add the pork and stir-fry for 2–3 minutes, until lightly coloured.

❋ Add the pak choi, soy sauce and sesame oil to the wok and stir-fry for 2–3 minutes. Remove from the heat and set aside to cool.

❋ Spread out the spring roll wrappers on a work surface and spoon 2 tablespoons of the pork mixture along one edge of each. Roll the wrapper over once and fold in the sides. Roll up completely to make a sausage shape, brushing the edges with a little water to seal. Set the pancake rolls aside for 10 minutes to seal firmly.

❋ To make the chilli sauce, heat the sugar, vinegar and water in a small saucepan, stirring until the sugar dissolves. Bring the mixture to the boil and boil rapidly until a light syrup forms. Remove from the heat and stir in the chillies. Leave the sauce to cool before serving.

❋ Heat the oil for deep-frying in a wok until almost smoking. Reduce the heat slightly and fry the pancake rolls, in batches if necessary, for 3–4 minutes, until golden brown. Remove from the oil with a slotted spoon and drain on absorbent kitchen paper. Serve with the chilli sauce.

Prawn Rolls

2 tbsp vegetable oil
3 shallots, very finely chopped
1 carrot, cut into matchsticks
7-cm/2$\frac{3}{4}$-inch piece
  cucumber, cut into
  matchsticks
60 g/2 oz bamboo shoots,
  finely shredded
125 g/4$\frac{1}{2}$ oz peeled
  prawns
90 g/3 oz cooked long-grain
  rice
1 tbsp fish sauce or light soy
  sauce

1 tsp sugar
2 tsp cornflour, blended in
  2 tbsp cold water
8 x 25-cm/10-inch spring roll
  wrappers
salt and pepper
oil, for deep-frying
plum sauce, to serve
spring onion tassels (see
  page 66) and sprigs of fresh
  coriander, to garnish

❋ Heat the oil in a wok and add the shallots, carrot, cucumber and bamboo shoots. Stir-fry briskly for 2–3 minutes. Add the prawns and cooked rice, and cook for a further 2 minutes. Season.

❋ Mix together the fish sauce, sugar and blended cornflour. Add to the stir-fry and cook, stirring constantly, for about 1 minute, until thickened. Leave to cool slightly.

❋ Place spoonfuls of the shrimp and vegetable mixture on the spring roll wrappers. Dampen the edges and roll them up to enclose the filling completely.

❋ Heat the oil for deep-frying and fry the spring rolls until crisp and golden brown. Drain on kitchen paper. Serve the rolls garnished with the spring onion tassels and coriander sprigs and accompanied by the plum sauce.

Thai-Style Noodle Cakes

125 g/4 oz vermicelli rice noodles
2 spring onions, finely shredded
1 lemon grass stalk, finely shredded
3 tbsp fresh coconut, finely shredded
salt and pepper
vegetable oil for frying

TO SERVE
115 g/4 oz beansprouts
1 small red onion, thinly sliced
1 avocado, thinly sliced
2 tbsp lime juice
2 tbsp rice wine
1 tsp chilli sauce
whole red chillies, to garnish

❈ Break the rice noodles into short pieces and soak in hot water for about 4 minutes, or according to package directions. Drain thoroughly and pat dry with paper towels.

❈ Stir together the noodles, spring onions, lemon grass and coconut.

❈ Heat a small amount of oil until very hot in a heavy-based frying pan. Brush a 9-cm/3¹/₂-inch round biscuit cutter with oil and place in the pan. Spoon a small amount of noodle mixture into the cutter to just cover the base of the pan, then press down lightly with the back of a spoon.

❈ Fry for 30 seconds, then carefully remove the cutter and continue frying the cake until it is golden brown, turning it over once. Remove and drain on kitchen paper. Repeat with the remaining noodles, to make about 12 cakes.

❈ To serve, arrange the noodle cakes in small stacks, with the beansprouts, onion and avocado slices between the layers. Mix the lime juice, rice wine and chilli sauce together and spoon over just before serving, garnished with the chillies.

Sweetcorn Patties

❖ **SERVES 6** ❖

325 g/11½ oz canned sweetcorn, drained
1 onion, finely chopped
1 tsp curry powder
1 garlic clove, crushed
1 tsp ground coriander
2 spring onions, chopped
3 tbsp plain flour
½ tsp baking powder
1 large egg
4 tbsp sunflower oil
salt
1 spring onion, sliced, to garnish

❖ Lightly mash the sweetcorn in a medium-sized bowl. Add the onion, curry powder, garlic, coriander, spring onions, flour, baking powder and egg. Stir well and season with salt.

❖ Heat the sunflower oil in a frying pan. Drop tablespoonfuls of the mixture carefully on to the hot oil, far enough apart for them not to run into each other as they cook.

❖ Cook for about 4–5 minutes, turning each patty once, until they are golden brown and firm to the touch. Take care not to turn them too soon, or they will break up in the pan.

❖ Remove the patties from the pan with a fish slice and drain them well on absorbent kitchen paper. Serve at once, garnished with the spring onion slices.

Spicy Sweetcorn Fritters

❖ **SERVES 4** ❖

225 g/8 oz canned or frozen sweetcorn
2 red chillies, deseeded and very finely chopped
2 cloves garlic, crushed
10 lime leaves, very finely chopped
2 tbsp fresh coriander, chopped
1 large egg
75 g/2¾ oz polenta
100 g/3½ oz French beans, very finely sliced
groundnut oil, for frying

❖ Place the sweetcorn, chillies, garlic, lime leaves, coriander, egg and polenta in a large mixing bowl, and stir to combine.

❖ Add the beans to the ingredients in the bowl and mix well, using a wooden spoon.

❖ Divide the mixture into small even-sized balls. Flatten the balls of mixture between the palms of your hands to form rounds.

❖ Heat a little groundnut oil in a preheated wok or large frying pan until really hot. Cook the fritters, in batches, until brown and crispy on the outside, turning occasionally.

❖ Leave the fritters to drain on absorbent kitchen paper while frying the remaining fritters.

❖ Transfer the fritters to warmed serving plates and serve immediately.

Garlicky Mushroom Pakoras

175 g/6 oz gram flour
1/2 tsp salt
1/4 tsp baking powder
1 tsp cumin seeds
1/2–1 tsp chilli powder
200 ml/7 fl oz water
2 garlic cloves, crushed
1 small onion, finely chopped

vegetable oil, for deep-frying
500 g/1 lb 2 oz button
    mushrooms, trimmed
    and wiped
sea salt, to serve
lemon wedges and sprigs of
    fresh coriander, to garnish

❄ Put the gram flour, salt, baking powder, cumin and chilli powder into a bowl and mix well together. Make a well in the centre of the mixture and gradually stir in the water, mixing thoroughly to form a batter.

❄ Stir the crushed garlic and the chopped onion into the batter and leave the mixture to infuse for 10 minutes. One-third fill a deep-fat fryer or saucepan with vegetable oil and heat to 180°C/350°F or until a cube of bread browns in 30 seconds. Lower the basket into the hot oil.

❄ Meanwhile, mix the mushrooms into the batter, stirring to coat. Remove a few at a time and place them in the hot oil. Fry for about 2 minutes or until golden brown.

❄ Remove the mushrooms from the pan with a slotted spoon and drain on kitchen paper while you are cooking the remainder in the same way.

❄ Serve hot, sprinkled with sea salt and garnished with lemon wedges and coriander sprigs.

Seven-Spice Aubergines

450 g/1 lb aubergines,
    wiped
1 egg white
50 g/1 3/4 oz cornflour

1 tsp salt
1 tbsp seven-spice powder
oil, for deep-frying

❄ Using a sharp knife, thinly slice the aubergines. Place the aubergine slices in a colander, sprinkle with salt and leave to stand for 30 minutes. This will remove all the bitter juices.

❄ Rinse the aubergine slices thoroughly and pat dry with absorbent kitchen paper.

❄ Place the egg white in a small bowl and whisk until light and foamy.

❄ Using a spoon, mix together the cornflour, salt and seven-spice powder on a large plate.

❄ Heat the oil for deep-frying in a large preheated wok or heavy-based frying pan.

❄ Dip the aubergine slices into the egg white, and then into the cornflour and seven-spice mixture to coat evenly.

❄ Deep-fry the coated aubergine slices, in batches, for 5 minutes or until pale golden and crispy.

❄ Transfer the aubergine slices to absorbent kitchen paper and leave to drain. Arrange on serving plates and serve hot.

Minted Onion Bhajis

125 g/4¹/₂ oz gram flour
¹/₄ tsp cayenne pepper
¹/₄–¹/₂ tsp ground coriander
¹/₄–¹/₂ tsp ground cumin
1 tbsp chopped fresh mint
4 tbsp Greek-style yogurt
65 ml/2¹/₂ fl oz cold water
1 large onion, quartered and
thinly sliced
salt and pepper
vegetable oil, for frying
sprigs of fresh mint, to garnish

❉ Put the gram flour into a bowl, add the cayenne pepper, coriander, cumin and mint and season to taste with salt and pepper. Stir in the yogurt, water and sliced onion and mix well.

❉ One-third fill a large deep frying pan with oil and heat until very hot. Drop heaped spoonfuls of the mixture, a few at a time, into the hot oil and use two forks to neaten the mixture into rough ball shapes.

❉ Fry the bhajis until golden brown and cooked through, turning frequently.

❉ Drain the bhajis on absorbent kitchen paper and keep warm while cooking the remainder in the same way.

❉ Arrange the bhajis on a platter and garnish with sprigs of fresh mint. Serve hot or warm.

Samosas

PASTRY
100 g/3½ oz self-raising flour
½ tsp salt
40 g/1½ oz butter, cut into
small pieces
4 tbsp water

FILLING
3 potatoes, boiled
1 tsp finely chopped root ginger

1 tsp crushed garlic
½ tsp white cumin seeds
½ tsp mixed onion and
mustard seeds
1 tsp salt
½ tsp crushed red chillies
2 tbsp lemon juice
2 small green chillies, finely
chopped
ghee or oil, for deep-frying

❖ Sift the flour and salt into a bowl. Add the butter and rub into the flour until the mixture resembles fine breadcrumbs.

❖ Pour in the water and mix with a fork to form a dough. Pat it into a ball and knead for 5 minutes or until smooth. Cover and leave to rise.

❖ To make the filling, mash the boiled potatoes gently and mix with the ginger, garlic, white cumin seeds, onion and mustard seeds, salt, crushed red chillies, lemon juice and green chillies.

❖ Form the dough into 12 small balls and roll out very thinly to form a round. Cut in half, dampen the edges and shape into cones. Fill the cones with a little of the filling, dampen the top and bottom edges of the cones and pinch together to seal. Set aside.

❖ Fill a deep saucepan one-third full with oil and heat to 180°C/350°F or until a cube of bread browns in 30 seconds. Carefully lower the samosas into the oil, a few at a time, and fry for 2–3 minutes, or until golden brown. Remove from the oil and drain thoroughly on kitchen paper. Serve hot or cold.

Falafel

675 g/1 lb 8 oz canned
chickpeas, drained
1 red onion, chopped
3 garlic cloves, crushed
100 g/3½ oz wholemeal
bread
2 small fresh red chillies
1 tsp ground cumin
1 tsp ground coriander
½ tsp turmeric

1 tbsp chopped fresh
coriander, plus extra
to garnish
1 egg, beaten
100 g/3½ oz wholemeal
breadcrumbs
salt and pepper
vegetable oil, for deep-frying
tomato and cucumber salad
and lemon wedges, to serve

❖ Put the chickpeas, onion, garlic, bread, chillies, spices, and coriander into a food processor and process for 30 seconds. Stir the mixture and season to taste with salt and pepper.

❖ Remove the mixture from the food processor and shape into walnut-sized balls.

❖ Place the beaten egg in a shallow bowl and put the breadcrumbs on a plate. First dip the chickpea balls into the egg to coat them thoroughly and then roll them in the breadcrumbs, shaking off any excess crumbs.

❖ Heat the oil for deep-frying to 180°C/350°F or until a cube of bread browns in 30 seconds. Cook the falafel, in batches if necessary, for 2–3 minutes until crisp and browned. Carefully remove them from the oil with a slotted spoon and dry on absorbent kitchen paper.

❖ Garnish the falafel with the reserved chopped coriander and serve with the tomato and cucumber salad and lemon wedges.

Toasted Cheese Nibbles

❄ SERVES 4 ❄

125 g/4½ oz ricotta cheese
125 g/4½ oz finely grated
Double Gloucester cheese
2 tsp chopped parsley
60 g/2 oz chopped mixed nuts

3 tbsp chopped herbs, such as
parsley, chives, marjoram,
lovage and chervil
2 tbsp mild paprika
pepper
fresh herb sprigs, to garnish

❄ Mix together the ricotta and Double Gloucester cheeses. Add the parsley and a little pepper and work together until thoroughly combined.

❄ Form the mixture into small balls and place on a plate. Cover and chill in the refrigerator for about 20 minutes until they are firm.

❄ Scatter the chopped nuts on a baking tray and place them under a preheated grill until lightly browned. Take care, as they can easily burn. Leave them to cool.

❄ Sprinkle the nuts, herbs and paprika into 3 separate small bowls. Remove the cheese balls from the refrigerator and divide into 3 equal piles. Roll 1 quantity of the cheese balls in the nuts, 1 quantity in the herbs and 1 quantity in the paprika until they are all well coated.

❄ Arrange the coated cheese balls alternately on a large serving platter. Chill in the refrigerator until ready to serve and then garnish with the sprigs of fresh herbs.

Chicken Balls with Sauce

❄ SERVES 4 ❄

2 chicken breasts
3 tbsp vegetable oil
2 shallots, finely chopped
½ celery stick, finely chopped
1 garlic clove, crushed
2 tbsp light soy sauce
1 small egg

1 bunch of spring onions
salt and pepper
spring onion tassels, to garnish
(see page 66)

DIPPING SAUCE
3 tbsp dark soy sauce
1 tbsp rice wine
1 tsp sesame seeds

❄ Skin and bone the chicken breasts and cut into 2-cm/¾-inch pieces. Heat half of the oil in a frying pan or wok and stir-fry the chicken over a high heat for 2–3 minutes until golden. Remove from the pan or wok with a slotted spoon and set aside. Add the shallots, celery and garlic to the pan and stir-fry for 1–2 minutes until soft.

❄ Place the chicken, shallots, celery and garlic in a food processor and process until finely ground. Add 1 tablespoon of the light soy sauce and just enough egg to make a fairly firm mixture. Season to taste with salt and pepper.

❄ Trim the spring onions and cut into 5-cm/2-inch lengths.

❄ To make the dipping sauce, mix together the dark soy sauce, rice wine and sesame seeds in a small serving bowl and set aside.

❄ Shape the chicken mixture into 16–18 walnut-sized balls. Heat the remaining oil in the pan and stir-fry the chicken balls in small batches for 4–5 minutes until golden brown. Drain each batch on kitchen paper and keep hot.

❄ Add the spring onions to the pan and stir-fry for 1–2 minutes until they begin to soften, then stir in the remaining light soy sauce. Serve immediately with the chicken balls and the bowl of dipping sauce on a plate, garnished with the spring onion tassels.

Chicken & Banana Patties

450 g/1 lb floury potatoes, diced
225 g/8 oz chicken mince
1 large banana
2 tbsp plain flour
1 tsp lemon juice
1 onion, finely chopped
2 tbsp chopped fresh sage
2 tbsp butter
2 tbsp vegetable oil
150 ml/5 fl oz single cream
150 ml/5 fl oz chicken stock
salt and pepper
fresh sage leaves, to garnish

❖ Cook the diced potatoes in a saucepan of boiling water for about 10 minutes until tender. Drain well and mash until smooth. Stir in the chicken.

❖ Mash the banana and add it to the potato with the flour, lemon juice, onion and half the chopped sage. Season to taste with salt and pepper and stir the mixture together.

❖ Divide the mixture into 8 equal portions. With lightly floured hands, shape each portion into a round patty.

❖ Heat the butter and oil in a frying pan, add the potato cakes and cook for 12–15 minutes or until cooked through, turning once. Remove from the pan and keep warm.

❖ Stir the cream and stock into the pan with the remaining chopped sage. Cook over a low heat for 2–3 minutes.

❖ Arrange the potato cakes on a warmed serving plate, garnish with the sage leaves and serve immediately with the cream and sage sauce.

Chicken & Herb Fritters

500 g/1 lb 2 oz mashed potato, with butter added
250 g/9 oz chopped, cooked chicken
125 g/4½ oz cooked ham, finely chopped
1 tbsp mixed herbs
2 eggs, lightly beaten
milk
125 g/4½ oz fresh brown breadcrumbs
salt and pepper
oil, for shallow frying
sprig of fresh parsley, to garnish
mixed salad, to serve

❉ In a large bowl, blend the potatoes, chicken, ham, herbs and half of the beaten egg, and season well.

❉ Shape the mixture into small balls or flat pancakes.

❉ Add a little milk to the remaining beaten egg.

❉ Place the breadcrumbs on a plate. Dip the balls in the egg and milk mixture, then roll in the breadcrumbs to coat completely.

❉ Heat the cooking oil in a large frying pan and cook the fritters until they are golden brown. Garnish with the parsley and serve with the salad.

Deep-Fried Risotto Balls

2 tbsp olive oil
1 medium onion, finely chopped
1 garlic clove, chopped
½ red pepper, diced
150 g/5½ oz arborio rice, washed
1 tsp dried oregano
400 ml/14 fl oz hot vegetable or chicken stock
100 ml/3½ fl oz dry white wine
75 g/2¾ oz mozzarella cheese
oil, for deep-frying
sprig of fresh basil, to garnish

❉ Heat the oil in a frying pan and cook the onion and garlic for 3–4 minutes or until just soft.

❉ Add the red pepper, rice and oregano to the pan. Cook for 2–3 minutes, stirring to coat the rice in the oil.

❉ Mix the stock together with the wine and add to the pan a ladleful at a time, waiting for the liquid to be absorbed by the rice before you add the next ladleful.

❉ Once all of the liquid has been absorbed and the rice is tender (it should take about 15 minutes in total), remove the pan from the heat and leave until the mixture is cool enough to handle.

❉ Cut the cheese into 12 pieces. Taking about 1 tablespoon of risotto, shape the mixture around the cheese pieces to make 12 balls.

❉ Heat the oil to 180°C/350°F or until a cube of bread browns in 30 seconds. Cook the risotto balls, in batches of 4, for 2 minutes or until golden.

❉ Remove the risotto balls with a slotted spoon and drain thoroughly on absorbent kitchen paper. Serve hot, garnished with the sprig of basil.

Mozzarella in Carriages

8 slices bread, preferably
slightly stale,
crusts removed
100 g/3^1/$_2$ oz mozzarella
cheese, thickly sliced
50 g/1^3/$_4$ oz black olives,
stoned and chopped

8 canned anchovy fillets,
drained and chopped
16 fresh basil leaves
4 eggs, beaten
150 ml/5 fl oz milk
salt and pepper
oil, for deep-frying

❖ Cut each slice of bread into 2 triangles. Top 8 of the bread triangles with the mozzarella cheese slices, the olives and the chopped anchovies.

❖ Place the basil leaves on top and season to taste with salt and pepper.

❖ Lay the other 8 triangles of bread over the top and press down round the edges to seal.

❖ Mix the eggs and milk and pour into an ovenproof dish. Add the sandwiches and leave to soak for about 5 minutes.

❖ Heat the oil in a large saucepan to 180°C/350°F or until a cube of bread browns in 30 seconds.

❖ Before cooking the sandwiches, squeeze the edges together again.

❖ Carefully place the sandwiches in the oil and deep-fry for 2 minutes or until golden, turning once. Remove the sandwiches with a slotted spoon and drain on absorbent kitchen paper. Serve immediately while still hot.

Three-Cheese Fondue

1 garlic clove
300 ml/10 fl oz dry white wine
250 g/8 oz mild Cheddar
cheese, grated
125 g/4^1/$_2$ oz Gruyère
cheese, grated
125 g/4^1/$_2$ oz mozzarella
cheese, grated
2 tbsp cornflour
pepper

TO SERVE
French bread
vegetables, such as courgettes,
mushrooms, baby sweetcorn
and cauliflower

❖ Bruise the garlic by placing the flat side of a knife on top and pressing down with the heel of your hand.

❖ Rub the garlic around the inside of a large bowl. Discard the garlic.

❖ Pour the wine into the bowl and heat in a microwave oven, uncovered, on HIGH power for 3–4 minutes until hot but not boiling.

❖ Gradually add the Cheddar and Gruyère cheeses, stirring well after each addition, then add the mozzarella cheese. Stir until all the cheese is completely melted.

❖ Mix the cornflour with a little water to form a smooth paste and stir it into the cheese mixture. Season to taste with pepper.

❖ Cover and cook on MEDIUM power for 6 minutes, stirring twice during cooking, until the sauce is smooth.

❖ Cut the French bread into bite-sized cubes and the vegetables into batons, slices or florets. To serve, keep the fondue warm over a spirit lamp or reheat as necessary in the microwave oven. Dip in the cubes of French bread and batons, slices or florets of vegetables.

Roast Garlic with Goat's Cheese

2 garlic bulbs, outer papery
layers removed
3 tbsp water
6 tbsp olive oil
2 sprigs fresh rosemary
1 bay leaf
200 g/7 oz soft goat's cheese
1 tbsp chopped fresh mixed
herbs, such as parsley
and oregano
1 loaf French bread, sliced
salt and pepper
salad leaves, to garnish

❖   Preheat the oven to 200°C/400°F/Gas Mark 6. Place the garlic in an ovenproof dish. Add the water, half the oil, the rosemary and the bay leaf. Season to taste with salt and pepper. Cover with foil and roast for 30 minutes.

❖   Remove the dish from the oven and baste the garlic with the cooking juices. Re-cover and roast for a further 15 minutes or until tender.

❖   Meanwhile, beat the cheese in a bowl until smooth, then beat in the mixed herbs. Heat the remaining oil in a frying pan. Fry the bread on both sides for 3–4 minutes, or until golden brown.

❖   Arrange the bread and cheese on serving plates garnished with salad leaves. Remove the garlic from the oven. Break up the bulbs but do not peel. Divide between the plates and serve immediately. Each diner squeezes the garlic pulp on to the bread and eats it with the cheese.

Paprika Potato Crisps

2 large potatoes
3 tbsp olive oil
1/2 tsp paprika
salt

❊ Using a sharp knife, slice the potatoes very thinly so that they are almost transparent. Drain the potato slices thoroughly and pat dry with kitchen paper.

❊ Heat the oil in a large frying pan and add the paprika, stirring constantly to ensure that the paprika doesn't burn.

❊ Add the potato slices to the pan and cook them in a single layer for about 5 minutes or until they just begin to curl slightly at the edges.

❊ Remove the potato slices from the pan using a slotted spoon and transfer them to kitchen paper to drain thoroughly.

❊ Thread the potato slices on to several wooden kebab skewers.

❊ Sprinkle the potato slices with a little salt and cook under a medium grill, turning frequently, for 10 minutes until the potato slices begin to go crisp. Sprinkle with a little more salt, if preferred, and serve immediately.

Spiced Corn & Nut Mix

2 tbsp vegetable oil
55 g/2 oz popping corn
60 g/2 oz butter
1 garlic clove, crushed
55 g/2 oz unblanched almonds
55 g/2 oz unsalted cashew nuts
55 g/2 oz unsalted peanuts
1 tsp Worcestershire sauce
1 tsp curry powder or paste
1/4 tsp chilli powder
55 g/2 oz seedless raisins
salt

❊ Heat the oil in a saucepan. Add the corn, stir well, then cover and cook over a fairly high heat for 3–5 minutes, holding the saucepan lid firmly and shaking the pan frequently until the popping stops.

❊ Turn the popped corn into a dish, discarding any unpopped kernels.

❊ Melt the butter in a frying pan and add the garlic, almonds, cashew nuts and peanuts, then stir in the Worcestershire sauce, the curry powder and the chilli powder and cook the mixture over a medium heat, stirring frequently, for 2–3 minutes until the nuts are lightly toasted.

❊ Remove the pan from the heat and stir in the raisins and popped corn. Season to taste with salt and mix thoroughly. Transfer to a serving bowl and serve warm or cold.

Crispy Seaweed

❄ **SERVES 4** ❄

1 kg/2 lb 4 oz pak choi
1 tsp salt
1 tsp sugar
2½ tbsp toasted pine kernels
900 ml/1½ pints groundnut oil,
for deep-frying

❄ Rinse the pak choi leaves under cold running water and then pat dry thoroughly with absorbent kitchen paper.

❄ Discarding any tough outer leaves, roll each pak choi leaf up, then slice through thinly so that the leaves are finely shredded. Alternatively, use a food processor to shred the pak choi.

❄ Heat the groundnut oil in a large wok or heavy-based frying pan.

❄ Carefully add the shredded pak choi leaves to the wok and fry for about 30 seconds or until they shrivel up and become crispy, resembling seaweed (you will probably need to do this in several batches, depending on the size of your wok).

❄ Remove the crispy seaweed from the wok with a slotted spoon and drain on absorbent kitchen paper.

❄ Transfer the crispy seaweed to a large bowl and toss with the salt, sugar and pine kernels. Serve immediately on warmed serving plates.

Son-in-Law Eggs

❄ **SERVES 4** ❄

6 eggs, hard-boiled and shelled
4 tbsp sunflower oil
1 onion, thinly sliced
2 fresh red chillies, deseeded
and sliced
2 tbsp sugar
1 tbsp water
2 tsp tamarind pulp
1 tbsp liquid seasoning, such
as Maggi
rice, to serve

❄ Prick the hard-boiled eggs 2 or 3 times with a cocktail stick.

❄ Heat the sunflower oil in a wok and fry the eggs until crispy and golden. Drain on absorbent kitchen paper.

❄ Halve the eggs lengthways and put on a serving dish.

❄ Reserve one tablespoon of the oil, pour off the rest, then heat the tablespoonful in the wok.

❄ Cook the onion and chillies over a high heat until golden and slightly crisp. Drain on kitchen paper.

❄ Heat the sugar, water, tamarind pulp and liquid seasoning in the wok and simmer over a low heat for 5 minutes, until the mixture has thickened.

❄ Pour the tamarind sauce over the eggs and spoon over the onion and chilli mix to garnish. Serve immediately with the rice.

Stuffed Eggs

4 large eggs
100 g/3^1/$_2$ oz pork mince
175 g/6 oz canned white crabmeat, drained
1 garlic clove, crushed
1 tsp Thai fish sauce
^{1}/$_2$ tsp lemon grass, ground
1 tbsp chopped fresh coriander
1 tbsp desiccated coconut
100 g/3^1/$_2$ oz plain flour
about 150 ml/5 fl oz coconut milk
salt and pepper
sunflower oil, for deep-frying
green salad, to serve
cucumber flower, to garnish

❉ Place the eggs in a saucepan of simmering water and bring to the boil, then simmer for 10 minutes. Drain the eggs, crack the shells and cool under cold running water. Peel off the shells.

❉ Cut the eggs lengthways down the middle and scoop out the yolks. Place the yolks in a bowl with the pork, crabmeat, garlic, fish sauce, lemon grass, coriander and coconut. Season with salt and pepper and mix the ingredients together thoroughly.

❉ Divide the mixture into 8 equal portions, then fill each of the egg whites with the mixture, pressing together with your hands to form the shape of a whole egg.

❉ Whisk together the flour and enough coconut milk to make a thick coating batter, then season with salt and pepper. Heat a 5-cm/2-inch depth of oil in a large saucepan to 180°C/350°F or until a cube of bread browns in 30 seconds. Dip each egg into the coconut batter, then shake off the excess.

❉ Fry the eggs, in 2 batches, for about 5 minutes, turning occasionally, until golden brown. Remove with a slotted spoon and drain on kitchen paper. Serve warm or cold with the green salad, garnished with the cucumber flower.

Cauliflower Roulade

1 small cauliflower, divided
into florets
4 eggs, separated
90 g/3 oz Cheddar cheese,
grated
60 g/2 oz cottage cheese
pinch of grated nutmeg
1/2 tsp mustard powder
salt and pepper

FILLING
1 bunch watercress, trimmed
55 g/2 oz butter
25 g/1 oz flour
175 ml/6 fl oz natural yogurt
25 g/1 oz Cheddar cheese,
grated
55 g/2 oz cottage cheese

❖ Line a Swiss roll tin with baking paper.

❖ Steam the cauliflower until just tender, then drain under cold water. Process the cauliflower in a food processor.

❖ Beat the egg yolks, then stir in the cauliflower, 55 g/ 2 oz of the Cheddar cheese and the cottage cheese. Season with nutmeg, mustard and salt and pepper. Whisk the egg whites until stiff but not dry, then fold them in. Spread the mixture evenly in the tin. Bake the roulade in a preheated oven, 190°C/375°F/Gas Mark 5, for about 20–25 minutes, until risen and golden.

❖ Chop the watercress, reserving a few sprigs for garnish. Melt the butter in a small saucepan. Cook the watercress, stirring, for 3 minutes, until wilted. Blend in the flour, then stir in the yogurt and simmer for 2 minutes. Stir in the cheeses.

❖ Turn out the roulade on to a damp tea towel covered with a fresh sheet of baking paper. Peel off the paper and leave for a minute to allow the steam to escape. Using the new sheet of baking paper, roll up the roulade, starting from one narrow end. Unroll the roulade, spread the filling to within 2.5 cm/1 inch of the edges, and roll it up again. Transfer to a baking tray, sprinkle with the remaining Cheddar cheese and return it to the oven for 5 minutes. Serve immediately if serving hot, or allow to cool completely.

Vegetable Cake

BASE
2 tbsp vegetable oil, plus extra
for brushing
1.25 kg/2 lb 12 oz waxy
potatoes, thinly sliced

TOPPING
1 tbsp vegetable oil
1 leek, chopped
1 courgette, grated
1 red pepper, deseeded and
diced

1 green pepper, deseeded and
diced
1 carrot, grated
2 tsp chopped parsley
225 g/8 oz full-fat soft cheese
4 tbsp grated mature Cheddar
cheese
2 eggs, beaten
salt and pepper
shredded cooked leek,
to garnish
salad, to serve

❖ Brush a 20-cm/8-inch springform cake tin with oil.

❖ To make the base, heat the oil in a frying pan. Cook the potato slices until softened and browned. Drain on kitchen paper and place in the base of the tin.

❖ To make the topping, heat the oil in a separate frying pan. Add the leek and fry over a low heat, stirring frequently, for 3–4 minutes until softened.

❖ Add the courgette, peppers, carrot and parsley to the pan and cook over a low heat for 5–7 minutes or until the vegetables have softened.

❖ Meanwhile, beat the cheeses and eggs together in a bowl. Stir in the vegetables and season to taste with salt and pepper. Spoon the mixture evenly over the potato base.

❖ Cook in a preheated oven, 190°C/ 375°F/Gas Mark 5, for 20–25 minutes until the cake is set.

❖ Remove the vegetable cake from the tin, transfer to a warmed serving plate, garnish with the shredded leek and serve with the salad.

Spanish Tortilla

1 kg/2 lb 4 oz waxy potatoes, thinly sliced
4 tbsp vegetable oil
1 onion, sliced
2 garlic cloves, crushed
1 green pepper, seeded and diced
2 tomatoes, seeded and chopped
25 g/1 oz canned sweetcorn, drained
6 large eggs, beaten
2 tbsp chopped parsley
salt and pepper

❖ Bring a saucepan of lightly salted water to the boil and parboil the potatoes for 5 minutes. Drain well.

❖ Heat the oil in a large frying pan, add the potato and onions and sauté over a low heat, stirring constantly, for 5 minutes until the potatoes have browned.

❖ Add the garlic, diced pepper, tomatoes and sweetcorn, mixing well.

❖ Pour in the eggs and add the chopped parsley. Season well with salt and pepper. Cook for 10–12 minutes, until the underside is cooked through.

❖ Remove the pan from the heat and continue to cook the tortilla under a preheated medium grill for 5–7 minutes, or until the tortilla is set and the top is golden brown.

❖ Cut the tortilla into wedges or squares, depending on your preference, and transfer to serving dishes. Serve with salad. In Spain tortillas are served hot, cold or warm.

Vegetable Frittata

3 tbsp olive oil
1 onion, chopped
2 garlic cloves, chopped
225 g/8 oz courgettes, thinly sliced
4 eggs
400 g/14 oz canned borlotti beans, rinsed and drained
3 tomatoes, peeled and chopped
2 tbsp chopped fresh parsley
1 tbsp chopped fresh basil
55 g/2 oz grated Gruyère cheese
salt and pepper

❖ Heat 2 tablespoons of the oil in a frying pan. Add the onion and garlic and cook over a medium heat, stirring occasionally, for 2–3 minutes or until soft. Add the courgettes and cook, stirring occasionally, for 3–4 minutes or until softened.

❖ Break the eggs into a bowl and season to taste with salt and pepper. Beat lightly and stir in the onion and courgette mixture, the beans, tomatoes, parsley and basil.

❖ Heat the remaining oil in a 24-cm/9½-inch omelette pan, add the egg mixture and cook over a low heat for about 5 minutes until the eggs have almost set and the underside of the frittata is golden brown.

❖ Sprinkle the cheese over the top and place the pan under a preheated moderate grill for 3–4 minutes or until set on the top but still moist in the middle. Cut into wedges and serve warm or at room temperature.

Mushroom & Goat's Cheese Frittata

4 large eggs
2 tbsp cold water
200 g/7 oz goat's cheese log
4 tbsp olive oil
225 g/8 oz large mushrooms, thinly sliced
2 garlic cloves, finely chopped
2 tbsp chopped fresh parsley
pepper

✻ Preheat the grill to medium. Beat the eggs and water together in a small bowl and season to taste with pepper. Remove the rind from the cheese and cut into cubes.

✻ Heat the oil in an 18-cm/7-inch omelette pan or frying pan with a heatproof handle. Add the mushrooms and garlic and cook until the mushrooms are beginning to crisp at the edges.

✻ Pour the beaten eggs over the mushrooms and cook over a low heat for 3 minutes, until set underneath.

✻ Scatter the cubes of goat's cheese on top of the frittata and place the omelette pan under the hot grill until the eggs are set and the cheese is beginning to melt. Sprinkle with chopped parsley, then cut into wedges and serve immediately.

Italian Omelette

900 g/2 lb potatoes
1 tbsp vegetable oil
1 large onion, sliced
2 garlic cloves, chopped
6 sun-dried tomatoes in oil, drained and cut into strips
400 g/14 oz canned artichoke hearts, drained and halved
250 g/9 oz ricotta cheese
4 large eggs, beaten
2 tbsp milk
55 g/2 oz Parmesan cheese, grated
3 tbsp chopped fresh thyme
salt and pepper

❄ Peel the potatoes and place them in a bowl of cold water. Cut the potatoes into thin slices.

❄ Bring a large saucepan of water to the boil and add the potato slices. Bring back to the boil, then simmer for 5–6 minutes or until just tender.

❄ Heat the oil in a large, heavy-based frying pan. Add the onions and garlic and cook over a low heat, stirring occasionally, for about 3–4 minutes until soft but not brown.

❄ Add the sun-dried tomatoes and cook for a further 2 minutes.

❄ Arrange a third of the potatoes in the bottom of a deep, ovenproof dish. Cover with half the onion mixture, then half the artichokes, followed by half the ricotta. Repeat the layers in the same order, finishing with a layer of potato slices on top.

❄ Combine the eggs, milk, half the cheese and the thyme and season to taste with salt and pepper. Pour the mixture over the potatoes. Sprinkle the remaining cheese on top and bake in a preheated oven, 190°C/375°F/Gas Mark 5, for 20–25 minutes or until golden brown. Cut the omelette into slices and serve immediately.

Feta & Spinach Omelette

75 g/2¾ oz butter
1.3 kg/3 lb waxy potatoes, diced
3 garlic cloves, crushed
1 tsp paprika
2 tomatoes, peeled, deseeded and diced
12 eggs
pepper

FILLING
225 g/8 oz baby spinach
1 tsp fennel seeds
125 g/4½ oz feta cheese, diced
4 tbsp natural yogurt

❄ Heat 25 g/1 oz of the butter in a frying pan and cook the potatoes over a low heat, stirring constantly, for 7–10 minutes until golden. Transfer to a bowl.

❄ Add the garlic, paprika and diced tomatoes to the pan and cook for a further 2 minutes.

❄ Whisk the eggs together and season with pepper. Pour the eggs into the potatoes and mix well.

❄ Cook the spinach in boiling water for 1 minute, until just wilted. Drain and refresh under cold running water. Pat dry with kitchen paper. Stir in the fennel seeds, feta cheese and yogurt.

❄ Heat a quarter of the remaining butter in a 15-cm/6-inch omelette pan. Ladle a quarter of the egg and potato mixture into the pan. Cook, turning over once, for 2 minutes, until set.

❄ Transfer the omelette to a serving plate. Spoon a quarter of the spinach mixture on to one half of the omelette, then fold the omelette in half over the filling. Repeat to make 4 omelettes.

Chinese Omelette

8 eggs	2 tbsp chopped chives
225 g/8 oz cooked chicken, shredded	2 tsp light soy sauce
	dash of chilli sauce
12 tiger prawns, peeled and deveined	2 tbsp vegetable oil

❖ Lightly beat the eggs in a large mixing bowl.

❖ Add the chicken and the prawns to the eggs, mixing well.

❖ Stir in the chopped chives, soy sauce and chilli sauce, mixing well to combine all the ingredients.

❖ Heat the vegetable oil in a large preheated frying pan over a medium heat.

❖ Add the egg mixture to the frying pan, tilting the pan to coat the base completely.

❖ Cook over a medium heat, gently stirring the omelette with a fork, until the surface is just set and the underside is a golden brown colour.

❖ When the omelette is set, slide it out of the pan, with the aid of a palette knife.

❖ Cut the omelette into squares or wedges and serve immediately. Alternatively, serve the omelette as a main course for two people.

Potato & Tuna Quiche

450 g/1 lb floury potatoes, diced	175 g/6 oz canned tuna, drained
25 g/1 oz butter	50 g/1¾ oz canned sweetcorn, drained
6 tbsp plain flour	150 ml/5 fl oz skimmed milk
sprigs of fresh dill and lemon wedges, to garnish	3 eggs, beaten
	1 tbsp chopped fresh dill
FILLING	50 g/1¾ oz mature Cheddar cheese, grated
1 tbsp vegetable oil	salt and pepper
1 shallot, chopped	
1 garlic clove, crushed	
1 red pepper, diced	

❖ Bring a saucepan of lightly salted water to the boil and cook the potatoes for 10 minutes or until tender. Drain and mash the potatoes. Add the butter and flour and mix to form a dough.

❖ Knead the potato dough on a floured surface and press the mixture into a 20-cm/8-inch flan tin. Prick the base with a fork. Line with baking paper and baking beans and bake blind in a preheated oven, 200°C/400°F/Gas Mark 6, for 20 minutes.

❖ Heat the oil in a frying pan, add the shallot, garlic and red pepper and fry gently for 5 minutes. Drain well and spoon the mixture into the flan case. Flake the tuna and arrange it over the top with the sweetcorn.

❖ In a bowl, mix the milk, eggs and chopped dill and season with salt and pepper.

❖ Pour the egg and dill mixture into the flan case and sprinkle the grated cheese on top.

❖ Bake in the oven for 20 minutes or until the filling has set. Garnish the quiche with the fresh dill and lemon wedges.

Baked Eggs with Spinach

❊ **SERVES 4** ❊

- 1 tbsp olive oil
- 3 shallots, finely chopped
- 500 g/1 lb 2 oz baby spinach leaves
- 4 tbsp single cream
- freshly grated nutmeg
- 4 large eggs
- 4 tbsp finely grated Parmesan cheese
- pepper
- toasted granary bread, to serve

❊ Preheat the oven to 200°C/400°F/Gas Mark 6. Heat the oil in a frying pan over a medium heat, add the shallots and cook, stirring frequently, for 4–5 minutes, or until soft. Add the spinach, cover and cook for 2–3 minutes, or until the spinach has wilted. Remove the lid and cook until all the liquid has evaporated.

❊ Add the cream to the spinach and season to taste with nutmeg and pepper. Spread the spinach mixture over the base of a shallow gratin dish and make 4 wells in the mixture with the back of a spoon.

❊ Crack an egg into each well and scatter over the cheese. Bake in the preheated oven for 12–15 minutes, or until the eggs are set. Serve with the bread.

Curried Crab Pancakes

115 g/4 oz buckwheat flour
1 large egg, beaten
300 ml/10 fl oz skimmed milk
125 g/4 1/2 oz frozen spinach, thawed, well-drained and chopped
2 tsp vegetable oil
green salad and lemon wedges, to serve

FILLING
350 g/12 oz crabmeat
1 tsp mild curry powder
1 tbsp mango chutney
1 tbsp mayonnaise
2 tbsp natural yogurt
2 tbsp fresh coriander, chopped
green salad and lemon wedges, to serve

❊ Sift the flour into a bowl and remove any husks that remain in the sieve. Make a well in the centre of the flour and add the egg. Whisk in the milk, then blend in the spinach. Transfer to a jug and leave for 30 minutes.

❊ To make the filling, mix together all the ingredients, except the coriander, in a bowl, cover and chill until required. Whisk the batter. Brush a small pancake pan with a little oil, heat until hot and pour in enough batter to cover the base thinly. Cook for 1–2 minutes, turn over and cook for 1 minute until golden. Repeat to make 8 pancakes, layering them on a plate with baking paper.

❊ Stir the coriander into the crab mixture. Fold each pancake into quarters. Open one fold and fill with the crab mixture. Serve warm, with the green salad and lemon wedges.

Mushroom & Garlic Soufflés

50 g/1 3/4 oz butter
75 g/2 3/4 oz chopped flat mushrooms,
2 tsp lime juice
2 garlic cloves, crushed
2 tbsp chopped marjoram

25 g/1 oz plain flour
225 ml/8 fl oz milk
salt and pepper
2 eggs, separated

❊ Lightly grease the inside of four 150-ml/1/4-pint individual soufflé dishes with a little butter.

❊ Melt 25 g/1 oz of the butter in a frying pan. Add the mushrooms, lime juice and garlic and sauté for 2–3 minutes. Remove the mushroom mixture from the pan with a slotted spoon and transfer to a mixing bowl. Stir in the marjoram.

❊ Melt the remaining butter in a saucepan. Add the flour and cook for 1 minute, then remove from the heat. Stir in the milk and return to the heat. Bring to the boil, stirring until thickened.

❊ Mix the sauce into the mushroom mixture and beat in the egg yolks.

❊ Whisk the egg whites until they form peaks and fold into the mushroom mixture until fully incorporated.

❊ Divide the mixture between the soufflé dishes. Place the dishes on a baking tray and cook in a preheated oven, 200°C/400°F/Gas Mark 6, for about 8–10 minutes, or until the soufflés have risen and are cooked through. Serve immediately.

Tomato Soufflés

6 beef tomatoes, halved	1/2 tsp mustard powder
25 g/1 oz butter	pinch of grated nutmeg
25 g/1 oz flour	5 egg whites
2 tbsp double cream	4 egg yolks
2 tbsp freshly grated	salt and pepper
Parmesan cheese	

❉ Scoop out the flesh and seeds of the tomatoes with a teaspoon. Place the shells upside down on kitchen paper to drain. Place the flesh and seeds in a small saucepan and simmer gently for 3 minutes. Rub the mixture through a fine sieve into a small bowl and reserve.

❉ Melt the butter in a small saucepan. Stir in the flour and cook, stirring constantly, for 1 minute. Remove the pan from the heat and gradually stir in the reserved tomato and the cream. Return the pan to the heat and cook, stirring constantly, for 2 minutes until smooth and thickened. Remove the pan from the heat, stir in the cheese and mustard and season to taste with nutmeg and salt and pepper. Set aside to cool for 10 minutes.

❉ Whisk the egg whites in a grease-free bowl until they form stiff peaks. Beat the egg yolks into the tomato mixture, 1 at a time. Fold 2 tablespoons of the egg whites into the mixture, then fold in the remainder. If necessary, pat dry the insides of the tomato shells, then divide the soufflé mixture between them.

❉ Place on a baking sheet and bake in a preheated oven, 220°C/425°F/Gas Mark 7, for 5 minutes. Reduce the oven temperature to 200°C/400°F/Gas Mark 6 and bake for 15–20 minutes more, until golden brown on top. Serve immediately.

Artichoke-Heart Soufflé

55 g/2 oz butter, plus extra for greasing	55 g/2 oz Emmenthal cheese, grated
55 g/2 oz plain flour	6 canned artichoke hearts,
300 ml/10 fl oz milk	drained and mashed
pinch of freshly grated nutmeg	4 egg yolks
2 tbsp single cream	5 egg whites
	salt and pepper

❉ Grease a 1.7-litre/3-pint soufflé dish with butter. Tie a double strip of greaseproof paper around the dish so that it protrudes about 5 cm/2 inches above the rim. Melt the butter in a heavy-based saucepan. Add the flour and cook, stirring constantly, for 2 minutes. Remove the pan from the heat and gradually stir in the milk. Return to the heat and bring to the boil, whisking constantly, for 2 minutes until thickened and smooth. Remove from the heat, season to taste with nutmeg and salt and pepper and beat in the cream, cheese and mashed artichoke hearts. Beat in the egg yolks, one at a time.

❉ Whisk the egg whites in a grease-free bowl until they form stiff peaks. Fold 2 tablespoons of the egg whites into the artichoke mixture to loosen, then gently fold in the remainder.

❉ Pour the mixture into the soufflé dish and bake in a preheated oven, 190°C/375°F/Gas Mark 5, for 35 minutes until the soufflé is well risen and the top is golden brown. Serve immediately.

Three-Cheese Soufflé

2 tbsp butter
2 tsp plain flour
900 g/2 lb floury potatoes
8 eggs, separated
4 tbsp grated Gruyère cheese
4 tbsp crumbled blue cheese
4 tbsp grated mature Cheddar
cheese
salt and pepper

❖ Butter a 2.25-litre/4-pint soufflé dish and dust with the flour. Set aside.

❖ Bring a saucepan of lightly salted water to the boil and cook the potatoes until tender. Mash until very smooth and then transfer to a mixing bowl to cool.

❖ Beat the egg yolks into the potato and stir in the Gruyère cheese, blue cheese and Cheddar cheese, mixing well. Season to taste with salt and pepper.

❖ Whisk the egg whites until standing in peaks, then gently fold them into the potato mixture with a metal spoon until fully incorporated.

❖ Spoon the potato mixture into the prepared soufflé dish.

❖ Cook in a preheated oven, 220°C/ 425°F/Gas Mark 7, for 35–40 minutes until risen and set. Serve immediately.

Garlic Mushrooms on Toast

❄ **SERVES 4** ❄

75 g/2¾ oz butter
2 garlic cloves, crushed
350 g/12 oz mixed mushrooms,
such as open-cup, button,
oyster and shiitake, sliced

8 diagonally cut slices of
French stick
1 tbsp chopped fresh parsley
salt and pepper

❄ Melt the butter in a frying pan. Add the crushed garlic and cook, stirring constantly, for 30 seconds.

❄ Add the mushrooms and cook, turning occasionally, for 5 minutes.

❄ Toast the bread under a preheated medium grill for 2–3 minutes, turning once. Transfer the toasts to a serving plate.

❄ Toss the parsley into the mushrooms, mixing well, and season well to taste with salt and pepper.

❄ Spoon the mushroom mixture over the toasts and serve immediately.

Chicken Liver Crostini

❄ **SERVES 4** ❄

2 tbsp olive oil
1 garlic clove, finely chopped
225 g/8 oz fresh or thawed
frozen chicken livers
2 tbsp white wine
2 tbsp lemon juice

4 fresh sage leaves, finely
chopped, or 1 tsp dried,
crumbled sage
4 slices ciabatta or other Italian
bread
salt and pepper
lemon wedges, to garnish

❄ Heat the olive oil in a heavy-based frying pan and cook the garlic over a low heat, stirring constantly, for 1 minute. Remove the pan from the heat.

❄ Rinse and roughly chop the chicken livers, using a sharp knife.

❄ Return the pan to a medium heat. Add the chicken livers with the white wine and lemon juice. Cook, stirring frequently, for 3–4 minutes or until the juices from the chicken livers run clear. Stir in the sage and season to taste.

❄ Toast the bread under a preheated grill for 2 minutes on both sides or until golden brown.

❄ Spoon the hot chicken liver mixture on top of the toasted bread and serve, garnished with the wedges of lemon.

Bruschetta

❖ **SERVES 4** ❖

55 g/2 oz dry-pack sun-dried tomatoes
300 ml/10 fl oz boiling water
35-cm/14-inch granary or wholemeal French stick
1 large garlic clove, halved
25 g/1 oz black olives in brine, stoned, drained and quartered
2 tsp olive oil
2 tbsp chopped fresh basil
40 g/1½ oz mozzarella cheese, grated
salt and pepper
fresh basil leaves, to garnish

❖ Place the sun-dried tomatoes in a heatproof bowl and pour over the boiling water.

❖ Set aside for 30 minutes to allow the tomatoes to soften. Drain well and pat dry with kitchen paper. Slice into thin strips and set aside.

❖ Trim and discard the ends from the bread and cut into 12 slices. Arrange on a grill rack, place under a preheated hot grill and cook for 1–2 minutes on each side until lightly golden.

❖ Rub both sides of each piece of bread with the cut sides of the garlic. Top with strips of sun-dried tomato and olives.

❖ Brush lightly with olive oil and season well. Sprinkle with the basil and mozzarella cheese and return to the grill for 1–2 minutes until the cheese is melted and bubbling.

❖ Transfer to a warmed serving platter and garnish with fresh basil leaves.

Red Onion Bruschetta

❖ **SERVES 4** ❖

6 tbsp extra virgin olive oil
4 red onions, thickly sliced
2 tbsp balsamic vinegar
8 black olives, stoned and chopped
1 tsp fresh thyme leaves
115 g/4 oz goat's cheese, sliced
4 thick slices of rustic bread, such as ciabatta
4 garlic cloves, cut lengthways

❖ Heat 2 tablespoons of the oil in a large heavy-based frying pan. Add the onions and cook over a low heat, stirring occasionally, for 5 minutes until softened. Increase the heat to medium and cook, stirring occasionally, until the onions have begun to colour. Add the vinegar to the pan and cook, stirring constantly, until it has almost completely evaporated. Stir in the olives and thyme leaves.

❖ Toast the bread on 1 side only. Rub the toasted sides with the garlic cloves. Place the bread, toasted side down, on the grill rack and drizzle with the remaining olive oil. Toast the second side.

❖ Divide the onion mixture between the slices of toast and top with the goat's cheese. Return the toast to the grill for 2 minutes, or until the cheese has melted. Serve immediately.

Tomato & Basil Toasts

300 g/10¹/₂ oz cherry tomatoes
4 sun-dried tomatoes
4 tbsp extra virgin olive oil
16 fresh basil leaves, shredded
8 slices ciabatta
2 garlic cloves, peeled
salt and pepper

❖ Using a sharp knife, cut the cherry tomatoes in half.

❖ Using a sharp knife, slice the sun-dried tomatoes into strips.

❖ Place the cherry tomatoes and sun-dried tomatoes in a bowl. Add the olive oil and the shredded basil leaves and toss to mix well. Season to taste with a little salt and pepper.

❖ Lightly toast the ciabatta bread on both sides. Using a sharp knife, cut the garlic cloves in half.

❖ Rub the garlic, with the cut side down, over both sides of the toasted ciabatta bread.

❖ Top the ciabatta bread with the tomato mixture and serve at once on warmed plates.

Fresh Figs with Gorgonzola

❖ **SERVES 4** ❖

4 fresh figs
8 slices French stick, ciabatta
or bloomer

115 g/4 oz Gorgonzola or other
strong blue cheese, sliced
or crumbled

❖ Cut the figs into thin slices. Preheat the grill to medium. Place the bread on the grill rack and toast on 1 side until golden. Remove the rack.

❖ Turn the bread over and top with cheese, making sure that it covers each slice right to the edge.

❖ Arrange the figs on top of the cheese.

❖ Return the rack to the grill and cook for 3–4 minutes, or until the cheese is soft and the fruit is hot. Transfer to a serving dish and serve immediately.

Mini Pitta Pizzas

❖ **MAKES 16** ❖

8 thin asparagus spears
16 mini pitta breads
about 6 tbsp ready-made
tomato pizza sauce
25 g/1 oz mild Cheddar cheese,
grated

25 g/1 oz ricotta cheese
60 g/2¼ oz smoked salmon
olive oil, for drizzling
pepper
sprigs of fresh flat-leaf parsley,
to garnish

❖ Preheat the oven to 200°C/400°F/Gas Mark 6. Cut the asparagus spears into 2.5-cm/1-inch lengths, then cut each piece in half lengthways.

❖ Blanch the asparagus in a saucepan of boiling water for 1 minute. Drain the asparagus, plunge into cold water and drain again.

❖ Place the pitta breads on 2 baking trays. Spread about 1 teaspoon of tomato sauce on each pitta.

❖ Mix the cheeses together and divide between the 16 pitta breads.

❖ Cut the smoked salmon into 16 long, thin strips. Arrange 1 strip on each pitta bread and add the asparagus spears.

❖ Drizzle over a little oil and season to taste with pepper.

❖ Bake in the preheated oven for 8–10 minutes. Garnish with the sprigs of parsley and serve.

Mini Pepperoni Pizzas

BASES
525 g/1 lb 3 oz self-raising
flour, plus extra for dusting
1 tsp salt
85 g/3 oz butter, diced
300–350 ml/10–12 fl oz milk
olive oil, for oiling

PEPPERONI TOPPING
175 ml/6 fl oz ready-made
tomato pizza sauce

115 g/4 oz rindless smoked
bacon, diced
1 orange pepper, deseeded
and chopped
85 g/3 oz pepperoni sausage,
sliced
55 g/2 oz mozzarella cheese,
grated
1/2 tsp dried oregano
salt and pepper
olive oil, for drizzling

❊ Preheat the oven to 200°C/400°F/Gas Mark 6. To make the bases, sift the flour and salt into a bowl, add the butter and rub in with your fingertips until the mixture resembles breadcrumbs. Make a well in the centre of the mixture. Add 300 ml/10 fl oz of the milk and mix with the blade of a knife to a soft dough, adding the remaining milk if necessary.

❊ Turn out on to a lightly floured work surface and knead gently. Divide the dough into 12 equal pieces and roll out each piece into a round. Place on a lightly oiled baking tray and gently push up the edges of each pizza to form a rim.

❊ For the topping, spread the tomato sauce over the bases almost to the edge. Arrange the bacon, chopped pepper and pepperoni on top and sprinkle with the cheese. Sprinkle with the oregano, drizzle with a little oil and season to taste with salt and pepper.

❊ Bake in the preheated oven for 10–15 minutes or until the edges are crisp and the cheese is bubbling. Serve immediately.

Cheese, Garlic & Herb Pâté

15 g/1/2 oz butter
1 garlic clove, crushed
3 spring onions, finely chopped
125 g/41/2 oz full-fat soft
cheese
2 tbsp chopped mixed herbs,
such as parsley, chives,
marjoram, oregano and basil
175 g/6 oz finely grated
mature Cheddar cheese

4–6 slices of white bread from
a medium-cut sliced loaf
pepper
mixed salad leaves and cherry
tomatoes, to serve
ground paprika and sprigs of
fresh herbs, to garnish

❊ Melt the butter in a small frying pan and gently fry the garlic and spring onions together for 3–4 minutes, until soft. Allow to cool.

❊ Beat the soft cheese in a large mixing bowl until smooth, then add the garlic and spring onions. Stir in the herbs, mixing well.

❊ Add the Cheddar cheese and work the mixture together to form a stiff paste. Cover and chill until ready to serve.

❊ Toast the slices of bread on both sides, then cut off the crusts. Using a sharp bread knife, cut through the slices horizontally to make very thin slices. Cut into triangles and then lightly grill the untoasted sides until golden.

❊ Arrange the mixed salad leaves on 4 serving plates with the cherry tomatoes. Pile the cheese pâté on top and sprinkle with a little paprika. Garnish with the herbs and serve with the toast.

Potato & Bean Pâté

100 g/3 1/2 oz floury potatoes,
diced
225 g/8 oz mixed canned beans,
such as borlotti, flageolet and
kidney, drained
1 garlic clove, crushed
2 tsp lime juice
1 tbsp chopped fresh coriander
2 tbsp natural yogurt
salt and pepper
chopped fresh coriander,
to garnish

❀ Bring a saucepan of lightly salted water to the boil and cook the potatoes for 10 minutes until tender. Drain well and mash.

❀ Transfer the mashed potato to a food processor or blender and add the beans, garlic, lime juice and the fresh coriander. Season the mixture and process for 1 minute to make a smooth purée. Alternatively, mix the beans with the potato, garlic, lime juice and coriander and mash well.

❀ Turn the purée into a bowl and add the yogurt. Mix together thoroughly.

❀ Spoon the pâté into a serving dish and garnish with the chopped coriander. Serve at once or cover with clingfilm and leave to chill before use.

Black Olive Pâté

225 g/8 oz stoned juicy black olives
1 garlic clove, crushed
finely grated rind of 1 lemon
4 tbsp lemon juice
25 g/1 oz fresh breadcrumbs
55 g/2 oz full-fat soft cheese
salt and pepper
lemon wedges, to garnish
thick slices of bread and a mixture of olive oil and butter, to serve

❄ Roughly chop the olives and mix with the garlic, lemon rind, lemon juice, breadcrumbs and soft cheese. Pound the mixture until smooth, or place in a food processor and work until fully blended. Season to taste with salt and pepper.

❄ Store the pâté in a screw-top jar and chill for several hours before using – this allows the flavours to develop.

❄ For a delicious cocktail snack, use a pastry cutter to cut out small rounds from a thickly sliced loaf.

❄ Fry the bread rounds in a mixture of olive oil and butter until they are a light golden brown colour. Drain thoroughly on paper towels.

❄ Top each round with a little of the pâté, garnish with lemon wedges and serve immediately. This pâté will keep chilled in an airtight jar for up to 2 weeks.

Parsley, Chicken & Ham Pâté

225 g/8 oz lean, skinless chicken, cooked
100 g/3½ oz lean ham
small bunch fresh parsley
1 tsp lime rind, grated
2 tbsp lime juice
1 garlic clove, peeled
125 ml/4 fl oz natural fromage frais
salt and pepper
1 tsp lime zest, to garnish

TO SERVE
wedges of lime
crisp bread
green salad, to serve

❄ Dice the chicken and ham and place in a blender or food processor.

❄ Add the parsley, lime rind, lime juice and garlic to the chicken and ham, and process well until finely minced. Alternatively, finely chop the chicken, ham, parsley and garlic and place in a bowl. Mix gently with the lime rind and juice.

❄ Transfer the mixture to a bowl and mix in the fromage frais. Season to taste with salt and pepper, cover and leave to chill in the refrigerator for about 30 minutes.

❄ Pile the pâté into individual serving dishes and garnish with lime zest. Serve the pâtés with the lime wedges, bread and salad.

Potted Smoked Chicken

❉ **SERVES 4–6** ❉

350 g/12 oz chopped smoked chicken
pinch each of grated nutmeg and mace
125 g/4 oz butter, softened
2 tbsp port

2 tbsp double cream
1 tbsp clarified butter
salt and pepper
sprig of fresh parsley, to garnish
buttered brown bread, to serve

❉ Place the smoked chicken in a large bowl with the nutmeg, mace, butter, port and cream and season to taste with salt and pepper.

❉ Pound until the mixture is very smooth or blend in a food processor.

❉ Transfer the mixture to individual earthenware pots or one large pot.

❉ Cover each pot with buttered baking paper and weigh down with cans or weights. Chill in the refrigerator for 4 hours.

❉ Remove the paper and cover with clarified butter. Garnish with a sprig of parsley and serve with the slices of buttered brown bread.

Tuna & Anchovy Pâté

❉ **SERVES 6** ❉

PÂTÉ
50 g/1¾ oz canned anchovy fillets, drained
about 400 g/14 oz canned tuna in brine, drained
175 g/6 oz low-fat cottage cheese
125 g/4½ oz low-fat soft cheese

1 tbsp horseradish relish
½ tsp grated orange rind
white pepper
orange slices and sprigs of fresh dill, to garnish

MELBA CROÛTONS
4 thick slices wholemeal bread

❉ To make the pâté, separate the anchovy fillets and pat well with kitchen paper to remove all traces of oil.

❉ Place the anchovy fillets and all the remaining pâté ingredients into a blender or food processor. Process for a few seconds until smooth. Alternatively, finely chop the anchovy fillets and flake the tuna, then beat together with the remaining ingredients; this will make a more textured pâté.

❉ Transfer to a mixing bowl, cover and chill for 1 hour.

❉ To make the Melba croûtons, place the bread slices under a preheated medium grill for 2–3 minutes on each side until lightly browned.

❉ Using a serrated knife, slice off the crusts and slide the knife between the toasted edges of the bread.

❉ Stamp out circles using a 5-cm/2-inch round cutter and place on a baking tray. Alternatively, cut each piece of toast in half diagonally. Bake in a preheated oven, 150°C/300°F/Gas Mark 2, for 15–20 minutes until curled and dry.

❉ Spoon the pâté on to serving plates and garnish with the orange slices and fresh dill. Serve with the freshly baked Melba croûtons.

Watercress & Cheese Tartlets

100 g/4 oz plain flour,
plus extra for dusting
pinch of salt
85 g/3 oz butter or margarine
2–3 tbsp cold water
2 bunches of watercress
2 garlic cloves, crushed
1 shallot, chopped
150 g/5½ oz Cheddar cheese,
grated
4 tbsp natural yogurt
½ tsp paprika

❖ Sift the flour into a mixing bowl and add the salt. Rub 55 g/2 oz of the butter into the flour until the mixture resembles breadcrumbs. Stir in enough of the cold water to make a smooth dough.

❖ Roll out the dough on a lightly floured surface and use to line 4 x 10-cm/4-inch tartlet tins. Prick the bases with a fork and set aside to chill in the refrigerator.

❖ Heat the remaining butter in a frying pan. Discard the stems from the watercress. Add the leaves to the pan with the garlic and shallot and cook for 1–2 minutes until wilted.

❖ Remove the pan from the heat and stir in the grated cheese, yogurt and paprika.

❖ Spoon the mixture into the pastry cases and cook in a preheated oven, 180°C/350°F/Gas Mark 4, for 20 minutes or until the filling is just firm. Turn out the tartlets and serve immediately, if serving hot, or place on a wire rack to cool, if serving cold.

Garlic & Pine Kernel Tartlets

❋ SERVES 4 ❋

4 slices wholemeal or granary
bread
50 g/1¾ oz pine kernels
150 g/5½ oz butter
5 garlic cloves, peeled
and halved

2 tbsp fresh oregano, chopped,
plus extra for garnish
4 black olives, stoned and
halved
fresh oregano leaves, to
garnish

❋ Using a rolling pin, flatten the bread slightly. Using a pastry cutter, cut out 4 circles of bread to fit your individual tart tins – they should measure about 10 cm/4 inches across. Reserve the offcuts of bread and leave them in the refrigerator for 10 minutes or until required.

❋ Meanwhile, place the pine kernels on a baking tray. Toast the pine kernels under a preheated grill for 2–3 minutes or until golden.

❋ Put the bread offcuts, pine kernels, butter, garlic and oregano into a food processor and blend for about 20 seconds. Alternatively, pound the ingredients by hand in a mortar with a pestle. The mixture should have a rough texture.

❋ Spoon the pine kernel butter mixture into the lined tin and top with the olives. Bake in a preheated oven, 200°C/400°F/ Gas Mark 6, for 10–15 minutes or until golden.

❋ Transfer the tartlets to serving plates and serve warm, garnished with the oregano leaves.

Onion & Mozzarella Tartlets

❋ SERVES 4 ❋

250 g/9 oz packet puff pastry,
thawed, if frozen
2 medium red onions
1 red pepper

8 cherry tomatoes, halved
100 g/3½ oz mozzarella
cheese, cut into chunks
8 sprigs fresh thyme

❋ Roll out the pastry to make 4 x 7.5-cm/3-inch squares. Using a sharp knife, trim the edges of the pastry, reserving the trimmings. Leave the pastry to chill in the refrigerator for 30 minutes.

❋ Place the pastry squares on a baking tray. Brush a little water along each edge of the pastry squares and use the reserved pastry trimmings to make a rim around each tart.

❋ Cut the red onions into thin wedges and halve and deseed the red pepper.

❋ Place the onions and the red pepper in a roasting tin. Cook under a preheated grill for 15 minutes or until charred.

❋ Place the roasted pepper halves in a polythene bag and leave to sweat for 10 minutes. Peel off the skin from the peppers and cut the flesh into strips.

❋ Line the pastry squares with squares of foil. Bake in a preheated oven, 200°C/400°F/Gas Mark 6, for 10 minutes. Remove the foil squares and bake for a further 5 minutes.

❋ Place the onions, pepper strips, tomatoes and cheese in each tart and sprinkle with the fresh thyme.

❋ Return to the oven for 15 minutes or until the pastry is golden. Serve hot.

Pissaladière with Marjoram

❊ **SERVES 8** ❊

4 tbsp olive oil
700 g/1 lb 9 oz red onions,
   thinly sliced
2 garlic cloves, crushed
2 tsp caster sugar
2 tbsp red wine vinegar
350 g/12 oz ready-made puff
   pastry
salt and pepper

TOPPING
100 g/3 1/2 oz canned anchovy
   fillets
12 green olives, stoned
1 tsp dried marjoram

❊ Lightly grease a Swiss roll tin. Heat the olive oil in a large saucepan. Add the onions and garlic and cook over a low heat for about 30 minutes, stirring occasionally.

❊ Add the sugar and vinegar to the pan and season with plenty of salt and pepper.

❊ On a lightly floured surface, roll out the pastry to a rectangle about 33 x 23 cm/13 x 9 inches. Place the pastry rectangle on the prepared tin, pushing the pastry well into the corners of the tin.

❊ Spread the onion mixture evenly over the pastry.

❊ Arrange the anchovy fillets and olives on top, then sprinkle with the marjoram.

❊ Bake in a preheated oven, 220°C/ 425°F/Gas Mark 7, for 20–25 minutes, or until the pissaladière is lightly golden. Serve piping hot, straight from the oven.

Mini Vegetable Puff Pastries

❊ **SERVES 4** ❊

PASTRY
450 g/1 lb ready-made puff
   pastry
1 egg, beaten

FILLING
225 g/8 oz sweet potatoes,
   diced
100 g/3 1/2 oz baby asparagus
   spears

2 tbsp butter or margarine
1 leek, sliced
2 small open-cup mushrooms,
   sliced
1 tsp lime juice
1 tsp chopped fresh thyme
pinch of mustard powder
salt and pepper

❊ Cut the pastry into 4 equal pieces. Roll each piece out on a lightly floured work surface to form a 13-cm/5-inch square. Place on a dampened baking tray and score a smaller 6-cm/2 1/2-inch square inside.

❊ Brush with the beaten egg and cook in a preheated oven, 200°C/400°F/Gas Mark 6, for 20 minutes or until risen and golden brown.

❊ While the pastry is cooking, start the filling. Cook the sweet potato in boiling water for 15 minutes, then drain. Blanch the asparagus in boiling water for 10 minutes or until tender. Drain and reserve.

❊ Remove the pastry squares from the oven. Carefully cut out the central square of pastry, lift out and reserve.

❊ Melt the butter in a saucepan and sauté the leek and mushrooms for 2–3 minutes. Add the lime juice, thyme and mustard, season well and stir in the sweet potatoes and asparagus. Spoon into the pastry cases, top with the reserved pastry squares and serve immediately.

Mini Cheese & Onion Tartlets

PASTRY
100 g/3¹/₂ oz plain flour, plus extra for dusting
¹/₄ tsp salt
5¹/₂ tbsp butter, cut into small pieces
1–2 tbsp water

FILLING
1 egg, beaten
100 ml/3¹/₂ fl oz single cream
50 g/1³/₄ oz Red Leicester cheese, grated
3 spring onions, finely chopped
salt
cayenne pepper

❖ To make the pastry, sift the flour and salt into a large bowl. Add the butter and rub in with your fingertips until the mixture resembles breadcrumbs. Stir in the water and mix to form a dough. Form the dough into a ball, cover with clingfilm and chill in the refrigerator for 30 minutes.

❖ Preheat the oven to 180°C/350°F/Gas Mark 4. Roll out the pastry on a lightly floured work surface. Using a 7.5-cm/3-inch plain cutter, cut out 12 rounds from the pastry and use them to line a 12-hole tartlet tin.

❖ To make the filling, whisk the beaten egg, cream, cheese and spring onions together in a jug. Season to taste with salt and cayenne pepper. Carefully pour the filling mixture into the pastry cases and bake in the preheated oven for 20–25 minutes, or until the filling is just set and the pastry is golden brown. Serve the tartlets warm or cold.

Fresh Tomato Tartlets

❋ **SERVES 6** ❋

250 g/9 oz puff pastry, thawed, if frozen
1 egg, beaten
2 tbsp ready-made pesto
6 plum tomatoes, sliced
salt and pepper
fresh thyme leaves, to garnish (optional)

❋ On a lightly floured surface, roll out the pastry to a rectangle measuring 30 x 25 cm/12 x 10 inches.

❋ Cut the rectangle in half and divide each half into 3 pieces to make 6 even-sized rectangles. Leave in the refrigerator to chill for 20 minutes.

❋ Lightly score the edges of the pastry rectangles and brush them with the beaten egg.

❋ Spread the pesto over the rectangles, dividing it equally between them, leaving a 2¹/2-cm/1-inch border around each rectangle.

❋ Arrange the tomato along the centre of each rectangle on top of the pesto.

❋ Season well to taste with salt and pepper and lightly sprinkle with the thyme leaves, if using.

❋ Bake in a preheated oven, 200°C/ 400°F/Gas Mark 6, for 15–20 minutes until well risen and golden brown.

❋ Transfer the tomato tartlets to warmed serving plates, garnish and serve while they are still piping hot.

Feta Cheese Tartlets

❋ **SERVES 4** ❋

8 slices bread from a medium-cut large loaf
125 g/4¹/2 oz butter, melted
125 g/4¹/2 oz feta cheese, cut into small cubes
4 cherry tomatoes, cut into wedges
8 black or green olives, stoned and halved
8 hard-boiled quail's eggs
2 tbsp olive oil
1 tbsp wine vinegar
1 tsp wholegrain mustard
pinch of caster sugar
salt and pepper
sprigs of fresh parsley, to garnish

❋ Remove the crusts from the bread. Trim the bread into squares and flatten each piece with a rolling pin.

❋ Brush the bread with melted butter, and then arrange them in bun tins. Press a piece of crumpled foil into each bread case to secure in place. Bake in a preheated oven, 190°C/375°F/Gas Mark 5, for about 10 minutes, or until crisp and browned.

❋ Meanwhile, mix together the feta cheese, tomatoes and olives. Shell the eggs and quarter them. Mix together the olive oil, vinegar, mustard and sugar. Season to taste with salt and pepper.

❋ Remove the bread cases from the oven and discard the foil. Leave to cool.

❋ Just before serving, fill the bread cases with the cheese and tomato mixture. Arrange the eggs on top and spoon over the dressing. Garnish with the parsley.

Filo Parcels

❁ **SERVES 6** ❁

55 g/2 oz butter	2 tbsp single cream
1 tbsp sunflower oil	140 g/4½ oz Gruyère or
4 leeks, sliced	Emmenthal cheese, grated
2 onions, chopped	12 sheets filo pastry, thawed
1 garlic clove, finely chopped	if frozen
2 tsp chopped fresh thyme	salt and pepper

❁ Melt half the butter with the oil in a large heavy-based frying pan. Add the leeks, onions, garlic and thyme and season to taste with salt and pepper. Cook, stirring frequently, for 10 minutes. Stir in the cream and cook for a further 2–3 minutes, until all the liquid has been absorbed. Remove the pan from the heat and set aside to cool. Stir in the cheese, cover with clingfilm and chill in the refrigerator for 30 minutes.

❁ Melt the remaining butter and brush a little on to a baking tray. Brush 2 sheets of filo with butter and place them one on top of the other. Place a heaped spoonful of the leek mixture close to one corner. Fold the corner over the filling, fold in the sides and roll up the parcel. Place the parcel, seam side down, on the baking tray and make 5 more parcels in the same way.

❁ Brush the pastry parcels with the remaining melted butter and bake in a preheated oven, 180°C/350°F/Gas Mark 4, for 30 minutes until crisp and golden. Serve immediately.

Spinach Filo Baskets

❁ **MAKES 2** ❁

125 g/4½ oz fresh leaf spinach,	90 g/3 oz mature Cheddar
washed and roughly chopped,	cheese, grated
or 90 g/3 oz thawed frozen	pinch of mixed spice
spinach	1 egg yolk
2–4 spring onions, trimmed	4 sheets filo pastry
and chopped, or 1 tbsp finely	25 g/1 oz butter, melted
chopped onion	salt and pepper
1 garlic clove, crushed	2 spring onions, to garnish
2 tbsp grated Parmesan	
cheese	

❁ If using fresh spinach, cook it in the minimum of boiling salted water for 3–4 minutes, until tender. Drain thoroughly, using a potato masher to remove excess liquid, then chop and put into a bowl. If using frozen spinach, simply drain and chop. Add the spring onions, garlic, cheeses, mixed spice, egg yolk and seasoning and mix well.

❁ Grease 2 individual Yorkshire pudding tins, or ovenproof dishes or tins about 12 cm/5 inches in diameter, and 4 cm/ 1½ inches deep. Cut the filo pastry sheets in half to make 8 pieces and brush each piece lightly with melted butter.

❁ Place one piece of filo pastry in a tin or dish and then cover with a second piece at right angles to the first. Add two more pieces at right angles, so that all the corners are in different places. Line the other tin in the same way.

❁ Spoon the spinach mixture into the 'baskets' and cook in a preheated oven, 180°C/350°F/Gas Mark 4, for about 20 minutes, or until the pastry is golden brown. Garnish with a spring onion tassel and serve hot or cold.

❁ Make spring onion tassels about 30 minutes before required. Trim off the root end and cut to a length of 5–7 cm/2–3 inches. Make a series of cuts from the green end to within 2 cm/¾ inch of the other end. Place in a bowl of iced water to open out. Drain well before use.

Filo Mushroom Purses

5 tbsp oil
115 g/4 oz button mushrooms, sliced
2 celery sticks, cut into thin shreds
1 carrot, cut into thin shreds
4 spring onions, cut into thin shreds
2.5-cm/1-inch piece of root ginger, grated
juice of 1 small lemon
5 large sheets filo pastry, about 45 x 30 cm/18 x 12 inches each
salt and pepper

❊ Heat 2 tablespoons of the oil in a large frying pan. Add the mushrooms, celery, carrot, spring onions and ginger and stir-fry over a high heat for 3–4 minutes, or until beginning to soften.

❊ Add the lemon juice and stir-fry until the vegetables are tender and the moisture has evaporated. Season to taste with salt and pepper, then leave to cool. Preheat the oven to 200°C/400°F/Gas Mark 6.

❊ Cut the pastry sheets into 4 pieces to make 20 rectangles. Lightly brush each piece with oil and layer them in 6 piles of 3 pieces. There will be 2 pieces left over. These can be used for patching any damaged pastry.

❊ Divide the vegetable mixture between the 6 pastry rectangles, draw up the pastry around the filling and pinch the tops together. Place on a baking tray and brush with oil. Bake for 20 minutes until browned and crisp.

Mini Prawn Cocktail Puffs

❊ **MAKES 22** ❊

CHOUX PASTRY
55 g/2 oz butter, plus extra for greasing
150 ml/5 fl oz water
70 g/2½ oz plain flour, sifted
2 eggs, beaten

FILLING
2 tbsp mayonnaise
1 tsp tomato purée

140 g/5 oz small cooked peeled prawns
1 tsp Worcestershire sauce
salt
Tabasco sauce
1 Little Gem lettuce, shredded, to serve
cayenne pepper, to garnish

❊ Preheat the oven to 180°C/350°F/Gas Mark 4. Grease a baking tray. To make the choux pastry, put the butter and water into a large heavy-based saucepan and bring to the boil. Add the flour, all at once, and beat thoroughly until the mixture leaves the sides of the pan. Let cool slightly, then vigorously beat in the beaten egg, a little at a time. Place 22 walnut-sized spoonfuls of the mixture on to the baking tray, spaced 2 cm/¾ inch apart. Bake in the preheated oven for 35 minutes, or until light, crisp and golden. Transfer to a cooling rack to cool. Cut a 5-mm/¼-inch slice from the top of each puff.

❊ To make the filling, place the mayonnaise, tomato paste, prawns and Worcestershire sauce in a bowl. Add salt and Tabasco sauce to taste, and mix together until combined.

❊ Place a few lettuce shreds in the bottom of each puff, making some protrude at the top. Spoon the prawn mixture on top and dust with a little cayenne pepper before serving.

Deep-Fried Diamond Pastries

❊ **SERVES 4** ❊

150 g/5½ oz plain flour
1 tsp baking powder
½ tsp salt
1 tbsp black cumin seeds

100 ml/3½ fl oz water
300 ml/10 fl oz oil
dhal, to serve

❊ Place the flour in a large mixing bowl. Add the baking powder, salt and cumin seeds and stir to mix.

❊ Add the water to the dry ingredients and mix together until combined to form a soft, elastic dough.

❊ Roll out the dough on a clean work surface to about 6 mm/¼ inch thick.

❊ Using a sharp knife, score the dough to form diamond shapes. Re-roll the trimmings and cut out more diamond shapes until the dough has been used up.

❊ Heat the oil in a large saucepan to 180°F/350°C or until a cube of bread browns in 30 seconds.

❊ Carefully place the pastry diamonds in the oil, in batches if necessary, and deep-fry until golden brown.

❊ Remove the diamond pastries with a slotted spoon and drain on kitchen paper. Serve with a dhal for dipping or store and serve when required.

Refried Bean Nachos

400 g/14 oz canned refried beans

400 g/14 oz canned pinto beans, drained

large pinch of ground cumin

large pinch of mild chilli powder

175 g/6 oz tortilla chips

225 g/8 oz grated cheese, such as Cheddar

salsa of your choice

1 avocado, stoned, diced and tossed with lime juice

1/2 small onion or 3–5 spring onions, chopped

2 ripe tomatoes, diced

handful of shredded lettuce

3–4 tbsp chopped fresh coriander

soured cream, to serve

❋ Place the refried beans in a pan with the pinto beans, cumin and chilli powder. Add enough water to make a thick soup-like consistency, stirring gently so that the beans do not lose their texture.

❋ Heat the bean mixture over a medium heat until hot, then reduce the heat and keep the mixture warm while you prepare the rest of the dish.

❋ Arrange half the tortilla chips in the bottom of a flameproof casserole or gratin dish and cover with the bean mixture. Sprinkle with the cheese and bake in a preheated oven, 200°C/400°F/Gas Mark 6, until the cheese melts.

❋ Alternatively, place the casserole under a preheated grill and grill for 5–7 minutes or until the cheese melts and lightly sizzles in places.

❋ Arrange the salsa, avocado, onion, tomato, lettuce and fresh coriander on top of the melted cheese. Surround with the remaining tortilla chips and serve immediately with the soured cream.

Potatoes with a Spicy Filling

4 large baking potatoes

1 tbsp vegetable oil (optional)

430 g/15 1/2 oz canned chickpeas, drained

1 tsp ground coriander

1 tsp ground cumin

4 tbsp chopped fresh coriander

150 ml/5 fl oz low-fat natural yogurt

salt and pepper

SALAD

2 tomatoes

4 tbsp chopped fresh coriander

1/2 cucumber

1/2 red onion

❋ Scrub the potatoes and pat them dry with absorbent kitchen paper. Prick them all over with a fork, brush with the oil, if using, and season with salt and pepper.

❋ Place the potatoes on a baking tray and bake in a preheated oven, 200°C/400°F/Gas Mark 6, for 1–1 1/4 hours or until cooked through. Cool for 10 minutes.

❋ Meanwhile, mash the chickpeas with a fork or potato masher. Stir in the ground coriander, cumin and half the fresh coriander. Cover and set aside.

❋ Halve the cooked potatoes and scoop the flesh into a bowl, keeping the shells intact. Mash the flesh and gently mix into the chickpea mixture with the yogurt. Season to taste.

❋ Fill the potato shells with the potato and chickpea mixture and place on a baking tray. Return the potatoes to the oven and bake for 10–15 minutes until heated through.

❋ Meanwhile, make the salad. Using a sharp knife, chop the tomatoes. Slice the cucumber and cut the onion into thin slices. Toss all the ingredients together in a serving dish.

❋ Serve the potatoes sprinkled with the remaining chopped coriander and the prepared salad.

Feta & Potato Cakes

500 g/1 lb 2 oz floury
potatoes, unpeeled
salt and pepper
4 spring onions, chopped
115 g/4 oz feta cheese,
crumbled
2 tsp chopped fresh thyme
1 egg, beaten
1 tbsp lemon juice
plain flour, for dusting
3 tbsp corn oil
fresh chives, to garnish

❖ Bring a saucepan of lightly salted water to the boil and cook the potatoes for about 25 minutes or until tender. Drain and peel. Place the potatoes in a bowl and mash well with a potato masher or fork.

❖ Add the spring onions, feta cheese, thyme, egg and lemon juice and season to taste with salt and pepper. Mix thoroughly. Cover the bowl with clingfilm and chill in the refrigerator for 1 hour.

❖ Take small handfuls of the potato mixture and roll into balls about the size of a walnut between the palms of your hands. Flatten each one slightly and dust all over with flour. Heat the oil in a frying pan over a high heat and cook the potato cakes, in batches, if necessary, until golden brown on both sides. Drain on kitchen paper and serve, garnished with the chives.

70

Sweet Potato Patties

500 g/1 lb 2 oz sweet potatoes
2 garlic cloves, crushed
1 small fresh green chilli, chopped
2 sprigs fresh coriander, chopped
1 tbsp dark soy sauce
plain flour, for shaping
vegetable oil, for frying
sesame seeds, for sprinkling

SOY-TOMATO SAUCE
2 tsp vegetable oil
1 garlic clove, finely chopped
1 1/2 tsp finely chopped fresh root ginger
3 tomatoes, peeled and chopped
2 tbsp dark soy sauce
1 tbsp lime juice
2 tbsp chopped fresh coriander

❄ To make the soy-tomato sauce, heat the oil in a wok and stir-fry the garlic and ginger for about 1 minute. Add the tomatoes and stir-fry for a further 2 minutes. Remove from the heat and stir in the soy sauce, lime juice and chopped coriander. Set aside and keep warm.

❄ Peel the sweet potatoes and grate finely (you can do this quickly with a food processor). Place the garlic, chilli and coriander in a mortar and crush to a smooth paste with a pestle. Stir in the soy sauce and mix with the sweet potatoes.

❄ Divide the mixture into 12 equal portions. Dip into flour and pat into a flat, round patty shape.

❄ Heat a shallow layer of oil in a wide frying pan. Fry the patties in batches over a high heat until golden, turning once.

❄ Drain on kitchen paper and sprinkle with sesame seeds. Serve hot, with a spoonful of the soy-tomato sauce.

Potato & Mushroom Hash

675 g/1 lb 8 oz potatoes, diced
1 tbsp olive oil
2 garlic cloves, crushed
1 green pepper, deseeded and diced
1 yellow pepper, deseeded and diced
3 tomatoes, diced

75 g/3 oz button mushrooms, halved
1 tbsp Worcestershire sauce
2 tbsp chopped fresh basil
salt and pepper
sprigs of fresh basil, to garnish
warmed crusty bread, to serve

❄ Bring a saucepan of lightly salted water to the boil and cook the potatoes for 7–8 minutes. Drain well and reserve.

❄ Heat the oil in a large heavy-based frying pan and cook the potatoes for 8–10 minutes, stirring until browned.

❄ Add the garlic and peppers to the frying pan and cook for 2–3 minutes.

❄ Stir the tomatoes and mushrooms into the mixture and continue to cook, stirring, for a further 5–6 minutes.

❄ Stir in the Worcestershire sauce and basil and season well.

❄ Transfer the hash to a warmed serving dish, garnish with the fresh basil and serve at once with crusty bread.

Tapas Potatoes with Chillies

❖ **SERVES 4–6** ❖

1 kg/2 lb 4 oz small new
potatoes, unpeeled
3 dried red chillies
4 tbsp olive oil
2 garlic cloves,
finely chopped

4 spring onions, chopped
200 g/7 oz canned tomatoes
1 tbsp passata
1 tbsp sherry vinegar
1/2 tsp saffron threads, crushed
salt and pepper

❖ Bring a large saucepan of lightly salted water to the boil and cook the potatoes for 10–15 minutes or until only just tender. Drain and leave until cool enough to handle.

❖ Meanwhile, crush the chillies in a mortar with a pestle. Heat the oil in a heavy-based saucepan. Add the garlic and spring onions and cook over a medium heat for 5 minutes, until softened. Stir in the crushed chillies, tomatoes with their juices, passata, vinegar and saffron and season to taste with salt and pepper. Reduce the heat and simmer gently, stirring occasionally, for 10 minutes.

❖ Cut the potatoes in half and add to the saucepan, stirring well to coat. Cover and simmer gently for a further 10 minutes. Taste, adjust the seasoning and serve hot or at room temperature.

Pork Dim Sum

❖ **SERVES 4** ❖

400 g/14 oz pork mince
2 spring onions, chopped
50 g/1³/4 oz canned bamboo
shoots, drained, rinsed and
chopped
1 tbsp light soy sauce

1 tbsp dry sherry
2 tsp sesame oil
2 tsp caster sugar
1 egg white, lightly beaten
4¹/2 tsp cornflour
24 wonton wrappers

❖ Place the pork, spring onions, bamboo shoots, soy sauce, dry sherry, sesame oil, sugar and beaten egg white in a large mixing bowl and mix until all the ingredients are thoroughly combined.

❖ Stir in the cornflour, mixing until thoroughly incorporated with the other ingredients.

❖ Spread out the wonton wrappers on a work surface. Place a spoonful of the pork and vegetable mixture in the centre of each wonton wrapper and lightly brush the edges of the wrappers with water.

❖ Bring the sides of the wrappers together in the centre of the filling, pinching firmly together.

❖ Line a steamer with a damp tea towel and arrange the wontons inside.

❖ Cover and steam for 5–7 minutes, until the dim sum are cooked through. Serve immediately.

Barbecued Spare Ribs

500 g/1 lb 2 oz pork finger
spare ribs
1 tbsp sugar
1 tbsp light soy sauce
1 tbsp dark soy sauce
3 tbsp hoisin sauce
1 tbsp rice wine or dry sherry
4–5 tbsp water or
Chinese stock
coriander leaves,
to garnish
mild chilli sauce, to dip

❉ Using a sharp knife, trim off any excess fat from the spare ribs and cut into pieces. Place the ribs in a baking dish.

❉ Mix together the sugar, light and dark soy sauce, hoisin sauce and wine. Pour over the ribs in the baking dish. Turn to coat the ribs thoroughly in the mixture and leave to marinate for about 2–3 hours.

❉ Add the water to the ribs and spread them out in the dish. Roast in a preheated hot oven for 15 minutes.

❉ Turn the ribs over, reduce the oven temperature and cook for a further 30–35 minutes.

❉ To serve, chop each rib into 3–4 small bite-sized pieces with a large knife or meat cleaver and arrange neatly on a serving dish.

❉ Pour the sauce from the baking dish over the spare ribs and garnish with a few coriander leaves. Place some mild chilli sauce into a small dish and serve with the ribs as a dip. Serve immediately.

Barbecued Pork

500 g/1 lb 2 oz pork fillet	1 tbsp light soy sauce
150 ml/5 fl oz boiling water	1 tbsp hoisin sauce
1 tbsp honey, dissolved with a	1 tbsp oyster sauce
little hot water	1/2 tsp chilli sauce
	1 tbsp brandy or rum
MARINADE	1 tsp sesame oil
1 tbsp sugar	shredded lettuce, to serve
1 tbsp crushed yellow bean	
sauce	

❊ Using a sharp knife or meat cleaver, cut the pork into strips about 2.5 cm/1 inch thick and 18–20 cm/7–8 inches long and place in a large shallow dish. Mix the marinade ingredients together and pour over the pork, turning until well coated. Cover, and leave to marinate for at least 3–4 hours, turning occasionally.

❊ Remove the pork strips from the dish with a slotted spoon, reserving the marinade. Arrange the pork strips on a rack over a roasting tin. Place the tin in a preheated oven and pour in the boiling water. Roast the pork for about 10–15 minutes.

❊ Reduce the oven temperature. Baste the pork strips with the reserved marinade and turn over using metal tongs. Roast for a further 10 minutes.

❊ Remove the pork from the oven, brush with the honey syrup and lightly brown under a medium–hot grill for about 3–4 minutes, turning once or twice.

❊ To serve, allow the pork to cool slightly before cutting it. Cut across the grain into thin slices and arrange neatly on a bed of shredded lettuce. Make a sauce by boiling the marinade and the drippings in the roasting tin for a few minutes, strain and pour over the pork.

Pork Satay

8 bamboo satay sticks, soaked	pinch of ground turmeric
in warm water	1 tbsp dark muscovado sugar
500 g/1 lb 2 oz pork fillet	salt

SAUCE	**TO GARNISH**
125 g/4 1/2 oz unsalted peanuts	fresh flat-leaf parsley or
2 tsp hot chilli sauce	coriander
175 ml/6 fl oz coconut milk	cucumber leaves
2 tbsp soy sauce	red chillies
1 tbsp ground coriander	

❊ To make the sauce, scatter the peanuts on a baking tray and toast under a preheated grill until golden brown, turning them once or twice. Leave to cool, then grind them in a food processor, blender or food mill. Alternatively, chop the peanuts very finely.

❊ Put the ground peanuts into a small saucepan with the hot chilli sauce, coconut milk, soy sauce, coriander, turmeric, sugar and salt. Heat gently, stirring constantly and taking care not to burn the sauce on the bottom of the pan. Reduce the heat to very low and cook gently for 5 minutes.

❊ Meanwhile, trim any fat from the pork. Cut the pork into small cubes and thread it on to the bamboo satay sticks. Place the kebabs on a rack covered with foil in a grill pan.

❊ Put half the peanut sauce into a small serving bowl. Brush the skewered pork with the remaining satay sauce and place under a preheated grill for about 10 minutes, turning and basting frequently, until cooked.

❊ Serve the pork with the reserved peanut sauce and garnish with the parsley, cucumber leaves and chillies.

Pork Sesame Toasts

250 g/9 oz lean pork
250 g/9 oz uncooked peeled
    prawns, deveined
4 spring onions, trimmed
1 garlic clove, crushed
1 tbsp chopped fresh
    coriander, leaves and stems
1 tbsp fish sauce
1 egg

8–10 slices of thick-cut white
    bread
3 tbsp sesame seeds
150 ml/5 fl oz vegetable oil
salt and pepper
sprigs of fresh coriander and
    finely sliced red pepper,
    to garnish

❀ Put the pork, prawns, spring onions, garlic, coriander, fish sauce, egg and seasoning into a food processor or blender. Process for a few seconds until the ingredients are finely chopped. Transfer the mixture to a bowl. Alternatively, chop the pork, prawns and spring onions very finely, and mix with the garlic, coriander, fish sauce, beaten egg and seasoning until all the ingredients are well combined.

❀ Spread the pork and prawn mixture thickly over the bread so that it reaches right up to the edges. Cut off the crusts and slice each piece of bread into 4 squares or triangles.

❀ Sprinkle the topping liberally with sesame seeds.

❀ Heat the oil in a wok or frying pan. Fry a few pieces of the bread, topping side down first so that it sets the egg, for about 2 minutes or until golden brown. Turn the pieces over to cook on the other side, about 1 minute.

❀ Drain the pork and prawn toasts and place them on kitchen paper. Fry the remaining pieces. Serve garnished with the coriander and slices of red pepper.

Honeyed Chicken Wings

450 g/1 lb chicken wings
2 tbsp groundnut oil
2 tbsp light soy sauce
2 tbsp hoisin sauce
2 tbsp clear honey
2 garlic cloves, crushed
1 tsp sesame seeds

MARINADE
1 dried red chilli
1/2–1 tsp chilli powder
1/2–1 tsp ground ginger
finely grated rind of 1 lime

❀ To make the marinade, crush the dried chilli in a mortar with a pestle. Mix together the crushed dried chilli, chilli powder, ground ginger and lime rind in a small mixing bowl.

❀ Thoroughly rub the spice mixture into the chicken wings with your fingertips. Set aside for at least 2 hours to allow the flavours to penetrate the chicken wings.

❀ Heat the oil in a large wok or frying pan.

❀ Add the chicken wings and fry, turning frequently, for about 10–12 minutes, until golden and crisp. Drain off any excess oil.

❀ Add the soy sauce, hoisin sauce, honey, garlic and sesame seeds to the wok, turning the chicken wings to coat.

❀ Reduce the heat and cook for 20–25 minutes, turning the chicken wings frequently, until completely cooked through. Serve hot.

Bang-Bang Chicken

1 litre/1¾ pints water
4 chicken pieces, breasts
and legs
1 cucumber, cut into
matchstick shreds
1 tsp white sesame seeds,
to garnish

SAUCE
2 tbsp light soy sauce
1 tsp sugar
1 tbsp finely chopped spring
onion, plus extra to garnish
1 tsp red chilli oil
¼ tsp pepper
2 tbsp peanut butter, creamed
with a little sesame oil

❖ Bring the water to a rolling boil in a wok or a large saucepan. Add the chicken pieces, reduce the heat, cover and cook for 30–35 minutes.

❖ Remove the chicken from the wok and immerse in a bowl of cold water for at least 1 hour to cool it, ready for shredding.

❖ Remove the chicken pieces, drain and dry on absorbent kitchen paper. Take the meat off the bone.

❖ On a flat surface, pound the chicken with a rolling pin, then tear the meat into shreds with 2 forks. Mix the chicken with the shredded cucumber and arrange in a serving dish.

❖ To serve, mix together all the sauce ingredients until thoroughly combined and pour over the chicken and cucumber in the serving dish. Sprinkle some sesame seeds and chopped spring onions over the sauce and serve.

76

Griddled Smoked Salmon

350 g/12 oz sliced
smoked salmon
115 g/4 oz mixed salad leaves
sprigs of fresh dill, to garnish

VINAIGRETTE
1 tsp Dijon mustard
1 garlic clove, crushed
2 tsp chopped fresh dill
2 tsp sherry vinegar
4 tbsp olive oil
salt and pepper

❖ Take the slices of smoked salmon, 1 at a time, and carefully fold them, making 2 folds accordion style, so that they form little parcels.

❖ To make the vinaigrette, whisk the mustard, garlic, dill and sherry vinegar together. Season to taste with salt and pepper. Gradually whisk in the olive oil until thoroughly combined.

❖ Heat a griddle pan until smoking. Cook the salmon parcels on 1 side only for 2–3 minutes until heated through and marked from the pan. Cook in batches, if necessary.

❖ Meanwhile, toss the salad leaves with some of the vinaigrette and divide them equally between 4 serving plates. Top with the cooked smoked salmon, cooked side up. Drizzle with the remaining dressing, garnish with the dill and serve immediately.

Salmon Tartare

900 g/2 lb very fresh salmon
fillet, skinned
3 tbsp lemon juice
3 tbsp lime juice
2 tsp sugar
1 tsp Dijon mustard
1 tbsp chopped fresh dill
1 tbsp chopped fresh basil
2 tbsp olive oil

55 g/2 oz rocket
handful of fresh basil leaves
55 g/2 oz mixed salad leaves
salt and pepper

TO GARNISH
sprigs of fresh dill
fresh basil leaves

❖ Cut the salmon into very tiny dice and season to taste with salt and pepper. Put into a large bowl.

❖ Combine the lemon juice, lime juice, sugar, mustard, dill, chopped basil and olive oil. Pour the mixture over the salmon and mix well. Set aside for 15–20 minutes until the fish becomes opaque.

❖ Meanwhile, mix together the rocket, basil leaves and salad leaves. Divide between 4 serving plates.

❖ To serve the salmon, fill 4 small ramekins or mini pudding basins with the mixture and turn out on to the centre of the salad leaves. Garnish with dill sprigs and basil leaves.

Prawn Parcels

1 tbsp sunflower oil
1 red pepper, deseeded and very thinly sliced
75 g/2¾ oz beansprouts
finely grated zest and juice of 1 lime
1 red chilli, deseeded and very finely chopped
1-cm/½-inch piece of root ginger, peeled and grated

225 g/8 oz peeled prawns
1 tbsp fish sauce
½ tsp arrowroot
2 tbsp chopped fresh coriander
8 sheets filo pastry
25 g/1 oz butter
2 tsp sesame oil, for frying
spring onion tassels, to garnish (see page 66)
chilli sauce, to serve

❊ Heat the sunflower oil in a large preheated wok. Add the red pepper and beansprouts and stir-fry for 2 minutes, or until the vegetables have softened.

❊ Remove the wok from the heat and toss in the lime zest and juice, chilli, ginger and prawns, stirring well.

❊ Mix the fish sauce with the arrowroot and stir the mixture into the wok juices. Return the wok to the heat and cook, stirring, for 2 minutes, or until the juices thicken. Toss in the coriander and mix well.

❊ Lay out the sheets of filo pastry on a board. Melt the butter and sesame oil and brush each pastry sheet with the mixture.

❊ Spoon a little of the prawn filling on to the top of each sheet, fold over each end, and roll up to enclose the filling.

❊ Heat the oil in a large wok. Cook the parcels, in batches, for 2–3 minutes, or until crisp and golden. Garnish with the spring onion tassels and serve hot with a chilli dipping sauce.

Spicy Salt & Pepper Prawns

250–300 g/9–10½ oz raw prawns in their shells, thawed, if frozen
1 tbsp light soy sauce
1 tsp Chinese rice wine or dry sherry
2 tsp cornflour
vegetable oil, for deep-frying

2–3 spring onions, to garnish

SPICY SALT AND PEPPER
1 tbsp salt
1 tsp ground Szechuan peppercorns
1 tsp Chinese five-spice powder

❊ Pull the soft legs off the prawns, but keep the body shell on. Dry well on absorbent kitchen paper.

❊ Place the prawns in a bowl with the soy sauce, rice wine and cornflour. Turn the prawns to coat thoroughly in the mixture and leave to marinate for about 25–30 minutes.

❊ To make the spicy salt and pepper, mix the salt, ground Szechuan peppercorns and five-spice powder together. Place in a dry frying pan and stir-fry for about 3–4 minutes over a low heat, stirring constantly to prevent the spices burning on the bottom of the pan. Remove from the heat and allow to cool.

❊ Heat the vegetable oil in a preheated wok or large frying pan until smoking, then deep-fry the prawns in batches until golden brown. Remove the prawns from the wok with a slotted spoon and drain on kitchen paper.

❊ Place the spring onions in a bowl, pour on 1 tablespoon of the hot oil and leave for 30 seconds. Serve the prawns garnished with the spring onions, with the spicy salt and pepper as a dip.

Butterfly Prawns

12 raw tiger prawns
in their shells
2 tbsp light soy sauce
1 tbsp Chinese rice wine or
dry sherry
1 tbsp cornflour
vegetable oil, for deep-frying
2 eggs, lightly beaten
8–10 tbsp breadcrumbs
salt and pepper
shredded lettuce leaves,
to serve
chopped spring onions,
either raw or soaked for about
30 seconds in hot oil, to garnish

❋ Peel and devein the prawns, leaving the tails on. Split them in half from the underbelly about halfway along, leaving the tails still firmly attached. Mix together the salt, pepper, soy sauce, wine and cornflour, add the prawns and turn to coat. Leave to marinate for 10–15 minutes.

❋ Heat the oil in a preheated wok. Pick up each prawn by the tail, dip it in the beaten egg then roll it in the breadcrumbs to coat well.

❋ Deep-fry the prawns in batches until golden brown. Remove them with a slotted spoon and drain on kitchen paper.

❋ To serve, arrange the prawns neatly on a bed of lettuce leaves and garnish with the spring onions.

Sesame Prawn Toasts

❖ **SERVES 4** ❖

4 slices medium-cut white bread	1 tbsp sesame oil
225 g/8 oz cooked peeled prawns	1 egg
	25 g/1 oz sesame seeds
1 tbsp soy sauce	oil, for deep-frying
2 cloves garlic, crushed	sweet chilli sauce, to serve

❖ Remove the crusts from the bread, if desired, then set aside until required.

❖ Place the prawns, soy sauce, garlic, sesame oil and egg into a food processor and blend until a smooth paste has formed.

❖ Spread the prawn paste evenly over the 4 slices of bread. Sprinkle the sesame seeds over the top of the prawn mixture and press the seeds down with your hands so that they stick to the mixture. Cut each slice in half and in half again to form 4 triangles.

❖ Heat the oil in a large wok or frying pan and deep-fry the toasts, sesame seed side up, for 4–5 minutes or until golden and crispy.

❖ Remove the toasts with a slotted spoon, transfer to absorbent kitchen paper and leave to drain thoroughly.

❖ Serve the sesame prawn toasts warm with the sweet chilli sauce for dipping.

Deep-Fried Seafood

❖ **SERVES 4** ❖

200 g/7 oz prepared squid	50 g/1¾ oz plain flour
200 g/7 oz blue tiger prawns, peeled	1 tsp dried basil
	salt and pepper
150 g/5½ oz whitebait	lemon wedges, to serve
oil, for deep-frying	

❖ Carefully rinse the squid, prawns and whitebait under cold running water, completely removing any dirt or grit.

❖ Using a sharp knife, slice the squid into rings, leaving the tentacles whole.

❖ Heat the oil in a large saucepan to 180°C/350°F or until a cube of bread browns in 30 seconds.

❖ Place the flour in a bowl, add the basil and season with salt and pepper to taste. Mix together well.

❖ Roll the squid, prawns and whitebait in the seasoned flour until coated all over. Carefully shake off any excess flour.

❖ Cook the seafood in the heated oil, in batches, for 2–3 minutes or until crispy and golden all over. Remove all of the seafood with a slotted spoon and leave to drain thoroughly on kitchen paper.

❖ Transfer the deep-fried seafood to serving plates and serve with a few lemon wedges.

Roasted Seafood

600 g/1 lb 5 oz new potatoes	4 tbsp olive oil
3 red onions, cut into wedges	350 g/12 oz shell-on prawns,
2 courgettes, sliced into	preferably uncooked
chunks	2 small squid, chopped into
8 garlic cloves, peeled	rings
2 lemons, cut into wedges	4 tomatoes, quartered
4 sprigs fresh rosemary	

❄ Scrub the potatoes to remove any excess dirt. Cut any large potatoes in half. Place the potatoes in a large roasting tin, together with the onions, courgettes, garlic, lemons and rosemary.

❄ Pour over the oil and toss to coat all of the vegetables in the oil. Cook in a preheated oven, at 200°C/400°F/Gas Mark 6, for 40 minutes, turning occasionally, until the potatoes are tender.

❄ Add the prawns, squid and tomatoes, tossing to coat them in the oil, and roast for 10 minutes. All of the vegetables should be cooked through and slightly charred for full flavour.

❄ Transfer the roasted seafood and vegetables to warmed serving plates and serve hot.

Crispy Crab Wontons

175 g/6 oz white crabmeat, flaked	1 tbsp cornflour
50 g/1¾ oz canned water chestnuts, drained, rinsed and chopped	1 tsp dry sherry
	1 tsp light soy sauce
	½ tsp lime juice
1 small fresh red chilli, chopped	24 wonton wrappers
	vegetable oil, for deep-frying
1 spring onion, chopped	sliced lime, to garnish

❄ To make the filling, mix together the crabmeat, water chestnuts, chilli, spring onion, cornflour, sherry, soy sauce and lime juice.

❄ Spread out the wonton wrappers on a work surface and spoon one portion of the filling into the centre of each wonton wrapper.

❄ Dampen the edges of the wonton wrappers with a little water and fold them in half to form triangles. Fold the two pointed ends in towards the centre, moisten with a little water to secure and then pinch together to seal.

❄ Heat the oil for deep-frying in a wok or deep-fat fryer to 180°C/350°F or until a cube of bread browns in 30 seconds. Fry the wontons, in batches, for 2–3 minutes until golden brown and crisp. Remove the wontons from the oil and leave to drain on kitchen paper.

❄ Serve the wontons hot, garnished with slices of lime.

Thai Fish Cakes

350 g/12 oz white fish fillet, such as cod or haddock, skinned
1 tbsp Thai fish sauce
2 tsp Thai red curry paste
1 tbsp lime juice
1 garlic clove, crushed
4 dried kaffir lime leaves, crumbled
1 egg white
3 tbsp chopped fresh coriander
vegetable oil, for frying
green salad leaves, to serve

PEANUT DIP
1 small fresh red chilli
1 tbsp light soy sauce
1 tbsp lime juice
1 tbsp soft light brown sugar
3 tbsp chunky peanut butter
4 tbsp coconut milk
salt and pepper

❊ Put the fish fillet in a food processor with the fish sauce, curry paste, lime juice, garlic, lime leaves and egg white, and process until a smooth paste forms.

❊ Add the chopped coriander and quickly process again until mixed. Divide the mixture into 8–10 pieces and roll into balls between the palms of your hands, then flatten to make small round patties and set aside.

❊ For the dip, halve and deseed the chilli, then chop finely. Place in a small pan with the soy sauce, lime juice, sugar, peanut butter and coconut milk and heat gently, stirring constantly, until thoroughly blended. Adjust the seasoning, adding more lime juice or sugar to taste.

❊ Heat the oil in a frying pan and fry the fish cakes in batches for 3–4 minutes on each side until golden brown. Drain on kitchen paper and serve them hot on a bed of green salad leaves with the chilli-flavoured peanut dip.

Mussels with Pesto

❊ **SERVES 4** ❊

900 g/2 lb live mussels
6 tbsp chopped fresh basil
2 garlic cloves, crushed
1 tbsp pine kernels, toasted
2 tbsp freshly grated
Parmesan cheese

100 ml/3 ½ fl oz olive oil
115 g/4 oz fresh white
breadcrumbs
salt and pepper
tomato slices and fresh basil
leaves, to garnish

❊ Clean the mussels by scrubbing or scraping the shells and pulling out any beards that are attached to them. Discard any with broken shells or any that do not close when tapped. Put the mussels into a large saucepan with just the water on their shells, cover and cook over a high heat for 3–4 minutes, shaking the pan occasionally, until all the mussels have opened. Discard any mussels that remain closed. Drain, reserving the cooking liquid, and set aside until cool enough to handle.

❊ Strain the cooking liquid into a clean pan and simmer until reduced to about 1 tablespoon. Put the liquid into a food processor with the basil, garlic, pine kernels and cheese and process until finely chopped. Add the olive oil and breadcrumbs and process until well mixed.

❊ Open the mussels and loosen from their shells, discarding the empty half of the shell. Divide the pesto breadcrumbs between the mussels.

❊ Cook under a preheated grill until the breadcrumbs are crisp and golden and the mussels are heated through. Serve immediately, garnished with slices of tomato and basil leaves.

Provençal Mussels

❊ **SERVES 4** ❊

900 g/2 lb live mussels
3 tbsp olive oil
1 onion, finely chopped
3 garlic cloves, finely chopped
2 tsp fresh thyme leaves
150 ml/5 fl oz red wine

800 g/1 lb 12 oz canned
chopped tomatoes
2 tbsp chopped fresh parsley
salt and pepper
crusty bread, to serve

❊ Clean the mussels by scrubbing or scraping the shells and pulling out any beards. Discard any with broken shells or that do not close when tapped sharply. Put the mussels in a large saucepan with just the water that clings to their shells. Cover and cook over a high heat, vigorously shaking the pan occasionally, for 3–4 minutes until all the mussels have opened. Discard any mussels that remain closed. Drain, reserving the cooking liquid. Set aside.

❊ Heat the oil in a large saucepan and add the onion. Cook over a low heat for 8–10 minutes until soft, but not coloured. Add the garlic and thyme and cook for a further minute. Add the wine and simmer rapidly until reduced and syrupy. Add the tomatoes and strain in the mussel cooking liquid. Bring to the boil, cover and simmer for 30 minutes. Uncover the pan and cook for a further 15 minutes.

❊ Add the mussels and cook for a further 5 minutes until heated through. Stir in the parsley, season to taste with salt and pepper and serve with plenty of crusty bread.

Stuffed Squid

12 baby squid, cleaned
4 tbsp olive oil
1 small onion, finely chopped
1 garlic clove, finely chopped
40 g/1½ oz basmati rice
1 tbsp seedless raisins
1 tbsp pine kernels, toasted
1 tbsp chopped fresh flat-leaf
parsley

400 g/14 oz canned chopped
tomatoes
25 g/1 oz sun-dried tomatoes
in oil, drained and finely
chopped
125 ml/4 fl oz dry white wine
salt and pepper
crusty bread, to serve

❄ Chop off the tentacles from the squid. Chop the tentacles and set aside. Rub the squid tubes inside and out with 1 teaspoon salt and set aside.

❄ Heat 1 tablespoon of the olive oil in a frying pan and add the onion and garlic. Cook, stirring occasionally, for 4–5 minutes until soft and lightly browned. Add the tentacles and fry for 2–3 minutes. Add the rice, raisins, pine kernels and parsley and season to taste. Remove the pan from the heat.

❄ Allow the rice mixture to cool slightly, then spoon it into the squid tubes, so they are about three-quarters full. Secure each filled squid with a cocktail stick.

❄ Heat the remaining oil in a large flameproof casserole. Add the squid and fry for a few minutes on all sides until lightly browned. Add the tomatoes, sun-dried tomatoes, wine and seasoning. Bake in a preheated oven, 180°C/350°F/ Gas Mark 4, for 45 minutes. Serve hot or cold with plenty of crusty bread.

Citrus Fish Kebabs

450 g/1 lb firm white fish fillet,
such as cod or monkfish
450 g/1 lb thick salmon fillet
2 large oranges
1 pink grapefruit
1 bunch of fresh bay leaves
1 tsp finely grated lemon rind

3 tbsp lemon juice
2 tsp clear honey
2 garlic cloves, crushed
salt and pepper
crusty bread and a mixed
salad, to serve

❄ Skin the white fish fillet and the salmon, then rinse and pat dry on kitchen paper. Cut up to give 16 pieces of each fish.

❄ Using a sharp knife, remove the skin and pith from the oranges and grapefruit. Cut out the segments of flesh, removing all remaining traces of the pith and dividing membranes.

❄ Thread the pieces of fish alternately with the orange and grapefruit segments and the bay leaves on to 8 skewers. Place the fish kebabs in a shallow dish.

❄ In a small bowl, mix together the lemon rind, lemon juice, honey and crushed garlic. Pour the mixture over the fish kebabs and season to taste with salt and pepper. Cover with clingfilm and set aside in the refrigerator to marinate for 2 hours, turning occasionally.

❄ Remove the kebabs from the marinade and place on a grill rack. Cook under a preheated medium grill, turning once, for 7–8 minutes until cooked through and the fish is opaque.

❄ Transfer the kebabs to warmed individual serving plates and serve immediately with the bread and salad.

Grilled Sardines

12 sardines
olive oil
fresh flat-leaf parsley sprigs,
to garnish
lemon wedges, to serve

DRESSING
150 ml/5 fl oz extra virgin
olive oil
finely grated rind of
1 large lemon
4 tbsp lemon juice
4 shallots, thinly sliced
1 small fresh red chilli,
deseeded and finely chopped
1 large garlic clove,
finely chopped
salt and pepper

❖ To make the dressing, place all the ingredients in a screw-top jar, season with salt and pepper, then shake until blended. Pour into a non-metallic dish that is large enough to hold the sardines in a single layer. Set aside.

❖ To prepare the sardines, chop off the heads and make a slit all along the length of each belly. Pull out the insides, rinse the fish inside and out with cold water and pat dry with kitchen paper.

❖ Line the grill pan with foil, shiny side up. Brush the foil with a little olive oil to prevent the sardines from sticking. Arrange the sardines on the foil in a single layer and brush with a little of the dressing. Grill under a preheated grill for about 90 seconds.

❖ Turn the fish over, brush with a little more dressing and continue grilling for a further 90 seconds or until they are cooked through and flake easily.

❖ Transfer the fish to the dish with the dressing. Spoon the dressing over the fish and set aside to cool completely. Cover with clingfilm and leave to chill in the refrigerator for at least 2 hours to allow the flavours to blend.

❖ Transfer the sardines to a serving platter and garnish with the parsley sprigs. Serve with the lemon wedges for squeezing over the fish.

Simple
soups & salads

Creamy Tomato Soup

50 g/1¾ oz butter
700 g/1 lb 9 oz ripe tomatoes, preferably plum, roughly chopped
850 ml/1½ pints vegetable stock
50 g/1¾ oz ground almonds
150 ml/5 fl oz milk or single cream
1 tsp sugar
2 tbsp shredded basil leaves
salt and pepper

❖ Melt the butter in a large saucepan. Add the tomatoes and cook for 5 minutes until the skins start to wrinkle. Season to taste with salt and pepper.

❖ Add the stock to the pan, bring to the boil, cover and simmer for 10 minutes.

❖ Meanwhile, under a preheated grill, lightly toast the ground almonds until they are golden brown. This will take only 1–2 minutes, so watch them closely.

❖ Remove the soup from the heat, place in a food processor and blend the mixture to form a smooth consistency. Alternatively, mash the soup with a potato masher until smooth.

❖ Pass the soup through a sieve to remove any tomato skin or pips.

❖ Place the soup in the pan and return to the heat. Stir in the milk or cream, toasted ground almonds and sugar. Warm the soup through and add the shredded basil leaves just before serving.

❖ Transfer the creamy tomato soup to warmed soup bowls and serve hot.

Tomato & Pasta Soup

60 g/2 oz butter
1 large onion, chopped
600 ml/1 pint vegetable stock
900 g/2 lb Italian plum tomatoes, peeled and roughly chopped
pinch of bicarbonate of soda
225 g/8 oz dried fusilli
1 tbsp caster sugar
150 ml/5 fl oz double cream
salt and pepper
fresh basil leaves, to garnish

❖ Melt the butter in a large saucepan, add the onion and fry for 3 minutes, stirring. Add 300 ml/10 fl oz of the stock to the pan, with the chopped tomatoes and bicarbonate of soda. Bring the soup to the boil and simmer for 20 minutes.

❖ Remove the pan from the heat and set aside to cool a little. Purée the soup in a blender or food processor and then pour it through a fine sieve back into the pan.

❖ Add the remaining stock and the fusilli to the pan, and season to taste with salt and pepper.

❖ Add the sugar to the pan, bring to the boil, then reduce the heat and simmer for about 15 minutes.

❖ Pour the soup into a warmed tureen or individual warmed bowls, swirl the cream around the surface of the soup and garnish with the basil leaves. Serve immediately.

Chunky Vegetable Soup

2 carrots, sliced
1 onion, diced
1 garlic clove, crushed
350 g/12 oz new potatoes, diced
115 g/4 oz closed-cup mushrooms, quartered
2 celery sticks, sliced
400 g/14 oz canned chopped tomatoes in tomato juice
600 ml/1 pint vegetable stock
1 bay leaf

1 tsp dried mixed herbs or 1 tbsp chopped fresh mixed herbs
85 g/3 oz sweetcorn kernels, frozen or canned, drained
55 g/2 oz green cabbage, shredded
pepper
few sprigs of fresh basil, to garnish
crusty wholemeal or white bread rolls, to serve

❖ Put the carrots, onion, garlic, potatoes, mushrooms, celery, tomatoes and stock into a large saucepan. Stir in the bay leaf and herbs. Bring to the boil, then reduce the heat, cover and simmer for 25 minutes.

❖ Add the sweetcorn and cabbage and return to the boil. Reduce the heat, cover and simmer for 5 minutes, or until the vegetables are tender. Remove and discard the bay leaf. Season to taste with pepper.

❖ Ladle into warmed bowls and garnish with the basil. Serve immediately with the bread rolls.

Vegetable Chowder

1 tbsp vegetable oil
1 red onion, diced
1 red pepper, deseeded and diced
3 garlic cloves, crushed
300 g/10 oz potatoes, diced
2 tbsp plain flour
600 ml/1 pint milk
300 ml/10 fl oz vegetable stock

55 g/2 oz broccoli florets
300 g/10 oz canned sweetcorn, drained
75 g/2¾ oz Cheddar cheese, grated
salt and pepper
1 tbsp chopped fresh coriander, to garnish

❖ Heat the oil in a large saucepan. Add the onion, red pepper, garlic and potatoes and sauté over a low heat, stirring frequently, for 2–3 minutes.

❖ Stir in the flour and cook, stirring, for 30 seconds. Gradually stir in the milk and stock.

❖ Add the broccoli and sweetcorn. Bring the mixture to the boil, stirring constantly, then reduce the heat and simmer for about 20 minutes, or until all the vegetables are tender.

❖ Stir in 50 g/1¾ oz of the cheese until it melts.

❖ Season to taste, then spoon the chowder into a warmed soup tureen. Sprinkle with the remaining cheese, garnish with the coriander and serve.

Golden Vegetable Soup

1 tbsp olive oil
1 onion, finely chopped
1 garlic clove, finely chopped
1 carrot, halved and
thinly sliced
450 g/1 lb green cabbage,
shredded
400 g/14 oz canned chopped
tomatoes
1/2 tsp dried thyme
2 bay leaves
1.5 litres/2¾ pints vegetable
stock
200 g/7 oz Puy lentils
450 ml/16 fl oz water
salt and pepper
fresh coriander leaves or
parsley, to garnish

❊ Heat the oil in a large saucepan over a medium heat. Add the onion, garlic and carrot and cook, stirring occasionally, for 3–4 minutes. Add the cabbage and cook for a further 2 minutes.

❊ Add the tomatoes, thyme and 1 bay leaf, then pour in the stock. Bring to the boil, reduce the heat, partially cover and simmer for about 45 minutes until the vegetables are tender.

❊ Meanwhile, put the lentils in another saucepan with the remaining bay leaf and the water. Bring just to the boil, reduce the heat and simmer for about 25 minutes until tender. Drain off any remaining water and set aside.

❊ Remove the soup pan from the heat and set aside to cool slightly, then transfer to a blender or food processor and process to a smooth purée, working in batches, if necessary. (If using a food processor, strain off the cooking liquid and reserve. Purée the soup solids with enough cooking liquid to moisten them, then combine with the remaining liquid.)

❊ Return the soup to the pan and add the cooked lentils. Taste and adjust the seasoning, if necessary, and cook for about 10 minutes to heat through. Ladle into warmed bowls and garnish with the coriander leaves.

Mexican Vegetable Soup

2 tbsp vegetable or extra virgin
olive oil
1 onion, finely chopped
4 garlic cloves, finely chopped
1/4–1/2 tsp ground cumin
2–3 tsp mild chilli powder
1 carrot, sliced
1 waxy potato, diced
350 g/12 oz diced fresh or
canned tomatoes
1 courgette, diced
1/4 small cabbage, shredded
1 litre/1 3/4 pints vegetable or
chicken stock or water

1 sweetcorn cob, kernels cut
off the cob
about 10 French beans, cut into
bite-sized lengths
salt and pepper

TO SERVE
4–6 tbsp chopped fresh
coriander
salsa of your choice or
chopped fresh chilli, to taste
tortilla chips

❉ Heat the oil in a heavy-based saucepan. Add the onion
and garlic and cook for a few minutes until soft, then
sprinkle in the cumin and chilli powder. Stir in the carrot,
potato, tomatoes, courgettes and cabbage and cook, stirring
occasionally, for 2 minutes.

❉ Pour in the stock. Cover and cook over a medium heat
for about 20 minutes until the vegetables are tender.

❉ Add extra water if necessary, then stir in the sweetcorn
and French beans and cook for a further 5–10 minutes or
until the beans are tender. Season to taste with salt and
pepper, bearing in mind that the tortilla chips may be salty.

❉ Ladle the soup into soup bowls and sprinkle each portion
with fresh coriander. Top with a tablespoon of salsa, then
add a handful of tortilla chips.

Gazpacho

1/2 small cucumber
1/2 small green pepper,
deseeded and very finely
chopped
500 g/1 lb 2 oz ripe tomatoes,
peeled, or 400 g/14 oz
canned chopped tomatoes
1/2 onion, coarsely chopped
2–3 garlic cloves, crushed
3 tbsp olive oil

2 tbsp white wine vinegar
1–2 tbsp lemon or lime juice
2 tbsp tomato purée
450 ml/16 fl oz tomato juice
salt and pepper

TO SERVE
chopped green pepper
thinly sliced onion rings
garlic croûtons

❉ Coarsely grate the cucumber into a large bowl and add
the chopped green pepper.

❉ Process the tomatoes, onion and garlic in a food
processor or blender, then add the oil, vinegar, lemon or
lime juice and tomato purée and process until smooth.
Alternatively, finely chop the tomatoes and finely grate the
onion, then mix both with the garlic, oil, vinegar, lemon juice
and tomato purée.

❉ Add the tomato mixture to the bowl and mix well, then
add the tomato juice and mix again.

❉ Season to taste, cover the bowl with clingfilm and chill
thoroughly – for at least 6 hours and preferably longer so
that the flavours have time to meld together.

❉ Prepare the side dishes of green pepper, onion rings and
garlic croûtons, and arrange in individual serving bowls.

❉ Ladle the soup into bowls, preferably from a soup tureen
set on the table with the side dishes placed around it. Hand
the dishes around to allow the people to help themselves.

Red Pepper Soup

225 g/8 oz red peppers, deseeded and sliced
1 onion, sliced
2 garlic cloves, crushed
1 fresh green chilli, chopped
300 ml/10 fl oz passata
600 ml/1 pint vegetable stock
2 tbsp chopped fresh basil
fresh basil sprigs, to garnish

❋ Put the red peppers in a large heavy-based saucepan with the onion, garlic and chilli. Add the passata and vegetable stock and bring to the boil over a medium heat, stirring constantly.

❋ Reduce the heat to low and simmer for 20 minutes or until the peppers are soft. Drain, reserving the liquid and vegetables separately.

❋ Sieve the vegetables by pressing through a sieve with the back of a spoon. Alternatively, process in a food processor to a smooth purée.

❋ Transfer the vegetable purée to a clean saucepan and add the reserved cooking liquid. Add the basil and heat through until hot. Garnish the soup with fresh basil sprigs and serve.

Carrot & Cumin Soup

3 tbsp butter or margarine
1 large onion, chopped
1–2 garlic cloves, crushed
350 g/12 oz carrots, sliced
900 ml/1½ pints vegetable stock
¾ tsp ground cumin
2 celery sticks, thinly sliced
115 g/4 oz potato, diced
2 tsp tomato purée
2 tsp lemon juice
2 bay leaves
300 ml/10 fl oz skimmed milk
salt and pepper
celery leaves, to garnish

❋ Melt the butter or margarine in a large saucepan. Add the onion and garlic and cook very gently until soft.

❋ Add the carrots and cook gently for a further 5 minutes, stirring frequently and taking care they do not brown.

❋ Add the stock, cumin, seasoning, celery, potato, tomato purée, lemon juice and bay leaves and bring to the boil. Cover and simmer for about 30 minutes until the vegetables are tender.

❋ Remove and discard the bay leaves, cool the soup a little and then press it through a sieve or process in a food processor or blender until smooth.

❋ Pour the soup into a clean saucepan, add the milk and bring to the boil over a low heat. Taste and adjust the seasoning if necessary.

❋ Ladle the soup into warmed bowls, garnish each serving with a small celery leaf and serve.

Pumpkin & Orange Soup

2 tbsp olive oil
2 medium onions, chopped
2 garlic cloves, chopped
900 g/2 lb pumpkin, peeled
and cut into 2.5-cm/1-inch
chunks
1.5 litres /2¾ pints boiling
vegetable or chicken stock
finely grated rind and juice of
1 orange
3 tbsp fresh thyme, stalks
removed
150 ml/5 fl oz milk
salt and pepper
crusty bread, to serve

❊ Heat the olive oil in a large saucepan. Add the onions to the pan and cook for 3–4 minutes or until softened. Add the garlic and pumpkin and cook for a further 2 minutes, stirring well.

❊ Add the boiling vegetable or chicken stock, orange rind and juice and 2 tablespoons of the thyme to the pan. Leave to simmer, covered, for 20 minutes or until the pumpkin is tender.

❊ Place the mixture in a food processor and blend until smooth. Alternatively, mash the mixture with a potato masher until smooth. Season to taste.

❊ Return the soup to the pan and add the milk. Reheat the soup for 3–4 minutes or until it is piping hot but not boiling.

❊ Sprinkle with the remaining fresh thyme just before serving.

❊ Divide the soup between 4 warmed soup bowls and serve with lots of fresh crusty bread.

Cream of Artichoke Soup

750 g/1 lb 10 oz Jerusalem artichokes
1 lemon, thickly sliced
60 g/2 oz butter or margarine
2 onions, chopped
1 garlic clove, crushed
1.25 litres/2¼ pints chicken or vegetable stock
2 bay leaves

½ tsp ground mace or ground nutmeg
1 tbsp lemon juice
150 ml/5 fl oz single cream or natural fromage frais
salt and pepper
coarsely grated carrot and chopped fresh parsley or coriander, to garnish

❖ Peel and slice the artichokes. Put into a bowl of water with the lemon slices.

❖ Melt the butter in a large saucepan. Add the onions and garlic and fry gently for 3–4 minutes until soft but not coloured.

❖ Drain the artichokes (discarding the lemon) and add to the pan. Mix well and cook gently for 2–3 minutes without allowing to colour.

❖ Add the stock, seasoning, bay leaves, mace or nutmeg and lemon juice. Bring slowly to the boil, then cover and simmer gently for about 30 minutes until the vegetables are very tender.

❖ Discard the bay leaves. Cool the soup slightly then press through a sieve or blend in a food processor until smooth. If liked, a little of the soup may be only partially puréed and added to the rest of the puréed soup, to give extra texture.

❖ Pour into a clean saucepan and bring to the boil. Adjust the seasoning and stir in the cream. Reheat gently without boiling. Garnish with the grated carrot and chopped parsley.

Spicy Courgette Soup

2 tbsp vegetable oil
4 garlic cloves, thinly sliced
1–2 tbsp mild red chilli powder
¼–½ tsp ground cumin
1.5 litres/2¾ pints chicken, vegetable or beef stock
2 courgettes, cut into bite-sized chunks

4 tbsp long-grain rice
salt and pepper
sprigs of fresh oregano, to garnish
lime wedges, to serve (optional)

❖ Heat the oil in a heavy-based saucepan, add the garlic and cook, stirring frequently, for about 2 minutes until soft and just beginning to change colour. Stir in the chilli powder and cumin and cook over a medium–low heat, stirring constantly, for a minute.

❖ Stir in the stock, courgettes and rice, then cook over a medium–high heat for about 10 minutes until the courgettes are just tender and the rice is cooked through. Season the soup to taste with salt and pepper.

❖ Ladle into warmed bowls, garnish with the oregano and serve with the lime wedges, if using.

Celery & Stilton Soup

60 g/2 oz butter
2 shallots, chopped
3 celery sticks, chopped
1 garlic clove, crushed
2 tbsp plain flour
600 ml/1 pint vegetable stock
300 ml/10 fl oz milk
150 g/5 1/2 oz Stilton cheese, crumbled, plus extra to garnish

2 tbsp roughly chopped walnut halves
150 ml/5 fl oz natural yogurt
salt and pepper
chopped celery leaves, to garnish

❄ Melt the butter in a large heavy-based saucepan and sauté the shallots, celery and garlic, stirring occasionally, for 2–3 minutes, until they are soft.

❄ Reduce the heat, add the flour and continue to cook, stirring constantly, for 30 seconds.

❄ Gradually stir in the vegetable stock and milk and bring to the boil.

❄ Reduce the heat to a gentle simmer and add the cheese and the walnut halves. Cover and simmer for 20 minutes.

❄ Stir in the yogurt and heat through for a further 2 minutes, but be careful not to let the soup boil.

❄ Season the soup to taste with salt and pepper, then transfer to a warmed soup tureen or individual serving bowls, garnish with the chopped celery leaves and extra cheese and serve at once.

Speedy Broccoli Soup

350 g/12 oz broccoli
1 leek, sliced
1 celery stick, sliced
1 garlic clove, crushed
350 g/12 oz potato, diced
1 litre/1 3/4 pints vegetable stock

1 bay leaf
pepper
crusty bread or toasted croûtons, to serve

❄ Cut the broccoli into florets and set aside. Cut the thicker broccoli stalks into 1-cm/1/2-inch dice and put into a large saucepan with the leek, celery, garlic, potato, stock and bay leaf. Bring to the boil, then reduce the heat, cover and simmer for 15 minutes.

❄ Add the broccoli florets to the soup and return to the boil. Reduce the heat, cover and simmer for a further 3–5 minutes, or until the potato and broccoli stalks are tender.

❄ Remove from the heat and leave the soup to cool slightly. Remove and discard the bay leaf. Purée the soup, in small batches, in a food processor or blender until smooth.

❄ Return the soup to the saucepan and heat through thoroughly. Season to taste with pepper. Ladle the soup into warmed bowls and serve immediately with crusty bread or toasted croûtons.

Cauliflower & Cider Soup

25 g/1 oz butter
1 onion, finely chopped
1 garlic clove, crushed
1 carrot, thinly sliced
500 g/1 lb 2 oz cauliflower
florets
600 ml/1 pint dry cider
freshly grated nutmeg
125 ml/4 fl oz milk
125 ml/4 fl oz double cream
salt and pepper
snipped fresh chives, to garnish

❖ Melt the butter in a saucepan over a medium heat. Add the onion and garlic and cook for about 5 minutes, stirring occasionally, until just soft.

❖ Add the carrot and cauliflower to the pan and pour over the cider. Season with salt and pepper and a generous grating of nutmeg. Bring to the boil, then reduce the heat to low. Cover and cook very gently for about 50 minutes until the vegetables are very soft.

❖ Allow the soup to cool slightly, then transfer to a blender or food processor and purée until smooth, working in batches if necessary. (If using a food processor, strain off the cooking liquid and reserve. Purée the soup solids with enough cooking liquid to moisten them, then combine with the remaining liquid.)

❖ Return the soup to the pan and stir in the milk and cream. Taste and adjust the seasoning, if necessary. Simmer the soup over a low heat, stirring occasionally, until heated through.

❖ Ladle the soup into warmed bowls, garnish with chives and serve.

Spiced Cauliflower Soup

350 g/12 oz cauliflower, divided
into small florets
350 g/12 oz swede, diced
1 onion, chopped
1 tbsp vegetable oil
3 tbsp water
1 garlic clove, crushed
2 tsp grated fresh root ginger
1 tsp cumin seeds

1 tsp black mustard seeds
2 tsp ground coriander
2 tsp ground turmeric
850 ml/1½ pints hot vegetable
stock
300 ml/10 fl oz low fat yogurt
salt and pepper
chopped fresh coriander,
to garnish

❉ Place the cauliflower, swede, onion, oil, and water in a large bowl. Cover and cook in a microwave oven on HIGH power for 10 minutes, stirring halfway through.

❉ Add the garlic, ginger, cumin, mustard seeds, ground coriander, and turmeric. Stir well, cover, and cook on HIGH power for 2 minutes.

❉ Pour in the stock, cover, and cook on HIGH power for 10 minutes. Stand, covered, for 5 minutes.

❉ Strain the vegetables and reserve the liquid. Process the vegetables with a little of the reserved liquid in a food processor or blender until smooth and creamy. Alternatively, either mash the soup or press it through a sieve.

❉ Pour the vegetable purée and remaining reserved liquid into a clean bowl and mix well. Season to taste with salt and pepper.

❉ Stir in the yogurt and cook on HIGH power for 3–4 minutes until hot, but not boiling, otherwise the yogurt will curdle. Ladle into warmed bowls and serve, garnished with the chopped coriander.

Celeriac & Potato Soup

1 tbsp butter
1 onion, chopped
2 large leeks, halved
lengthways and sliced
750 g/1 lb 10 oz celeriac,
peeled and cubed
1 potato, cubed
1 carrot, quartered and
thinly sliced

1.2 litres/2 pints water
1/8 tsp dried marjoram
1 bay leaf
freshly grated nutmeg
salt and pepper
celery leaves, to garnish

❉ Melt the butter in a large saucepan over a medium–low heat. Add the onion and leeks and cook for about 4 minutes, stirring frequently, until just soft; do not allow to colour.

❉ Add the celeriac, potato, carrot, water, marjoram and bay leaf, with a large pinch of salt. Bring to the boil, reduce the heat, cover and simmer for about 25 minutes until the vegetables are tender. Remove the bay leaf.

❉ Allow the soup to cool slightly. Transfer to a blender or food processor and purée until smooth. (If using a food processor, strain off the cooking liquid and reserve. Purée the soup solids with enough cooking liquid to moisten them, then combine with remaining liquid.)

❉ Return the puréed soup to the saucepan and stir to blend. Season with salt and pepper and nutmeg. Simmer over a medium–low heat until reheated.

❉ Ladle the soup into warmed bowls, garnish with the celery leaves and serve.

Beetroot Soup

1 onion	1 tbsp white wine vinegar
3 celery sticks	1 tbsp sugar
55 g/2 oz butter	115 g/4 oz white cabbage,
350 g/12 oz beetroot, cut into	shredded
thin batons	1 beetroot, grated
1 carrot, cut into thin batons	salt and pepper
2 tomatoes, peeled, deseeded	150 ml/5 fl oz soured cream,
and chopped	to garnish
2 tbsp chopped fresh dill	rye bread, to serve
1.4 litres/2$\frac{1}{2}$ pints vegetable	
stock	

❈ Slice the onion into rings and the celery sticks thinly. Melt the butter in a large heavy-based saucepan. Add the onion and cook over a low heat, stirring occasionally, for 3–5 minutes until soft. Add the beetroot and carrot batons, celery and tomatoes to the pan and cook, stirring frequently, for 4–5 minutes.

❈ Add the stock, vinegar, sugar and half the dill to the pan and season to taste with salt and pepper. Bring to the boil, reduce the heat and simmer for 35–40 minutes, until all the vegetables are tender.

❈ Stir in the cabbage, cover and simmer for 10 minutes. Stir in the grated beetroot, with any juices, and cook for a further 10 minutes.

❈ Ladle into warmed bowls, garnish with spoonfuls of soured cream and the remaining dill and serve immediately with rye bread.

Tuscan Onion Soup

50 g/1$\frac{3}{4}$ oz pancetta, diced	4 slices ciabatta or other
1 tbsp olive oil	Italian bread
4 large white onions, sliced	50 g/1$\frac{3}{4}$ oz butter
thinly into rings	75 g/2$\frac{3}{4}$ oz Gruyère or
3 garlic cloves, chopped	Cheddar cheese
850 ml/1$\frac{1}{2}$ pints hot chicken or	salt and pepper
ham stock	

❈ Dry fry the pancetta in a large saucepan for 3–4 minutes until it begins to brown. Remove the pancetta from the pan and set aside until required.

❈ Add the oil to the pan and cook the onions and garlic over a high heat for 4 minutes. Reduce the heat, cover and cook for 15 minutes or until the onions are lightly caramelized.

❈ Add the stock to the pan and bring to the boil. Reduce the heat and leave the mixture to simmer, covered, for about 10 minutes.

❈ Toast the slices of ciabatta on both sides, under a preheated grill, for 2–3 minutes or until golden. Spread the ciabatta with butter and top with the Gruyère cheese. Cut the bread into bite-sized pieces.

❈ Add the reserved pancetta to the soup and season to taste with salt and pepper.

❈ Pour into 4 soup bowls and top with the toasted bread.

Curried Parsnip Soup

1 tbsp vegetable oil
15 g/¹/₂ oz butter
1 red onion, chopped
3 parsnips, chopped
2 garlic cloves, crushed
2 tsp garam masala
¹/₂ tsp chilli powder
1 tbsp plain flour
850 ml/1¹/₂ pints vegetable stock
grated rind and juice of 1 lemon
salt and pepper
lemon rind, to garnish

❊ Heat the oil and butter in a large saucepan until the butter has melted. Add the onion, parsnips and garlic and sauté, stirring frequently, for about 5–7 minutes, until the vegetables are soft but not coloured.

❊ Add the garam masala and chilli powder and cook, stirring constantly, for 30 seconds. Sprinkle in the flour, mixing well and cook, stirring constantly, for a further 30 seconds.

❊ Stir in the stock, lemon rind and juice and bring to the boil. Reduce the heat and simmer for 20 minutes.

❊ Remove some of the vegetable pieces with a slotted spoon and reserve until required. Process the remaining soup and vegetables in a food processor or blender for about 1 minute, or until a smooth purée is formed. Alternatively, press the vegetables through a sieve with the back of a wooden spoon.

❊ Transfer the soup to a clean saucepan and stir in the reserved vegetables. Heat the soup through for 2 minutes until piping hot.

❊ Season to taste with salt and pepper, then transfer to soup bowls, garnish with the grated lemon rind and serve.

Spinach & Ginger Soup

2 tbsp sunflower oil
1 onion, chopped
2 garlic cloves, finely chopped
2 tsp finely chopped root ginger
250 g/9 oz young spinach leaves
1 small lemongrass stalk, finely chopped
1 litre/1¾ pints vegetable stock
225 g/8 oz potatoes, chopped
1 tbsp rice wine or dry sherry
1 tsp sesame oil
salt and pepper

❈ Heat the oil in a large saucepan. Add the onion, garlic and ginger and fry over a low heat, stirring occasionally, for 3–4 minutes until soft.

❈ Reserve 2–3 small spinach leaves. Add the remaining leaves and lemongrass to the pan, stirring until the spinach is wilted. Add the stock and potatoes to the pan and bring to the boil. Reduce the heat, cover the pan and simmer for about 10 minutes.

❈ Remove the pan from the heat and set aside to cool slightly, then tip the soup into a blender or food processor and process until completely smooth.

❈ Return the soup to the pan and add the rice wine, then adjust the seasoning to taste with salt and pepper. Heat until just about to boil.

❈ Finely shred the reserved spinach leaves and sprinkle some over the top. Drizzle a few drops of sesame oil into the soup. Ladle into warmed soup bowls, sprinkle the remaining shredded spinach on each and serve the soup immediately.

Calabrian Mushroom Soup

2 tbsp olive oil
1 onion, chopped
450 g/1 lb mixed mushrooms, such as ceps, oyster and button
300 ml/10 fl oz milk
850 ml/1½ pints hot vegetable stock
8 slices of rustic bread or French stick
2 garlic cloves, crushed
50 g/1¾ oz butter, melted
75 g/2¾ oz Gruyère cheese, finely grated
salt and pepper

❈ Heat the oil in a large frying pan and cook the onion for 3–4 minutes or until soft and golden.

❈ Wipe each mushroom with a damp cloth and cut any large mushrooms into smaller bite-sized pieces.

❈ Add the mushrooms to the pan, stirring quickly to coat them in the oil.

❈ Add the milk to the pan, bring to the boil, cover and leave to simmer for about 5 minutes. Gradually stir in the hot vegetable stock and season with salt and pepper to taste.

❈ Under a preheated grill, toast the bread on both sides until golden.

❈ Mix together the garlic and butter and spoon generously over the toast.

❈ Place the toast in the bottom of a large tureen or divide it between 4 individual serving bowls and pour over the hot soup. Top with the grated Gruyère cheese and serve at once.

Mushroom & Barley Soup

60 g/2 oz pearl barley
1.5 litres/2¾ pints chicken or
vegetable stock
1 bay leaf
1 tbsp butter
350 g/12 oz mushrooms,
thinly sliced
1 tsp olive oil
1 onion, finely chopped
2 carrots, thinly sliced
1 tbsp chopped fresh tarragon
1 tbsp chopped fresh parsley
salt and pepper
1 tbsp chopped fresh parsley or
tarragon, to garnish

❊ Rinse and drain the barley. Bring 450 ml/16 fl oz of the stock to the boil in a small saucepan. Add the bay leaf and a pinch of salt. Stir in the barley, reduce the heat, cover and simmer for 40 minutes.

❊ Melt the butter in a large frying pan over a medium heat. Add the mushrooms and season to taste with salt and pepper. Cook, stirring occasionally, for about 8 minutes until they are golden brown. Stir more often after the mushrooms start to colour. Remove the mushrooms from the heat.

❊ Heat the oil in a large saucepan over a medium heat and add the onion and carrots. Cook, stirring occasionally, for about 3 minutes until the onion is softened and translucent.

❊ Add the remaining stock and bring to the boil. Stir in the barley with its cooking liquid and add the mushrooms. Reduce the heat, cover and simmer gently, stirring occasionally, for about 20 minutes or until the carrots are tender.

❊ Stir in the tarragon and parsley. Ladle into warmed bowls, garnish with fresh parsley and serve.

Mushroom Noodle Soup

125 g/4½ oz flat or open-cup
mushrooms
½ cucumber
2 spring onions
1 garlic clove
2 tbsp vegetable oil
600 ml/1 pint water
25 g/1 oz Chinese rice noodles
¾ tsp salt
1 tbsp soy sauce

❊ Wash the mushrooms and pat them dry on kitchen paper. Slice thinly. Do not remove the mushroom peel as this adds more flavour.

❊ Cut the cucumber in half lengthways. Taking care not to damage the flesh, scoop out the seeds, using a teaspoon, and slice the cucumber thinly.

❊ Chop the spring onions finely and cut the garlic clove into thin strips.

❊ Heat the vegetable oil in a large saucepan or wok.

❊ Add the spring onions and garlic to the pan and stir-fry for 30 seconds. Add the mushrooms and stir-fry for a further 2–3 minutes.

❊ Stir in the water. Break the noodles into short lengths and add to the soup. Bring to the boil, stirring occasionally.

❊ Add the cucumber slices, salt and soy sauce, and simmer for 2–3 minutes.

❊ Serve the mushroom noodle soup in warmed bowls, distributing the noodles and vegetables evenly.

Minestrone

1 tbsp olive oil
100 g/3^1/$_2$ oz pancetta, diced
2 medium onions, chopped
2 garlic cloves, crushed
1 potato, peeled and cut into
1-cm/^{1}/$_2$-inch cubes
1 carrot, peeled and
cut into chunks
1 leek, sliced into rings
^{1}/$_4$ green cabbage, shredded
1 stick celery, chopped
450 g/1 lb canned chopped
tomatoes
200 g/7 oz canned flageolet
beans, drained and rinsed
600 ml/1 pint hot ham or
chicken stock, diluted with
600 ml/1 pint boiling water
bouquet garni (2 bay leaves, 2
sprigs rosemary and 2 sprigs
thyme, tied together)
salt and pepper
freshly grated Parmesan
cheese, to serve

❊ Heat the olive oil in a large saucepan. Add the pancetta, onions and garlic and fry for about 5 minutes, stirring, or until the onions are soft and golden.

❊ Add the prepared potato, carrot, leek, cabbage and celery to the saucepan. Cook for a further 2 minutes, stirring frequently to coat all of the vegetables in the oil.

❊ Add the tomatoes, flageolet beans, hot stock and bouquet garni to the pan, stirring to mix. Leave the soup to simmer, covered, for 15–20 minutes or until all of the vegetables are just tender.

❊ Remove the bouquet garni, season to taste with salt and pepper and serve with plenty of freshly grated Parmesan cheese.

Soup with Chilli Pesto

1 litre/1¾ pints fresh cold water
bouquet garni of 1 sprig fresh parsley, 1 sprig fresh thyme and 1 bay leaf, tied together with clean string
2 celery sticks, chopped
3 baby leeks, chopped
4 baby carrots, chopped
150 g/5½ oz new potatoes, scrubbed and cut into bite-sized chunks
4 tbsp shelled broad beans or peas
175 g/6 oz canned cannellini or flageolet beans, drained and rinsed
3 heads pak choi
150 g/5½ oz rocket
pepper

CHILLI PESTO

2 large handfuls fresh basil leaves
1 fresh green chilli, deseeded
2 garlic cloves
4 tbsp olive oil
1 tsp finely grated Parmesan cheese

❉ Put the water and bouquet garni into a large saucepan and add the celery, leeks, carrots and potatoes. Bring to the boil, then reduce the heat and simmer for 10 minutes.

❉ Stir in the broad beans and canned beans and simmer for a further 10 minutes. Stir in the pak choi, rocket and pepper to taste and simmer for a further 2–3 minutes. Remove and discard the bouquet garni.

❉ Meanwhile, to make the pesto, put the basil, chilli, garlic and oil into a food processor and pulse to form a thick paste. Stir in the cheese.

❉ Stir most of the pesto into the soup, then ladle into warmed bowls. Top with the remaining pesto and serve immediately.

Tuscan Bean Soup

❉ SERVES 4 ❉

225 g/8 oz dried butter beans, soaked overnight, or
800 g/1 lb 12 oz canned butter beans
1 tbsp olive oil
2 garlic cloves, crushed
1 vegetable or chicken stock cube, crumbled
150 ml/5 fl oz milk
2 tbsp chopped fresh oregano
salt and pepper

❉ If you are using dried beans that have been soaked overnight, drain them thoroughly. Bring a large saucepan of water to the boil, add the beans and boil for 10 minutes. Cover the pan and simmer for a further 30 minutes or until tender. Drain the beans, reserving the cooking liquid. If you are using canned beans, drain them thoroughly and reserve the liquid.

❉ Heat the oil in a large frying pan and fry the garlic for 2–3 minutes or until just beginning to brown.

❉ Add the beans and 400 ml/14 fl oz of the reserved liquid to the pan, stirring. You may need to add a little water if there is insufficient liquid. Stir in the crumbled stock cube. Bring the mixture to the boil and then remove the pan from the heat.

❉ Place the bean mixture in a food processor and blend to form a smooth purée. Alternatively, mash the bean mixture to a smooth consistency. Season to taste with salt and pepper and stir in the milk.

❉ Pour the soup back into the pan and gently heat to just below boiling point. Stir in the chopped oregano just before serving.

Beans & Greens Soup

250 g/9 oz dried haricot or
cannellini beans
1 tbsp olive oil
2 onions, finely chopped
4 garlic cloves, finely chopped
1 celery stick, thinly sliced
2 carrots, halved and
thinly sliced
1.2 litres/2 pints water

¼ tsp dried thyme
¼ tsp dried marjoram
1 bay leaf
115 g/4 oz leafy greens,
such as chard, spinach and
kale, washed
salt and pepper

❖ Cover the beans with cold water and soak for 6 hours or overnight. Drain, put in a pan and add water to cover by 5 cm/2 inches. Bring to the boil and boil for 10 minutes. Drain and rinse.

❖ Heat the olive oil in a large pan over a medium heat. Add the onion and cook, stirring occasionally, for about 3–4 minutes until just soft. Add the garlic, celery and carrots and continue cooking for 2 minutes.

❖ Add the water, beans, thyme, marjoram and bay leaf. When the mixture begins to simmer, reduce the heat to low. Cover and simmer gently, stirring occasionally, for about 1¼ hours until the beans are tender. The cooking time will vary depending on the type of bean. Season to taste with salt and pepper.

❖ Remove the pan from the heat and set aside to cool slightly, then transfer 450 ml/16 fl oz to a blender or food processor. Process to a smooth purée and recombine with the soup.

❖ Cut the greens crossways into thin ribbons, keeping tender leaves, such as spinach, separate. Add the thicker leaves and cook gently for 10 minutes. Stir in any remaining greens and cook for a further 5–10 minutes until all the greens are tender. Taste and adjust the seasoning. Ladle the soup into warmed bowls and serve immediately.

Chickpea & Tomato Soup

2 tbsp olive oil
2 leeks, sliced
2 courgettes, diced
2 garlic cloves, crushed
800 g/1 lb 12 oz canned
chopped tomatoes
1 tbsp tomato purée
1 bay leaf
850 ml/1½ pints vegetable
stock

400 g/14 oz canned chickpeas,
drained and rinsed
225 g/8 oz spinach
salt and pepper
freshly grated Parmesan
cheese and warmed sun-
dried tomato bread, to serve

❖ Heat the olive oil in a large saucepan, then add the leeks and courgettes and cook them briskly for 5 minutes, stirring constantly.

❖ Add the garlic, tomatoes, tomato purée, bay leaf, stock and chickpeas.

❖ Bring the soup to the boil and simmer for 5 minutes.

❖ Shred the spinach finely, add to the soup and cook for 2 minutes. Season to taste.

❖ Discard the bay leaf. Serve the soup immediately with the cheese and some warmed sun-dried tomato bread.

Tunisian Garlic & Chickpea Soup

8 tbsp olive oil
12 garlic cloves, very finely chopped
350 g/12 oz chickpeas, soaked overnight in cold water and drained
2.5 litres/4$\frac{1}{2}$ pints water
1 tsp ground cumin
1 tsp ground coriander
2 carrots, very finely chopped
2 onions, very finely chopped
6 celery sticks, very finely chopped
juice of 1 lemon
salt and pepper
4 tbsp chopped fresh coriander

❖ Heat half the oil in a large heavy-based saucepan. Add the garlic and cook over a low heat, stirring frequently, for 2 minutes. Add the chickpeas to the pan with the measured water, cumin and ground coriander. Bring to the boil, then reduce the heat and simmer for 2$\frac{1}{2}$ hours or until tender.

❖ Meanwhile, heat the remaining oil in a separate saucepan. Add the carrots, onions and celery, cover and cook over a medium–low heat, stirring occasionally, for 20 minutes.

❖ Stir the vegetable mixture into the pan of chickpeas. Transfer about half the soup to a food processor or blender and process until smooth. Return the purée to the pan, add about half the lemon juice and stir. Taste and add more lemon juice as required. Season to taste with salt and pepper. Ladle into warmed bowls, sprinkle with the fresh coriander and serve.

Rice & Bean Soup

250 g/9 oz dried black-eyed beans
1 tbsp olive oil
1 large onion, finely chopped
2 garlic cloves, finely chopped or crushed
2 carrots, finely chopped
2 celery sticks, finely chopped
1 small red pepper, deseeded and finely chopped
85 g/3 oz lean smoked ham, finely diced
1/2 tsp fresh thyme leaves
1 bay leaf
1.2 litres/2 pints chicken or vegetable stock
600 ml/1 pint water
100 g/3 1/2 oz brown rice
salt and pepper
chopped fresh parsley or chives, to garnish

❖ Put the beans in a bowl, cover generously with cold water and set aside to soak for at least 6 hours or overnight. Drain the beans, put in a pan and add enough cold water to cover by 5 cm/2 inches. Bring to the boil and boil for 10 minutes. Drain and rinse well.

❖ Heat the oil in a large heavy-based saucepan over a medium heat. Add the onion, cover and cook, stirring frequently, for 3–4 minutes until just soft. Add the garlic, carrots, celery and pepper, stir well and cook for a further 2 minutes.

❖ Transfer to a larger saucepan if necessary. Add the beans, ham, thyme, bay leaf, stock and water. Bring to the boil, reduce the heat, cover and simmer gently, stirring occasionally, for 1 hour or until the beans are just tender.

❖ Stir in the rice and season the soup with salt, if needed, and pepper. Continue cooking for 30 minutes or until the rice and beans are tender.

❖ Remove and discard the bay leaf. Taste the soup and adjust the seasoning if necessary. Ladle into warmed bowls and serve garnished with parsley.

Lentil & Parsnip Soup

3 rashers streaky bacon, chopped
1 onion, chopped
2 carrots, chopped
2 parsnips, chopped
55 g/2 oz red lentils
1 litre/1 3/4 pints vegetable stock or water
salt and pepper
chopped fresh chives to garnish

❖ Heat a large saucepan, add the bacon and dry-fry for 5 minutes until crisp and golden.

❖ Add the onion, carrots and parsnips and cook for about 5 minutes without browning.

❖ Add the lentils to the pan and stir to mix with the vegetables. Add the stock or water to the pan and bring to the boil. Cover and simmer for 30–40 minutes until tender.

❖ Transfer the soup to a blender or food processor and blend for about 15 seconds until smooth. Alternatively, press the soup through a sieve.

❖ Return the soup to the pan and reheat gently until almost boiling.

❖ Season to taste with salt and pepper. Garnish with the chopped chives and serve at once.

Lentil & Ham Soup

225 g/8 oz red lentils
1.5 litres/2¾ pints stock or water
2 onions, chopped
1 garlic clove, crushed
2 large carrots, chopped
1 lean ham knuckle or 175 g/6 oz lean bacon, chopped
4 large tomatoes, peeled and chopped

2 bay leaves
250 g/9 oz potatoes, chopped
1 tbsp white wine vinegar
¼ tsp mixed spice
salt and pepper
chopped spring onions or chopped fresh parsley, to garnish

❊ Put the lentils and stock in a saucepan and set aside to soak for 1–2 hours.

❊ Add the onions, garlic, carrots, ham knuckle, tomatoes and bay leaves. Season to taste with salt and pepper.

❊ Bring the mixture to the boil over a medium heat, then reduce the heat, cover and simmer for about 1 hour until the lentils are tender, stirring occasionally to prevent them from sticking to the base of the pan.

❊ Add the potatoes and continue to simmer for about 20 minutes until the potatoes and the meat on the ham knuckle are tender.

❊ Remove and discard the bay leaves. Remove the knuckle, chop 125 g/4½ oz of the meat and reserve. If liked, press half the soup through a sieve or process in a food processor or blender until smooth. Return to the pan with the rest of the soup.

❊ Adjust the seasoning, add the vinegar and mixed spice and the reserved ham. Simmer gently for a further 5–10 minutes. Serve sprinkled liberally with the spring onions.

Warming Red Lentil Soup

225 g/8 oz dried red split lentils
1 red onion, diced
2 large carrots, sliced
1 celery stick, sliced
1 parsnip, diced
1 garlic clove, crushed

1.2 litres/2 pints vegetable stock
2 tsp paprika
pepper
1 tbsp snipped fresh chives, to garnish

❊ Put the lentils, onion, carrots, celery, parsnip, garlic, stock and paprika into a large saucepan. Bring to the boil and boil rapidly for 10 minutes. Reduce the heat, cover and simmer for 20 minutes, or until the lentils and vegetables are tender.

❊ Leave the soup to cool slightly, then purée in small batches in a food processor or blender. Process until the mixture is smooth.

❊ Return the soup to the pan and heat through thoroughly. Season to taste with pepper.

❊ To serve, ladle the soup into warmed bowls. Sprinkle the chives over the soup to garnish and serve immediately.

Minted Pea & Yogurt Soup

2 tbsp vegetable ghee or oil
2 onions, peeled and coarsely chopped
225 g/8 oz potato, peeled and coarsely chopped
2 garlic cloves, peeled
2.5-cm/1-inch piece root ginger, peeled and chopped
1 tsp ground coriander
1 tsp ground cumin
1 tbsp plain flour
850 ml/1½ pints vegetable stock
500 g/1 lb 2 oz frozen peas
2–3 tbsp chopped fresh mint, to taste
150 ml/5 fl oz low-fat natural yogurt, plus extra to garnish
½ tsp cornflour
300 ml/10 fl oz skimmed milk
salt and pepper
sprigs of fresh mint, to garnish

❖ Heat the ghee in a saucepan, add the onions and potato and cook gently for 3 minutes. Stir in the garlic, ginger, coriander, cumin and flour and cook for 1 minute, stirring. Add the stock, peas and half the mint and bring to the boil, stirring. Reduce the heat, cover and simmer gently for 15 minutes.

❖ Purée the soup in a blender or food processor. Return the mixture to the pan and season with salt and pepper to taste. Blend the yogurt with the cornflour and stir into the soup.

❖ Add the milk and bring almost to the boil, stirring all the time. Cook very gently for 2 minutes. Serve hot, sprinkled with the sprigs of mint and a swirl of yogurt.

Tarragon Pea Soup

40 g/1$\frac{1}{2}$ oz butter	1 vegetable stock cube
1 onion, finely chopped	$\frac{1}{2}$ tsp dried tarragon
2 leeks, finely chopped	salt and pepper
60 g/2 oz white rice	chopped hard-boiled egg or
500 g/1 lb 2 oz frozen peas	croûtons, to garnish
1 litre/1$\frac{3}{4}$ pints water	

❈ Melt the butter in a large saucepan over a low–medium heat. Add the onion, leeks and rice. Cover and cook for about 10 minutes, stirring occasionally, until the vegetables are soft.

❈ Add the peas, water, stock cube and tarragon and bring just to the boil. Season with a little pepper. Cover the pan and simmer the soup for about 35 minutes, stirring occasionally, until the vegetables are very tender.

❈ Allow the soup to cool slightly, then transfer to a blender or food processor and purée until smooth, working in batches if necessary. (If using a food processor, strain off the cooking liquid and reserve. Purée the soup solids with enough cooking liquid to moisten them, then combine with the remaining liquid.)

❈ Return the puréed soup to the pan. Taste and adjust the seasoning, adding plenty of pepper and, if needed, salt. Gently reheat the soup over a low heat for about 10 minutes until hot.

❈ Ladle into warmed bowls and garnish with hard-boiled egg or croûtons.

Split Pea & Ham Soup

500 g/1 lb 2 oz split green peas	1 litre/1$\frac{3}{4}$ pints water
1 tbsp olive oil	225 g/8 oz lean smoked ham,
1 large onion, finely chopped	finely diced
1 large carrot, finely chopped	$\frac{1}{4}$ tsp dried thyme
1 celery stick, finely chopped	$\frac{1}{4}$ tsp dried marjoram
1 litre/1$\frac{3}{4}$ pints chicken or	1 bay leaf
vegetable stock	salt and pepper

❈ Rinse the peas under cold running water. Put in a saucepan and cover generously with water. Bring to the boil and boil for 3 minutes, skimming off the foam from the surface. Drain the peas.

❈ Heat the oil in a large saucepan over a medium heat. Add the onion and cook, stirring occasionally, for about 3–4 minutes, until just soft.

❈ Add the carrot and celery and continue cooking for 2 minutes. Add the peas, pour in the stock and water and stir to combine.

❈ Bring just to the boil and stir the ham into the soup. Add the thyme, marjoram and bay leaf. Reduce the heat, cover and cook gently for 1–1$\frac{1}{2}$ hours until the ingredients are very soft. Remove and discard the bay leaf.

❈ Taste and adjust the seasoning if necessary. Ladle into warmed soup bowls and serve immediately.

Chilled Potato & Leek Soup

3 large leeks	pinch of ground nutmeg
40 g/1½ oz butter or	¼ tsp ground coriander
margarine	1 bay leaf
1 onion, thinly sliced	1 egg yolk
500 g/1 lb 2 oz potatoes,	150 ml/5 fl oz single cream
chopped	salt and white pepper
850 ml/1½ pints vegetable	freshly snipped chives,
stock	to garnish
2 tsp lemon juice	

❖ Trim the leeks and remove most of the green part. Slice the white part of the leeks very finely.

❖ Melt the butter in a saucepan. Add the leeks and onion and fry, stirring occasionally, for about 5 minutes without browning.

❖ Add the potatoes, vegetable stock, lemon juice, nutmeg, coriander and bay leaf to the pan, season to taste with salt and pepper and bring to the boil. Cover and simmer for about 30 minutes until all the vegetables are very soft.

❖ Cool the soup a little, remove and discard the bay leaf and then press through a sieve or process in a food processor or blender until smooth. Pour into a clean saucepan.

❖ Blend the egg yolk into the cream, add a little of the soup to the mixture and then whisk it all back into the soup and reheat gently, without boiling. Adjust the seasoning to taste. Cool and then chill thoroughly in the refrigerator.

❖ Serve the soup sprinkled with freshly snipped chives.

Sweet Potato & Onion Soup

2 tbsp vegetable oil	225 ml/8 fl oz low-fat natural
900 g/2 lb sweet potatoes,	yogurt
diced	2 tbsp chopped fresh coriander
1 carrot, diced	salt and pepper
2 onions, sliced	sprigs of fresh coriander and
2 garlic cloves, crushed	some orange rind, to garnish
600 ml/1 pint vegetable stock	
300 ml/10 fl oz orange juice	

❖ Heat the vegetable oil in a large, heavy-based saucepan and add the sweet potatoes, carrot, onions and garlic. Sauté the vegetables over a low heat, stirring constantly for 5 minutes until they are soft.

❖ Pour in the vegetable stock and orange juice and bring to the boil.

❖ Reduce the heat to a simmer, cover the pan and cook the vegetables for 20 minutes or until the sweet potatoes and carrot are tender.

❖ Transfer the mixture to a food processor or blender in batches and process for 1 minute until puréed. Return the purée to the rinsed-out pan.

❖ Stir in the yogurt and chopped coriander and season to taste with salt and pepper.

❖ Serve the soup in warmed bowls, garnished with the sprigs of coriander and the orange rind.

Cream of Chicken Soup

55 g/2 oz unsalted butter
1 large onion, peeled and chopped
300 g/10^1/$_2$ oz cooked chicken, finely shredded
600 ml/1 pint chicken stock
1 tbsp chopped fresh tarragon
150 ml/5 fl oz double cream
salt and pepper
fresh tarragon leaves, to garnish

✣ Melt the butter in a large saucepan and fry the onion for 3 minutes.

✣ Add the chicken to the pan with 300 ml/10 fl oz of the stock.

✣ Bring to the boil and simmer for 20 minutes. Allow to cool, then liquidize the soup.

✣ Add the remainder of the stock and season with salt and pepper.

✣ Add the chopped tarragon, pour the soup into a tureen or individual serving bowls and add a swirl of cream.

✣ Garnish the soup with fresh tarragon and serve.

Chicken Consommé

1.75 litres/3 pints chicken stock
150 ml/5 fl oz medium sherry
4 egg whites plus egg shells

125 g/4 oz cooked chicken,
thinly sliced
salt and pepper

❖ Place the chicken stock and sherry in a large saucepan and heat gently for 5 minutes.

❖ Add the egg whites and the egg shells to the stock and whisk until the mixture begins to boil.

❖ Remove the pan from the heat and allow the mixture to subside for 10 minutes. Repeat this process three times. This allows the egg white to trap the sediments in the stock to clarify the soup. Let the consommé cool for 5 minutes.

❖ Carefully place a piece of fine muslin over a clean saucepan. Ladle the soup over the muslin and strain into the pan.

❖ Repeat this process twice, then gently reheat the consommé. Season to taste with salt and pepper then add the cooked chicken slices. Pour the soup into a warmed serving dish or individual bowls.

Chicken Noodle Soup

1 sheet of dried egg noodles
from a 250 g/9 oz pack
1 tbsp oil
4 skinless, boneless
chicken thighs, diced
1 bunch spring onions, sliced
2 garlic cloves, chopped
2-cm/¾-inch piece of root
ginger, finely chopped

850 ml/1½ pints chicken stock
200 ml/7 fl oz coconut milk
3 tsp red curry paste
3 tbsp peanut butter
2 tbsp light soy sauce
1 small red pepper, chopped
55 g/2 oz frozen peas
salt and pepper

❖ Put the noodles in a shallow dish and soak in boiling water as the pack directs.

❖ Heat the oil in a large preheated saucepan or wok.

❖ Add the diced chicken to the pan and fry for 5 minutes, stirring until lightly browned.

❖ Add the white part of the spring onions, the garlic and ginger and fry for 2 minutes, stirring.

❖ Stir in the chicken stock, coconut milk, red curry paste, peanut butter and soy sauce.

❖ Season to taste with salt and pepper. Bring to the boil, stirring, then simmer for 8 minutes, stirring occasionally.

❖ Add the red pepper, peas and green spring onion tops and cook for 2 minutes.

❖ Add the drained noodles and heat through. Spoon the chicken noodle soup into warmed bowls and serve with a spoon and fork.

Chicken & Sweetcorn Soup

1 skinless, boneless chicken breast, about 175 g/6 oz
2 tbsp sunflower oil
2–3 spring onions, thinly sliced diagonally
1 small or ½ large red pepper, thinly sliced
1 garlic clove, crushed
125 g/4½ oz baby sweetcorn, thinly sliced
1 litre/1¾ pints chicken stock
200 g/7 oz canned sweetcorn kernels, well drained
2 tbsp sherry
2–3 tsp sweet chilli sauce
2–3 tsp cornflour
2 tomatoes, quartered and deseeded, then sliced
salt and pepper
chopped fresh coriander or parsley, to garnish

❈ Cut the chicken breast into 4 strips lengthways, then cut each strip into narrow slices across the grain.

❈ Heat the oil in a wok or frying pan, swirling it around until it is really hot.

❈ Add the chicken and stir-fry for 3–4 minutes, moving it around the wok until it is well sealed all over and almost cooked through.

❈ Add the spring onions, pepper and garlic, and stir-fry for 2–3 minutes. Add the sweetcorn and stock and bring to the boil.

❈ Add the sweetcorn kernels, sherry, sweet chilli sauce and salt to taste, and simmer for 5 minutes, stirring from time to time.

❈ Blend the cornflour with a little cold water. Add to the soup and bring to the boil, stirring until the sauce is thickened. Add the tomato slices, season to taste and simmer for 1–2 minutes.

❈ Serve hot, sprinkled with chopped coriander.

Thai Chicken & Coconut Soup

1.2 litres/2 pints chicken stock
200 g/7 oz skinless, boneless chicken
1 fresh chilli, split lengthways and deseeded
7.5-cm/3-inch piece of lemon grass, split lengthways
3–4 lime leaves
2.5-cm/1-inch piece of root ginger, peeled and sliced
120 ml/4 fl oz coconut milk
6–8 spring onions, sliced diagonally
¼ tsp chilli purée, or to taste
salt
fresh coriander leaves, to garnish

❈ Put the stock in a saucepan with the chicken, chilli, lemon grass, lime leaves and ginger. Bring almost to the boil, reduce the heat, cover and simmer for 20–25 minutes or until the chicken is cooked through and firm to the touch.

❈ Remove the chicken from the pan and strain the stock. When the chicken is cool, slice thinly or shred into bite-sized pieces.

❈ Return the stock to the pan and heat to simmering. Stir in the coconut milk and spring onions. Add the chicken and continue simmering for about 10 minutes, or until the soup is heated through and all the different flavours have mingled.

❈ Stir in the chilli purée. Season to taste with salt and, if wished, add a little more chilli purée.

❈ Ladle into warmed bowls and float the coriander leaves on top to serve.

Provençal Turkey Soup

1 tbsp olive oil
2 red, yellow or green peppers,
deseeded and finely chopped
1 celery stick, thinly sliced
1 large onion, finely chopped
125 ml/4 fl oz dry white wine
400 g/14 oz canned plum
tomatoes
3–4 garlic cloves,
finely chopped
1 litre/1¾ pints turkey or
chicken stock
¼ tsp dried thyme
1 bay leaf
2 courgettes, finely diced
350 g/12 oz cooked diced turkey
salt and pepper
fresh basil leaves, to garnish

❖ Heat the oil in a large saucepan over a medium heat. Add the peppers, celery and onion and cook for about 8 minutes until soft and just beginning to colour.

❖ Add the wine and simmer for 1 minute. Add the tomatoes and garlic.

❖ Stir in the stock. Add the thyme and bay leaf, season to taste with salt and pepper and bring to the boil. Reduce the heat, cover and simmer for about 25 minutes until the vegetables are tender.

❖ Add the courgettes and turkey. Continue cooking for a further 10–15 minutes until the courgettes are completely tender.

❖ Taste the soup and adjust the seasoning if necessary. Ladle into warmed bowls, garnish with basil leaves and serve immediately.

Hot & Sour Soup

4–6 dried Chinese mushrooms, soaked
125 g/4½ oz cooked lean pork or chicken
1 cake tofu
55 g/2 oz canned sliced bamboo shoots, drained
600 ml/1 pint Chinese stock or water
1 tbsp Chinese rice wine or dry sherry
1 tbsp light soy sauce
2 tbsp rice vinegar
1 tbsp cornflour paste
½ tsp ground white pepper
salt
2–3 spring onions, thinly sliced, to serve

❈ Drain the mushrooms, squeeze dry and discard the hard stalks. Thinly slice the mushrooms. Slice the meat, tofu and bamboo shoots into narrow shreds.

❈ Bring the stock to a rolling boil in a wok or large saucepan and add all the sliced ingredients. Bring back to the boil then simmer for about 1 minute.

❈ Add the wine, soy sauce, vinegar, pepper and salt to taste to the wok.

❈ Bring back to the boil once more, and add the cornflour paste to thicken the soup. Gently stir the soup while it is thickening. Serve the soup hot, sprinkled with the sliced spring onions.

Bacon, Bean & Garlic Soup

225 g/8 oz smoked lean back bacon rashers
1 carrot, thinly sliced
1 celery stick, thinly sliced
1 onion, chopped
1 tbsp oil
3 garlic cloves, sliced
700 ml/1¼ pints hot vegetable stock
200 g/7 oz canned chopped tomatoes
1 tbsp chopped fresh thyme
about 400 g/14 oz canned cannellini beans, drained
1 tbsp tomato purée
salt and pepper
grated Cheddar cheese, to garnish

❈ Chop 2 rashers of the bacon and place in a bowl. Cook in a microwave oven on HIGH power for 3–4 minutes until the fat runs and the bacon is well cooked. Stir the bacon halfway through cooking to separate the pieces. Transfer to a plate lined with kitchen paper and leave to cool. When cool, the bacon pieces should be crisp and dry. Place the carrot, celery, onion and oil in a large bowl. Cover and cook on HIGH power for 4 minutes.

❈ Chop the remaining bacon and add to the bowl with the garlic. Cover and cook on HIGH power for 2 minutes.

❈ Add the stock, tomatoes, thyme, beans and tomato purée. Cover and cook on HIGH power for 8 minutes, stirring halfway through. Season to taste. Ladle the soup into warmed bowls and sprinkle with the crisp bacon and grated cheese.

Chickpea Soup with Chorizo

250 g/9 oz dried chickpeas, soaked overnight in cold water to cover
115 g/4 oz lean chorizo, skinned and finely diced
1 onion, finely chopped
1 shallot, finely chopped
1 carrot, thinly sliced
2 garlic cloves, finely chopped
400 g/14 oz canned chopped tomatoes
1.2 litres/2 pints water
1 bay leaf
1/4 tsp dried thyme
1/4 tsp dried oregano
225 g/8 oz pumpkin, diced
225 g/8 oz potato, diced
115 g/4 oz curly kale leaves, finely chopped
salt and pepper

❄ Drain the chickpeas and put in a saucepan with enough cold water to cover generously. Bring to the boil over a high heat and cook for 10 minutes. Drain.

❄ Put the chorizo in a large dry frying pan over a medium–low heat. Cook, stirring frequently, for 5–10 minutes to render as much fat as possible. Remove with a slotted spoon and drain on absorbent kitchen paper.

❄ Pour off the excess fat from the pan and return to the heat. Add the onion, shallot, carrot and garlic and cook, stirring occasionally, for 3–4 minutes.

❄ Transfer to a larger saucepan if necessary. Add the chickpeas, tomatoes, water, herbs and chorizo. Bring almost to the boil, reduce the heat, cover and simmer gently for 30 minutes.

❄ Stir in the pumpkin and potato, cover and continue cooking for about 30 minutes until the chickpeas are tender. Season to taste with salt and pepper.

❄ Stir in the kale and continue to cook, uncovered, for 15–20 minutes or until it is tender. Taste and adjust the seasoning if necessary. Ladle the soup into warmed bowls and serve immediately.

Chilli Pork Soup

2 tsp olive oil
500 g/1 lb 2 oz lean pork mince
1 onion, finely chopped
1 celery stick, finely chopped
1 pepper, deseeded and finely chopped
2–3 garlic cloves, finely chopped
400 g/14 oz canned chopped tomatoes in juice
3 tbsp tomato purée
450 ml/16 fl oz chicken or meat stock
1/4 tsp ground coriander
1/4 tsp ground cumin
1/4 tsp dried oregano
1 tsp mild chilli powder
salt and pepper
chopped fresh coriander leaves or parsley, to garnish
soured cream, to serve

❄ Heat the oil in a large pan over a medium–high heat. Add the pork, season with salt and pepper, and cook, stirring frequently, until no longer pink. Reduce the heat to medium and add the onion, celery, pepper and garlic. Cover and cook, stirring occasionally, for a further 5 minutes until the onion is soft.

❄ Add the tomatoes, tomato purée and the stock. Stir in the coriander, cumin, oregano and chilli powder. Season to taste with salt and pepper.

❄ Bring just to the boil, then reduce the heat to low, cover and simmer for about 30–40 minutes until all the vegetables are very tender. Taste and adjust the seasoning, adding more chilli powder if you like it hotter.

❄ Ladle the soup into warmed bowls and sprinkle with the chopped coriander. You can either hand around the soured cream separately or top each serving with a spoonful.

Lamb & Barley Broth

❖ SERVES 4 ❖

1 tbsp vegetable oil
500 g/1 lb 2 oz lean neck
of lamb
1 large onion, sliced
2 carrots, sliced
2 leeks, sliced
1 litre/1¾ pints vegetable stock
1 bay leaf
few sprigs of fresh parsley
60 g/2 oz pearl barley

❖ Heat the vegetable oil in a large heavy-based saucepan and add the pieces of lamb, turning them to seal and brown on both sides.

❖ Lift the lamb out of the pan and set aside until required.

❖ Add the onion, carrots and leeks to the saucepan and cook gently for about 3 minutes.

❖ Return the lamb to the pan and add the stock, bay leaf, parsley and pearl barley to the pan.

❖ Bring the mixture in the pan to the boil, then reduce the heat. Cover and simmer for 1½ –2 hours.

❖ Discard the parsley. Lift the pieces of lamb from the broth and allow them to cool slightly.

❖ Remove the bones and any fat and chop the meat. Return the lamb to the broth and reheat gently.

❖ Ladle the lamb and parsley broth into warmed bowls and serve immediately.

Spicy Lamb Soup

❊ **SERVES 4** ❊

1–2 tbsp olive oil
450 g/1 lb lean boneless lamb, such as shoulder or neck fillet, trimmed of fat and cut into 1-cm/$\frac{1}{2}$-inch cubes
1 onion, finely chopped
2–3 garlic cloves, crushed
1.2 litres/2 pints water
400 g/14 oz canned chopped tomatoes in juice
1 bay leaf
$\frac{1}{2}$ tsp dried thyme
$\frac{1}{2}$ tsp dried oregano
pinch of ground cinnamon

$\frac{1}{4}$ tsp ground cumin
$\frac{1}{4}$ tsp ground turmeric
1 tsp harissa
400 g/14 oz canned chickpeas, rinsed and drained
1 carrot, diced
1 potato, diced
1 courgette, quartered lengthways and sliced
100 g/3$\frac{1}{2}$ oz fresh or frozen green peas
salt and pepper
chopped fresh mint or coriander, to garnish

❊ Heat the oil in a large saucepan or flameproof casserole over a medium–high heat. Add the lamb, in batches if necessary, and cook, stirring occasionally, until evenly browned on all sides, adding a little more oil if needed. Remove the meat with a slotted spoon.

❊ Reduce the heat and add the onion and garlic to the pan. Cook, stirring frequently, for 1–2 minutes.

❊ Add the water and return all the meat to the pan. Bring just to the boil and skim off any foam that rises to the surface. Reduce the heat and stir in the tomatoes, bay leaf, thyme, oregano, cinnamon, cumin, turmeric and harissa. Simmer for about 1 hour or until the meat is very tender.

❊ Discard the bay leaf. Stir in the chickpeas, carrot and potato and simmer for 15 minutes. Add the courgette and peas and simmer for a further 15–20 minutes or until all the vegetables are tender.

❊ Season to taste with salt and pepper and add more harissa if desired. Ladle the soup into warmed bowls, garnish with the chopped mint and serve immediately.

Chunky Potato & Beef Soup

❊ **SERVES 4** ❊

2 tbsp vegetable oil
225 g/8 oz lean stewing or frying steak, cut into strips
225 g/8 oz new potatoes, halved
1 carrot, diced
2 celery sticks, sliced
2 leeks, sliced
850 ml/1$\frac{1}{2}$ pints beef stock

8 baby sweetcorn cobs, sliced
1 bouquet garni
2 tbsp dry sherry
salt and pepper
chopped fresh parsley, to garnish
crusty bread, to serve

❊ Heat the vegetable oil in a large saucepan. Add the strips of steak to the pan and cook for 3 minutes, turning constantly.

❊ Add the halved potatoes, diced carrot and sliced celery and leeks. Cook, stirring constantly, for a further 5 minutes.

❊ Pour in the stock and bring to the boil over a medium heat. Reduce the heat until the liquid is simmering gently, then add the sweetcorn and the bouquet garni.

❊ Cook the soup for a further 20 minutes or until the meat and all the vegetables are tender.

❊ Remove the bouquet garni from the pan and discard. Stir the dry sherry into the soup and season to taste with salt and pepper.

❊ Pour the soup into warmed soup bowls and garnish with the chopped parsley. Serve immediately with the bread.

Beef & Spring Vegetable Soup

12 small new potatoes, quartered
4 slim carrots, quartered lengthways and cut into 4-cm/1½-inch lengths
150 g/5½ oz tiny French beans, cut into 4-cm/1½-inch lengths
1.5 litres/2¾ pints beef stock
2 tbsp soy sauce
3 tbsp dry sherry
350 g/12 oz beef fillet, about 5 cm/2 inches thick
150 g/5½ oz shiitake mushrooms, sliced
1 tbsp chopped fresh parsley
1 tbsp chopped fresh chives
salt and pepper

❋ Bring a saucepan of lightly salted water to the boil and add the potatoes and carrots. Reduce the heat, cover and boil gently for about 15 minutes until tender. Bring another saucepan of lightly salted water to the boil, add the beans and boil for about 5 minutes until just tender. Drain the vegetables and reserve.

❋ Bring the stock to the boil in a saucepan and add the soy sauce and sherry. Season with salt and pepper. Reduce the heat, add the beef and simmer gently for 10 minutes. (The beef should be very rare, as it will continue cooking in the bowls.)

❋ Add the mushrooms and simmer for a further 3 minutes. Warm the bowls in a low oven.

❋ Remove the meat and set aside to rest on a carving board. Taste the stock and adjust the seasoning, if necessary. Bring the stock back to the boil.

❋ Cut the meat in half lengthways and slice each half into pieces about 3 mm/⅛ inch thick. Lightly season the meat with salt and pepper and divide between the warmed bowls.

❋ Drop the reserved vegetables into the stock and heat through for about 1 minute. Ladle the stock over the meat, dividing the vegetables as evenly as possible. Sprinkle over the parsley and chives and serve immediately.

Salmon Bisque

1–2 salmon heads or a tail piece of salmon weighing about 500 g/1 lb 2 oz
900 ml/1½ pints water
1 fresh or dried bay leaf
1 lemon, sliced
a few black peppercorns
25 g/1 oz butter or margarine
2 tbsp finely chopped onion or spring onions
25 g/1 oz plain flour
150 ml/5 fl oz dry white wine or fish stock
150 ml/5 fl oz single cream
1 tbsp chopped fresh fennel or dill
2–3 tsp lemon or lime juice
salt and pepper
30–45 g/1–1½ oz smoked salmon pieces, chopped (optional), and sprigs of fresh fennel or dill, to garnish

❋ Put the salmon, water, bay leaf, lemon and peppercorns into a saucepan. Bring to the boil, remove any scum from the surface, then cover the pan and simmer gently for 20 minutes until the fish is cooked through.

❋ Remove from the heat, strain the stock and reserve 600 ml/1 pint. Remove and discard all the skin and bones from the salmon and flake the flesh, removing all the pieces from the head, if using.

❋ Melt the butter in a saucepan and fry the onion gently for about 5 minutes until soft. Stir in the flour and cook for 1 minute, then stir in the reserved stock and wine or fish stock. Bring to the boil, stirring. Add the salmon, season well, then simmer gently for about 5 minutes.

❋ Add the cream and the chopped fennel or dill and reheat gently, but do not boil. Sharpen to taste with lemon juice and season again. Serve hot or chilled, garnished with the smoked salmon, if using, and the fennel.

Mediterranean Fish Soup

1 tbsp olive oil
1 large onion, chopped
2 garlic cloves, finely chopped
425 ml/15 fl oz fresh fish stock
150 ml/5 fl oz dry white wine
1 bay leaf
1 sprig each fresh thyme, rosemary and oregano
450 g/1 lb firm white fish fillets (such as cod, monkfish or halibut), skinned and cut into 2.5-cm/1-inch cubes
450 g/1 lb fresh mussels, prepared
400 g/14 oz canned chopped tomatoes
225 g/8 oz peeled prawns, thawed, if frozen
salt and pepper
sprigs of thyme, to garnish
lemon wedges and 4 slices of toasted French bread, rubbed with a cut garlic clove, to serve

❖ Heat the olive oil in a large saucepan and gently fry the onion and garlic for 2–3 minutes until just soft.

❖ Pour in the stock and wine and bring to the boil.

❖ Tie the bay leaf and herbs together with clean string and add to the pan together with the fish and mussels. Stir well, cover and simmer for 5 minutes.

❖ Stir in the tomatoes and prawns and continue to cook for a further 3–4 minutes until piping hot and the fish is cooked through.

❖ Discard the herbs and any mussels that have not opened. Season to taste, then ladle into warmed bowls.

❖ Garnish with the sprigs of thyme and serve with the lemon wedges and toasted bread.

Louisiana Seafood Soup

1 tbsp plain flour	600 ml/1 pint vegetable stock
1 tsp paprika	425 g/15 oz canned chopped
350 g/12 oz monkfish fillets,	tomatoes
cut into chunks	1 bouquet garni
2 tbsp olive oil	125 g/4½ oz peeled prawns
1 onion, chopped	juice of 1 lemon
1 green pepper, cored,	dash of Tabasco sauce
deseeded and chopped	2 tsp Worcestershire sauce
3 celery sticks, finely chopped	175 g/6 oz cooked long-grain
2 garlic cloves, crushed	rice
175 g/6 oz okra, sliced	

❄ Mix the flour with the paprika. Add the monkfish chunks and toss to coat well.

❄ Heat the olive oil in a large heavy-based saucepan. Add the monkfish pieces and fry until brown on all sides. Remove from the pan with a slotted spoon and set aside.

❄ Add the onion, green pepper, celery, garlic and okra and fry gently for 5 minutes until soft.

❄ Add the stock, tomatoes and bouquet garni. Bring to the boil, reduce the heat and simmer for 15 minutes.

❄ Return the monkfish to the pan with the prawns, lemon juice and the Tabasco and Worcestershire sauces. Simmer for a further 5 minutes.

❄ To serve, place a mound of cooked rice in each of 4 warmed serving bowls, then ladle over the seafood gumbo.

Thai-Style Seafood Soup

1.2 litres/2 pints fish stock	200 g/7 oz large or medium
1 lemon grass stalk,	raw prawns, peeled and
split lengthways	deveined
pared rind of ½ lime or	250 g/9 oz scallops
1 lime leaf	2 tbsp fresh coriander leaves
2.5-cm/1-inch piece of root	salt
ginger, sliced	finely chopped red pepper or
¼ tsp chilli purée	fresh red chilli rings,
4–6 spring onions, trimmed	to garnish

❄ Put the stock in a saucepan with the lemon grass, lime rind, ginger and chilli purée. Bring just to the boil, reduce the heat, cover and simmer for 10–15 minutes.

❄ Cut the spring onions in half lengthways, then slice crossways very thinly. Cut the prawns almost in half lengthways, keeping the tails intact.

❄ Strain the stock, return to the pan and bring to a simmer, with bubbles rising at the edges and the surface trembling. Add the spring onions and cook for 2–3 minutes. Taste and season with salt, if needed, and stir in a little more chilli purée, if liked.

❄ Add the scallops and prawns and poach for about 1 minute until the scallops turn opaque and the prawns curl.

❄ Add the coriander leaves, ladle the soup into warmed bowls and garnish with the chopped pepper.

Prawn Laksa

400 g/14 oz canned coconut milk
300 ml/10 fl oz vegetable stock
50 g/1¾ oz dried vermicelli rice noodles
1 red pepper, deseeded and cut into strips
225 g/8 oz canned bamboo shoots, drained and rinsed
5-cm/2-inch piece of root ginger, thinly sliced
3 spring onions, chopped
1 tbsp Thai red curry paste
2 tbsp Thai fish sauce
1 tsp palm sugar or soft light brown sugar
6 fresh Thai basil sprigs
12 cooked prawns, in their shells

❄ Put the coconut milk and stock in a saucepan over a medium heat and bring slowly to the boil.

❄ Add all the remaining ingredients, except the prawns, reduce the heat to low and simmer gently for 4–5 minutes until the noodles are cooked.

❄ Add the prawns and simmer for a further 1–2 minutes until heated through. Ladle the soup into small warmed bowls, dividing the prawns equally between them, and serve immediately.

Crab & Ginger Soup

1 carrot, chopped
1 leek, chopped
1 bay leaf
850 ml/1½ pints fish stock
2 medium-sized cooked crabs
2.5-cm/1-inch piece of root ginger, grated
1 tsp light soy sauce
½ tsp ground star anise
salt and pepper

❄ Put the carrot, leek, bay leaf and stock into a large saucepan and bring to the boil. Reduce the heat, cover and leave to simmer for about 10 minutes or until the vegetables are nearly tender.

❄ Meanwhile, remove all of the meat from the cooked crabs. Break off the claws, break the joints and remove the meat (you may require a fork or skewer for this). Reserve some crab claws to garnish. Add the crabmeat to the pan of fish stock.

❄ Add the ginger, soy sauce and star anise to the fish stock and bring to the boil. Leave to simmer for about 10 minutes or until the vegetables are tender and the crab is heated through. Season to taste with salt and pepper.

❄ Ladle the soup into warmed serving bowls and garnish with the reserved crab claws. Serve at once.

New England Clam Chowder

900 g/2 lb live clams
4 rashers rindless streaky
bacon, chopped
25 g/1 oz butter
1 onion, chopped
1 tbsp chopped fresh thyme
1 large potato, peeled and diced
300 ml/10 fl oz milk
1 bay leaf
150 ml/5 fl oz double cream
1 tbsp chopped fresh parsley
salt and pepper

❊ Scrub the clams and put into a large saucepan with a splash of water. Cook over a high heat for 3–4 minutes until all the clams have opened. Discard any that remain closed. Strain the clams, reserving the cooking liquid. Leave until cool enough to handle.

❊ Reserve 8 clams in their shells to garnish, then remove the rest of the clams from their shells. Roughly chop, if large, and reserve.

❊ Dry-fry the bacon in a clean saucepan over a medium–low heat until brown and crisp. Drain on kitchen paper. Add the butter to the same pan and, when it has melted, add the onion. Cook for 4–5 minutes until soft but not coloured. Add the thyme and cook briefly before adding the diced potato, reserved clam cooking liquid, milk and bay leaf. Bring to the boil and simmer for 10 minutes until the potato is tender but not falling apart. Transfer to a food processor and process until smooth. Alternatively, rub through a sieve into a bowl and return to the pan.

❊ Add the clams, bacon and cream. Simmer for 2–3 minutes until heated through. Season to taste with salt and pepper. Stir in the parsley and ladle into 4 soup bowls. Garnish with the reserved clams in their shells and serve.

Tabbouleh Salad

❋ **SERVES 2** ❋

125 g/4½ oz bulgar wheat
600 ml/1 pint boiling water
1 red pepper, deseeded
and halved
3 tbsp olive oil
1 garlic clove, crushed
grated rind of ½ lime
about 1 tbsp lime juice
1 tbsp chopped mint
1 tbsp chopped parsley

3–4 spring onions, trimmed
and thinly sliced
8 pitted black olives, halved
40 g/1½ oz large salted
peanuts or cashew nuts
1–2 tsp lemon juice
55–85 g/2–3 oz Gruyère cheese
salt and pepper
sprigs of fresh mint, to garnish
warmed pitta bread or crusty
rolls, to serve

❋ Put the bulgar wheat into a bowl and cover with the boiling water to reach about 2.5 cm/1 inch above the bulgar. Set aside to soak for up to 1 hour, until most of the water is absorbed and is cold.

❋ Meanwhile, put the halved red pepper, skin side upwards, on a grill rack and cook under a preheated medium grill until the skin is thoroughly charred and blistered. Leave to cool slightly. When cool enough to handle, peel off the skin and discard the seeds. Cut the pepper flesh into narrow strips.

❋ Whisk together the oil, garlic and lime rind and juice. Season to taste and whisk until thoroughly blended. Add 4½ teaspoons of the dressing to the peppers and mix lightly.

❋ Drain the soaked bulgar wheat thoroughly, squeezing it in a dry cloth to make it even drier, then place in a bowl.

❋ Add the chopped herbs, spring onions, olives and peanuts to the bulgar and toss. Add the lemon juice to the remaining dressing, and stir through the salad. Spoon the salad on to 2 serving plates. Cut the cheese into narrow strips and mix with the pepper strips. Spoon alongside the bulgar salad. Garnish with the sprigs of mint and serve with the warmed pitta bread.

Moroccan Salad

❋ **SERVES 6** ❋

175 g/6 oz couscous
1 bunch spring onions,
finely chopped
1 small green pepper, seeded
and chopped
10-cm/4-inch piece of
cucumber, chopped
175 g/6 oz canned chickpeas,
rinsed and drained
60 g/2 oz sultanas or raisins

2 oranges
salt and pepper
sprigs of fresh mint, to garnish
lettuce leaves, to serve

DRESSING
finely grated rind of 1 orange
1 tbsp chopped fresh mint
150 ml/5 fl oz natural yogurt

❋ Put the couscous into a bowl and cover with boiling water. Leave it to soak for about 15 minutes to swell the grains, then stir gently with a fork to separate them.

❋ Add the spring onions, green pepper, cucumber, chickpeas and sultanas to the couscous, stirring to combine. Season well with salt and pepper.

❋ To make the dressing, place the orange rind, mint and yogurt in a bowl and mix together until well combined. Pour over the couscous mixture and stir to mix well.

❋ Using a sharp serrated knife, remove the peel and pith from the oranges. Cut the flesh into segments, removing all the membrane.

❋ Arrange the lettuce leaves on 4 serving plates. Divide the couscous mixture between the plates and arrange the orange segments on top. Garnish with the sprigs of mint and serve.

Coleslaw

150 ml/5 fl oz mayonnaise
150 ml/5 fl oz natural yogurt
dash of Tabasco sauce
1 medium head white cabbage

4 carrots
1 green pepper
2 tbsp sunflower seeds
salt and pepper

❀ To make the dressing, combine the mayonnaise, yogurt, Tabasco sauce and salt and pepper to taste in a small bowl. Leave to chill until required.

❀ Cut the cabbage in half and then into quarters. Remove and discard the tough centre stalk. Shred the cabbage leaves finely. Wash the leaves and dry them thoroughly.

❀ Peel the carrots and shred using a food processor or mandolin. Alternatively, coarsely grate the carrot.

❀ Quarter and deseed the pepper and cut the flesh into thin strips.

❀ Combine the vegetables in a large mixing bowl and toss to mix. Pour over the dressing and toss until the vegetables are well coated. Leave to chill in the refrigerator until required.

❀ Just before serving, place the sunflower seeds on a baking tray and toast them in the oven or under the grill until golden brown. Transfer the salad to a large serving dish, scatter with sunflower seeds and serve.

Fruity Coleslaw

1/2 small red cabbage, thinly shredded
1/2 small white cabbage, thinly shredded
175 g/6 oz dried dates, stoned and chopped
1 red dessert apple
2 green dessert apples

4 tbsp lemon juice
25 g/1 oz pine kernels, toasted

DRESSING
5 tbsp olive oil
2 tbsp cider vinegar
1 tsp clear honey
salt and pepper

❀ Put the shredded red and white cabbage and the dates into a salad bowl and toss well to mix.

❀ Core the apples but do not peel them. Thinly slice them and place in another bowl. Add the lemon juice and toss well to coat to prevent the apples from turning brown. Add them to the salad bowl.

❀ To make the dressing, whisk together the olive oil, vinegar and honey in a small bowl and season to taste with salt and pepper. Pour the dressing over the salad and toss. Sprinkle with the pine kernels, toss lightly and serve.

Carrot & Mango Salad

4 carrots
1 small, ripe mango
200 g/7 oz firm tofu
1 tbsp chopped fresh chives

DRESSING
2 tbsp orange juice
1 tbsp lime juice
1 tsp clear honey
$\frac{1}{2}$ tsp orange-flower water
1 tsp sesame oil
1 tsp sesame seeds, toasted

❖ Peel and coarsely grate the carrots. Peel, stone and thinly slice the mango.

❖ Cut the tofu into 1-cm/$\frac{1}{2}$-inch dice and toss together with the carrots and mango in a wide salad bowl.

❖ For the dressing, place all the ingredients in a screw-top jar and shake vigorously to mix evenly.

❖ Pour the dressing over the salad and toss well to coat the salad evenly.

❖ Chill the salad for 1–2 hours, if wished. Just before serving, lightly toss the salad and sprinkle with chives. Serve immediately.

Salad with Garlic Dressing

75 g/2¾ oz cucumber,
cut into sticks
6 spring onions, halved
2 tomatoes, seeded and
cut into eighths
1 yellow pepper, cut into strips
2 celery sticks, cut into strips
4 radishes, quartered
75 g/2¾ oz rocket
1 tbsp chopped mint, to serve

DRESSING
2 tbsp lemon juice
1 garlic clove, crushed
150 ml/5 fl oz low-fat natural
yogurt
2 tbsp olive oil
salt and pepper

❖ To make the salad, mix the cucumber, spring onions, tomatoes, pepper, celery, radishes and rocket together in a large serving bowl.

❖ To make the dressing, stir the lemon juice, garlic, yogurt and olive oil together.

❖ Season well with salt and pepper.

❖ Spoon the dressing over the salad and toss to mix. Sprinkle the salad with the chopped mint and serve.

Caesar Salad

1 garlic clove, halved
1 lettuce
55 g/2 oz Parmesan cheese,
coarsely grated

GARLIC CROÛTONS
3 tbsp olive oil
1 large garlic clove, halved
4 slices wholemeal bread,
crusts removed, diced

DRESSING
1 egg
1 tsp Worcestershire sauce
2 tbsp lemon juice
2 tsp Dijon mustard
2 tbsp olive oil
salt and pepper

❖ First make the garlic croûtons. Pour the olive oil into a small saucepan and add the garlic. Heat gently for 5 minutes. Remove and discard the garlic. Place the cubes of bread in a bowl and pour in the oil. Toss well, then spread out on a baking tray. Bake in a preheated oven, 190°C/375°F/Gas Mark 5, for 10 minutes until crisp. Remove from the oven and set aside to cool.

❖ To make the dressing, boil the egg for 1 minute. Crack it into a bowl and scoop out any remaining egg white from the shell. Whisk in the Worcestershire sauce, lemon juice, mustard and oil and season to taste with salt and pepper.

❖ Rub the inside of a salad bowl with the garlic halves, then discard them.

❖ Arrange the lettuce leaves in the salad bowl and sprinkle with the Parmesan cheese. Drizzle the dressing over the salad and sprinkle the garlic croûtons on top. Toss the salad at the table and serve at once.

Provençal Pasta Salad

225 g/8 oz penne
1 tbsp olive oil
25 g/1 oz stoned black olives, drained and chopped
25 g/1 oz dry-pack sun-dried tomatoes, soaked, drained and chopped
400 g/14 oz canned artichoke hearts, drained and halved
115 g/4 oz baby courgettes, trimmed and sliced
115 g/4 oz baby plum tomatoes, halved
100 g/3$^{1}/_{2}$ oz assorted baby salad leaves
salt and pepper
shredded basil leaves, to garnish

DRESSING
4 tbsp passata
2 tbsp low-fat natural fromage frais
1 tbsp unsweetened orange juice
1 small bunch fresh basil, shredded

❃ Cook the penne according to the instructions on the packet. Do not overcook the pasta – it should still have 'bite'. Drain well and return to the saucepan.

❃ Stir in the olive oil, salt and pepper, olives and sun-dried tomatoes. Leave to cool.

❃ Gently mix the artichokes, courgettes and plum tomatoes into the pasta. Arrange the salad leaves in a serving bowl.

❃ To make the dressing, mix all the ingredients together and toss into the vegetables and pasta.

❃ Spoon the mixture on top of the salad leaves and garnish with shredded basil leaves.

Pasta & Garlic Mayo Salad

2 large lettuces
260 g/9 oz dried penne
1 tbsp olive oil
8 red eating apples
juice of 4 lemons
1 head of celery, sliced
115 g/4 oz shelled, halved walnuts
250 ml/9 fl oz fresh garlic mayonnaise
salt

❃ Wash, drain and pat dry the lettuce leaves with kitchen paper. Transfer them to the refrigerator for 1 hour or until crisp.

❃ Meanwhile, bring a large saucepan of lightly salted water to the boil. Add the pasta and olive oil and cook for 8–10 minutes or until the pasta is tender but still firm to the bite. Drain the pasta and refresh under cold running water. Drain thoroughly again and set aside.

❃ Core and dice the apples, place them in a small bowl and sprinkle with the lemon juice.

❃ Mix together the pasta, celery, apples and walnuts and toss the mixture in the garlic mayonnaise. Add more mayonnaise, if liked.

❃ Line a salad bowl with the lettuce leaves and spoon the pasta salad into the lined bowl. Serve when required.

Cheese, Nut & Pasta Salad

225 g/8 oz dried pasta shells
1 tbsp olive oil
115 g/4 oz shelled walnuts,
halved
mixed salad leaves, such as
radicchio, escarole, rocket,
lamb's lettuce and frisée
225 g/8 oz dolcelatte cheese,
crumbled
salt

DRESSING
2 tbsp walnut oil
4 tbsp extra virgin olive oil
2 tbsp red wine vinegar
salt and pepper

❖ Bring a large saucepan of lightly salted water the boil. Add the pasta shells and olive oil and cook for 8–10 minutes or until the pasta is tender but still firm to the bite. Drain the pasta, refresh under cold running water, drain again and set aside.

❖ Spread out the walnut halves on a baking tray and toast under a preheated grill for 2–3 minutes. Set aside to cool while you make the dressing.

❖ To make the dressing, whisk together the walnut oil, olive oil and vinegar in a small bowl, and season to taste.

❖ To make up the salad, arrange the salad leaves in a serving bowl. Pile the cooled pasta in the middle of the salad leaves and sprinkle over the dolcelatte cheese. Just before serving, pour the dressing over the pasta salad, scatter the walnut halves on top and toss together to coat with dressing. Serve immediately.

Hot Rice Salad

300 g/10$\frac{1}{2}$ oz brown rice	**DRESSING**
1 bunch spring onions	2 tbsp crunchy peanut butter
1 red pepper	1 tbsp groundnut oil
125 g/4$\frac{1}{2}$ oz radishes	2 tbsp light soy sauce
425 g/15 oz canned pineapple	2 tbsp white wine vinegar
pieces in natural juice,	2 tsp clear honey
drained	1 tsp chilli powder
125 g/4$\frac{1}{2}$ oz beansprouts	$\frac{1}{2}$ tsp garlic salt
90 g/3 oz dry-roasted peanuts	pepper

❃ Put the rice in a saucepan and cover with water. Bring to the boil, then cover and simmer for 30 minutes until tender.

❃ Meanwhile, chop the spring onions, using a sharp knife. Deseed and chop the red pepper and thinly slice the radishes.

❃ To make the dressing, place the peanut butter, oil, light soy sauce, vinegar, honey, chilli powder, garlic salt and pepper in a small bowl and whisk for a few seconds until well combined.

❃ Drain the rice thoroughly and place in a heatproof bowl.

❃ Heat the dressing in a small saucepan for 1 minute and then toss into the rice and mix well.

❃ Working quickly, stir the pineapple pieces, spring onions, pepper, beansprouts and peanuts into the mixture in the bowl.

❃ Pile the hot rice salad into a warmed serving dish.

❃ Arrange the radish slices around the outside of the salad and serve immediately.

Tropical Rice Salad

115 g/4 oz long-grain rice,	3 tbsp sultanas
rinsed	salt and pepper
225 g/8 oz canned pineapple	
pieces in natural juice	**DRESSING**
200 g/7 oz canned sweetcorn,	1 tbsp groundnut oil
drained	1 tbsp hazelnut oil
2 red peppers, deseeded and	1 tbsp light soy sauce
diced	1 garlic clove, finely chopped
4 spring onions, thinly sliced	1 tsp chopped root ginger

❃ Prepare the vegetables. Bring a saucepan of lightly salted water to the boil and cook the rice for 15 minutes. Drain and rinse with cold water. Place the rice in a serving bowl.

❃ Drain the pineapple pieces, reserving the juice in a jug. Add the pineapple, sweetcorn, red peppers, spring onions and sultanas to the rice and mix lightly.

❃ Add all the dressing ingredients to the fruit juice, whisking well, and season to taste with salt and pepper. Pour the dressing over the salad and toss to coat.

Gazpacho Rice Salad

❈ SERVES 4 ❈

7 tbsp extra virgin olive oil
1 onion, finely chopped
4 garlic cloves, finely chopped
200 g/7 oz long-grain white rice
350 ml/12 fl oz vegetable stock
  or water
1½ tsp dried thyme
3 tbsp sherry vinegar
1 tsp Dijon mustard
1 tsp clear honey
1 red pepper, deseeded and
  chopped
½ yellow pepper, deseeded
  and chopped
½ green pepper, deseeded
  and chopped

1 red onion, finely chopped
½ cucumber, peeled,
  deseeded and chopped
  (optional)
3 tomatoes, deseeded and
  chopped
2–3 tbsp chopped flat-leaf
  parsley
salt and pepper

TO GARNISH
12 cherry tomatoes, halved
12 black olives, stoned and
  coarsely chopped
1 tbsp flaked almonds, toasted

❈ Heat 2 tablespoons of the oil in a large saucepan. Add the onion and cook, stirring frequently, for 2 minutes until beginning to soften. Stir in half the garlic and cook for a further minute.

❈ Add the rice, stir to coat and cook for about 2 minutes until translucent. Stir in the stock and half the thyme and bring to the boil. Season to taste. Cover and simmer gently for about 20 minutes until tender. Stand, still covered, for about 15 minutes; uncover and cool completely.

❈ Whisk the vinegar with the remaining garlic and thyme, the mustard, honey and salt and pepper in a large bowl. Gradually whisk in the remaining olive oil. Using a fork, gently fluff the rice into the vinaigrette.

❈ Add the peppers, red onion, cucumber, tomatoes and parsley; toss and adjust the seasoning. Transfer the salad to a serving bowl and garnish with the cherry tomatoes, olives and toasted almonds. Serve warm.

Pepper Salad

❈ SERVES 4 ❈

1 onion
2 red peppers
2 yellow peppers
3 tbsp olive oil
2 large courgettes, sliced
2 garlic cloves, sliced
1 tbsp balsamic vinegar
50 g/1¾ oz anchovy fillets,
  chopped
25 g/1 oz black olives, halved
  and stoned

1 tbsp chopped fresh basil
salt and pepper

TOMATO TOASTS
small stick of French bread
1 garlic clove, crushed
1 tomato, peeled and chopped
2 tbsp olive oil, plus extra to
  drizzle

❈ Cut the onion into wedges. Core and deseed the peppers and cut into thick slices.

❈ Heat the oil in a large heavy-based frying pan. Add the onion, peppers, courgettes and garlic and fry gently for 20 minutes, stirring occasionally.

❈ Add the vinegar, anchovies, olives and seasoning to taste, mix thoroughly and leave to cool.

❈ Spoon on to individual plates and sprinkle with the basil.

❈ To make the tomato toasts, cut the French bread diagonally into 1-cm/½-inch slices.

❈ Mix the garlic, tomato, oil and seasoning together, and spread thinly over each slice of bread.

❈ Place the bread on a baking tray, drizzle with the olive oil and bake in a preheated oven, 220°C/425°F/Gas Mark 7, for 5–10 minutes until crisp. Serve the pepper salad with the tomato toasts.

Aubergine Salad

2 large aubergines,
about 1 kg/2 lb 4 oz
6 tbsp olive oil
1 small onion, finely chopped
2 garlic cloves, crushed
6–8 celery sticks, cut into
1-cm/½-inch slices
2 tbsp capers
12–16 green olives, stoned
and sliced
2 tbsp pine kernels
25 g/1 oz plain chocolate,
grated
4 tbsp wine vinegar
1 tbsp brown sugar
salt and pepper
2 hard-boiled eggs,
sliced, to serve
celery leaves or curly endive,
to garnish

❊ Cut the aubergines into 2.5-cm/1-inch cubes and sprinkle liberally with 2–3 tablespoons of salt. Leave to stand for 1 hour to extract the bitter juices, then rinse off the salt thoroughly under cold water, drain and dry on kitchen paper.

❊ Heat most of the oil in a frying pan and fry the aubergine cubes until golden brown all over. Drain on kitchen paper and put into a large bowl.

❊ Add the onion and garlic to the pan with the remaining oil and fry very gently until just soft. Add the celery to the pan and fry for a few minutes, stirring frequently, until lightly coloured but still crisp.

❊ Add the celery to the aubergines with the capers, olives and pine kernels and mix lightly.

❊ Add the chocolate, vinegar and sugar to the residue in the pan. Heat gently until melted, then bring to the boil. Season to taste with salt and pepper. Pour over the salad and mix lightly. Cover, leave until cold and chill thoroughly.

❊ Serve with the sliced hard-boiled eggs and garnish with the celery leaves.

Grilled Vegetable Salad

❄ **SERVES 4** ❄

1 courgette, sliced
1 yellow pepper, deseeded
and sliced
1 aubergine, sliced
1 fennel bulb, cut into
8 wedges
1 red onion, cut into 8 wedges
16 cherry tomatoes
3 tbsp olive oil
1 garlic clove, crushed

sprigs of fresh rosemary,
to garnish

DRESSING
4 tbsp olive oil
2 tbsp balsamic vinegar
2 tsp chopped fresh rosemary
1 tsp Dijon mustard
1 tsp clear honey
2 tsp lemon juice

❄ Spread out all of the vegetables, except the cherry tomatoes, on a baking tray.

❄ Mix the oil and garlic and brush over the vegetables. Cook under a medium–hot grill for 10 minutes until tender and beginning to char. Set aside to cool. Spoon the vegetables into a serving bowl with the cherry tomatoes.

❄ Mix the dressing ingredients and pour over the vegetables. Cover and chill for 1 hour. Garnish and serve.

Spicy Tomato Salad

❄ **SERVES 4** ❄

4 large ripe tomatoes
1 small fresh red chilli
1 garlic clove
25 g/1 oz fresh basil
4 tbsp extra virgin olive oil
1 tbsp lemon juice

2 tbsp balsamic vinegar
salt and pepper
fresh crusty bread, to serve
sprigs of fresh basil and lemon
wedges, to garnish

❄ Bring a kettle of water to the boil. Place the tomatoes in a heatproof bowl, then pour over enough boiling water to cover them. Leave them to soak for 2–4 minutes, then lift out of the water and leave to cool slightly.

❄ When the tomatoes are cool enough to handle, gently pierce the skins with the point of a knife. The skins should now be easy to remove. Discard the skins, then chop the tomatoes and place them in a large salad bowl.

❄ Deseed and finely chop the chilli, then chop the garlic. Rinse and finely chop the basil, then add it to the tomatoes in the bowl with the chilli and the garlic.

❄ Mix the oil, lemon juice and vinegar together in a separate bowl, then season to taste with salt and pepper. Pour the mixture over the salad and toss together well. Garnish with basil sprigs and lemon wedges, and serve immediately with fresh crusty bread.

Beetroot & Orange Salad

❈ SERVES 4 ❈

225 g/8 oz mixed long-grain
and wild rice
4 large oranges
450 g/1 lb cooked beetroot,
peeled and drained
2 heads of chicory
salt and pepper
fresh snipped chives,
to garnish

DRESSING
4 tbsp low-fat natural fromage
frais
1 garlic clove, crushed
1 tbsp wholegrain mustard
1/2 tsp finely grated orange rind
2 tsp clear honey

❈ Cook the long-grain and wild rice according to the packet instructions. Drain and set aside to cool.

❈ Meanwhile, slice the top and bottom off each orange. Using a sharp knife, remove the skin and pith. Holding the orange over a bowl to catch the juice, carefully slice between each segment. Place the segments in a separate bowl. Cover the juice and leave to chill.

❈ Dice the beetroot into small cubes. Mix with the orange segments, cover and chill.

❈ When the rice has cooled, mix in the reserved orange juice until thoroughly incorporated and season to taste with salt and pepper.

❈ Line 4 bowls or plates with the chicory leaves. Spoon over the rice and top with the beetroot and orange.

❈ Mix all the dressing ingredients together and spoon over the salad, or serve separately in a bowl, if preferred. Garnish with the chives.

Cucumber Salad

❈ SERVES 4 ❈

1/2 cucumber
1 tbsp rice vinegar
2 tbsp sugar

1/2 tsp salt
2 tbsp hot water
1 small shallot

❈ Wash the cucumber thoroughly and pat dry with absorbent kitchen paper.

❈ Peel the cucumber, halve it lengthways, and deseed it, using a teaspoon or a melon baller.

❈ Using a sharp knife, slice the cucumber thinly.

❈ Arrange the cucumber slices in an attractive pattern on a serving plate.

❈ To make the dressing, mix together the vinegar, sugar and salt in a bowl. Pour on the hot water and stir until the sugar has dissolved. Leave the dressing to cool slightly.

❈ Pour the dressing evenly over the cucumber slices.

❈ Using a sharp knife, thinly slice the shallot and sprinkle over the cucumber.

❈ Cover the cucumber salad with clingfilm and leave to chill in the refrigerator before serving. Serve as a cooling accompaniment to curries.

Courgette & Mint Salad

2 courgettes, cut into batons
100 g/3¹/2 oz French beans,
cut into thirds
1 green pepper, deseeded and
cut into strips
2 celery sticks, sliced
1 bunch of watercress

DRESSING
200 ml/7 fl oz natural yogurt
1 garlic clove, crushed
2 tbsp chopped fresh mint
pepper

❖ Bring a saucepan of lightly salted water to the boil and cook the courgette batons and beans for 7–8 minutes. Drain, rinse under cold running water and drain again. Set aside to cool completely.

❖ Mix the courgettes and beans with the green pepper strips, celery and watercress in a large serving bowl.

❖ To make the dressing, combine the yogurt, garlic and chopped mint in a small bowl. Season to taste with pepper.

❖ Spoon the dressing on to the salad and serve immediately.

Green Salad

25 g/1 oz pistachio nuts
5 tbsp extra virgin olive oil
1 tbsp rosemary, chopped
2 garlic cloves, chopped
4 slices rustic bread
1 tbsp red wine vinegar
1 tbsp wholegrain mustard

1 tsp sugar
25 g/1 oz rocket
25 g/1 oz red chard
50 g/1¾ oz green olives, stoned
2 tbsp fresh basil, shredded

❈ Shell the pistachio nuts and roughly chop them, using a sharp knife.

❈ Place 2 tablespoons of the olive oil in a frying pan. Add the rosemary and garlic and cook for 2 minutes.

❈ Add the slices of bread to the pan and fry for 2–3 minutes on both sides until golden. Remove the bread from the pan and drain on absorbent kitchen paper.

❈ To make the dressing, mix together the remaining olive oil with the vinegar, mustard and sugar.

❈ Place a slice of bread on a serving plate and top with the rocket and red chard. Sprinkle with the olives.

❈ Drizzle the dressing over the top of the salad leaves. Sprinkle with the chopped pistachio nuts and shredded basil leaves and serve the salad immediately.

Mixed Leaf Salad

½ head frisée
½ head oakleaf lettuce or quattro stagione
few leaves of radicchio
1 head chicory
25 g/1 oz rocket leaves
few sprigs fresh basil
edible flowers, to garnish

FRENCH DRESSING
1 tbsp white wine vinegar
pinch of sugar
½ tsp Dijon mustard
3 tbsp extra virgin olive oil
salt and pepper

❈ Tear the frisée, oakleaf lettuce and radicchio into pieces. Place the salad leaves in a large serving bowl or individual bowls if you prefer.

❈ Cut the chicory into diagonal slices and add to the bowl with the rocket leaves and basil.

❈ To make the dressing, beat the vinegar, sugar and mustard in a small bowl until the sugar has dissolved. Gradually beat in the olive oil until creamy and thoroughly mixed. Season to taste with salt and pepper.

❈ Pour the dressing over the salad and toss thoroughly. Sprinkle a mixture of edible flowers over the top and serve.

Warm Spinach Salad

❋ **SERVES 4** ❋

275 g/9¾ oz fresh baby
spinach leaves
2 tbsp olive oil
150 g/5½ oz pancetta, cubed
280 g/10 oz mixed wild
mushrooms, sliced

DRESSING
5 tbsp olive oil
1 tbsp balsamic vinegar
1 tsp Dijon mustard
pinch of sugar
salt and pepper

❋ To make the dressing, place the olive oil, vinegar, mustard, sugar and salt and pepper to taste in a small bowl and whisk together. Rinse the baby spinach under cold running water, then drain and place in a large salad bowl.

❋ Heat the oil in a large frying pan. Add the pancetta and fry for 3 minutes. Add the mushrooms and cook for 3–4 minutes or until tender.

❋ Pour the dressing into the pan and immediately turn the fried mixture and dressing into the bowl with the spinach. Toss until coated with the dressing and serve immediately.

Potato Salad

❋ **SERVES 4** ❋

700 g/1 lb 9 oz tiny new
potatoes
8 spring onions
1 hard-boiled egg (optional)
250 ml/9 fl oz low-fat
mayonnaise

1 tsp paprika
salt and pepper
2 tbsp snipped chives and
a pinch of paprika, to garnish

❋ Bring a large saucepan of lightly salted water to the boil. Add the potatoes and cook for 10–15 minutes or until they are just tender.

❋ Drain the potatoes in a colander and rinse them under cold running water until they are completely cold. Drain them again thoroughly. Transfer to a mixing bowl and set aside until required.

❋ Trim and slice the spring onions thinly on the diagonal.

❋ Shell and chop the hard-boiled egg, if using.

❋ Mix together the mayonnaise, paprika and salt and pepper to taste in a bowl until well blended. Pour the mixture over the potatoes.

❋ Add the sliced spring onions and chopped egg, if using, and toss together gently.

❋ Transfer the potato salad to a serving bowl and sprinkle with the snipped chives and a pinch of paprika. Cover and chill in the refrigerator until required.

Italian Potato Salad

450 g/1 lb baby potatoes, unpeeled, or larger potatoes, halved
4 tbsp natural yogurt
4 tbsp mayonnaise
8 sun-dried tomatoes
2 tbsp flat-leaf parsley, chopped
salt and pepper

❈ Rinse and clean the potatoes and place them in a large saucepan of lightly salted water. Bring to the boil and cook for 8–12 minutes or until just tender. (The cooking time will vary according to the size of the potatoes.)

❈ Using a sharp knife, cut the sun-dried tomatoes into thin slices.

❈ To make the dressing, mix together the yogurt and mayonnaise in a bowl and season to taste with a little salt and pepper. Stir in the sun-dried tomato slices and the chopped parsley.

❈ Remove the potatoes with a slotted spoon, drain them thoroughly and then set them aside to cool. If you are using larger potatoes, cut them into 5-cm/2-inch chunks.

❈ Pour the dressing over the potatoes and toss to mix.

❈ Leave the potato salad to chill in the refrigerator for about 20 minutes, then serve.

Potato & Apple Salad

❄ **SERVES 4** ❄

2 large potatoes, unpeeled
and sliced
2 green dessert apples, diced
1 tsp lemon juice
25 g/1 oz walnut pieces
125 g/4¹/₂ oz goat's cheese,
cubed
150 g/5¹/₂ oz rocket
salt and pepper

DRESSING
2 tbsp olive oil
1 tbsp red wine vinegar
1 tsp clear honey
1 tsp fennel seeds

❄ Bring a saucepan of lightly salted water to the boil and cook the potatoes for 15 minutes until tender. Drain and leave to cool. Transfer the cooled potatoes to a serving bowl.

❄ Toss the diced apples in the lemon juice, drain and stir into the cold potatoes.

❄ Add the walnut pieces, cheese cubes and rocket, then toss the salad to mix and season to taste.

❄ In a small bowl, whisk the dressing ingredients together and pour the dressing over the salad. Serve immediately.

Multi-Coloured Salad

❄ **SERVES 4** ❄

500 g/1 lb 2 oz waxy potatoes,
diced
4 small cooked beetroot, sliced
¹/₂ small cucumber,
thinly sliced
2 large dill pickles, sliced
1 red onion, halved and sliced
sprigs of fresh dill, to garnish

DRESSING
1 garlic clove, crushed
2 tbsp olive oil
2 tbsp red wine vinegar
2 tbsp chopped fresh dill
salt and pepper

❄ Cook the diced potatoes in a saucepan of boiling water for about 15 minutes, or until just tender. Drain and set aside to cool.

❄ When cool, mix the diced potato and beetroot together gently in a bowl and set aside.

❄ To make the dressing, whisk together the garlic, olive oil, vinegar and dill and season to taste with salt and pepper.

❄ When you are ready to serve the salad, line a large serving platter with the slices of cucumber, the dill pickles and the red onion.

❄ Spoon the potato and beetroot mixture on top of the other vegetables in the centre of the platter.

❄ Pour the dressing over the salad and serve immediately, garnished with the sprigs of dill.

Green Sesame Salad

125 g/4^1/$_2$ oz beansprouts	3 celery sticks
1^1/$_2$ tbsp chopped fresh	1 large green pepper,
coriander	deseeded
3 tbsp fresh lime juice	1 large Granny Smith apple
^{1}/$_2$ tsp mild chilli powder	2 tbsp toasted sesame seeds,
1 tsp sugar	to garnish
^{1}/$_2$ tsp salt	

❄ Rinse the beansprouts and drain thoroughly.

❄ Pick over the beansprouts, removing any that seem a little brown or limp – it is essential that they are fresh and crunchy for this recipe.

❄ To make the dressing, combine the coriander, lime juice, chilli powder, sugar and salt in a small bowl and mix thoroughly.

❄ Using a sharp knife, cut the celery into 2.5-cm/1-inch pieces. Cut the pepper into small pieces and the apple into small chunks.

❄ Place the beansprouts, celery, green pepper and apple in a large mixing bowl and stir gently to mix.

❄ Just before serving, pour the dressing over the salad, tossing well to mix.

❄ Garnish the salad with the toasted sesame seeds and serve.

Beansprout Salad

350 g/12 oz beansprouts	1 garlic clove, crushed
1 small cucumber	dash of chilli sauce
1 green pepper, deseeded and	2 tbsp light soy sauce
cut into matchsticks	1 tsp wine vinegar
1 carrot, cut into matchsticks	2 tsp sesame oil
2 tomatoes, finely chopped	16 fresh chives
1 celery stick, cut into	
matchsticks	

❄ Blanch the beansprouts in boiling water for 1 minute. Drain well and rinse under cold water. Drain thoroughly again.

❄ Cut the cucumber in half lengthways. Scoop out the seeds with a teaspoon and discard. Cut the flesh into matchsticks and mix with the beansprouts, green pepper, carrot, tomatoes and celery.

❄ Mix together the garlic, chilli sauce, soy sauce, vinegar and sesame oil. Pour the dressing over the vegetables, tossing well to coat. Spoon on to 4 individual serving plates. Garnish with the chives and serve.

Broccoli & Almond Salad

450 g/1 lb small broccoli florets
50 g/1¾ oz baby sweetcorn,
halved lengthways
1 red pepper, seeded and cut
into thin strips
50 g/1¾ oz blanched almonds

DRESSING
1 tbsp sesame seeds
1 tbsp groundnut oil
2 garlic cloves, crushed
2 tbsp light soy sauce
1 tbsp clear honey
2 tsp lemon juice
pepper
lemon zest, to garnish
(optional)

❊ Blanch the broccoli and sweetcorn in boiling water for 5 minutes. Drain well, rinse and drain again.

❊ Transfer to a large mixing bowl and add the red pepper and almonds.

❊ To make the dressing, heat a wok and add the sesame seeds. Dry-fry, stirring constantly, for about 1 minute or until the sesame seeds are lightly browned and are giving off a delicious aroma. Remove from the heat.

❊ Mix the peanut oil, garlic, soy sauce, honey, lemon juice and pepper to taste in a bowl. Add the sesame seeds and mix well.

❊ Pour the dressing over the salad, cover and set aside in the refrigerator for a minimum of 4 hours and preferably overnight.

❊ Garnish the salad with the lemon zest, if using, and serve.

Chicory Salad

❊ **SERVES 4** ❊

1 pink grapefruit
1 avocado
1 packet lamb's lettuce, washed thoroughly
2 heads chicory, sliced diagonally
1 tbsp chopped fresh mint

FRENCH DRESSING
3 tbsp olive oil
1 tbsp wine vinegar
1 small garlic clove, crushed
1/2 tsp Dijon or Meaux mustard
1 tsp clear honey
salt and pepper

❊ Peel the grapefruit with a serrated knife.

❊ Cut the grapefruit into segments by cutting between the membranes.

❊ To make the French dressing, put all the ingredients into a screw-top jar and shake vigorously.

❊ Halve the avocado and remove the stone by stabbing it with a sharp knife and twisting to loosen. Remove the avocado skin.

❊ Cut the avocado into small slices, put into a bowl and toss in the French dressing.

❊ Remove any stalks from the lamb's lettuce and put into a bowl with the grapefruit, chicory and mint.

❊ Add the avocado and 2 tablespoons of the French dressing. Toss well, transfer to serving plates, and serve immediately.

Tomato & Fennel Salad

❊ **SERVES 4** ❊

1 small fennel bulb
2 large beef tomatoes, cut into wedges
1 eating apple, quartered, cored and sliced
15-cm/6-inch piece of cucumber, peeled

4 tbsp olive oil
2 tbsp lemon juice
1/2 tsp Dijon mustard
salt and pepper
fennel fronds, to garnish

❊ Using a sharp knife, thinly slice the fennel bulb and place in a large serving dish with the tomato wedges and apple slices.

❊ Cut the cucumber in half lengthways and, using a teaspoon, scoop out the seeds and discard. Cut each half into thick slices and add to the salad.

❊ Mix the oil, lemon juice and mustard together in a small bowl. Season to taste with salt and pepper and pour over the salad. Toss gently until the salad is coated with the dressing. Snip the fennel fronds over the top to garnish and serve.

Red Cabbage & Pear Salad

350 g/12 oz red cabbage, finely shredded
2 Conference pears, cored and thinly sliced
4 spring onions, sliced
lollo biondo leaves
1 carrot, grated
fresh chives, to garnish

DRESSING
4 tbsp pear juice
1 tsp wholegrain mustard
3 tbsp olive oil
1 tbsp garlic wine vinegar
1 tbsp chopped chives

❖ Put the red cabbage, pears and spring onions into a bowl and toss gently together to mix.

❖ Line a serving dish with lollo biondo leaves and spoon the cabbage and pear mixture into the centre.

❖ Sprinkle the grated carrot into the centre of the cabbage to form a domed pile.

❖ To make the dressing, combine the pear juice, mustard, olive oil, garlic, wine vinegar and chives, stirring until well mixed.

❖ Pour the dressing over the salad, garnish and serve immediately. (Do not make the salad much in advance of serving because the colour from the red cabbage will bleed into the other ingredients, spoiling the appearance.)

Pear & Roquefort Salad

❖ **SERVES 4** ❖

50 g/1¾ oz Roquefort cheese
150 ml/5 fl oz low-fat natural yogurt
2 tbsp snipped chives
few leaves of lollo rosso

few leaves of radicchio
few leaves of lamb's lettuce
2 ripe pears
pepper
whole chives, to garnish

❖ Place the cheese in a bowl and mash with a fork. Gradually blend the yogurt into the cheese to make a smooth dressing. Add the chives and season to taste with pepper.

❖ Tear the salad leaves into manageable pieces and arrange on a serving platter or on individual serving plates.

❖ Quarter and core the pears and cut them into slices.

❖ Arrange the pear slices over the salad leaves.

❖ Drizzle the dressing over the pears and garnish with the chives.

Greek Salad

4 tomatoes, cut into wedges
1 onion, sliced
1/2 cucumber, sliced
225 g/8 oz Kalamata
olives, stoned
225 g/8 oz feta cheese, cubed
(drained weight)
2 tbsp fresh coriander leaves
fresh flat-leaf parsley,
to garnish
pitta bread, to serve

DRESSING
5 tbsp extra virgin olive oil
2 tbsp white wine vinegar
1 tbsp lemon juice
1/2 tsp sugar
1 tbsp chopped fresh coriander
salt and pepper

❅ To make the dressing, place the oil, vinegar, lemon juice, sugar and coriander in a large bowl. Season with salt and pepper and mix together well.

❅ Add the tomatoes, onion, cucumber, olives, feta cheese and coriander. Toss all the ingredients together, then divide between individual serving bowls. Garnish with the parsley and serve with the pitta bread.

143

Goat's Cheese Salad

❄ **SERVES 4** ❄

3 tbsp olive oil	4 small tomatoes
1 tbsp white wine vinegar	12 fresh basil leaves
1 tsp black olive paste	2 x 125-g/4^1/$_2$-oz logs goat's
1 garlic clove, crushed	cheese
1 tsp chopped fresh thyme	mixed salad leaves, including
1 ciabatta loaf	rocket and radicchio, to serve

❄ Mix the oil, vinegar, olive paste, garlic and thyme together in a screw-top jar and shake vigorously.

❄ Cut the ciabatta in half horizontally, then in half vertically to make 4 pieces.

❄ Drizzle some of the dressing over the bread, then arrange the tomatoes and basil leaves on the top.

❄ Cut each roll of goat's cheese into 6 slices and place 3 slices on each piece of ciabatta.

❄ Brush with some of the dressing and bake in a preheated oven, 230°C/ 450°F/Gas Mark 8, for 5–6 minutes until turning brown at the edges.

❄ Pour the remaining dressing over the salad leaves and serve with the baked bread.

Italian Tricolour Salad

❄ **SERVES 4** ❄

2 ripe beef tomatoes	1 tsp coarsegrain mustard
150 g/5^1/$_2$ oz fresh mozzarella	salt and pepper
cheese	few fresh basil leaves,
2 avocados	torn into pieces
4 tbsp olive oil	20 black olives
1^1/$_2$ tbsp white wine vinegar	fresh crusty bread, to serve

❄ Using a sharp knife, cut the tomatoes into thick wedges and place in a large serving dish. Drain the mozzarella cheese and roughly tear into pieces. Cut the avocados in half and remove the stones. Cut the flesh into slices, then arrange the mozzarella cheese and avocado with the tomatoes.

❄ Mix the oil, vinegar and mustard together in a small bowl, add salt and pepper to taste, then drizzle over the salad.

❄ Scatter the basil and olives over the top and serve immediately with the bread.

Italian Mozzarella Salad

200 g/7 oz baby spinach	225 g/8 oz cherry tomatoes
125 g/4$^{1}/_{2}$ oz watercress	2 tsp balsamic vinegar
125 g/4$^{1}/_{2}$ oz mozzarella	1$^{1}/_{2}$ tbsp extra virgin olive oil
cheese	salt and pepper

❖ Wash the spinach and watercress and drain thoroughly on absorbent kitchen paper. Remove any tough stalks. Place the spinach and watercress leaves in a large serving dish.

❖ Cut the cheese into small pieces and scatter them over the spinach and watercress leaves.

❖ Cut the cherry tomatoes in half and scatter them over the salad.

❖ Sprinkle over the vinegar and oil, and season to taste with salt and pepper. Toss the mixture together to coat the leaves. Serve at once or leave to chill in the refrigerator until required.

Capri Salad

2 beef tomatoes	1 tbsp balsamic vinegar
125 g/4$^{1}/_{2}$ oz mozzarella	1 tbsp olive oil
cheese	salt and pepper
12 black olives	basil leaves, to garnish
8 basil leaves	

❖ Using a sharp knife, cut the tomatoes into thin slices.

❖ Using a sharp knife, cut the cheese into slices.

❖ Stone the olives and slice them into rings.

❖ Layer the tomatoes, cheese and olives in a stack, finishing with a layer of cheese on top.

❖ Place each stack under a preheated hot grill for 2–3 minutes or just long enough to melt the cheese.

❖ Drizzle over the vinegar and olive oil, and season to taste with a little salt and pepper.

❖ Transfer to serving plates and garnish with basil leaves. Serve immediately.

Hot Lentil Salad

❖ **SERVES 6–8** ❖

175 g/6 oz Puy lentils, cooked
4 tbsp olive oil
1 small onion, sliced
4 sticks celery, sliced
2 cloves garlic, crushed
2 courgettes, trimmed and diced
125 g/4 1/2 oz French beans, trimmed and cut into short lengths
1/2 red pepper, deseeded and diced
1/2 yellow pepper, deseeded and diced
1 tsp Dijon mustard
1 tbsp balsamic vinegar
salt and pepper

❖   Place the lentils in a large mixing or serving bowl. The lentils can still be warm, if wished.

❖   Heat the oil in a saucepan and fry the onion and celery for 2–3 minutes until soft but not brown.

❖   Stir the garlic, courgettes and French beans into the pan and cook for a further 2 minutes.

❖   Add the peppers to the pan and cook for 1 minute.

❖   Stir the mustard and the vinegar into the pan and mix until warm and well combined.

❖   Pour the warm mixture over the lentils and toss together to mix well. Season to taste with salt and pepper and serve immediately.

Three-Bean Salad

❊ **SERVES 6** ❊

3 tbsp olive oil
1 tbsp lemon juice
1 tbsp tomato purée
1 tbsp light malt vinegar
1 tbsp snipped fresh chives, plus extra to garnish
175 g/6 oz thin French beans
400 g/14 oz canned soya beans, rinsed and drained
400 g/14 oz canned kidney beans, rinsed and drained
2 tomatoes, chopped
4 spring onions, trimmed and chopped
125 g/4½ oz feta cheese, cut into cubes
salt and pepper
mixed salad leaves, to serve

❊ Put the olive oil, lemon juice, tomato purée, vinegar and snipped fresh chives into a large bowl and mix thoroughly. Set aside until required.

❊ Bring a small saucepan of lightly salted water to the boil and cook the French beans for 4–5 minutes. Drain, refresh under cold water to prevent any further cooking and drain well again. Pat dry with absorbent kitchen paper.

❊ Add all the beans to the dressing, stirring well to mix.

❊ Add the tomatoes, spring onions and feta cheese to the bean mixture, tossing gently to coat in the dressing. Season to taste with salt and pepper.

❊ Arrange the salad leaves on serving plates. Pile the bean salad on top, garnish with extra chives and serve.

Cool Broad Bean Salad

❊ **SERVES 4** ❊

1 red onion, thinly sliced
350 g/12 oz broad beans, fresh or frozen
150 ml/5 fl oz natural yogurt
1 tbsp chopped fresh mint
1½ tsp lemon juice
1 garlic clove, halved
½ cucumber, peeled, halved and sliced
salt and ground white pepper

❊ Rinse the red onion slices briefly under cold running water and drain well.

❊ Cook the broad beans in a small pan of boiling water and until tender: 8–10 minutes for fresh beans, 5–6 minutes for frozen.

❊ Drain, rinse under cold running water and drain again.

❊ If you wish, shell the beans from their white outer shells to leave the sweet green bean.

❊ Combine the yogurt, mint, lemon juice, garlic and seasoning in a bowl.

❊ Combine the onion, cucumber and broad beans. Toss them in the yogurt dressing until well coated. Remove and discard the garlic halves.

❊ Spoon the salad on to 4 serving plates and serve immediately.

Bean & Tomato Salad

	DRESSING
1 lollo rosso lettuce	4 tbsp olive oil
2 ripe avocados	4 tbsp olive oil
2 tsp lemon juice	dash of chilli oil
4 tomatoes	2 tbsp garlic wine vinegar
1 onion	pinch of caster sugar
175 g/6 oz canned mixed	pinch of chilli powder
beans, rinsed and drained	1 tbsp chopped fresh parsley

❖ Line a serving bowl with the lettuce leaves.

❖ Cut the avocados in half and remove and discard the stones. Peel and thinly slice the flesh. Sprinkle with the lemon juice to prevent discoloration.

❖ Thinly slice the tomatoes and onion. Arrange the avocado, tomato and onion slices around the salad bowl, leaving a space in the centre. Spoon the beans into the centre of the salad.

❖ Whisk all the dressing ingredients together in a small bowl until thoroughly combined. Pour the dressing over the salad and serve immediately.

Tuscan Bean & Tuna Salad

1 small white onion or 2 spring	2 tbsp flat-leaf parsley,
onions, finely chopped	chopped
800 g/1 lb 12 oz canned butter	2 tbsp olive oil
beans, drained	1 tbsp lemon juice
2 tomatoes	2 tsp clear honey
185 g/6½ oz canned tuna,	1 garlic clove, crushed
drained	

❖ Place the chopped onions and the beans in a bowl and mix well to combine.

❖ Using a sharp knife, cut the tomatoes into wedges.

❖ Add the tomatoes to the onion and bean mixture.

❖ Flake the tuna with a fork and add it to the onion and bean mixture together with the parsley.

❖ In a screw-top jar, mix together the olive oil, lemon juice, honey and garlic. Shake the jar until the dressing emulsifies and thickens.

❖ Pour the dressing over the bean salad. Toss the ingredients together using 2 spoons and serve.

Sweet & Sour Tuna Salad

2 tbsp olive oil
1 onion, chopped
2 garlic cloves, chopped
2 courgettes, sliced
4 tomatoes, peeled
400 g/14 oz canned flageolet
beans, drained and rinsed
10 black olives, halved and
stoned
1 tbsp capers
1 tsp caster sugar
1 tbsp wholegrain mustard
1 tbsp white wine vinegar
200 g/7 oz canned tuna, drained
2 tbsp chopped fresh parsley,
plus extra to garnish
crusty bread, to serve

✿ Heat the olive oil in a large heavy-based frying pan. Add the onion and garlic and fry over a low heat, stirring occasionally, for 5 minutes until soft but not brown.

✿ Add the courgette slices and cook, stirring occasionally, for a further 3 minutes.

✿ Cut the tomatoes in half, then into thin wedges.

✿ Add the tomatoes to the pan with the beans, olives, capers, sugar, mustard and vinegar.

✿ Simmer for 2 minutes, stirring gently, then set aside to cool slightly.

✿ Flake the tuna and stir it into the bean mixture with the parsley. Transfer to a serving dish, garnish with the extra chopped parsley and serve lukewarm with crusty bread.

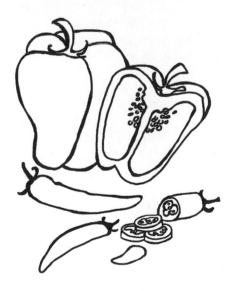

Tuna & Avocado Salad

2 avocados, stoned, peeled and cubed
250 g/9 oz cherry tomatoes, halved
2 red peppers, deseeded and chopped
1 bunch fresh flat-leaf parsley, chopped
2 garlic cloves, crushed
1 fresh red chilli, deseeded and finely chopped
juice of $^1/_2$ lemon
6 tbsp olive oil
3 tbsp sesame seeds
4 fresh tuna steaks, about 150 g/5$^1/_2$ oz each
8 cooked new potatoes, cubed
pepper
rocket leaves, to serve

❊ Toss the avocados, tomatoes, peppers, parsley, garlic, chilli, lemon juice and 2 tablespoons of the oil together in a large bowl. Season to taste with pepper, cover and chill in the refrigerator for 30 minutes.

❊ Lightly crush the sesame seeds in a mortar with a pestle. Tip the crushed seeds on to a plate and spread out. Press each tuna steak in turn into the crushed seeds to coat on both sides.

❊ Heat 2 tablespoons of the remaining oil in a frying pan, add the potatoes and cook, stirring frequently, for 5–8 minutes or until crisp and brown. Remove from the pan and drain on kitchen paper.

❊ Wipe out the pan, add the remaining oil and heat over a high heat until very hot. Add the tuna steaks and cook for 3–4 minutes on each side.

❊ To serve, divide the avocado salad between 4 serving plates. Top each with a tuna steak, then scatter over the potatoes and a handful of rocket leaves.

Pasta & Tuna Salad

225 g/8 oz farfalle
175 g/6 oz French beans, topped and tailed
350 g/12 oz fresh tuna steaks
115 g/4 oz baby plum tomatoes, halved
8 anchovy fillets, drained on absorbent kitchen paper
2 tbsp capers in brine, drained
25 g/1 oz stoned black olives in brine, drained
salt and pepper
fresh basil leaves, to garnish

DRESSING
1 tbsp olive oil
1 garlic clove, crushed
1 tbsp lemon juice
$^1/_2$ tsp finely grated lemon rind
1 tbsp shredded fresh basil leaves

❊ Cook the pasta in lightly salted boiling water according to the instructions on the packet until just cooked. Drain well, set aside and keep warm.

❊ Bring a small saucepan of lightly salted water to the boil and cook the French beans for 5–6 minutes until just tender. Drain well and toss into the pasta. Set aside and keep warm.

❊ Preheat the grill to medium. Rinse and pat the tuna steaks dry on absorbent kitchen paper. Season on both sides with pepper. Place the tuna steaks on the grill rack and cook for 4–5 minutes on each side until cooked through.

❊ Drain the tuna on absorbent kitchen paper and flake into bite-sized pieces. Toss the tuna into the pasta along with the tomatoes, anchovies, capers and olives. Set aside and keep warm.

❊ Meanwhile, prepare the dressing. Mix all the ingredients together and season well. Pour the dressing over the pasta mixture and mix carefully. Transfer the salad to a warmed serving bowl and serve sprinkled with fresh basil leaves.

Prawn & Rice Salad

175 g/6 oz mixed long-grain
and wild rice
350 g/12 oz cooked peeled
prawns
1 mango, peeled, stoned and
diced
4 spring onions, sliced
25 g/1 oz flaked almonds
1 tbsp finely chopped
fresh mint
salt and pepper

DRESSING
1 tbsp extra virgin olive oil
2 tsp lime juice
1 garlic clove, crushed
1 tsp clear honey
salt and pepper

❈ Bring a large saucepan of lightly salted water to the boil. Add the rice, return to the boil and cook for 35 minutes or until tender. Drain, then transfer to a large bowl and stir in the prawns.

❈ To make the dressing, combine the olive oil, lime juice, garlic and honey in a large jug, season to taste with salt and pepper and whisk until well blended. Pour the dressing over the rice and prawn mixture and leave to cool.

❈ Add the mango, spring onions, almonds and mint to the salad and season to taste with pepper. Stir thoroughly, transfer to a large serving dish and serve.

Smoked Salmon Salad

50 g/1¾ oz wild rocket
1 tbsp chopped fresh flat-leaf
parsley
2 spring onions, finely diced
2 large avocados
1 tbsp lemon juice
250 g/9 oz smoked salmon
lime wedges, to serve

LIME MAYONNAISE
150 ml/5 fl oz mayonnaise
2 tbsp lime juice
finely grated rind of 1 lime
1 tbsp chopped fresh flat-leaf
parsley, plus extra sprigs
to garnish

❈ Shred the rocket and arrange in 4 individual salad bowls or on 4 small plates. Scatter over the chopped parsley and spring onions.

❈ Halve, peel and stone the avocados and cut into thin slices or small chunks. Brush with the lemon juice to prevent discoloration, then divide between the salad bowls. Mix together gently. Cut the smoked salmon into strips and scatter over the top.

❈ Put the mayonnaise into a bowl, then add the lime juice and rind and the chopped parsley. Mix together well. Spoon some of the lime mayonnaise on top of each salad, garnish with the parsley sprigs and serve with the lime wedges for squeezing over.

Salmon & Avocado Salad

450 g/1 lb new potatoes
4 salmon steaks, about
115 g/4 oz each
1 avocado
juice of $^1/_2$ lemon
55 g/2 oz baby spinach leaves
125 g/4$^1/_2$ oz mixed small salad
leaves, including watercress
12 cherry tomatoes, halved
55 g/2 oz chopped walnuts

DRESSING
3 tbsp unsweetened clear
apple juice
1 tsp balsamic vinegar
pepper

❖ Cut the new potatoes into bite-sized pieces, put into a saucepan and cover with cold water. Bring to the boil, then reduce the heat, cover and simmer for 10–15 minutes or until just tender. Drain and keep warm.

❖ Meanwhile, preheat the grill to medium. Cook the salmon steaks under the preheated grill for 10–15 minutes, depending on the thickness of the steaks, turning halfway through cooking. Remove from the grill and keep warm.

❖ While the potatoes and salmon are cooking, cut the avocado in half, remove and discard the stone and peel the flesh. Cut the avocado flesh into slices and coat in the lemon juice to prevent discoloration.

❖ Toss the spinach leaves and mixed salad leaves together in a large serving bowl until combined. Arrange 6 cherry tomato halves on each plate of salad.

❖ Remove and discard the skin and any bones from the salmon. Flake the salmon and divide between the plates along with the potatoes. Sprinkle the walnuts over the salads.

❖ To make the dressing, mix the apple juice and vinegar together in a small bowl or jug and season well with pepper. Drizzle over the salads and serve immediately.

Neapolitan Seafood Salad

450 g/1 lb prepared squid, cut into strips
750 g/1 lb 10 oz cooked mussels
450 g/1 lb cooked cockles in brine
150 ml/5 fl oz white wine
300 ml/10 fl oz olive oil
225 g/8 oz dried campanelle or other small pasta shapes
juice of 1 lemon
1 bunch chives, snipped
1 bunch fresh parsley, finely chopped
4 large tomatoes
mixed salad leaves
salt and pepper
sprig of fresh basil, to garnish

❖ Put all of the seafood into a large bowl, pour over the wine and half the olive oil, and set aside for 6 hours.

❖ Put the seafood mixture into a saucepan and simmer over a low heat for 10 minutes. Set aside to cool.

❖ Bring a large saucepan of lightly salted water to the boil. Add the pasta and 1 tablespoon of the remaining olive oil and cook for 8–10 minutes or until tender, but still firm to the bite. Drain thoroughly and refresh in cold water.

❖ Strain off about half the cooking liquid from the seafood and discard the rest. Mix in the lemon juice, chives, parsley and the remaining olive oil. Season to taste with salt and pepper. Drain the pasta and add to the seafood.

❖ Cut the tomatoes into quarters. Shred the salad leaves and arrange them at the base of a salad bowl. Spoon in the seafood salad, sprinkle with the tomatoes, garnish with the basil and serve.

Cantaloupe & Crab Salad

350 g/12 oz fresh crabmeat
5 tbsp mayonnaise
50 ml/2 fl oz natural yogurt
4 tsp extra virgin olive oil
4 tsp lime juice
1 spring onion, finely chopped
4 tsp finely chopped fresh parsley
pinch of cayenne pepper
1 cantaloupe melon
leaves of 2 radicchio heads
few sprigs fresh parsley, to garnish

❖ Place the crabmeat in a large bowl and pick over it very carefully to remove any remaining shell or cartilage, but try not to break the meat up.

❖ Place the mayonnaise, yogurt, olive oil, lime juice, spring onion, chopped parsley and cayenne pepper in a separate bowl and mix until thoroughly blended. Fold in the crabmeat.

❖ Cut the melon in half and remove and discard the seeds. Thinly slice, then cut off the rind with a sharp knife.

❖ Arrange the melon slices and radicchio leaves on 4 large serving plates, then arrange the crabmeat mixture on top. Garnish with the sprigs of parsley and serve.

Mussel Salad

❖ **SERVES 4** ❖

2 large red peppers
350 g/12 oz cooked shelled
mussels, thawed, if frozen
1 head radicchio
25 g/1 oz rocket
8 cooked New Zealand
mussels in their shells
lemon wedges and crusty
bread, to serve

DRESSING
1 tbsp olive oil
1 tbsp lemon juice
1 tsp finely grated lemon rind
2 tsp clear honey
1 tsp French mustard
1 tbsp snipped fresh chives
salt and pepper

❖ Preheat the grill to hot. Halve and deseed the peppers and place them skin side up on the rack.

❖ Cook for 8–10 minutes until the skin is charred and blistered and the flesh is soft. Leave to cool for 10 minutes, then peel off the skin.

❖ Slice the pepper flesh into thin strips and place in a bowl. Gently mix in the shelled mussels and set aside until required.

❖ To make the dressing, mix all of the ingredients until well blended. Mix into the pepper and mussel mixture until coated.

❖ Remove the central core of the radicchio and shred the leaves. Place in a serving bowl with the rocket leaves and toss together.

❖ Pile the mussel mixture into the centre of the leaves and arrange the large mussels in their shells around the edge of the dish. Serve with the lemon wedges and the bread.

Waldorf Chicken Salad

❖ **SERVES 4** ❖

500 g/1 lb 2 oz red apples,
diced
3 tbsp fresh lemon juice
150 ml/5 fl oz mayonnaise
1 head of celery
4 shallots, sliced
1 garlic clove, crushed

85 g/3 oz walnuts, chopped
500 g/1 lb 2 oz lean cooked
chicken, cubed
1 cos lettuce
pepper
sliced apple and walnuts,
to garnish

❖ Place the apples in a bowl with the lemon juice and 1 tablespoon of mayonnaise. Leave for 40 minutes or until required.

❖ Slice the celery very thinly. Add the celery with the shallots, garlic and walnuts to the apple, mix and then add the remaining mayonnaise and blend thoroughly.

❖ Add the chicken and mix with the other ingredients.

❖ Line a glass salad bowl or serving dish with the lettuce.

❖ Pile the chicken salad into the centre, sprinkle with pepper and garnish with the apple slices and walnuts.

Layered Chicken Salad

750 g/1 lb 10 oz new potatoes, scrubbed
1 red pepper, halved, cored and deseeded
1 green pepper, halved, cored and deseeded
2 small courgettes, sliced
1 small onion, thinly sliced
3 tomatoes, sliced
350 g/12 oz cooked chicken, sliced
snipped fresh chives, to garnish

YOGURT DRESSING
150 g/5$\frac{1}{2}$ oz natural yogurt
3 tbsp mayonnaise
1 tbsp snipped fresh chives
salt and pepper

❄ Put the potatoes into a large saucepan of cold water. Bring to the boil, then reduce the heat. Cover and simmer for 15–20 minutes until tender.

❄ Meanwhile place the pepper halves, cut side down, under a preheated hot grill and grill until the skins blacken and begin to char.

❄ Remove the peppers and leave to cool, then peel off the skins and slice the flesh. Set aside.

❄ Bring a small saucepan of lightly salted water to the boil and cook the courgettes for 3 minutes. Rinse the courgettes with cold water to cool quickly and set aside.

❄ To make the dressing, mix together the yogurt, mayonnaise and chives in a small bowl. Season well with salt and pepper.

❄ Drain, cool and slice the potatoes. Add them to the dressing and mix well to coat evenly. Divide between 4 serving plates. Top each plate with one quarter of the pepper slices and cooked courgettes. Layer one quarter of the onion and tomato slices, then the sliced chicken, on top of each serving. Garnish with the snipped chives and serve.

Chicken & Paw-Paw Salad

❖ **SERVES 4** ❖

4 skinless, boneless chicken breasts
1 red chilli, deseeded and chopped
2 tbsp red wine vinegar
5 tbsp olive oil
1 paw-paw, peeled
1 avocado, peeled
125 g/4^1/$_2$ oz alfalfa sprouts
125 g/4^1/$_2$ oz beansprouts
salt and pepper
diced red pepper and diced cucumber, to garnish

❖ Poach the chicken breasts in boiling water for about 15 minutes or until cooked through.

❖ Remove the chicken with a slotted spoon and set aside to cool.

❖ Combine the chilli, vinegar and olive oil, season well with salt and pepper and set aside.

❖ Place the chicken breasts on a chopping board. Using a very sharp knife, cut them across the grain into thin diagonal slices. Set aside.

❖ Slice the paw-paw and avocado to the same thickness as the chicken.

❖ Arrange the slices of paw-paw and avocado, together with the chicken, in an alternating pattern on 4 serving plates.

❖ Arrange the alfalfa sprouts and beansprouts on the serving plates and garnish with the diced red pepper and cucumber. Serve the salad with the dressing.

Chicken & Noodle Salad

❖ **SERVES 4** ❖

1 tsp finely grated fresh root ginger
^{1}/$_2$ tsp Chinese five-spice powder
1 tbsp plain flour
^{1}/$_2$ tsp chilli powder
350 g/12 oz boned chicken breast, skinned and thinly sliced
55 g/2 oz rice noodles
125 g/4^1/$_2$ oz Chinese leaves or hard white cabbage, finely shredded
7-cm/2^3/$_4$-inch piece of cucumber, finely sliced
1 large carrot, thinly pared
1 tbsp olive oil
2 tbsp lime or lemon juice
2 tbsp sesame oil
salt and pepper
lemon or lime slices and fresh coriander leaves, to garnish

❖ Mix together the ginger, five-spice powder, flour and chilli powder in a shallow mixing bowl. Season with salt and pepper. Add the strips of chicken and roll in the mixture until well coated.

❖ Put the noodles in a large bowl and cover with warm water. Leave to soak for about 5 minutes, then drain well.

❖ Mix together the Chinese leaves or white cabbage, cucumber and carrot, and arrange in a salad bowl. Whisk together the olive oil and lime juice, season with salt and pepper and use to dress the salad.

❖ Heat the sesame oil in a wok or frying pan and add the chicken. Stir-fry for 5–6 minutes until brown and crispy on the outside. Remove from the wok with a slotted spoon and drain on absorbent kitchen paper.

❖ Add the noodles to the wok and stir-fry for 3–4 minutes until heated through. Remove from the wok, mix with the chicken and pile the mixture on top of the salad. Serve garnished with the lime slices and coriander leaves.

Potato & Chicken Salad

4 large waxy potatoes
300 g/10½ oz fresh pineapple, diced
2 carrots, grated
175 g/6 oz beansprouts
1 bunch spring onions, sliced
1 large courgette, cut into matchsticks
3 celery sticks, cut into matchsticks
175 g/6 oz unsalted peanuts

2 cooked chicken breast fillets, about 125 g/4½ oz each, sliced

DRESSING
6 tbsp crunchy peanut butter
6 tbsp olive oil
2 tbsp light soy sauce
1 red chilli, chopped
2 tsp sesame oil
4 tsp lime juice

❁ Using a sharp knife, cut the potatoes into small dice. Bring a saucepan of water to the boil.

❁ Cook the diced potatoes in a saucepan of boiling water for 10 minutes or until tender. Drain and leave to cool until required.

❁ Transfer the cooled potatoes to a salad bowl.

❁ Add the pineapple, carrots, beansprouts, spring onions, courgette, celery, peanuts and sliced chicken to the potatoes. Toss well to mix all the salad ingredients together.

❁ To make the dressing, put the peanut butter in a small mixing bowl and gradually whisk in the olive oil and light soy sauce.

❁ Stir in the chopped red chilli, sesame oil and lime juice. Mix until well combined.

❁ Pour the spicy dressing over the salad and toss lightly to coat all of the ingredients. Serve the potato and chicken salad immediately.

Hot Potato & Ham Salad

175 g/6 oz lean smoked ham
500 g/1 lb 2 oz salad potatoes
6 spring onions, white and green parts, sliced
3 pickled dill cucumbers, halved and sliced

DRESSING
4 tbsp mayonnaise
4 tbsp thick natural yogurt
2 tbsp chopped fresh dill
salt and pepper

❁ Cut the ham into 3.5-cm/1½-inch strips. Cut the potatoes into 1-cm/½-inch pieces. Bring a saucepan of lightly salted water to the boil and cook the potatoes for about 8 minutes until tender.

❁ Drain the potatoes well and return to the pan. Add the spring onions, ham and cucumbers.

❁ To make the dressing, combine the mayonnaise, yogurt and dill in a small bowl, beating well until thoroughly mixed. Season to taste with salt and pepper.

❁ Add the dressing to the pan and stir gently until the potatoes are coated with the dressing.

❁ Transfer the salad to a warmed dish and serve.

Spicy Sausage Salad

125 g/4½ oz small pasta shapes, such as elbow tubetti
3 tbsp olive oil
1 medium onion, chopped
2 cloves garlic, crushed
1 small yellow pepper, cored, deseeded and cut into matchstick strips
175 g/6 oz spicy pork sausage such as chorizo, skinned and sliced
2 tbsp red wine
1 tbsp red wine vinegar
mixed salad leaves, chilled
salt

❖ Bring a saucepan of lightly salted water to the boil, add the pasta with 1 tablespoon of the oil and cook for 8–10 minutes or until tender. Drain in a colander and set aside.

❖ Heat the remaining oil in a saucepan over a medium heat. Fry the onion until it is translucent, stir in the garlic, pepper and sliced sausage and cook for 3–4 minutes, stirring once or twice.

❖ Add the wine, vinegar and reserved pasta to the pan, stir to blend well and bring the mixture just to the boil.

❖ Arrange the chilled salad leaves on 4 individual serving plates and spoon on the warm sausage and pasta mixture. Serve at once.

Rare Beef Pasta Salad

450 g/1 lb rump or sirloin steak in a single piece	4 spring onions, sliced
450 g/1 lb dried fusilli	1 cucumber, peeled and cut into 2.5-cm/1-inch chunks
4 tbsp olive oil	3 tomatoes, cut into wedges
2 tbsp lime juice	1 tbsp finely chopped fresh mint
2 tbsp Thai fish sauce	
2 tsp clear honey	salt and pepper

❆ Season the steak with salt and pepper. Grill or pan-fry it for 4 minutes on each side. Allow to rest for 5 minutes, then slice thinly across the grain.

❆ Meanwhile, bring a large saucepan of lightly salted water to the boil. Add the pasta, bring back to the boil and cook for 8–10 minutes or until tender, but still firm to the bite. Drain the fusilli, refresh in cold water and drain again thoroughly. Toss the fusilli in the olive oil and set aside until required.

❆ Combine the lime juice, fish sauce and honey in a small saucepan and cook over a medium heat for 2 minutes.

❆ Add the spring onions, cucumber, tomatoes and mint to the pan, then add the steak and mix well. Season to taste with salt.

❆ Transfer the fusilli to a large warmed serving dish and top with the steak and salad mixture. Serve just warm or allow to cool completely.

Hot & Sour Beef Salad

1 tsp black peppercorns	2 tbsp groundnut oil
1 tsp coriander seeds	1 garlic clove, crushed
1 dried red bird's-eye chilli	1 tsp finely chopped lemon grass
1/4 tsp Chinese five-spice powder	1 tbsp chopped fresh mint
250 g/9 oz beef fillet	1 tbsp chopped fresh coriander
1 tbsp dark soy sauce	
6 spring onions	**DRESSING**
1 carrot	3 tbsp lime juice
1/4 cucumber	1 tbsp light soy sauce
8 radishes	2 tsp soft light brown sugar
1 red onion	1 tsp sesame oil
1/4 head Chinese leaves	

❆ Crush the peppercorns, coriander seeds and chilli in a mortar with a pestle, then mix with the five-spice powder and sprinkle on a plate. Brush the beef all over with soy sauce, then roll it in the spices to coat evenly.

❆ Cut the spring onions into 6-cm/2 1/2-inch lengths, then shred finely lengthways. Place in iced water until curled. Drain well.

❆ Trim the carrot and cut into very thin diagonal slices. Halve the cucumber, scoop out and discard the seeds, then slice the flesh thinly. Trim the radishes and cut into flower shapes.

❆ Slice the onion thinly. Roughly shred the Chinese leaves. Toss all the vegetables together in a large salad bowl.

❆ Heat the oil in a frying pan and fry the garlic and lemon grass until golden. Add the steak and cook for 3–4 minutes, turning once. Remove from the heat.

❆ Slice the steak thinly and toss into the salad with the mint and coriander. Mix together the dressing ingredients and stir into the pan, then spoon over the salad and serve.

Chef's Salad

1 Webbs lettuce, shredded
175 g/6 oz cooked ham, cut into thin strips
175 g/6 oz cooked tongue, cut into thin strips
350 g/12 oz cooked chicken, cut into thin strips
175 g/6 oz Gruyère cheese
4 tomatoes, quartered
3 hard-boiled eggs, shelled and quartered
400 ml/14 fl oz Thousand Island dressing

❊ Arrange the lettuce on a large serving platter. Arrange the cold meat decoratively on top.

❊ Cut the Gruyère cheese into batons. Arrange the cheese batons over the salad and the tomato and egg quarters around the edge of the platter.

❊ Serve the salad immediately, handing the dressing around separately.

Chorizo & Artichoke Salad

12 small globe artichokes
juice of 1/2 lemon
2 tbsp Spanish olive oil
1 small orange-fleshed melon, such as cantaloupe
200 g/7 oz chorizo sausage, outer casing removed
fresh tarragon or flat-leaf parsley sprigs, to garnish

DRESSING
3 tbsp Spanish extra virgin olive oil
1 tbsp red wine vinegar
1 tsp prepared mustard
1 tbsp chopped fresh tarragon
salt and pepper

❊ To prepare the artichokes, cut off the stalks. Break off the toughest outer leaves at the base until the tender inside leaves are visible. Using a pair of scissors, cut the spiky tips off the leaves. Using a sharp knife, pare the dark green skin from the base and down the stem. As you prepare them, brush the cut surfaces of the artichokes with lemon juice to prevent discoloration. Carefully remove the choke (the mass of silky hairs) by pulling it out with your fingers (the little barbs, if eaten, can irritate the throat). However, if you are using very young artichokes, you do not need to worry about removing the choke and you can include the stalk too, well scraped, as it will be quite tender. Cut the artichokes into quarters and brush again with lemon juice.

❊ Heat the olive oil in a large heavy-based frying pan. Add the prepared artichokes and fry, stirring frequently, for 5 minutes. Remove from the frying pan, transfer to a large serving bowl and leave to cool.

❊ To prepare the melon, cut in half and scoop out the seeds with a spoon. Cut the flesh into bite-sized cubes. Add to the cooled artichokes. Cut the chorizo into bite-sized chunks and add to the melon and artichokes.

❊ To make the dressing, place all the ingredients in a small bowl and whisk together. Just before serving, pour the dressing over the prepared salad ingredients and toss together. Serve the salad garnished with the tarragon.

Wild Rice & Bacon Salad

150 g/5½ oz wild rice
600 ml/1 pint water or more,
if necessary
55 g/2 oz pecan nuts or walnuts
2 tbsp vegetable oil
4 rashers smoked bacon,
diced or sliced
3–4 shallots, finely chopped
5 tbsp walnut oil
2–3 tbsp sherry or cider vinegar
2 tbsp chopped fresh dill
8–12 large scallops, cut in half
lengthways
salt and pepper
lemon and lime slices, to serve

❖ Put the rice in a saucepan with the water and bring to the boil, stirring once or twice. Reduce the heat, cover and simmer gently for 30–50 minutes, depending on whether you prefer a chewy or tender texture. Using a fork, fluff the rice into a large bowl and set aside to cool slightly.

❖ Meanwhile, dry-fry the nuts in a frying pan, stirring frequently, for 2–3 minutes until just beginning to colour. Cool and chop coarsely, then set aside.

❖ Heat 1 tablespoon of the vegetable oil in the pan. Stir in the bacon and cook, stirring occasionally, until crisp and brown. Transfer to kitchen paper to drain. Remove some of the oil from the pan and stir in the shallots. Cook, stirring occasionally, for 3–4 minutes until soft.

❖ Stir the toasted nuts, bacon and shallots into the rice. Add the walnut oil, vinegar, half the chopped dill and salt and pepper to taste. Toss well to combine the ingredients, then set aside.

❖ Brush a large non-stick frying pan with the remaining oil. Heat until very hot, add the scallops and cook for 1 minute on each side until golden (do not overcook). Remove them from the pan.

❖ Divide the wild rice salad between 4 plates. Top with the scallops and sprinkle with the remaining dill. Garnish with a sprig of dill, if desired, and serve immediately with the lemon and lime slices.

Simple
main dishes

Coriander Chicken

3 sprigs fresh coriander, chopped
4 garlic cloves
1/2 tsp salt
1 tsp pepper
4 tbsp lemon juice
4 tbsp olive oil
1 large chicken
sprig of fresh parsley, to garnish
boiled potatoes and carrots, to serve

❋ Place the chopped coriander, garlic, salt, pepper, lemon juice and olive oil in a mortar and pound together with a pestle or blend in a food processor. Chill for 4 hours to allow the flavours to develop.

❋ Place the chicken in a roasting tin. Coat generously with the coriander and garlic mixture.

❋ Sprinkle with more pepper and roast in a preheated oven, 190°C/375°F/Gas Mark 5, on a low shelf for 1 1/2 hours, basting every 20 minutes with the coriander mixture. If the chicken starts to turn brown, cover with foil. Garnish with fresh parsley and serve with the potatoes and carrots.

Potato-Topped Chicken Pie

500 g/1 lb 2 oz chicken mince
1 large onion, finely chopped
2 carrots, finely diced
25 g/1 oz plain flour
1 tbsp tomato purée
300 ml/1 1/2 pints chicken stock
pinch of fresh thyme
900 g/2 lb potatoes, creamed with butter and milk and highly seasoned
90 g/3 oz grated Lancashire cheese
salt and pepper
peas, to serve

❋ Dry-fry the chicken, onion and carrots in a non-stick saucepan for 5 minutes, stirring frequently.

❋ Sprinkle the chicken with the flour and simmer for a further 2 minutes.

❋ Gradually blend in the tomato purée and stock, then simmer for 15 minutes. Season and add the thyme.

❋ Transfer the chicken and vegetable mixture to an ovenproof casserole and allow to cool.

❋ Spoon the potato over the chicken mixture and sprinkle with the Lancashire cheese. Bake in a preheated oven, 200°C/400°F/Gas Mark 6, for 20 minutes or until the cheese is bubbling and golden, then serve with the peas.

Mediterranean Chicken

1 tbsp olive oil
6 skinless chicken breast fillets
250 g/9 oz mozzarella cheese
500 g/1 lb 2 oz courgettes, sliced
6 large tomatoes, sliced
1 small bunch fresh basil or oregano
pepper
rice or pasta, to serve

❖ Cut six pieces of foil, each about 25 cm/10 inches square. Brush the foil squares lightly with oil and set aside until required.

❖ With a sharp knife, slash each chicken breast at intervals, then slice the cheese and place between the cuts in the chicken.

❖ Divide the courgettes and tomatoes between the pieces of foil and sprinkle with pepper. Tear or roughly chop the basil or oregano and scatter over the vegetables in each parcel.

❖ Place the chicken on top of each pile of vegetables then wrap in the foil to enclose the chicken and vegetables, tucking in the ends.

❖ Place on a baking tray and bake in a preheated oven, 200°C/400°C/Gas Mark 6, for about 30 minutes.

❖ To serve, unwrap each foil parcel and serve with the rice.

Harlequin Chicken

10 skinless, boneless chicken thighs
1 medium onion
1 each medium red, green and yellow peppers
1 tbsp sunflower oil
400 g/14 oz canned chopped tomatoes
2 tbsp chopped fresh parsley
pepper
wholemeal bread and a green salad, to serve

❖ Using a sharp knife, cut the chicken thighs into bite-sized pieces.

❖ Peel and thinly slice the onion. Halve and deseed the peppers and cut into small diamond shapes.

❖ Heat the oil in a shallow frying pan. Add the chicken and onion and fry quickly until golden.

❖ Add the peppers, cook for 2–3 minutes, then stir in the tomatoes and parsley and season with pepper.

❖ Cover tightly and simmer for about 15 minutes until the chicken and vegetables are tender. Serve hot with bread and salad.

Devilled Chicken

❊ **SERVES 2–3** ❊

25 g/1 oz plain flour
1 tbsp cayenne pepper
1 tsp paprika
350 g/12 oz skinless, boneless chicken, diced
25 g/1 oz butter
1 onion, finely chopped
450 ml/16 fl oz milk, warmed
4 tbsp apple purée
125 g/4$\frac{1}{2}$ oz green grapes
150 ml/5 fl oz soured cream
sprinkle of paprika

❊ Mix the flour, cayenne pepper and paprika together and use to coat the chicken.

❊ Shake off any excess flour. Melt the butter in a saucepan and gently fry the chicken with the onion for 4 minutes.

❊ Stir in the flour and spice mixture. Add the milk slowly, stirring until the sauce thickens.

❊ Simmer until the sauce is smooth.

❊ Add the apple purée and grapes and simmer gently for 20 minutes.

❊ Transfer the chicken and devilled sauce to a serving dish and top with the soured cream and a sprinkle of paprika.

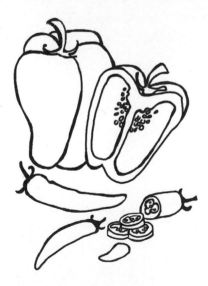

Chicken with Mushrooms

❋ **SERVES 4** ❋

1 tbsp olive oil
8 chicken pieces
300 ml/10 fl oz passata
200 ml/7 fl oz white wine
2 tsp dried mixed herbs
40 g/1½ oz butter, melted
2 garlic cloves, crushed
8 slices white bread

100 g/3½ oz mixed
  mushrooms (such as
  button, oyster and ceps)
40 g/1¾ oz black olives,
  chopped
1 tsp sugar
fresh basil, to garnish

❋ Using a sharp knife, remove the bone from each of the chicken pieces.

❋ Heat the oil in a large frying pan. Add the chicken pieces and cook for 4–5 minutes, turning occasionally, or until browned all over.

❋ Add the passata, wine and mixed herbs to the frying pan. Bring to the boil and then leave to simmer for 30 minutes or until the chicken is tender and the juices run clear when a skewer is inserted into the thickest part of the meat.

❋ Mix the melted butter and crushed garlic together. Lightly toast the slices of bread and brush with the garlic butter.

❋ Add the remaining oil to a separate frying pan and cook the mushrooms for 2–3 minutes or until just brown.

❋ Add the olives and sugar to the chicken mixture and warm through.

❋ Transfer the chicken and sauce to serving plates. Serve with the toasted bread and fried mushrooms.

Chicken with Onions & Peas

❋ **SERVES 4** ❋

250 g/9 oz fat pork,
  cut into small cubes
55 g/2 oz butter
16 small onions or shallots
1 kg/2 lb 4 oz boneless
  chicken pieces

25 g/1 oz plain flour
600 ml/1 pint chicken stock
bouquet garni
500 g/1 lb 2 oz fresh peas
salt and pepper

❋ Bring a saucepan of lightly salted water to the boil and simmer the pork cubes for three minutes. Drain and dry the pork on absorbent kitchen paper.

❋ Melt the butter in a large frying pan, add the pork and onions, fry gently for 3 minutes until lightly browned.

❋ Remove the pork and onions from the pan and set aside until required. Add the chicken pieces to the pan and cook until browned all over. Transfer the chicken to an ovenproof casserole.

❋ Add the flour to the pan and cook, stirring, until it begins to brown, then slowly blend in the chicken stock.

❋ Cook the chicken, with the sauce and bouquet garni, in a preheated oven, 200°C/400°F/Gas Mark 6, for 35 minutes.

❋ Remove the bouquet garni about 10 minutes before the end of cooking time and add the peas and the reserved pork and onions. Stir to mix and season to taste with salt and pepper.

❋ When cooked, place the chicken pieces on a large platter, surrounded with the pork, peas and onions.

Rich Chicken Casserole

8 chicken thighs
2 tbsp olive oil
1 medium red onion, sliced
2 garlic cloves, crushed
1 large red pepper, thickly sliced
thinly pared rind and juice of 1 small orange
125 ml/4 fl oz chicken stock
400 g/14 oz canned chopped tomatoes
25 g/1 oz sun-dried tomatoes, thinly sliced
1 tbsp chopped fresh thyme
50 g/1¾ oz stoned black olives
salt and pepper
sprigs of fresh thyme and orange rind, to garnish
crusty fresh bread, to serve

❖ In a large non-stick or heavy-based frying pan, fry the chicken without fat over a fairly high heat, turning occasionally until golden brown. Using a slotted spoon, drain off any excess fat from the chicken and transfer the chicken to a flameproof casserole.

❖ Fry the onion, garlic and pepper in the pan over a moderate heat for 3–4 minutes. Transfer to the casserole.

❖ Add the orange rind and juice, stock, canned tomatoes and sun-dried tomatoes and stir to combine.

❖ Bring to the boil, then cover the casserole with a lid and simmer very gently over a low heat for about 1 hour, stirring occasionally. Add the chopped thyme and the black olives, then adjust the seasoning with salt and pepper.

❖ Scatter the sprigs of thyme and the orange rind over the casserole to garnish, and serve with the crusty bread.

Chicken with White Wine

4 tbsp sunflower oil
900 g/1 lb 12 oz chicken meat, diced
250 g/9 oz button mushrooms
125 g/4½ oz rindless smoked bacon, diced
16 shallots
2 garlic cloves, crushed
1 tbsp plain flour
150 ml/5 fl oz white Burgundy wine
150 ml/5 fl oz chicken stock
1 bouquet garni (1 bay leaf, 1 sprig thyme, 1 celery stick, 1 sprig parsley and 1 sprig sage, tied with string)
salt and pepper
deep-fried croûtons and a selection of cooked vegetables, to serve

❖ Heat the sunflower oil in an ovenproof casserole and brown the chicken all over. Remove from the casserole with a slotted spoon.

❖ Add the mushrooms, bacon, shallots and garlic to the casserole and cook for 4 minutes.

❖ Return the chicken to the casserole and sprinkle with flour. Cook for a further 2 minutes, stirring.

❖ Add the wine and stock to the casserole and stir until boiling. Add the bouquet garni and season well with salt and pepper.

❖ Cover the casserole and bake in the centre of a preheated oven, 150°C/300°F/Gas Mark 2, for 1½ hours. Remove the bouquet garni.

❖ Deep fry some heart-shaped croûtons (about 8 large ones) in beef dripping and serve with the chicken.

Hungarian Chicken Goulash

750 g/1 lb 10 oz chicken meat, diced
125 g/4$\frac{1}{2}$ oz flour, seasoned with 1 tsp paprika, salt and pepper
2 tbsp olive oil
40 g/1$\frac{1}{2}$ oz butter
1 onion, sliced
24 shallots, peeled
1 red pepper, chopped
1 green pepper, chopped
1 tbsp paprika
1 tsp rosemary, crushed
4 tbsp tomato purée
300 ml/10 fl oz chicken stock
150 ml/5 fl oz claret
400 g/14 oz canned chopped tomatoes
150 ml/5 fl oz soured cream
1 tbsp chopped fresh parsley, to garnish
chunks of bread and a side salad, to serve

❊ Toss the chicken in the seasoned flour until it is coated all over.

❊ In a flameproof casserole, heat the oil and butter and sauté the onion, shallots and peppers for 3 minutes.

❊ Add the chicken and cook for a further 4 minutes.

❊ Sprinkle with the paprika and rosemary.

❊ Add the tomato purée, stock, claret and chopped tomatoes, cover and cook in the centre of a preheated oven, 160°C/325°F/Gas Mark 3, for 1$\frac{1}{2}$ hours.

❊ Remove the casserole from the oven, allow it to stand for 4 minutes, add the soured cream and garnish with the parsley.

❊ Serve with the bread and a side salad.

Chicken Chow Mein

250 g/9 oz packet
medium egg noodles
2 tbsp sunflower oil
275 g/9^1/2 oz cooked chicken
breasts, shredded
1 clove garlic, finely chopped
1 red pepper, deseeded
and thinly sliced

100 g/3^1/2 oz shiitake
mushrooms, sliced
6 spring onions, sliced
100 g/3^1/2 oz beansprouts
3 tbsp soy sauce
1 tbsp sesame oil

❋ Place the egg noodles in a large bowl or dish and break them up slightly. Pour over enough boiling water to cover the noodles and leave to stand.

❋ Heat the sunflower oil in a large preheated wok. Add the shredded chicken, finely chopped garlic, pepper slices, mushrooms, spring onions and beansprouts to the wok and stir-fry for about 5 minutes.

❋ Drain the noodles thoroughly. Add the noodles to the wok, toss well and stir-fry for a further 5 minutes.

❋ Drizzle the soy sauce and sesame oil over the chow mein and toss until well combined.

❋ Transfer to warmed serving bowls and serve immediately.

Chicken in Yellow Bean Sauce

❋ **SERVES 4** ❋

450 g/1 lb boneless chicken
breasts
2 tbsp vegetable oil
1 red onion, sliced
350 g/12 oz flat mushrooms,
sliced

90 g/3 oz cashew nuts
65 g/2^3/4 oz jar yellow bean
sauce
fresh coriander, to garnish
egg-fried rice or plain boiled
rice, to serve

❋ Using a sharp knife, remove the excess skin from the chicken breasts if desired. Cut the chicken into small bite-sized chunks.

❋ Heat the vegetable oil in a preheated wok.

❋ Add the chicken to the wok and stir-fry for 5 minutes.

❋ Add the red onion and mushrooms to the wok and continue to stir-fry for a further 5 minutes.

❋ Place the cashew nuts on a baking tray and toast under a preheated medium grill until just beginning to brown – this brings out their flavour.

❋ Toss the toasted cashew nuts into the wok together with the yellow bean sauce. Allow the sauce to bubble for 2–3 minutes.

❋ Transfer to warmed serving bowls and garnish with the coriander. Serve hot with the egg-fried rice.

Thai Red Chicken

1 tbsp sunflower oil
450 g/1 lb boneless, skinless chicken
2 cloves garlic, finely chopped
2 tbsp Thai red curry paste
2 tbsp fresh grated root ginger
1 tbsp tamarind paste
4 lime leaves
225 g/8 oz sweet potato
600 ml/1 pint coconut milk
225 g/8 oz cherry tomatoes, halved
3 tbsp chopped fresh coriander
cooked jasmine rice, to serve

❖ Heat the sunflower oil in a large preheated wok.

❖ Thinly slice the chicken. Add the chicken to the wok and stir-fry for 5 minutes.

❖ Add the garlic, curry paste, ginger, tamarind, and lime leaves to the wok and stir-fry for 1 minute.

❖ Using a sharp knife, peel and dice the sweet potato.

❖ Add the coconut milk and sweet potato to the mixture in the wok and bring to the boil. Allow to bubble over a medium heat for 20 minutes, or until the juices start to thicken and reduce.

❖ Add the cherry tomatoes and coriander to the curry and cook for a further 5 minutes, stirring occasionally. Transfer to serving plates and serve hot with the cooked jasmine rice.

Chicken Risotto alla Milanese

125 g/4½ oz butter
900 g/2 lb chicken meat, thinly sliced
1 large onion, chopped
500 g/1 lb 2 oz arborio rice
600 ml/1 pint chicken stock
150 ml/5 fl oz white wine
1 tsp crumbled saffron
salt and pepper
55 g/2 oz grated Parmesan cheese, to serve

❖ Heat 55 g/2 oz of the butter in a deep frying pan and fry the chicken and onion until golden brown.

❖ Add the rice, stir well and cook for 15 minutes.

❖ Heat the stock until boiling and gradually add to the rice. Add the white wine, saffron and salt and pepper to taste and mix well. Simmer gently for 20 minutes, stirring occasionally and adding more stock if the risotto becomes too dry.

❖ Leave to stand for a few minutes and just before serving add a little more stock and simmer for a further 10 minutes. Serve the risotto, sprinkled with the grated Parmesan cheese and the remaining butter.

Golden Chicken Risotto

2 tbsp sunflower oil
15 g/½ oz butter or margarine
1 medium leek, thinly sliced
1 large yellow pepper, diced
3 skinless, boneless chicken breasts, diced
350 g/12 oz arborio rice
few strands saffron
1.5 litres/2¾ pints chicken stock
200 g/7 oz canned sweetcorn
55 g/2 oz toasted unsalted peanuts
55 g/2 oz grated Parmesan cheese
salt and pepper

❉ Heat the oil and butter in a large saucepan. Fry the leek and pepper for 1 minute, then stir in the chicken and cook, stirring until golden brown.

❉ Stir in the rice and cook for 2–3 minutes.

❉ Stir in the saffron strands and salt and pepper to taste. Add the stock, a little at a time, cover and cook over a low heat, stirring occasionally, for about 20 minutes until the rice is tender and most of the liquid is absorbed. Do not let the risotto dry out – add more stock if necessary.

❉ Stir in the sweetcorn, peanuts and Parmesan cheese, then adjust the seasoning to taste. Serve hot.

One-Pot Chicken

❋ **SERVES 2** ❋

1 tbsp sunflower oil	300 ml/10 fl oz chicken stock
4 chicken thighs	1 small red chilli
1 small onion, diced	250 g/9 oz okra
2 celery sticks, diced	1 tbsp tomato purée
1 small green pepper, diced	salt and pepper
90 g/3 oz long-grain rice	

❋ Heat the oil in a wide saucepan and fry the chicken until golden. Remove the chicken from the pan using a slotted spoon. Stir in the onion, celery and pepper and fry for 1 minute. Pour off any excess fat.

❋ Add the rice and fry, stirring briskly, for a further minute. Add the stock and heat until boiling.

❋ Thinly slice the chilli and trim the okra. Add to the pan with the tomato purée. Season to taste.

❋ Return the chicken to the pan and stir. Cover tightly and simmer gently for 15 minutes, or until the rice is tender, the chicken is thoroughly cooked and all the liquid absorbed. Stir occasionally and, if the mixture becomes too dry, add a little extra stock to moisten. Serve immediately.

Honey & Mustard Chicken

❋ **SERVES 4–6** ❋

8 chicken portions	1 tsp paprika
55 g/2 oz butter, melted	salt and pepper
4 tbsp mild mustard	3 tbsp poppy seeds
4 tbsp clear honey	tomato and sweetcorn salad,
2 tbsp lemon juice	to serve

❋ Place the chicken pieces, skinless side down, on a large baking tray.

❋ Place all the remaining ingredients except the poppy seeds in a large bowl and blend together thoroughly.

❋ Brush half the mixture over the chicken portions.

❋ Bake in the centre of a preheated oven, 200°C/400°F/Gas Mark 6, for 15 minutes.

❋ Carefully turn over the chicken pieces and coat the top side of the chicken with the remaining honey and mustard mixture.

❋ Sprinkle the chicken with poppy seeds and return to the oven for a further 15 minutes.

❋ Arrange the chicken on a serving dish, pour over the cooking juices and serve with a tomato and sweetcorn salad, if wished.

Mexican Chicken

2 tbsp oil	400 g/14 oz canned chopped
8 chicken drumsticks	tomatoes
1 medium onion, finely	2 tbsp tomato purée
chopped	125 g/4¹/₂ oz frozen sweetcorn
1 tsp chilli powder	salt and pepper
1 tsp ground coriander	rice and mixed pepper salad,
	to serve

❖ Heat the oil in a large frying pan, add the chicken drumsticks and cook over a medium heat until lightly browned. Remove the chicken drumsticks from the pan with a slotted spoon and set aside until required.

❖ Add the chopped onion to the pan and cook for 3–4 minutes until soft, then stir in the chilli powder and coriander and cook for a few seconds, stirring briskly so the spices do not burn on the base of the pan. Add the chopped tomatoes with their juice and the tomato purée and stir well to incorporate.

❖ Return the chicken drumsticks to the pan and simmer the casserole gently for 20 minutes until the chicken is tender and thoroughly cooked. Add the sweetcorn and cook for a further 3–4 minutes. Season to taste with salt and pepper.

❖ Serve with the rice and mixed pepper salad.

Spicy Chicken Skewers

500 g/1 lb 2 oz skinless,	1 tbsp chopped fresh rosemary
boneless chicken breasts	250 g/9 oz cherry tomatoes
3 tbsp tomato purée	couscous or rice, to serve
2 tbsp clear honey	sprigs of fresh rosemary,
2 tbsp Worcestershire sauce	to garnish

❖ Using a sharp knife, cut the chicken into 2.5-cm/1-inch chunks and place in a bowl.

❖ Mix together the tomato purée, honey, Worcestershire sauce and rosemary. Add to the chicken, stirring to coat evenly.

❖ Alternating the chicken pieces and tomatoes, thread them on to 8 presoaked wooden skewers.

❖ Spoon over any remaining glaze. Cook under a preheated hot grill for 8–10 minutes, turning occasionally, until the chicken is thoroughly cooked. Serve on a bed of couscous and garnish with the sprigs of rosemary.

Grilled Chicken with Pesto Toasts

❊ **SERVES 4** ❊

8 part-boned chicken thighs
olive oil, for brushing
400 ml/14 fl oz passata
120 ml/4 fl oz green or red pesto
12 slices French bread
85 g/3 oz freshly grated Parmesan cheese
55 g/2 oz pine kernels or flaked almonds
salad leaves, to serve

❊ Arrange the chicken in a single layer in a wide flameproof dish and brush lightly with oil. Place under a preheated grill for about 15 minutes, turning occasionally, until golden brown.

❊ Pierce the chicken with a skewer to ensure that there is no trace of pink in the juices.

❊ Pour off any excess fat. Warm the passata and half the pesto in a small saucepan and pour over the chicken. Grill for a few more minutes, turning until coated.

❊ Meanwhile, spread the remaining pesto on to the slices of bread. Arrange the bread over the chicken and sprinkle with the Parmesan cheese. Scatter the pine kernels over the cheese. Grill for 2–3 minutes, or until browned and bubbling. Serve with the salad leaves.

Hearty Chicken Casserole

❖ **SERVES 4** ❖

1 roasting chicken, about 1.5 kg/ 3 lb 5 oz, cut into 6 or 8 serving pieces
125 g/4^1/$_2$ oz plain flour
3 tbsp olive oil
150 ml/5 fl oz dry white wine
1 green pepper, deseeded and sliced
1 red pepper, deseeded and sliced
1 carrot, finely chopped
1 celery stalk, finely chopped
1 garlic clove, crushed
200 g/7 oz canned chopped tomatoes
salt and pepper

❖ Rinse and pat dry the chicken pieces with kitchen paper. Lightly dust them with seasoned flour.

❖ Heat the oil in a large frying pan. Add the chicken and fry over a medium heat until browned all over. Remove from the pan and set aside.

❖ Drain off all but 2 tablespoons of the fat in the pan. Add the wine and stir for a few minutes. Then add the peppers, carrots, celery and garlic, season to taste with salt and pepper and simmer together for about 15 minutes.

❖ Add the chopped tomatoes to the pan. Cover and simmer for 30 minutes, stirring often, until the chicken is completely cooked through.

❖ Check the seasoning before serving piping hot.

Sweet-Sour Chicken

❖ **SERVES 4** ❖

4 boneless chicken breasts, about 125 g/4^1/$_2$ oz each
2 tbsp clear honey
1 tbsp dark soy sauce
2 tsp lemon rind, finely grated
1 tbsp lemon juice
225 g/8 oz rice noodles
2 tsp sesame oil
1 tbsp sesame seeds
salt and pepper
1 tbsp chopped fresh chives and some grated lemon rind, to garnish

❖ Preheat the grill to medium. Skin and trim the chicken breasts to remove any excess fat, then wash and pat them dry with absorbent kitchen paper. Using a sharp knife, score the chicken breasts with a criss-cross pattern on both sides (making sure that you do not cut all the way through the meat).

❖ Mix together the honey, soy sauce, 1 teaspoon of the lemon rind and the lemon juice in a small bowl, and then season well with pepper.

❖ Arrange the chicken breasts on the grill rack and brush with half the honey mixture. Cook for 10 minutes, turn over and brush with the remaining mixture. Cook for a further 8–10 minutes or until cooked through.

❖ Meanwhile, prepare the noodles according to the instructions on the packet. Drain well and transfer to a warmed serving bowl. Mix the noodles with the sesame oil, sesame seeds and the remaining lemon rind. Season and keep warm.

❖ Drain the chicken and serve with a small mound of noodles, garnished with the chopped chives and grated lemon rind.

Garlic Chicken Casserole

4 tbsp sunflower oil	225 ml/8 fl oz chicken stock
900 g/2 lb chicken meat, chopped	1 bouquet garni (1 bay leaf, 1 sprig each thyme, parsley
225 g/8 oz mushrooms, sliced	and sage, and 1 celery stick,
16 shallots	tied with string)
6 garlic cloves, crushed	400 g/14 oz canned borlotti
1 tbsp plain flour	beans
225 ml/8 fl oz white wine	salt and pepper

❈ Heat the sunflower oil in an ovenproof casserole and fry the chicken until browned all over. Remove from the casserole with a slotted spoon.

❈ Add the mushrooms, shallots and garlic to the oil in the casserole and cook for 4 minutes.

❈ Return the chicken to the casserole and sprinkle with the flour, then cook for a further 2 minutes.

❈ Add the wine and stock, stir until boiling, then add the bouquet garni. Season well with salt and pepper.

❈ Stir in the borlotti beans, cover and place in the centre of a preheated oven, 150°C/300°F/Gas Mark 2, for 2 hours.

❈ Remove the bouquet garni and serve piping hot.

Turkey with Cheese Pockets

4 turkey breast portions, each about 225 g/8 oz	4 tbsp olive oil
4 portions full-fat cheese (such	2 tbsp lemon juice
as Bel Paese), 15 g/½ oz each	salt and pepper
4 sage leaves or ½ tsp	
dried sage	**TO SERVE**
8 rashers rindless streaky	garlic bread
bacon	salad leaves
	cherry tomatoes

❈ Carefully cut a pocket into the side of each turkey breast. Open out each breast a little and season inside to taste with salt and pepper.

❈ Place a portion of cheese in each pocket, spreading it a little with a knife. Tuck a sage leaf into each pocket or sprinkle with a little dried sage.

❈ Stretch out the bacon with the back of a knife. Wrap 2 pieces of bacon around each turkey breast, so that the pocket opening is completely covered.

❈ Combine the oil and lemon juice in a small bowl.

❈ Grill the turkey under a medium–hot grill for about 10 minutes on each side, basting with the oil and lemon mixture frequently.

❈ Lightly toast the garlic bread.

❈ Transfer the turkey to warmed serving plates. Serve with the toasted garlic bread, salad leaves and cherry tomatoes.

Turkey with Cranberry Glaze

1 turkey breast
2 tbsp sunflower oil
15 g/$\frac{1}{2}$ oz stem ginger
50 g/1$\frac{3}{4}$ oz fresh or frozen cranberries
100 g/3$\frac{1}{2}$ oz canned chestnuts
4 tbsp cranberry sauce
3 tbsp light soy sauce
salt and pepper

❊ Remove any skin from the turkey breast. Using a sharp knife, thinly slice the turkey breast.

❊ Heat the sunflower oil in a large preheated wok or heavy-based frying pan.

❊ Add the turkey to the wok and stir-fry for 5 minutes or until cooked through.

❊ Using a sharp knife, finely chop the ginger.

❊ Add the ginger and the cranberries to the wok and stir-fry for 2–3 minutes or until the cranberries are soft.

❊ Add the chestnuts, cranberry sauce and soy sauce, season to taste with salt and pepper and allow to bubble for 2–3 minutes.

❊ Transfer the turkey stir-fry to warmed serving dishes and serve immediately.

Curried Turkey with Apricots

❄ **SERVES 4** ❄

1 tbsp vegetable oil
1 large onion, chopped
450 g/1 lb skinless
  turkey breast, cut into
  2.5-cm/1-inch cubes
3 tbsp mild curry paste
300 ml/10 fl oz chicken stock
175 g/6 oz frozen peas
400 g/14 oz canned apricot
  halves in natural juice

50 g/1¾ oz sultanas
350 g/12 oz basmati rice,
  freshly cooked
1 tsp ground coriander
4 tbsp fresh coriander,
  chopped
1 green chilli, deseeded
  and sliced
salt and pepper

❄ Heat the oil in a large saucepan and gently fry the onion and turkey for 4–5 minutes until the onion is soft but not brown and the turkey is a light golden colour.

❄ Stir in the curry paste. Pour in the stock, stirring, and bring to the boil. Cover and simmer for 15 minutes. Stir in the peas and bring back to the boil. Cover and simmer for 5 minutes.

❄ Drain the apricots, reserving the juice, and cut into thick slices. Add to the curry, stirring in a little of the juice if the mixture is becoming dry. Add the sultanas and cook for 2 minutes.

❄ Mix the rice with the ground and fresh coriander, stir in the sliced green chilli and season well. Transfer the rice to warmed plates and top with the curry.

Duck with Chilli & Lime

❄ **SERVES 4** ❄

4 boneless duck breast
  portions
2 garlic cloves, crushed
4 tsp light brown sugar
3 tbsp lime juice
1 tbsp soy sauce

1 tsp chilli sauce
1 tsp vegetable oil
2 tbsp plum jam
125 ml/4 fl oz chicken stock
salt and pepper

❄ Using a small, sharp knife, cut deep slashes in the skin of the duck to make a diamond pattern. Place the duck breasts in a wide, non-metallic dish.

❄ Combine the garlic, sugar, lime juice, soy and chilli sauces, then spoon over the duck, turning well to coat them evenly. Cover the dish with clingfilm and set aside to marinate in the refrigerator for at least 3 hours or overnight.

❄ Drain the duck, reserving the marinade. Heat a large, heavy-based saucepan until very hot and brush with the oil. Add the duck breast portions, skin side down, and cook for about 5 minutes or until the skin is brown and crisp. Carefully tip away the excess fat. Turn the duck breasts over.

❄ Continue cooking on the other side for 2–3 minutes to brown. Add the reserved marinade, plum jam and stock and simmer for 2 minutes. Season to taste with salt and pepper. Serve hot, with the juices spooned over.

Roast Duck with Apple

4 duckling portions,
350 g/12 oz each
4 tbsp dark soy sauce
2 tbsp light muscovado sugar
2 red eating apples
2 green eating apples
juice of 1 lemon
2 tbsp clear honey
few bay leaves

salt and pepper
assorted fresh vegetables,
to serve

SAUCE
400 g/14 oz canned apricots,
in natural juice
4 tbsp sweet sherry

❀ Preheat the oven to 190°C/375°F/Gas Mark 5. Wash the duck and trim away any excess fat. Place on a wire rack over a roasting tin and prick all over with a fork.

❀ Brush the duck with the soy sauce. Sprinkle over the sugar and season with pepper. Cook in the oven, basting occasionally, for 50–60 minutes until the meat is cooked through – the juices should run clear when a skewer is inserted into the thickest part of the meat.

❀ Meanwhile, core the apples and cut each into 6 wedges. Place in a small roasting tin and mix with the lemon juice and honey. Add a few bay leaves and season. Cook alongside the duck, basting occasionally, for 20–25 minutes until tender. Discard the bay leaves.

❀ To make the sauce, place the apricots in a blender or food processor together with the juice from the can and the sherry. Process for a few seconds until smooth. Alternatively, mash the apricots with a fork until smooth and mix with the juice and sherry.

❀ Just before serving, heat the apricot sauce in a small pan. Remove the skin from the duck and pat the flesh with kitchen paper to absorb any fat. Serve the duck with the apple wedges, apricot sauce and fresh vegetables.

Spaghetti Bolognese

1 tbsp olive oil
1 onion, finely chopped
2 garlic cloves, chopped
1 carrot, scraped and chopped
1 stick celery, chopped
50 g/1¾ oz pancetta or streaky
bacon, diced
350 g/12 oz lean beef mince

400 g/14 oz canned chopped
tomatoes
2 tsp dried oregano
125 ml/4 fl oz red wine
2 tbsp tomato purée
675 g/1 lb 8 oz fresh spaghetti
or 350 g/12 oz dried spaghetti
salt and pepper

❀ Heat the oil in a large frying pan. Add the onions and cook for 3 minutes.

❀ Add the garlic, carrot, celery and pancetta or bacon and sauté for 3–4 minutes or until just beginning to brown.

❀ Add the beef and cook, stirring, over a high heat for another 3 minutes or until all of the meat is brown.

❀ Stir in the tomatoes, oregano and red wine and bring to the boil. Reduce the heat and leave to simmer for about 45 minutes.

❀ Stir in the tomato purée and season with salt and pepper.

❀ Bring a saucepan of lightly salted water to the boil and cook for 8–10 minutes until tender but still firm to the bite. Drain thoroughly.

❀ Transfer the spaghetti to a serving plate and pour over the bolognese sauce. Toss to mix well and serve hot.

Chilli con Carne

750 g/1 lb 10 oz lean stewing
steak
2 tbsp vegetable oil
1 large onion, sliced
2–4 garlic cloves, crushed
1 tbsp plain flour
425 ml/15 fl oz tomato juice
400 g/14 oz canned tomatoes
1–2 tbsp sweet chilli sauce
1 tsp ground cumin
425 g/15 oz canned red kidney
beans, drained
1/2 teaspoon dried oregano
1–2 tbsp chopped fresh parsley
salt and pepper
chopped fresh herbs, to garnish
boiled rice and tortillas,
to serve

❖ Cut the beef into 2-cm/3/4-inch cubes. Heat the oil in a flameproof casserole and fry the beef until well sealed. Remove from the casserole.

❖ Add the onion and garlic to the casserole and cook until lightly browned. Stir in the flour and cook for 1–2 minutes. Stir in the tomato juice and tomatoes and bring to the boil. Replace the beef and add the chilli sauce, cumin and seasoning. Cover and place in a preheated oven, 160°C/325°F/Gas Mark 3, for 1 1/2 hours or until almost tender.

❖ Stir in the beans, oregano and parsley and adjust the seasoning to taste. Cover the casserole and return to the oven for 45 minutes. Serve, sprinkled with herbs, with the boiled rice and tortillas.

Rich Beef Stew

1 tbsp oil
15 g/$\frac{1}{2}$ oz butter
225 g/8 oz baby onions, peeled
   and halved
600 g/1 lb 5 oz stewing steak,
   diced into 4-cm/1$\frac{1}{2}$-inch
   chunks
300 ml/10 fl oz beef stock
150 ml/5 fl oz red wine

4 tbsp chopped oregano
1 tbsp sugar
1 orange
25 g/1 oz ceps or other
   dried mushrooms
225 g/8 oz fresh plum
   tomatoes
cooked rice or potatoes,
   to serve

❋ Heat the oil and butter in a large frying pan. Add the onions and sauté for 5 minutes or until golden. Remove the onions with a slotted spoon, set aside and keep warm.

❋ Add the beef to the pan and cook, stirring, for 5 minutes or until browned all over.

❋ Return the onions to the pan and add the stock, wine, oregano and sugar, stirring to mix well. Transfer the mixture to an ovenproof casserole dish.

❋ Pare the rind from the orange and cut it into strips. Slice the orange flesh into rings. Add the orange rings and the rind to the casserole. Cook in a preheated oven, 180°C/350°F/Gas Mark 4, for 1$\frac{1}{4}$ hours.

❋ Soak the mushrooms for 30 minutes in a small bowl containing 4 tablespoons of warm water.

❋ Peel and halve the tomatoes. Add the tomatoes, mushrooms and their soaking liquid to the casserole. Cook for a further 20 minutes until the beef is tender and the juices thickened. Serve with the cooked rice.

Beef with Red Wine

2 tbsp olive oil
1 large onion, cut into wedges
2 celery sticks, chopped
1 green pepper, cored,
   deseeded and chopped
1 kg/2 lb 4 oz lean stewing
   steak, cubed
55 g/2 oz plain flour, seasoned
   with salt and pepper
600 ml/1 pint beef stock

2 garlic cloves, crushed
150 ml/5 fl oz red wine
2 tbsp red wine vinegar
2 tbsp tomato purée
$\frac{1}{2}$ tsp Tabasco sauce
1 tsp chopped fresh thyme
2 bay leaves
$\frac{1}{2}$ tsp Cajun spice mix
French stick, to serve

❋ Heat the oil in a large heavy-based flameproof casserole. Add the onion wedges and cook until browned on all sides. Remove with a slotted spoon and set aside.

❋ Add the celery and pepper to the casserole and cook until soft. Remove the vegetables with a slotted spoon and set aside.

❋ Coat the meat in the seasoned flour, add to the casserole and sauté until browned on all sides.

❋ Add the stock, garlic, wine, vinegar, tomato purée, Tabasco sauce and thyme and heat gently.

❋ Return the onions, celery and peppers to the pan. Tuck in the bay leaves and sprinkle with the Cajun seasoning.

❋ Bring to the boil, transfer to the oven and cook for 2$\frac{1}{2}$–3 hours or until the meat and vegetables are tender.

❋ Serve with the French stick.

Chilli Beef

❊ **SERVES 4–6** ❊

about 3 tbsp plain flour
1 kg/2 lb 4 oz stewing beef, cut
into large bite-sized pieces
2 tbsp vegetable oil
2 onions, chopped
5 garlic cloves, chopped
400 g/14 oz tomatoes, diced
1½ dried chipotle chillies,
reconstituted, deseeded
and cut into thin strips,
or a few shakes of bottled
chipotle salsa

1.5 litres/2¾ pints beef stock
350 g/12 oz French beans
pinch of sugar
salt and pepper
simmered beans and cooked
rice, to serve

❊ Place the flour in a large bowl and season with salt and pepper. Add the beef and toss to coat well. Remove from the bowl, shaking off the excess flour.

❊ Heat the oil in a frying pan and brown the meat briefly over a high heat. Reduce the heat to medium, add the onions and garlic and cook for 2 minutes.

❊ Add the tomatoes, chillies and stock, cover and simmer over a low heat for 1½ hours or until the meat is very tender, adding the French beans 15 minutes before the end of the cooking time. Skim off any fat that rises to the surface.

❊ Transfer to individual bowls and serve with the simmered beans and rice.

Beef with Wild Mushrooms

❊ **SERVES 4** ❊

4 fillet or sirloin steaks
2 tbsp butter
1–2 garlic cloves, crushed
150 g/5½ oz mixed wild
mushrooms

2 tbsp chopped fresh parsley
salad leaves and halved cherry
tomatoes, to serve

❊ Place the steaks on a chopping board and, using a sharp knife, cut a pocket in the side of each steak.

❊ To make the stuffing, heat the butter in a frying pan, add the garlic and cook gently for about 1 minute.

❊ Add the mushrooms to the pan and cook gently for 4–6 minutes until tender. Stir in the parsley.

❊ Divide the mushroom mixture into 4 and insert a portion into the pocket of each steak. Seal the pocket closed with a cocktail stick. If preparing ahead, let the mixture cool before stuffing the steaks.

❊ Grill the steaks under a preheated hot grill, for about 2 minutes on each side. Reduce the heat and grill for a further 4–10 minutes on each side, depending on how well done you like your steaks.

❊ Transfer the steaks to serving plates and remove the cocktail sticks. Serve with the salad leaves and cherry tomato halves.

Hot Beef & Coconut Curry

400 ml/14 fl oz coconut milk
2 tbsp Thai red curry paste
2 garlic cloves, crushed
500 g/1 lb 2 oz stewing steak
2 kaffir lime leaves, shredded
3 tbsp kaffir lime juice
2 tbsp Thai fish sauce
1 large fresh red chilli,
deseeded and sliced
$\frac{1}{2}$ tsp ground turmeric
2 tbsp chopped fresh
basil leaves
2 tbsp chopped fresh
coriander leaves
salt and pepper
shredded coconut, to garnish
boiled rice, to serve

✤ Place the coconut milk in a large saucepan and bring to the boil. Lower the heat and simmer gently over a low heat for about 10 minutes until the milk has thickened. Stir in the red curry paste and garlic and simmer for a further 5 minutes.

✤ Cut the beef into 2-cm/$\frac{3}{4}$-inch chunks, add to the pan and bring to the boil, stirring. Lower the heat and add the lime leaves, lime juice, fish sauce, chilli, turmeric and $\frac{1}{2}$ teaspoon salt. Cover the pan and simmer gently for a further 20–25 minutes until the meat is tender and cooked through, adding a little water if the sauce looks too dry.

✤ Stir in the basil and coriander and adjust the seasoning with salt and pepper to taste. Transfer to a warmed serving dish, sprinkle with coconut and serve with boiled rice.

Red Spiced Beef

625 g/1 lb 6 oz sirloin or rump
steak
2 tbsp paprika
2–3 tsp mild chilli powder
¹/₂ tsp salt
6 celery sticks
6 tbsp stock or water
2 tbsp tomato purée
2 tbsp clear honey
3 tbsp wine vinegar

1 tbsp Worcestershire sauce
2 tbsp sunflower oil
4 spring onions, thinly sliced
diagonally
4 tomatoes, peeled, deseeded
and sliced
1–2 garlic cloves, crushed
celery leaves, to garnish
(optional)
Chinese noodles, to serve

❋ Using a sharp knife or meat cleaver, cut the steak across the grain into narrow strips about 1 cm/¹/₂ inch thick and place in a bowl.

❋ Combine the paprika, chilli powder and salt, add to the beef and mix until the meat strips are evenly coated with the spices. Set the beef aside to marinate in a cool place for at least 30 minutes.

❋ Cut the celery into 5-cm/2-inch lengths, then cut the lengths into strips about 5 mm/¹/₄ inch thick.

❋ Combine the stock, tomato purée, honey, vinegar and Worcestershire sauce and set aside.

❋ Heat the oil in the wok until really hot. Add the spring onion, celery, tomatoes and garlic and stir-fry for about 1 minute until the vegetables are beginning to soften, then add the steak strips. Stir-fry over a high heat for 3–4 minutes until the meat is well sealed.

❋ Add the sauce to the wok and continue to stir-fry briskly until thoroughly coated and sizzling.

❋ Garnish with the celery leaves, if using, and serve with the noodles.

Beef & Broccoli Stir-Fry

225 g/8 oz lean steak, trimmed
2 garlic cloves, crushed
dash of chilli oil
1-cm/¹/₂-inch piece of root
ginger, grated
¹/₂ tsp Chinese five-spice
powder
2 tbsp dark soy sauce

2 tbsp vegetable oil
150 g/5¹/₂ oz broccoli florets
1 tbsp light soy sauce
150 ml/5 fl oz beef stock
2 tsp cornflour
4 tsp water
carrot strips, to garnish

❋ Using a sharp knife, cut the steak into thin strips and place in a shallow glass dish.

❋ Mix together the garlic, chilli oil, grated ginger, Chinese five-spice powder and dark soy sauce in a small bowl and pour over the beef, tossing to coat the strips evenly.

❋ Cover the bowl and leave the meat to marinate in the refrigerator for several hours to allow the flavours to develop fully.

❋ Heat 1 tablespoon of the vegetable oil in a preheated wok or large frying pan. Add the broccoli and stir-fry over a medium heat for 4–5 minutes. Remove from the wok with a slotted spoon and set aside until required.

❋ Heat the remaining oil in the wok. Add the steak together with the marinade, and stir-fry for 2–3 minutes, until the steak is browned and sealed.

❋ Return the broccoli to the wok and stir in the light soy sauce and stock.

❋ Blend the cornflour with the water to form a smooth paste and stir into the wok. Bring to the boil, stirring, until thickened and clear. Cook for 1 minute. Transfer the stir-fry to a warmed serving dish, arrange the carrot strips in a lattice on top and serve immediately.

Beef Chow Mein

❖ **SERVES 4** ❖

450 g/1 lb egg noodles	1 carrot, thinly sliced
4 tbsp groundnut oil	2 celery sticks, sliced
450 g/1 lb lean beef steak, cut into thin strips	8 spring onions
	1 tsp dark brown sugar
2 garlic cloves, crushed	1 tbsp dry sherry
1 tsp grated root ginger	2 tbsp dark soy sauce
1 green pepper, thinly sliced	few drops of chilli sauce

❖ Bring a saucepan of lightly salted water to the boil and cook the noodles for 4–5 minutes. Drain well, rinse under cold running water and drain again thoroughly.

❖ Toss the noodles in 1 tablespoon of the oil.

❖ Heat the remaining oil in a preheated wok. Add the beef and stir-fry for 3–4 minutes, stirring constantly.

❖ Add the garlic and ginger to the wok and stir-fry for 30 seconds.

❖ Add the pepper, carrot, celery and spring onions and stir-fry for about 2 minutes.

❖ Add the sugar, sherry, soy sauce and chilli sauce to the mixture in the wok and cook, stirring, for 1 minute.

❖ Stir in the noodles, mixing well, and cook until completely warmed through.

❖ Transfer the noodles to warmed serving bowls and serve immediately.

Neapolitan Pork Steaks

❖ **SERVES 4** ❖

2 tbsp olive oil	75 g/2¾ oz black olives, stoned
1 garlic clove, chopped	2 tbsp fresh basil, shredded
1 large onion, sliced	freshly grated Parmesan
400 g/14 oz canned tomatoes	cheese, to serve
2 tsp yeast extract	
4 pork loin steaks, each about 125 g/4½ oz	

❖ Heat the oil in a large frying pan. Add the onions and garlic and cook, stirring, for 3–4 minutes or until they just begin to soften.

❖ Add the tomatoes and yeast extract to the pan and leave to simmer for about 5 minutes or until the sauce starts to thicken.

❖ Cook the steaks under a preheated grill for 5 minutes on both sides, until the meat is cooked through. Set the pork aside and keep warm.

❖ Add the olives and fresh shredded basil to the sauce in the pan and stir quickly to combine.

❖ Transfer the steaks to warmed serving plates. Top the steaks with the sauce, sprinkle with the grated cheese and serve immediately.

Pork with Ratatouille Sauce

4 lean, boneless pork chops,
about 125 g/4^1/$_2$ oz each
1 tsp dried mixed herbs
salt and pepper
jacket potatoes, to serve

SAUCE
1 medium onion
1 garlic clove
1 small green pepper,
deseeded
1 small yellow pepper,
deseeded
1 medium courgette, trimmed
100 g/3^1/$_2$ oz button mushrooms
400 g/14 oz canned chopped
tomatoes
2 tbsp tomato purée
1 tsp dried mixed herbs
1 tsp caster sugar
salt and pepper

❖ To make the sauce, peel and chop the onion and garlic. Dice the peppers and the courgette. Wipe and halve the mushrooms.

❖ Place all of the vegetables in a saucepan and stir in the chopped tomatoes and tomato purée. Add the dried herbs, sugar and plenty of seasoning. Bring to the boil, cover and simmer for 20 minutes.

❖ Meanwhile, preheat the grill to medium. Trim away any excess fat from the chops, then season on both sides and rub in the dried mixed herbs. Cook the chops for 5 minutes, then turn over and cook for a further 6–7 minutes or until cooked through.

❖ Drain the chops on absorbent kitchen paper and serve accompanied by the sauce and jacket potatoes.

Sweet & Sour Pork

450 g/1 lb pork fillet
2 tbsp sunflower oil
225 g/8 oz courgettes
1 red onion, cut into thin wedges
2 cloves garlic, crushed
225 g/8 oz carrots, cut into matchsticks
1 red pepper, deseeded and sliced
100 g/3½ oz baby sweetcorn
100 g/3½ oz button mushrooms, halved
175 g/6 oz fresh pineapple, cubed
100 g/3½ oz beansprouts
150 ml/5 fl oz pineapple juice
1 tbsp cornflour
2 tbsp soy sauce
3 tbsp tomato ketchup
1 tbsp white wine vinegar
1 tbsp clear honey

❊ Using a sharp knife, thinly slice the pork into even-sized pieces.

❊ Heat the oil in a large preheated wok. Add the pork to the wok and stir-fry for 10 minutes, or until the pork is completely cooked through and beginning to turn crispy at the edges.

❊ Meanwhile, cut the courgettes into thin sticks.

❊ Add the onion, garlic, carrots, courgettes, pepper, sweetcorn and mushrooms to the wok and stir-fry for a further 5 minutes.

❊ Add the pineapple cubes and beansprouts to the wok and stir-fry for 2 minutes.

❊ Mix together the pineapple juice, cornflour, soy sauce, tomato ketchup, vinegar and honey.

❊ Pour the sweet and sour mixture into the wok and cook over a high heat, tossing frequently, until the juices thicken. Transfer to serving bowls and serve hot.

Pork Chow Mein

250 g/9 oz egg noodles
4–5 tbsp vegetable oil
250 g/9 oz pork fillet, cooked
125 g/4½ oz French beans
2 tbsp light soy sauce
1 tsp salt
½ tsp sugar
1 tbsp Chinese rice wine or dry sherry
2 spring onions, finely shredded
a few drops sesame oil
chilli sauce, to serve (optional)

❊ Cook the noodles in boiling water according to the instructions on the packet, then drain and rinse under cold water. Drain again, then toss with 1 tablespoon of the oil.

❊ Slice the pork into thin shreds and top and tail the beans.

❊ Heat 3 tablespoons of oil in a preheated wok until hot. Add the noodles and stir-fry for 2–3 minutes with 1 tablespoon of the soy sauce, then remove to a serving dish. Keep warm.

❊ Heat the remaining oil and stir-fry the beans and meat for 2 minutes. Add the salt, sugar, wine, the remaining soy sauce and about half the spring onions to the wok.

❊ Stir the mixture in the wok, adding a little water if necessary, then pour on top of the noodles, and sprinkle with sesame oil and the remaining spring onions.

❊ Serve the chow mein hot or cold with chilli sauce, if using.

Pork Satay Stir-Fry

❈ SERVES 4 ❈

150 g/5½ oz carrots
2 tbsp sunflower oil
350 g/12 oz pork fillet, thinly
sliced
1 onion, sliced
2 cloves garlic, crushed
1 yellow pepper, deseeded
and sliced
150 g/5½ oz mangetout
75 g/2¾ oz fine asparagus

chopped salted peanuts,
to serve

SATAY SAUCE
6 tbsp crunchy peanut butter
6 tbsp coconut milk
1 tsp chilli flakes
1 clove garlic, crushed
1 tsp tomato purée

❈ Using a sharp knife, slice the carrots into matchsticks.

❈ Heat the oil in a large, preheated wok. Add the pork, onion and garlic and stir-fry for 5 minutes or until cooked through.

❈ Add the carrots, pepper, mangetout and asparagus to the wok and stir-fry for 5 minutes.

❈ To make the satay sauce, place the peanut butter, coconut milk, chilli flakes, garlic and tomato purée in a small saucepan and heat gently, stirring, until well combined. Be careful not to let the sauce stick to the bottom of the pan.

❈ Transfer the stir-fry to warmed serving plates. Spoon the satay sauce over the stir-fry and scatter with chopped peanuts. Serve immediately.

Chilli Pork Noodles

❈ SERVES 4 ❈

350 g/12 oz pork mince
1 tbsp light soy sauce
1 tbsp dry sherry
350 g/12 oz egg noodles
2 tsp sesame oil
2 tbsp vegetable oil
2 garlic cloves, crushed
2 tsp grated fresh root ginger

2 fresh red chillies, sliced
1 red pepper, seeded and
finely sliced
25 g/1 oz unsalted peanuts
3 tbsp peanut butter
3 tbsp dark soy sauce
dash of chilli oil
300 ml/10 fl oz pork stock

❈ Mix together the pork, light soy sauce and sherry in a large bowl. Cover and leave to marinate for 30 minutes.

❈ Meanwhile, bring a saucepan of water to the boil and cook the noodles for 4 minutes. Drain well, rinse in cold water and drain again. Toss the noodles in the sesame oil.

❈ Heat the vegetable oil in a preheated wok and stir-fry the garlic, ginger, chillies and red pepper for 30 seconds.

❈ Add the pork to the mixture in the wok, together with the marinade. Continue cooking for about 1 minute until the pork is sealed.

❈ Add the peanuts, peanut butter, dark soy sauce, chilli oil and stock and cook for 2–3 minutes.

❈ Toss the noodles in the mixture and serve at once.

Pork with Fennel & Juniper

❖ SERVES 4 ❖

$1/2$ fennel bulb
1 tbsp juniper berries
about 2 tbsp olive oil
finely grated rind and
juice of 1 orange
4 pork chops, each
about 150 g/5$1/2$ oz
fresh bread and a crisp salad,
to serve

✻ Finely chop the fennel bulb, discarding the green parts.

✻ Grind the juniper berries in a pestle and mortar. Mix the crushed juniper berries with the fennel flesh, olive oil and orange rind.

✻ Using a sharp knife, score a few cuts all over each chop.

✻ Place the pork chops in a roasting tin or an ovenproof dish. Spoon the fennel and juniper mixture over the chops.

✻ Pour the orange juice over the top of each chop, cover and marinate in the refrigerator for about 2 hours.

✻ Cook the pork chops under a preheated grill for 10–15 minutes, depending on the thickness of the meat, or until the meat is tender and cooked through, turning occasionally.

✻ Transfer the pork chops to serving plates and serve with the bread and the salad.

Pork Stroganoff

350 g/12 oz lean pork fillet
1 tbsp vegetable oil
1 medium onion, chopped
2 garlic cloves, crushed
25 g/1 oz plain flour
2 tbsp tomato purée
425 ml/15 fl oz fresh chicken
  or vegetable stock
125 g/4½ oz button
  mushrooms, sliced

1 large green pepper,
  deseeded and diced
½ tsp ground nutmeg, plus
  extra to garnish
4 tbsp low-fat natural yogurt,
  plus extra to serve
salt and pepper
white rice, freshly boiled,
  to serve

❄ Trim away any excess fat and silver skin from the pork, then cut the meat into slices 1 cm/½ inch thick.

❄ Heat the oil in a large saucepan and gently fry the pork, onion and garlic for 4–5 minutes until lightly browned.

❄ Stir in the flour and tomato purée, pour in the stock and stir to mix thoroughly.

❄ Add the mushrooms, green pepper, seasoning and nutmeg. Bring to the boil, cover and simmer for 20 minutes until the pork is tender and cooked through.

❄ Remove the saucepan from the heat and stir in the yogurt.

❄ Serve the pork and sauce on a bed of rice with an extra spoonful of yogurt, and garnish with a dusting of ground nutmeg.

Pan-Cooked Pork Medallions

8 lean pork medallions, about
  50 g/1¾ oz each
2 tsp vegetable oil
1 medium onion, finely sliced
1 tsp caster sugar
1 tsp dried sage
150 ml/5 fl oz dry cider
150 ml/5 fl oz fresh chicken
  or vegetable stock

1 green eating apple
1 red eating apple
1 tbsp lemon juice
salt and pepper
fresh sage leaves, to garnish
freshly cooked vegetables,
  to serve

❄ Trim away any excess fat from the pork and set aside until required.

❄ Heat the oil in a frying pan and gently fry the onion for 5 minutes until soft. Add the sugar and cook for 3–4 minutes until golden. Add the pork to the pan and cook for 2 minutes on each side until browned.

❄ Add the sage, cider and stock. Bring to the boil and then simmer for 20 minutes.

❄ Meanwhile, core and cut each apple into 8 wedges. Toss the apple wedges in lemon juice so that they do not turn brown.

❄ Add the apples to the pork and mix gently. Season and cook for a further 3–4 minutes until tender.

❄ Serve immediately, garnished with the sage leaves and accompanied by the freshly cooked vegetables.

Sausage & Bean Casserole

8 Italian sausages
1 tbsp olive oil
1 large onion, chopped
2 garlic cloves, chopped
1 green pepper
225 g/8 oz fresh tomatoes, peeled and chopped or 400 g/14 oz canned tomatoes, chopped

2 tbsp sun-dried tomato paste
400 g/14 oz canned cannellini beans
mashed potato or cooked rice, to serve

❖ Using a sharp knife, deseed the pepper and cut it into thin strips.

❖ Prick the sausages all over with a fork. Cook the sausages under a preheated grill for 10–12 minutes, turning occasionally, until brown all over. Set aside and keep warm.

❖ Heat the oil in a large frying pan. Add the onion, garlic and pepper to the pan and cook, stirring occasionally, for 5 minutes or until soft.

❖ Add the tomatoes to the pan and leave the mixture to simmer, stirring occasionally, for about 5 minutes or until slightly reduced and thickened.

❖ Stir the sun-dried tomato paste, cannellini beans and sausages into the mixture in the pan. Cook for 4–5 minutes or until the mixture is piping hot. Add 4–5 tablespoons of water if the mixture becomes too dry during cooking.

❖ Transfer the casserole to serving plates and serve with the mashed potato.

Spicy Pork Balls

450 g/1 lb pork mince
2 shallots, finely chopped
2 cloves garlic, crushed
1 tsp cumin seeds
1/2 tsp chilli powder
25 g/1 oz wholemeal breadcrumbs
1 egg, beaten

2 tbsp sunflower oil
400 g/14 oz canned chopped tomatoes, flavoured with chilli
2 tbsp soy sauce
200 g/7 oz canned water chestnuts, drained
3 tbsp chopped fresh coriander

❖ Place the pork in a large mixing bowl. Add the shallots, garlic, cumin seeds, chilli powder, breadcrumbs and beaten egg and mix together well.

❖ Form the mixture into balls between the palms of your hands.

❖ Heat the oil in a large preheated wok. Add the pork balls and stir-fry, in batches, over a high heat for about 5 minutes or until sealed on all sides.

❖ Add the tomatoes, soy sauce and water chestnuts and bring to the boil. Return the pork balls to the wok, reduce the heat and leave to simmer for 15 minutes.

❖ Scatter with chopped fresh coriander and serve hot.

Pot-Roasted Leg of Lamb

1.6 kg/3 lb 8 oz leg of lamb
3–4 sprigs fresh rosemary
115 g/4 oz streaky bacon
rashers
4 tbsp olive oil
2–3 garlic cloves, crushed
2 onions, sliced
2 carrots, sliced
2 celery sticks, sliced
300 ml/10 fl oz dry white wine
1 tbsp tomato purée
300 ml/10 fl oz lamb stock
350 g/12 oz tomatoes, peeled,
quartered and deseeded
1 tbsp chopped fresh parsley
1 tbsp chopped fresh oregano
or marjoram
salt and pepper
sprigs of fresh rosemary,
to garnish

❖ Wipe the leg of lamb all over, trimming off any excess fat, then season with salt and pepper, rubbing well in. Lay the rosemary over the lamb, cover evenly with the bacon rashers and tie in place with string.

❖ Heat the oil in a frying pan and fry the lamb for about 10 minutes, turning several times. Remove from the pan.

❖ Transfer the oil from the frying pan to a large flameproof casserole and cook the garlic and onion for 3–4 minutes until beginning to soften. Add the carrots and celery and cook for a few minutes longer.

❖ Lay the lamb on top of the vegetables and press down to partly submerge. Pour the wine over the lamb, add the tomato purée and simmer for about 3–4 minutes. Add the stock, tomatoes and herbs and season to taste with salt and pepper. Bring back to the boil for a further 3–4 minutes.

❖ Cover the casserole tightly and cook in a moderate oven, 180°C/350°F/Gas Mark 4, for 2–2½ hours until very tender.

❖ Remove the lamb from the casserole and, if preferred, take off the bacon and herbs along with the string. Keep warm. Strain the juices, skimming off any excess fat, and serve in a jug. The vegetables may be put around the joint or in a serving dish. Garnish with the sprigs of rosemary.

Lamb with Bay & Lemon

4 lamb chops   150 ml/5 fl oz lamb or
1 tbsp oil   vegetable stock
15 g/$\frac{1}{2}$ oz butter   2 bay leaves
150 ml/5 fl oz white wine   pared rind of 1 lemon
salt and pepper

❃ Using a sharp knife, carefully remove the bone from each lamb chop, keeping the meat intact. Shape the meat into rounds and secure with a length of string. Alternatively, ask the butcher to prepare the lamb noisettes for you.

❃ In a large frying pan, heat together the oil and butter until the mixture starts to froth.

❃ Add the lamb noisettes to the pan and cook for 2–3 minutes on each side or until browned all over.

❃ Remove the pan from the heat, drain off all of the excess fat and discard.

❃ Return the pan to the heat. Add the wine, stock, bay leaves and lemon rind to the pan and cook for 20–25 minutes or until the lamb is tender. Season the lamb noisettes and sauce to taste with a little salt and pepper.

❃ Transfer to serving plates. Remove the string from each noisette and serve with the sauce.

Fruity Lamb Casserole

450 g/1 lb lean lamb,   2 tbsp tomato purée
trimmed and cut into   125 g/4$\frac{1}{2}$ oz dried apricots
2.5-cm/1-inch cubes   1 tsp caster sugar
1 tsp ground cinnamon   300 ml/10 fl oz vegetable stock
1 tsp ground coriander   salt and pepper
1 tsp ground cumin   1 small bunch fresh coriander,
2 tsp olive oil   to garnish
1 medium red onion,   brown rice, steamed couscous
finely chopped   or bulgar wheat, to serve
1 garlic clove, crushed
400 g/14 oz canned chopped
tomatoes

❃ Preheat the oven to 180°C/350°F/Gas Mark 4. Place the meat in a mixing bowl and add the spices and oil. Mix thoroughly so that the lamb is well coated in the spices.

❃ Heat a non-stick frying pan for a few seconds until it is hot, then add the spiced lamb. Reduce the heat and cook for 4–5 minutes, stirring, until browned all over. Using a slotted spoon, remove the lamb and transfer to a large ovenproof casserole.

❃ In the same frying pan, cook the onion, garlic, tomatoes and tomato purée for 5 minutes. Season to taste. Stir in the apricots and sugar, add the stock and bring to the boil.

❃ Spoon the sauce over the lamb and mix well. Cover and cook in the oven for 1 hour, removing the lid for the last 10 minutes.

❃ Roughly chop the coriander and sprinkle over the casserole to garnish. Serve with the brown rice.

Lamb & Potato Moussaka

1 large aubergine, sliced
1 tbsp olive or vegetable oil
1 onion, finely chopped
1 garlic clove, crushed
350 g/12 oz lean lamb mince
250 g/9 oz mushrooms, sliced
425 g/15 oz canned chopped
 tomatoes with herbs
150 ml/5 fl oz lamb or
 vegetable stock
2 tbsp cornflour
2 tbsp water
500 g/1 lb 2 oz potatoes,
 parboiled for 10 minutes
 and sliced
2 eggs
125 g/4½ oz soft cheese
150 ml/5 fl oz natural yogurt
60 g/2 oz mature Cheddar
 cheese, grated
salt and pepper
fresh flat-leaf parsley,
 to garnish
green salad, to serve

❊ Lay the aubergine slices on a clean surface and sprinkle liberally with salt to extract the bitter juices. Leave for 10 minutes then turn the slices over and repeat. Put in a colander, rinse and drain well.

❊ Meanwhile, heat the oil in a saucepan and fry the onion and garlic for 3–4 minutes. Add the lamb and mushrooms and cook for 5 minutes until browned. Stir in the tomatoes and stock, bring to the boil and simmer for 10 minutes. Mix the cornflour with the water and stir into the pan. Cook, stirring, until thickened.

❊ Spoon half the mixture into an ovenproof dish. Cover with the aubergine slices, then the remaining lamb mixture. Arrange the sliced potatoes on top.

❊ Beat together the eggs, soft cheese, yogurt and seasoning. Pour over the potatoes to cover them completely. Sprinkle with the grated cheese.

❊ Bake in a preheated oven, 190°C/375°F/Gas Mark 5, for 45 minutes until the topping is set and golden brown. Garnish with the parsley and serve with the green salad.

Lamb with Olives

1.25 kg/2 lb 12 oz boned leg
 of lamb
90 ml/3 fl oz olive oil
2 garlic cloves, crushed
1 onion, sliced
1 small red chilli, cored,
 deseeded and finely chopped
175 ml/6 fl oz dry white wine
175 g/6 oz stoned black olives
salt
chopped fresh parsley,
 to garnish

❊ Using a sharp knife, cut the lamb into 2.5-cm/1-inch cubes.

❊ Heat the oil in a frying pan and fry the garlic, onion and chilli for 5 minutes.

❊ Add the meat and wine and cook for a further 5 minutes.

❊ Stir in the olives, then transfer the mixture to a casserole. Place in a preheated oven, 180°C/350°F/Gas Mark 4, and cook for 1 hour 20 minutes or until the meat is tender. Season to taste with salt and serve garnished with the parsley.

Lamb Mince with Peas

6 tbsp oil
1 medium onion, sliced
3 fresh green chillies
1 bunch of fresh coriander
2 tomatoes, chopped
1 tsp salt
1 tsp finely chopped
root ginger
1 tsp fresh garlic, crushed
1 tsp chilli powder
450 g/1 lb lean lamb mince
100 g/3¹/₂ oz peas

❖ Heat the oil in a medium-sized saucepan. Add the onion slices and cook, stirring constantly, until golden brown.

❖ Add 2 of the chillies, half of the fresh coriander and the chopped tomatoes to the pan and reduce the heat to a gentle simmer.

❖ Add the salt, ginger, garlic and chilli powder to the pan and stir thoroughly to combine.

❖ Add the lamb to the pan and stir-fry the mixture for 7–10 minutes until the meat turns brown.

❖ Stir in the peas and cook, stirring occasionally, for 3–4 minutes.

❖ Transfer the lamb and pea mixture to warmed serving plates and garnish with the remaining chopped green chilli and coriander.

Lamb Pilau

2–3 tbsp vegetable oil
650 g/1 lb 7 oz boneless
lamb shoulder, cut into
2.5-cm/1-inch cubes
2 onions, coarsely chopped
1 tsp ground cumin
200 g/7 oz arborio, long-grain
or basmati rice
1 tbsp tomato purée
1 tsp saffron threads
100 ml/3½ fl oz pomegranate
juice

850 ml/1½ pints lamb or
chicken stock or water
115 g/4 oz dried apricots or
prunes, soaked
and halved
2 tbsp raisins
salt and pepper
2 tbsp chopped fresh mint
and 2 tbsp chopped fresh
watercress, to serve

❄   Heat the oil in a large flameproof casserole or wide saucepan over a high heat. Add the lamb, in batches, and cook, stirring and turning frequently, for about 7 minutes until lightly browned.

❄   Add the onions, reduce the heat to medium–high and cook for about 2 minutes until beginning to soften. Add the cumin and rice and cook, stirring to coat, for about 2 minutes until the rice is translucent. Stir in the tomato purée and the saffron threads.

❄   Add the pomegranate juice and stock and bring to the boil, stirring. Stir in the apricots and raisins. Reduce the heat to low, cover and simmer for 20–25 minutes until the lamb and rice are tender and the liquid is absorbed.

❄   To serve, season to taste, sprinkle the chopped mint and watercress over the pilau and serve from the casserole.

Red Lamb Curry

500 g/1 lb 2 oz boneless lean
leg of lamb
2 tbsp vegetable oil
1 large onion, sliced
2 garlic cloves, crushed
2 tbsp red curry paste
150 ml/5 fl oz coconut milk
1 tbsp soft light brown sugar
1 large red pepper, deseeded
and thickly sliced

125 ml/4 fl oz lamb or beef stock
1 tbsp Thai fish sauce
2 tbsp lime juice
225 g/8 oz canned water
chestnuts, drained
2 tbsp fresh coriander, chopped
2 tbsp fresh basil, chopped
salt and pepper
boiled jasmine rice, to serve
fresh basil leaves, to garnish

❄   Trim the meat and cut it into 3-cm/1¼-inch cubes. Heat the oil in a large frying pan or wok over a high heat and stir-fry the onion and garlic for 2–3 minutes to soften. Add the meat and stir-fry until lightly browned.

❄   Stir in the curry paste and cook for a few seconds, then add the coconut milk and sugar and bring to the boil. Reduce the heat and simmer for 15 minutes, stirring occasionally.

❄   Stir in the red pepper, stock, fish sauce and lime juice, cover and continue simmering for a further 15 minutes or until the meat is tender.

❄   Add the water chestnuts, coriander and basil and adjust the seasoning to taste. Serve with the jasmine rice, garnished with the basil.

Lamb & Black Bean Burritos

❖ **SERVES 4** ❖

650 g/1 lb 5 oz lean lamb
3 garlic cloves, finely chopped
juice of 1/2 lime
1/2 tsp mild chilli powder
1/2 tsp ground cumin
pinch of dried oregano
1–2 tbsp extra virgin olive oil

400 g/14 oz cooked or canned
black beans, seasoned with
cumin, salt and pepper
4 large flour tortillas
3 tbsp chopped fresh coriander
salsa of your choice
salt and pepper

❖ Slice the lamb into thin strips, then combine with the garlic, lime juice, chilli powder, cumin, oregano and olive oil. Season with salt and pepper. Set aside to marinate in the refrigerator for 4 hours.

❖ Warm the black beans with a little water in a saucepan.

❖ Heat the tortillas in an ungreased non-stick frying pan, sprinkling them with a few drops of water as they heat; wrap the tortillas in a clean tea towel as you work to keep them warm. Alternatively, heat through in a stack in the pan, alternating the top and bottom tortillas so that they warm evenly.

❖ Stir-fry the lamb in a heavy-based non-stick frying pan over a high heat until browned on all sides. Remove from the heat.

❖ Spoon some of the beans and lamb into a tortilla, sprinkle with coriander, then top with salsa and roll up. Repeat with the remaining tortillas and serve immediately.

Salmon with Pineapple

❖ **SERVES 4** ❖

100 g/3 1/2 oz baby sweetcorn
2 tbsp sunflower oil
1 red onion, sliced
1 orange pepper, deseeded
and sliced
1 green pepper, deseeded
and sliced
450 g/1 lb salmon fillet,
skinned

1 tbsp paprika
225 g/8 oz canned cubed
pineapple in natural juice,
drained
100 g/3 1/2 oz beansprouts
2 tbsp tomato ketchup
2 tbsp soy sauce
2 tbsp medium sherry
1 tsp cornflour

❖ Cut each piece of sweetcorn in half. Heat the oil in a large preheated wok. Add the onion, peppers and sweetcorn to the wok and stir-fry for 5 minutes.

❖ Rinse the salmon fillet under cold running water and pat dry with kitchen paper.

❖ Cut the salmon flesh into thin strips and place in a large bowl. Sprinkle with the paprika and toss well to coat.

❖ Add the salmon to the wok together with the pineapple and stir-fry for a further 2–3 minutes or until the fish is tender.

❖ Add the beansprouts to the wok and toss well.

❖ Mix together the tomato ketchup, soy sauce, sherry and cornflour. Add to the wok and cook until the juices start to thicken. Transfer to warmed serving plates and serve immediately.

Thai Spiced Salmon

2.5-cm/1-inch piece of root
ginger, grated
1 tsp coriander seeds, crushed
1/4 tsp chilli powder
1 tbsp lime juice
1 tsp sesame oil
4 salmon fillets with skin, about
150 g/5 1/2 oz each
2 tbsp vegetable oil
boiled rice and stir-fried
vegetables, to serve

❖ Combine the ginger, coriander, chilli powder, lime juice and sesame oil.

❖ Place the salmon in a wide, non-metallic dish or on a plate and spoon the mixture over the flesh side of the fillets, spreading it to coat each piece of salmon evenly.

❖ Cover the dish with clingfilm and chill the salmon in the refrigerator for 30 minutes.

❖ Heat a wide, heavy-based frying pan or griddle pan with the oil over a high heat. Place the salmon on the hot pan, skin side down.

❖ Cook the salmon for 4–5 minutes, without turning, until it is crusty underneath and the flesh flakes easily. Serve immediately with the boiled rice and stir-fried vegetables.

Salmon with Red Curry

4 salmon steaks, about 175 g/6 oz each
2 banana leaves, halved
1 garlic clove, crushed
1 tsp grated fresh root ginger
1 tbsp Thai red curry paste
1 tbsp soft light brown sugar
1 tbsp Thai fish sauce
2 tbsp lime juice
lime wedges and finely chopped fresh red chilli, to garnish

❊ Place a salmon steak on the centre of each half banana leaf.

❊ Combine the garlic, ginger, curry paste, sugar and fish sauce. Spread this mixture evenly over the surface of each steak and sprinkle with lime juice.

❊ Wrap the banana leaves around the fish, tucking in the sides as you go to make a neat, compact bundle. Alternatively, use baking paper or foil.

❊ Place the parcels seam side down on a baking tray and bake in a preheated oven, 220°C/425°F/Gas Mark 7, for 15–20 minutes until the fish is cooked and the banana leaves are beginning to brown. Serve garnished with the lime wedges and chopped chilli.

Fragrant Tuna Steaks

4 tuna steaks, 175 g/6 oz each
$1/2$ tsp finely grated lime rind
1 garlic clove, crushed
2 tsp olive oil
1 tsp ground cumin
1 tsp ground coriander
pepper
1 tbsp lime juice
chopped fresh coriander, to garnish

TO SERVE
avocado relish
lime wedges
tomato wedges

❊ Trim the skin from the tuna steaks, then rinse and pat dry on absorbent kitchen paper.

❊ In a small bowl, mix together the lime rind, garlic, olive oil, cumin, ground coriander and pepper to make a paste.

❊ Spread the paste thinly on both sides of the tuna. Heat a non-stick griddle pan until hot and press the tuna steaks into the pan to seal them. Reduce the heat and cook for 5 minutes. Turn the fish over and cook for a further 4–5 minutes until cooked through. Drain on kitchen paper and transfer to a serving plate.

❊ Sprinkle the lime juice and chopped coriander over the fish. Serve with the avocado relish and lime and tomato wedges.

Sweet & Sour Tuna

❊ **SERVES 4** ❊

4 fresh tuna steaks, about
500 g/1 lb 2 oz total weight
¼ tsp pepper
2 tbsp groundnut oil
1 onion, diced
1 small red pepper, deseeded
and cut into thin batons
1 garlic clove, crushed
½ cucumber, deseeded and
cut into thin batons

2 pineapple slices, diced
1 tsp finely chopped
root ginger
1 tbsp soft light brown sugar
1 tbsp cornflour
1½ tbsp lime juice
1 tbsp Thai fish sauce
250 ml/9 fl oz fish stock
lime and cucumber slices,
to garnish

❊ Sprinkle the tuna steaks with pepper on both sides. Heat a heavy frying pan or griddle pan and brush with a little of the oil. Cook the tuna steaks for about 8 minutes, turning them over once.

❊ Heat the remaining oil in another frying pan and gently cook the onion, red pepper and garlic for 3–4 minutes to soften.

❊ Turn off the heat and stir in the cucumber, pineapple, ginger and sugar.

❊ Blend the cornflour with the lime juice and fish sauce, then stir into the stock and add to the pan. Stir over a medium heat until boiling, then cook for 1–2 minutes until thickened and clear.

❊ Spoon the sauce over the tuna and serve immediately, garnished with the lime slices and cucumber.

Maltese Swordfish

❊ **SERVES 4** ❊

1 tbsp fennel seeds
2 tbsp extra virgin olive oil,
plus extra for brushing
and drizzling
2 large onions, thinly sliced
1 small garlic clove, crushed
4 swordfish steaks,
about 175 g/6 oz each

1 large lemon, halved
2 large tomatoes, finely
chopped
4 sprigs fresh thyme
salt and pepper

❊ Place the fennel seeds in a dry frying pan over a medium–high heat and toast, stirring constantly, until they give off their aroma. Watch carefully, as they can easily burn. Immediately tip the seeds out of the pan on to a plate. Set aside.

❊ Heat 2 tablespoons of the oil in the pan. Add the onions and cook over a low heat, stirring occasionally, for 5 minutes. Add the garlic and continue to cook until the onions are very soft and tender, but not brown. Remove the pan from the heat.

❊ Cut out 4 x 30-cm/12-inch circles of baking paper. Very lightly brush the centre of each paper circle with oil. Divide the onions equally between the paper circles, flattening them out to about the size of the fish steaks.

❊ Top the onions in each parcel with a swordfish steak. Squeeze lemon juice over the fish steaks and drizzle with a little olive oil. Sprinkle the tomatoes and fennel seeds over the top, add a sprig of thyme to each swordfish steak and season to taste with salt and pepper.

❊ Fold the edges of the paper together tightly. Place on a baking tray and cook in a preheated oven, 200°C/400°F/ Gas Mark 6, for 20 minutes.

❊ To test if the fish is cooked, open 1 parcel and pierce the flesh with a knife – it should flake easily. Serve straight from the paper parcels.

Swordfish Steaks

4 swordfish steaks,
about 150 g/5¹/₂ oz each
4 tbsp olive oil
1 garlic clove, crushed
1 tsp lemon rind
lemon wedges, to garnish

SALSA VERDE
25 g/1 oz flat-leaf parsley
leaves
15 g/¹/₂ oz mixed fresh herbs,
such as basil, mint and chives
1 garlic clove, chopped
1 tbsp capers, drained
and rinsed
1 tbsp green peppercorns
in brine, drained
4 anchovies in oil, drained
and roughly chopped
1 tsp Dijon mustard
125 ml/4 fl oz extra virgin
olive oil
salt and pepper

❧ Wash and dry the swordfish steaks and place in a non-metallic dish. Combine the olive oil, garlic and lemon rind. Pour over the swordfish steaks and set aside to marinate for 2 hours.

❧ For the salsa verde, put all the ingredients into a food processor or blender. Process to a smooth paste, adding a little warm water if necessary.

❧ Remove the swordfish steaks from the marinade. Cook in a preheated griddle pan for 2–3 minutes each side until tender. Serve immediately with the salsa verde, garnished with the lemon wedges.

Cajun Spiced Fish

❉ SERVES 4 ❉

1 tbsp lime juice
2 tbsp low-fat natural yogurt
4 swordfish steaks,
about 175 g/6 oz each
sunflower or corn oil,
for brushing
lemon wedges, to serve

SPICE MIX
1 tsp paprika
1 tsp cayenne pepper
1 tsp ground cumin
1 tsp mustard powder
1 tsp dried oregano

❉ First make the spice mix by blending all the ingredients in a bowl. Mix the lime juice and yogurt in a separate bowl.

❉ Pat the fish steaks dry with kitchen paper, then brush both sides with the yogurt mixture. Use your hands to coat both sides of the fish with the spice mix, rubbing it well into the flesh.

❉ Brush a griddle pan with a little sunflower oil. Add the fish steaks and cook for 5 minutes over a medium heat, then turn over and cook for a further 4 minutes or until the flesh flakes easily when tested with a fork. Serve straight from the pan with the lemon wedges.

Mediterranean Monkfish

❉ SERVES 4–6 ❉

600 g/1 lb 4 oz cherry
tomatoes, a mixture of yellow
and red, if available
2 monkfish fillets,
about 350 g/12 oz each

8 tbsp pesto
salt and pepper
sprigs of fresh basil, to garnish
new potatoes, to serve

❉ Cut the tomatoes in half and scatter, cut sides up, on the base of an ovenproof serving dish. Set aside.

❉ Using your fingers, rub off the thin grey membrane that covers monkfish.

❉ If the skin has not been removed, place the fish skin side down on the work surface. Loosen enough skin at one end of the fillet so you can grip it. Work from the front to the back. Insert the knife, almost flat, and, using a gentle sawing action, remove the skin. Rinse the fillets well and pat dry with kitchen paper.

❉ Place the fillets on top of the tomatoes, tucking the thin end under, if necessary. Spread 4 tablespoons of the pesto over each fillet and season with pepper.

❉ Cover the dish tightly with foil, shiny side down. Place in a preheated oven, 230°C/450°F/Gas Mark 8, and roast for 16–18 minutes until the fish is cooked through, the flesh flakes easily and the tomatoes are collapsing into a thick sauce.

❉ Adjust the seasoning, if necessary. Garnish with the basil and serve immediately with the new potatoes.

Stuffed Monkfish Tail

❊ **SERVES 6** ❊

750 g/1 lb 10 oz monkfish tail, skinned and trimmed
6 slices Parma ham
4 tbsp chopped fresh mixed herbs, such as parsley, chives, basil and sage
1 tsp finely grated lemon rind
2 tbsp olive oil
salt and pepper
stir-fried vegetables and new potatoes, to serve

❊ Using a sharp knife, carefully cut down each side of the central bone of the monkfish to leave 2 fillets. Wash the fillets and pat dry with kitchen paper.

❊ Lay the Parma ham slices widthways on a clean work surface so that they overlap slightly. Lay the fish fillets lengthways on top of the ham so that the 2 cut sides face each other.

❊ Combine the herbs and lemon rind. Season well. Pack this mixture on to the cut surface of 1 monkfish fillet. Press the 2 fillets together and wrap tightly with the Parma ham slices. Secure with string or cocktail sticks.

❊ Heat the olive oil in a large ovenproof frying pan and place the fish in the pan, seam side down first, and brown the wrapped monkfish tail all over.

❊ Cook in a preheated oven, 200°C/400°F/Gas Mark 6, for 25 minutes until golden and the fish is tender. Remove from the oven and set aside to rest for 10 minutes before slicing thickly. Serve with the stir-fried vegetables and potatoes.

Spicy Monkfish Rice

❊ **SERVES 4** ❊

1 fresh hot red chilli, deseeded and chopped
1 tsp crushed chilli flakes
2 garlic cloves, chopped
pinch of saffron
3 tbsp roughly chopped fresh mint leaves
4 tbsp olive oil
2 tbsp lemon juice
375 g/12 oz monkfish fillet, cut into bite-sized pieces
1 onion, finely chopped
225 g/8 oz long-grain rice
400 g/14 oz canned chopped tomatoes
200 ml/7 fl oz coconut milk
115 g/4 oz peas
salt and pepper
2 tbsp chopped fresh coriander, to garnish

❊ Process the chilli, chill flakes, garlic, saffron, mint, olive oil and lemon juice in a food processor or blender until combined but not smooth.

❊ Put the monkfish into a non-metallic dish and pour over the spice paste, turning to coat. Cover and set aside for 20 minutes to marinate.

❊ Heat a large saucepan until very hot. Using a slotted spoon, lift the monkfish from the marinade and add, in batches, to the hot pan. Cook for 3–4 minutes until browned and firm. Remove with a slotted spoon and set aside.

❊ Add the onion and remaining marinade to the pan and cook for 5 minutes until soft and lightly browned. Add the rice and stir until well coated. Add the tomatoes and coconut milk. Bring to the boil, cover and simmer very gently for 15 minutes. Stir in the peas, season and arrange the fish over the top. Cover with foil and continue to cook over a very low heat for 5 minutes. Serve garnished with the chopped coriander.

Goan Fish Curry

750 g/1 lb 10 oz monkfish fillet,
cut into chunks
1 tbsp cider vinegar
1 tsp salt
1 tsp ground turmeric
3 tbsp vegetable oil
2 garlic cloves, crushed
1 small onion, finely chopped
2 tsp ground coriander
1 tsp cayenne pepper
2 tsp paprika
2 tbsp tamarind pulp plus
2 tbsp boiling water
85 g/3 oz creamed coconut,
cut into pieces
300 ml/10 fl oz warm water
plain boiled rice, to serve

❖ Put the fish on a plate and drizzle the vinegar over it. Combine half the salt and half the turmeric and sprinkle evenly over the fish. Cover and set aside for 20 minutes.

❖ Heat the oil in a heavy-based frying pan and add the garlic. Brown slightly, then add the onion and cook, stirring occasionally, for 3–4 minutes until soft but not brown. Add the ground coriander and stir for 1 minute.

❖ Mix the remaining turmeric, the cayenne pepper and paprika with about 2 tablespoons water to make a paste. Add to the pan and cook over a low heat for 1–2 minutes.

❖ Stir the tamarind pulp and boiling water. When thickened and the pulp has come away from the seeds, rub through a sieve. Discard the seeds.

❖ Add the coconut, warm water and tamarind paste to the pan and stir until the coconut has dissolved. Add the fish and any juices on the plate and simmer gently for 4–5 minutes until the sauce has thickened and the fish is just tender. Serve on a bed of plain boiled rice.

Whole Sea Bass with Ginger

800 g/1 lb 12 oz whole sea bass, cleaned and scaled
4 tbsp light soy sauce
5 spring onions, cut into long, fine shreds
2 tbsp finely shredded root ginger
4 tbsp fresh coriander leaves
5 tsp sunflower oil
1 tsp sesame oil
4 tbsp hot fish stock
steamed rice, to serve
lime wedges, to garnish

❄ Wash the fish and pat dry with kitchen paper. Brush all over with 2 tablespoons of the soy sauce. Sprinkle half the spring onions and all the ginger over a steaming tray or large plate and put the fish on top.

❄ Half fill a large saucepan with water and fit a steamer on top. Bring the water to the boil. Put the steaming plate with the sea bass into the steamer and cover with a tight-fitting lid. Keeping the water boiling, steam the fish for 10–12 minutes until tender and cooked through.

❄ Carefully remove the plate and lift the fish on to a serving platter, leaving behind the spring onions and ginger. Scatter over the remaining spring onions and coriander leaves.

❄ Put the sunflower oil into a small pan and heat until almost smoking. Add the sesame oil and immediately pour the mixture over the fish and spring onions. Mix the remaining soy sauce with the fish stock and pour this over the fish. Serve immediately with the steamed rice, garnished with the lime wedges.

Baked Sea Bass

1.4 kg/3 lb fresh sea bass or 2 x 750 g/1 lb 10 oz sea bass, gutted
2–4 sprigs fresh rosemary
1/2 lemon, thinly sliced
2 tbsp olive oil
bay leaves and lemon wedges, to garnish

GARLIC SAUCE
2 tsp coarse sea salt
2 tsp capers
2 garlic cloves, crushed
4 tbsp water
2 fresh bay leaves
1 tsp lemon juice or wine vinegar
2 tbsp olive oil
pepper

❄ Scrape off the scales from the fish and cut off the sharp fins. Make diagonal cuts along both sides. Wash and dry thoroughly. Place a sprig of rosemary in the cavity of each of the smaller fish with half the lemon slices, or put two sprigs and all the lemon in the large fish.

❄ Place the fish in a foil-lined dish or roasting tin brushed with oil, and brush the fish with the rest of the oil. Cook in a preheated oven, 190°C/375°F/Gas Mark 5, for 30 minutes for the small fish or 45–50 minutes for the large fish, until the thickest part of the fish is opaque.

❄ To make the garlic sauce, crush the salt and capers with the garlic in a mortar with a pestle and then work in the water. Alternatively, work in a food processor or blender until smooth.

❄ Bruise the bay leaves and remaining sprigs of rosemary and put into a bowl. Add the garlic mixture, lemon juice or vinegar and oil and pound together until the flavours are released. Season to taste with pepper.

❄ Place the fish on a serving dish and, if liked, remove the skin. Spoon some of the sauce over the fish and serve the rest separately. Garnish with fresh bay leaves and lemon wedges.

Grilled Stuffed Sole

1 tbsp olive oil	1 tbsp lemon juice
25 g/1 oz butter	4 small whole sole, gutted
1 small onion, finely chopped	and cleaned
1 garlic clove, chopped	salt and pepper
3 sun-dried tomatoes, chopped	lemon wedges, to garnish
2 tbsp lemon thyme	fresh green salad leaves,
50 g/1¾ oz breadcrumbs	to serve

❊ Heat the oil and butter in a frying pan until it just begins to froth.

❊ Add the onion and garlic to the frying pan and cook, stirring, for 5 minutes until just soft.

❊ To make the stuffing, mix the tomatoes, thyme, breadcrumbs and lemon juice in a bowl, and season.

❊ Add the stuffing mixture to the pan, and stir to mix.

❊ Using a sharp knife, pare the skin from the bone inside the gut hole of the fish to make a pocket. Spoon the tomato and herb stuffing into the pocket.

❊ Cook the fish under a preheated grill for 6 minutes on each side or until golden brown.

❊ Transfer the stuffed fish to serving plates and garnish with the lemon wedges. Serve immediately with the salad leaves.

Sole Florentine

600 ml/1 pint milk	300 ml/10 fl oz double cream
2 strips of lemon rind	pinch of freshly grated nutmeg
2 tsp fresh tarragon	450 g/1 lb fresh spinach
1 bay leaf	4 x 750 g/1 lb 10 oz Dover sole,
½ onion, sliced	quarter-cut fillets (2 from
2 tbsp butter, plus extra	each side of the fish)
for greasing	salt and pepper
4 tbsp plain flour	crisp green salad and crusty
2 tsp mustard powder	bread, to serve
3 tbsp freshly grated Parmesan	
cheese	

❊ Put the milk, lemon rind, tarragon, bay leaf and onion into a saucepan and bring to the boil over a low heat. Remove from the heat and set aside for 30 minutes for the flavours to infuse.

❊ Melt the butter in a clean saucepan and stir in the flour and mustard powder. Strain the infused milk, discarding the lemon, herbs and onion. Gradually whisk in the milk until smooth. Bring to the boil over a low heat, stirring constantly until thickened. Simmer gently for 2 minutes. Remove from the heat and stir in the cheese, cream, nutmeg and seasoning. Cover the surface with clingfilm.

❊ Grease a large ovenproof dish. Blanch the spinach leaves in boiling salted water for 30 seconds. Drain and refresh under cold water. Drain and pat dry. Put the spinach in the base of the dish.

❊ Wash and dry the fish fillets. Season and roll up. Arrange on top of the spinach and pour over the cheese sauce. Transfer to a preheated oven, 200°C/400°F/Gas Mark 6, and cook for 35 minutes until bubbling and golden. Serve immediately with a crisp green salad and crusty bread.

Fresh Baked Sardines

2 tbsp olive oil
2 large onions, sliced into rings
3 garlic cloves, chopped
2 large courgettes,
cut into sticks
3 tbsp fresh thyme,
stalks removed
8 sardine fillets or about
1 kg/2 lb 4 oz whole
sardines, filleted
75 g/2¾ oz Parmesan
cheese, grated
4 eggs, beaten
150 ml/5 fl oz milk
salt and pepper

❄ Heat 1 tablespoon of the oil in a frying pan. Add the onions and garlic and sauté for 2–3 minutes.

❄ Add the courgettes to the pan and cook for about 5 minutes or until golden.

❄ Stir 2 tablespoons of the thyme into the mixture.

❄ Place half of the onions and courgettes in the base of a large ovenproof dish. Top with the sardine fillets and half the cheese.

❄ Place the remaining onions and courgettes on top and sprinkle with the remaining thyme.

❄ Mix the eggs and milk together in a bowl and season to taste with salt and pepper. Pour the mixture over the vegetables and sardines in the dish. Sprinkle the remaining cheese over the top.

❄ Bake in a preheated oven, 180°C/350°F/Gas Mark 4, for 20–25 minutes or until golden and set. Serve hot, straight from the oven.

Spicy Prawns

❖ **SERVES 4** ❖

2 tbsp corn oil
1 onion
2 cloves garlic, crushed
1 tsp cumin seeds
1 tbsp demerara sugar
400 g/14 oz canned chopped tomatoes
1 tbsp sun-dried tomato purée
1 tbsp chopped fresh basil
450 g/1 lb peeled king prawns
salt and pepper

❖ Heat the corn oil in a large preheated wok.

❖ Using a sharp knife, finely chop the onion. Add the onion and crushed garlic to the wok and stir-fry for 2–3 minutes, or until soft.

❖ Stir in the cumin seeds and stir-fry for 1 minute.

❖ Add the sugar, chopped tomatoes and tomato purée to the wok.

❖ Bring the mixture to the boil, then reduce the heat and leave the sauce to simmer for 10 minutes.

❖ Add the basil and prawns to the mixture in the wok. Season to taste with salt and pepper.

❖ Increase the heat and cook for a further 2–3 minutes or until the prawns are completely cooked through. Transfer to a warmed serving dish and serve immediately.

Prawn Bhuna

❖ **SERVES 4–6** ❖

2 dried red chillies, deseeded, if liked
3 fresh green chillies, finely chopped
1 tsp ground turmeric
1/2 tsp pepper
1 tsp paprika
3 garlic cloves, crushed
2 tsp white wine vinegar
1/2 tsp salt
500 g/1 lb 2 oz uncooked peeled king prawns
3 tbsp oil
1 onion, very finely chopped
175 ml/6 fl oz water
2 tbsp lemon juice
2 tsp garam masala
fresh coriander, to garnish

❖ Combine the chillies, spices, garlic, vinegar and salt in a non-metallic bowl. Stir in the prawns and set aside for 10 minutes.

❖ Heat the oil in a large frying pan or wok, add the onion and cook, stirring occasionally, for 3–4 minutes until soft.

❖ Add the prawns and the spice mixture to the pan and stir-fry over a high heat for 2 minutes. Reduce the heat, add the water and boil for 10 minutes, stirring occasionally, until the water has evaporated and the curry is fragrant.

❖ Stir in the lemon juice and garam masala, then transfer the mixture to a warmed serving dish and garnish with the coriander. Serve immediately.

Curried Prawn Noodles

225 g/8 oz rice noodles
4 tbsp vegetable oil
1 onion, sliced
2 ham slices, shredded
2 tbsp Chinese curry powder
150 ml/5 fl oz fish stock
225 g/8 oz peeled raw prawns
2 garlic cloves, crushed

6 spring onions, chopped
1 tbsp light soy sauce
2 tbsp hoisin sauce
1 tbsp dry sherry
2 tsp lime juice
freshly snipped chives,
to garnish

❉ Bring a saucepan of lightly salted water to the boil and cook the noodles for 3–4 minutes. Drain well, rinse under cold water and drain again.

❉ Heat 2 tablespoons of the oil in a wok. Add the onion and ham and stir-fry for 1 minute. Add the curry powder and stir-fry for a further 30 seconds.

❉ Stir the noodles and fish stock into the wok and cook for 2–3 minutes. Remove the noodles from the wok and keep warm.

❉ Heat the remaining oil in the wok. Add the prawns, garlic and spring onions and stir-fry for about 1 minute.

❉ Stir in the remaining ingredients. Pour the mixture over the noodles, toss to mix and garnish with fresh chives.

Jambalaya

2 tbsp vegetable oil
2 onions, roughly chopped
1 green pepper, deseeded and
roughly chopped
2 celery sticks,
roughly chopped
3 garlic cloves, finely chopped
2 tsp paprika
300 g/10 1/2 oz skinless,
boneless chicken breasts,
chopped
100 g/3 1/2 oz kabanos
sausages, chopped

3 tomatoes, peeled and
chopped
450 g/1 lb long-grain rice
850 ml/1 1/2 pints hot chicken
or fish stock
1 tsp dried oregano
2 bay leaves
12 large prawn tails
4 spring onions, finely chopped
2 tbsp chopped fresh parsley
salt and pepper
salad, to serve

❉ Heat the vegetable oil in a large frying pan and add the onions, pepper, celery and garlic. Cook over a low heat, stirring occasionally, for about 8–10 minutes until all the vegetables have softened. Add the paprika and cook for a further 30 seconds. Add the chicken and sausages and cook for 8–10 minutes until lightly browned. Add the tomatoes and cook for 2–3 minutes until collapsed.

❉ Add the rice to the pan and stir well. Pour in the hot stock and stir in the oregano and bay leaves. Cover and simmer for 10 minutes over a very low heat.

❉ Add the prawns and stir well. Cover again and cook for a further 6–8 minutes until the rice is tender and the prawns are cooked through.

❉ Stir in the spring onions and parsley and season to taste. Serve with salad.

Seafood Medley

2 tbsp dry white wine
1 egg white, lightly beaten
^{1}/2 tsp Chinese five-spice
powder
1 tsp cornflour
300 g/10^1/2 oz raw prawns,
peeled and deveined
125 g/4^1/2 oz prepared squid,
cut into rings
125 g/4^1/2 oz white fish fillets,
cut into strips
vegetable oil, for deep-frying
1 green pepper, deseeded and
cut into thin strips
1 carrot, cut into thin strips
4 baby sweetcorn cobs, halved
lengthways

❖ Mix the wine, egg white, five-spice powder and cornflour in a large bowl. Add the prawns, squid rings and fish fillets and stir to coat evenly. Remove the fish and seafood with a slotted spoon, reserving any leftover cornflour mixture.

❖ Heat the oil in a preheated wok and deep-fry the prawns, squid and fish for 2–3 minutes. Remove the seafood mixture from the wok with a slotted spoon and set aside.

❖ Pour off all but 1 tablespoon of oil from the wok and return to the heat. Add the pepper, carrot and sweetcorn and stir-fry for 4–5 minutes.

❖ Return the seafood to the wok with any remaining cornflour mixture. Heat through, stirring, and serve.

Prawns in Red Curry Sauce

1 tbsp vegetable oil	2 tbsp Thai red curry paste
6 spring onions, sliced	1 tbsp Thai fish sauce
1 lemon grass stalk	500 g/1 lb 2 oz raw king
1-cm/$\frac{1}{2}$-inch piece of	prawns
root ginger	1 tbsp chopped fresh coriander
250 ml/9 fl oz coconut milk	fresh chillies, to garnish

❈ Heat the vegetable oil in a wok or large frying pan. Add the spring onions and cook gently for about 2 minutes until soft.

❈ Bruise the lemon grass using a meat mallet or rolling pin. Peel and finely grate the ginger.

❈ Add the lemon grass and ginger to the wok or frying pan with the coconut milk, Thai red curry paste and Thai fish sauce. Heat gently until the coconut milk is almost boiling.

❈ Peel the prawns, leaving the tails intact. Remove the black vein along the back of each prawn.

❈ Add the prawns to the wok with the coriander and cook gently for 5 minutes.

❈ Transfer the prawns with the sauce to a warmed serving bowl, garnish with the chillies and serve immediately.

Squid & Macaroni Stew

225 g/8 oz dried short-cut	350 g/12 oz tomatoes, peeled
macaroni or other small	and thinly sliced
pasta shapes	2 tbsp tomato purée
7 tbsp olive oil	1 tsp dried oregano
2 onions, sliced	2 bay leaves
350 g/12 oz prepared squid,	2 tbsp chopped fresh parsley
cut into 4-cm/1$\frac{1}{2}$-inch strips	salt and pepper
225 ml/8 fl oz fish stock	fresh crusty bread, to serve
150 ml/5 fl oz red wine	

❈ Bring a large saucepan of lightly salted water to the boil. Add the pasta and 1 tablespoon of the olive oil and cook for 3 minutes. Drain, return to the pan, cover and keep warm.

❈ Heat the remaining oil in a saucepan over a medium heat. Add the onions and fry until they are translucent. Add the squid and stock and simmer for 5 minutes. Pour in the wine and add the tomatoes, tomato purée, oregano and bay leaves. Bring the sauce to the boil, season to taste and cook for 5 minutes.

❈ Stir the pasta into the pan, cover and simmer for about 10 minutes, or until the squid and macaroni are tender and the sauce has thickened. If the sauce remains too liquid, uncover the pan and continue cooking for a few minutes longer.

❈ Remove and discard the bay leaves. Reserve a little parsley and stir the remainder into the pan. Transfer to a warmed serving dish and sprinkle over the remaining parsley. Serve with the bread to soak up the sauce.

Seafood Risotto

❖ **SERVES 4** ❖

1.2 litres/2 pints hot fish or chicken stock
350 g/12 oz arborio rice, washed
50 g/1¾ oz butter
2 garlic cloves, chopped

250 g/9 oz mixed seafood, preferably raw, such as prawns, squid, mussels, clams and shrimps
2 tbsp chopped oregano, plus extra to garnish
50 g/1¾ oz pecorino or Parmesan cheese, grated

❖ In a large saucepan, bring the stock to the boil. Add the rice and cook, stirring, for about 12 minutes or until the rice is tender. Drain thoroughly, reserving any excess liquid.

❖ Heat the butter in a large frying pan and add the garlic, stirring.

❖ Add the raw mixed seafood to the pan and cook for 5 minutes. If you are using cooked seafood, fry for 2–3 minutes.

❖ Stir the oregano into the seafood mixture in the frying pan.

❖ Add the cooked rice to the pan and cook for 2–3 minutes, stirring, or until hot. Add the reserved stock if the mixture gets too sticky.

❖ Add the cheese and mix well.

❖ Transfer the risotto to warmed serving dishes and serve immediately.

Prawn & Asparagus Risotto

❖ **SERVES 4** ❖

1.2 litres/2 pints vegetable stock
375 g/12 oz asparagus, cut into 5-cm/2-inch lengths
2 tbsp olive oil
1 onion, finely chopped
1 garlic clove, finely chopped
375 g/12 oz arborio rice

450 g/1 lb raw tiger prawns, peeled and deveined
2 tbsp olive paste or tapenade
2 tbsp chopped fresh basil
salt and pepper
Parmesan cheese shavings, to garnish

❖ Bring the vegetable stock to the boil in a large saucepan. Add the asparagus and cook for 3 minutes until just tender. Strain, reserving the stock, and refresh the asparagus under cold running water. Drain and set aside.

❖ Heat the oil in a large heavy-based frying pan. Add the onion and cook over a low heat, stirring occasionally, for 5 minutes until soft. Add the garlic and cook for a further 30 seconds. Add the rice and cook, stirring constantly, for about 1–2 minutes until coated with the oil and slightly translucent.

❖ Keep the stock on a low heat. Increase the heat under the frying pan to medium and begin adding the stock, a ladleful at a time, stirring well between additions. Continue until almost all the stock has been absorbed. This should take 20–25 minutes.

❖ Add the prawns and asparagus with the last ladleful of stock and cook for a further 5 minutes until the prawns and the rice are tender and the stock has been absorbed. Remove from the heat.

❖ Stir in the olive paste, basil and seasoning and set aside for 1 minute. Serve immediately, garnished with the cheese shavings.

Crab Risotto

❖ **SERVES 4–6** ❖

2–3 large red peppers
3 tbsp olive oil
1 onion, finely chopped
1 small fennel bulb, finely chopped
2 celery sticks, finely chopped
¼–½ tsp cayenne pepper
350 g/12 oz arborio or carnaroli rice
800 g/1 lb 12 oz canned Italian peeled plum tomatoes, drained and chopped
50 ml/2 fl oz dry white vermouth (optional)
1.5 litres/2¾ pints fish or chicken stock, simmering
450 g/1 lb fresh cooked crabmeat
50 ml/2 fl oz lemon juice
2–4 tbsp chopped fresh parsley or chervil
salt and pepper

❖ Grill the peppers until the skins are charred. Transfer to a polythene bag and twist to seal. When cool enough to handle, peel off the charred skins, working over a bowl to catch the juices. Remove the cores and seeds. Chop the flesh and set aside, reserving the juices.

❖ Heat the olive oil in a large heavy-based saucepan. Add the onion, fennel and celery and cook over a low heat, stirring occasionally, for 2–3 minutes until the vegetables are soft. Add the cayenne pepper and rice and cook, stirring frequently, for about 2 minutes until the rice is translucent and well coated.

❖ Stir in the chopped tomatoes and vermouth, if using. The liquid will bubble and steam rapidly. When the liquid is almost absorbed, add a ladleful (about 225 ml/8 fl oz) of the simmering stock. Cook, stirring constantly, until the liquid is completely absorbed.

❖ Continue adding the stock, about half a ladleful at a time, allowing each addition to be absorbed before adding the next. This should take 20–25 minutes. The risotto should have a creamy consistency and the rice should be tender but still firm to the bite.

❖ Stir in the peppers and their reserved juices, the crabmeat, lemon juice and parsley and heat. Season to taste with salt and pepper. Serve the risotto immediately.

Thai Steamed Mussels

❁ **SERVES 2** ❁

1 kg/2 lb 4 oz fresh mussels in their shells
2 shallots, finely chopped
1 lemon grass stalk, thinly sliced
1 garlic clove, finely chopped
3 tbsp Chinese rice wine or sherry
2 tbsp lime juice
1 tbsp Thai fish sauce
2 tbsp butter
4 tbsp chopped fresh basil
salt and pepper
fresh basil leaves, to garnish
crusty bread, to serve

❁ Scrub the mussels, removing any beards. Rinse them under cold running water and lightly scrub to remove any sand from the shells. Using a small sharp knife, remove the beards from the shells. Discard any that do not close when tapped or that have damaged shells.

❁ Place the shallots, lemon grass, garlic, rice wine, lime juice and fish sauce in a large saucepan and place over a high heat.

❁ Add the mussels, cover and steam for about 2–3 minutes, shaking the pan occasionally during cooking until the mussel shells open.

❁ Discard any mussels that have not opened, then stir in the chopped basil and season with salt and pepper.

❁ Lift out the mussels with a slotted spoon and divide between 2 deep bowls. Quickly whisk the butter into the pan juices until incorporated, then pour the juices over the mussels.

❁ Garnish each bowl with fresh basil leaves and serve with plenty of crusty bread to mop up the juices.

Mussels Marinara

❁ **SERVES 4** ❁

2 kg/4 lb 8 oz fresh mussels
4 tbsp olive oil
4–6 large garlic cloves, halved
800 g/1 lb 12 oz canned chopped tomatoes
300 ml/10 fl oz dry white wine
2 tbsp finely chopped fresh flat-leaf parsley, plus extra to garnish
1 tbsp finely chopped fresh oregano
salt and pepper
French bread, to serve

❁ Scrub the mussels, removing any beards. Rinse them under cold running water and lightly scrub to remove any sand from the shells. Using a small sharp knife, remove the beards from the shells. Discard any that do not close when tapped or that have damaged shells. Rinse the mussels again, then set aside in a colander.

❁ Heat the olive oil in a large saucepan over a medium–high heat. Add the garlic and cook, stirring, for about 3 minutes. Using a slotted spoon, remove the garlic from the pan.

❁ Add the tomatoes and their juice, the wine, parsley and oregano and bring to the boil, stirring. Reduce the heat, cover and simmer for 5 minutes to allow the flavours to blend.

❁ Add the mussels, cover the pan and simmer for 5–8 minutes, shaking the pan regularly, until the mussels open. Using a draining spoon, transfer the mussels to serving bowls, discarding any that remain closed.

❁ Season the sauce with salt and pepper to taste. Ladle the sauce over the mussels, sprinkle with the extra chopped parsley and serve immediately with plenty of the French bread to mop up the delicious juices.

Mexican Pan-Fried Scallops

❖ **SERVES 4–8** ❖

2 tbsp butter
2 tbsp extra virgin olive oil
650 g/1 lb 7 oz scallops,
shelled
4–5 spring onions, thinly sliced
3–4 garlic cloves,
finely chopped

½ fresh green chilli, deseeded
and finely chopped
2 tbsp finely chopped
fresh coriander
juice of ½ lime
salt and pepper
lime wedges, to serve

❖ Heat half the butter and olive oil in a heavy-based frying pan until the butter foams.

❖ Add the scallops and cook quickly until just turning opaque; do not overcook. Remove from the pan with a slotted spoon and keep warm.

❖ Add the remaining butter and oil to the pan, then toss in the spring onions and garlic and cook over a medium heat until the spring onions are wilted. Return the scallops to the pan.

❖ Remove the pan from the heat and add the chopped chilli and coriander. Squeeze in the lime juice. Season to taste with salt and pepper and stir to mix well.

❖ Serve immediately with the lime wedges for squeezing over the scallops.

Spicy Lime Scallops

❖ **SERVES 4** ❖

16 large scallops
1 tbsp butter
1 tbsp vegetable oil
1 tsp crushed garlic
1 tsp grated fresh root ginger
1 bunch of spring onions,
thinly sliced

finely grated rind of
1 kaffir lime
1 small fresh red chilli,
deseeded and
very finely chopped
3 tbsp kaffir lime juice
lime wedges and boiled
rice, to serve

❖ Trim the scallops, then wash and pat dry. Separate the corals from the white parts, then horizontally slice each white part in half, making 2 rounds.

❖ Heat the butter and oil in a frying pan or wok. Add the garlic and ginger and stir-fry for 1 minute without browning. Add the spring onions and stir-fry for a further minute.

❖ Add the scallops and stir-fry over a high heat for 4–5 minutes. Stir in the lime rind, chilli and lime juice and cook for a further minute.

❖ Serve the scallops hot, with the juices spooned over them, accompanied by the lime wedges and boiled rice.

Fettuccine with Walnut Sauce

2 thick slices wholemeal bread,
crusts removed
300 ml/10 fl oz milk
275 g/9¹/2 oz shelled walnuts
2 garlic cloves, crushed
115 g/4 oz stoned black olives
55 g/2 oz freshly grated
Parmesan cheese
8 tbsp extra virgin olive oil
150 ml/5 fl oz double cream
450 g/1 lb fresh fettuccine
salt and pepper
2–3 tbsp chopped fresh parsley

❋ Put the bread in a shallow dish, pour over the milk and set aside to soak until the liquid has been absorbed.

❋ Spread out the walnuts on a baking tray and toast in a preheated oven, 190°C/375°F/Gas Mark 5, for about 5 minutes or until golden. Set aside to cool.

❋ Put the soaked bread, walnuts, garlic, olives, Parmesan cheese and 6 tablespoons of the olive oil in a food processor and work to make a purée. Season to taste with salt and pepper and stir in the cream.

❋ Bring a large pan of lightly salted water to the boil. Add the fettuccine and 1 tablespoon of the remaining oil and cook for 2–3 minutes, or until tender but still firm to the bite. Drain the fettuccine thoroughly and toss with the remaining olive oil.

❋ Divide the fettuccine between individual serving plates and spoon the olive, garlic and walnut sauce on top. Sprinkle over the fresh parsley and serve.

Tagliatelle with Broccoli

300 g/10½ oz dried tagliatelle tricolore (plain, spinach- and tomato-flavoured)
225 g/8 oz broccoli, broken into small florets
350g/12 oz mascarpone cheese
125 g/4½ oz blue cheese, chopped
1 tbsp chopped fresh oregano
25 g/1 oz butter
salt and pepper
sprigs of fresh oregano, to garnish
freshly grated Parmesan cheese, to serve

❖ Bring a saucepan of lightly salted water to the boil and cook the tagliatelle for 8–10 minutes or until just tender.

❖ Meanwhile, bring another saucepan of lightly salted water to the boil and cook the broccoli florets. Avoid overcooking the broccoli, so that it retains much of its colour and texture.

❖ Heat the mascarpone and blue cheeses together gently in a large saucepan until they are melted. Stir in the oregano and season to taste with salt and pepper.

❖ Drain the pasta thoroughly. Return it to the saucepan and add the butter, tossing the tagliatelle to coat it. Drain the broccoli well and add to the pasta with the sauce, tossing gently to mix.

❖ Divide the pasta between 4 warmed serving plates. Garnish with the sprigs of oregano and serve with the Parmesan cheese.

Pasta Provençale

3 tbsp olive oil
1 onion, sliced
2 garlic cloves, chopped
3 red peppers, deseeded and cut into strips
3 courgettes, sliced
400 g/14 oz canned chopped tomatoes
3 tbsp sun-dried tomato purée
2 tbsp chopped fresh basil
225 g/8 oz fresh pasta spirals
125 g/4½ oz grated Gruyère cheese
salt and pepper
sprigs of fresh basil, to garnish

❖ Heat the oil in a heavy-based saucepan or flameproof casserole. Add the onion and garlic and cook, stirring occasionally, until softened. Add the peppers and courgettes and fry, stirring occasionally, for 5 minutes.

❖ Add the tomatoes, sun-dried tomato purée and basil and season to taste with salt and pepper. Cover and cook for a further 5 minutes.

❖ Meanwhile, bring a large saucepan of lightly salted water to the boil and add the pasta. Stir and bring back to the boil. Reduce the heat slightly and cook, uncovered, for 3 minutes, until just tender. Drain thoroughly and add to the vegetables. Toss gently to mix well.

❖ Transfer to a shallow flameproof dish and sprinkle with the cheese.

❖ Cook under a preheated grill for 5 minutes, until the cheese is golden brown and bubbling. Garnish with the sprigs of basil and serve immediately.

Spaghetti & Mushroom Sauce

❖ SERVES 4 ❖

55 g/2 oz butter
2 tbsp olive oil
6 shallots, sliced
450 g/1 lb sliced button
mushrooms
1 tsp plain flour
150 ml/5 fl oz double cream
2 tbsp port

115 g/4 oz sun-dried
tomatoes, chopped
freshly grated nutmeg
450 g/1 lb dried spaghetti
1 tbsp freshly chopped parsley
salt and pepper
6 triangles of fried white bread,
to serve

❖ Heat the butter and 1 tablespoon of the oil in a large saucepan. Add the shallots and cook over a medium heat for 3 minutes. Add the mushrooms and cook over a low heat for 2 minutes. Season with salt and pepper, sprinkle over the flour and cook, stirring constantly, for 1 minute.

❖ Gradually stir in the cream and port, add the sun-dried tomatoes and a pinch of grated nutmeg and cook over a low heat for 8 minutes.

❖ Meanwhile, bring a large saucepan of lightly salted water to the boil. Add the spaghetti and the remaining olive oil and cook for 12–14 minutes, until the pasta tender but still firm to the bite.

❖ Drain the spaghetti and return to the pan. Pour over the mushroom sauce and cook for 3 minutes. Transfer the spaghetti and mushroom sauce to a large serving plate and sprinkle over the chopped parsley. Serve with crispy triangles of fried bread.

Vegetable Cannelloni

❖ SERVES 4 ❖

1 aubergine
125 ml/4 fl oz olive oil
225 g/8 oz spinach
2 garlic cloves, crushed
1 tsp ground cumin
85 g/3 oz mushrooms, chopped
salt and pepper
12 cannelloni tubes

TOMATO SAUCE
1 tbsp olive oil
1 onion, chopped
2 garlic cloves, crushed
800 g/1 lb 12 oz canned
chopped tomatoes
1 tsp caster sugar
2 tbsp chopped fresh basil
55 g/2 oz sliced mozzarella
cheese

❖ Cut the aubergine into small dice. Heat the oil in a frying pan. Add the aubergine and cook over a moderate heat, stirring frequently, for 2–3 minutes.

❖ Add the spinach, garlic, cumin and mushrooms and reduce the heat. Season to taste with salt and pepper and cook, stirring constantly, for 2–3 minutes. Spoon the mixture into the cannelloni tubes and place in an ovenproof dish in a single layer.

❖ To make the sauce, heat the olive oil in a saucepan and cook the onion and garlic for 1 minute. Add the tomatoes, sugar and basil and bring to the boil. Reduce the heat and simmer gently for about 5 minutes. Spoon the sauce over the cannelloni tubes.

❖ Arrange the sliced mozzarella on top of the sauce and cook in a preheated oven, 190°C/375°F/Gas Mark 5, for about 30 minutes or until the cheese is bubbling and golden brown. Serve immediately.

Penne with Three Cheeses

butter, for greasing
400 g/14 oz dried penne pasta
2 eggs, beaten
350 g/12 oz ricotta cheese
4 fresh basil sprigs
115 g/4 oz mozzarella or
halloumi cheese, grated
70 g/2½ oz Parmesan cheese,
freshly grated
salt and pepper
fresh basil leaves, to garnish
(optional)
selection of cooked vegetables,
to serve

❖ Lightly grease a large ovenproof dish with butter.

❖ Bring a saucepan of lightly salted water to the boil. Add the pasta, bring back to the boil and cook for 8–10 minutes until just tender but still firm to the bite. Drain the pasta, set aside and keep warm.

❖ Beat the eggs into the ricotta cheese and season to taste.

❖ Spoon half the pasta into the base of the prepared dish and cover with half the basil leaves.

❖ Spoon over half of the ricotta cheese mixture. Sprinkle over the mozzarella or halloumi cheese and top with the remaining basil leaves. Cover with the remaining pasta and then spoon over the remaining ricotta cheese mixture. Lightly sprinkle the Parmesan cheese over the top.

❖ Bake in a preheated oven, 190°C/375°F/Gas Mark 5, for 30–40 minutes until golden brown and the cheese topping is hot and bubbling. Garnish with the basil leaves and serve immediately with a selection of cooked vegetables.

Macaroni Cheese

225 g/8 oz dried elbow macaroni
175 g/6 oz grated Cheddar
cheese
100 g/3 1/2 oz grated Parmesan
cheese
1 tbsp butter or margarine,
plus extra for greasing
4 tbsp fresh white
breadcrumbs
1 tbsp chopped fresh basil

TOMATO SAUCE

1 tbsp olive oil
1 shallot, finely chopped
2 garlic cloves, crushed
500 g/1 lb 2 oz canned chopped
tomatoes
1 tbsp chopped fresh basil
salt and pepper

❖ To make the tomato sauce, heat the oil in a heavy-based saucepan. Add the shallots and garlic and cook, stirring constantly, for 1 minute. Add the tomatoes and basil and season to taste with salt and pepper. Cook over a medium heat, stirring constantly, for 10 minutes.

❖ Meanwhile, bring a large saucepan of lightly salted water to the boil. Add the macaroni, bring back to the boil and cook for 8 minutes or until tender but still firm to the bite. Drain well.

❖ Combine the grated Cheddar and Parmesan cheeses in a bowl. Grease a deep ovenproof dish. Spoon one-third of the tomato sauce into the base of the dish, cover with one-third of the macaroni and then top with one-third of the mixed cheeses. Season to taste with salt and pepper. Repeat these layers twice, ending with a layer of grated cheese.

❖ Combine the breadcrumbs and basil and sprinkle evenly over the top. Dot the topping with the butter and cook in a preheated oven, 190°C/ 375°F/Gas Mark 5, for 25 minutes or until the topping is golden brown and bubbling. Serve immediately.

Roasted Pepper Tart

PASTRY

175 g/6 oz plain flour
pinch of salt
75 g/2 3/4 oz butter or
margarine
2 tbsp green olives, stoned
and finely chopped
3 tbsp cold water

FILLING

1 red pepper
1 green pepper
1 yellow pepper
2 garlic cloves, crushed
2 tbsp olive oil
100 g/3 1/2 oz mozzarella
cheese, grated
2 eggs
150 ml/5 fl oz milk
1 tbsp chopped fresh basil
salt and pepper

❖ To make the pastry, sift the flour and salt into a bowl. Rub in the butter until the mixture resembles breadcrumbs. Add the chopped olives and cold water, bringing the mixture together to form a dough.

❖ Roll out the dough on a floured surface and use to line a 20-cm/8-inch loose-based flan tin. Prick the base with a fork and leave to chill.

❖ Cut the peppers in half lengthways, deseed and place, skin side upwards, on a baking tray. Mix the garlic and oil and brush over the peppers. Cook in a preheated oven, 200°C/400°F/Gas Mark 6, for 20 minutes or until beginning to char slightly.

❖ Leave the peppers to cool slightly, then thinly slice them. Arrange the slices in the pastry case, layering with the grated mozzarella cheese.

❖ Beat the eggs and milk and add the basil. Season and pour over the peppers. Put the tart on a baking tray and bake in the oven for 20 minutes, or until set. Serve hot or cold.

Cauliflower & Broccoli Tart

PASTRY	FILLING
175 g/6 oz plain flour, plus	100 g/3$\frac{1}{2}$ oz cauliflower florets
extra for dusting	100 g/3$\frac{1}{2}$ oz broccoli florets
pinch of salt	1 onion, cut into 8 wedges
$\frac{1}{2}$ tsp paprika	2 tbsp butter or margarine
1 tsp dried thyme	1 tbsp plain flour
6 tbsp margarine	6 tbsp vegetable stock
3 tbsp water	125 ml/4 fl oz milk
	85 g/3 oz Cheddar cheese, grated
	salt and pepper
	paprika, to garnish

❊ To make the pastry, sift the flour and salt into a bowl. Add the paprika and thyme and rub in the margarine. Stir in the water and bind to form a dough.

❊ Roll out the pastry on a floured surface and use to line an 18-cm/7-inch loose-based tart tin. Prick the base with a fork and line with baking paper. Fill with baking beans and bake in a preheated oven, 190°C/375°F/ Gas Mark 5, for 15 minutes. Remove the paper and beans and return the pastry case to the oven for 5 minutes.

❊ To make the filling, bring a saucepan of lightly salted water to the boil and cook the cauliflower, broccoli and onion for 10–12 minutes until tender. Drain and reserve.

❊ Melt the butter in a saucepan. Add the flour and cook, stirring constantly, for 1 minute. Remove from the heat, stir in the stock and milk and return to the heat. Bring to the boil, stirring constantly, and add 55 g/2 oz of the cheese. Season to taste with salt and pepper.

❊ Spoon the cauliflower, broccoli and onion into the pastry case. Pour over the sauce and sprinkle with the remaining grated cheese. Return the tart to the oven for 10 minutes until the cheese is golden and bubbling. Garnish with the paprika and serve immediately.

Artichoke & Cheese Tart

PASTRY	FILLING
175 g/6 oz wholemeal flour,	2 tbsp olive oil
plus extra for dusting	1 red onion, halved and sliced
pinch of salt	10 canned artichoke hearts
2 garlic cloves, crushed	100 g/3$\frac{1}{2}$ oz Cheddar cheese,
6 tbsp butter or margarine	grated
3 tbsp water	55 g/2 oz Gorgonzola cheese,
	crumbled
	2 eggs, beaten
	1 tbsp chopped fresh rosemary
	150 ml/5 fl oz milk
	salt and pepper

❊ To make the pastry, sift the flour into a mixing bowl, add a pinch of salt and the crushed garlic. Rub in the butter with your fingertips until the mixture resembles fine breadcrumbs. Stir in the water and bring the mixture together to form a dough.

❊ Roll out the pastry on a lightly floured surface to fit a 20-cm/8-inch tart tin. Prick the pastry with a fork.

❊ Heat the oil in a frying pan. Add the onion and cook over a medium heat, stirring occasionally, for 3 minutes. Add the artichoke hearts and cook, stirring frequently, for a further 2 minutes.

❊ Combine the cheeses, beaten eggs, rosemary and milk in a large bowl. Remove the artichoke and onion mixture from the pan with a slotted spoon and transfer to the cheese mixture, stirring gently. Season to taste with salt and pepper.

❊ Spoon the artichoke and cheese mixture into the pastry case and cook in a preheated oven, 200°C/400°F/Gas Mark 6, for 25 minutes or until cooked and set. Remove the tart from the oven and serve hot or cold.

Spinach & Ricotta Pie

225 g/8 oz fresh spinach
25 g/1 oz pine kernels
100 g/3$\frac{1}{2}$ oz ricotta cheese
2 large eggs, beaten
50 g/1$\frac{3}{4}$ oz ground almonds
40 g/1$\frac{1}{2}$ oz Parmesan cheese,
freshly grated
250 g/9 oz puff pastry,
thawed, if frozen
1 small egg, beaten

❀ Rinse the spinach, place in a large saucepan and cook with just the water that clings to the leaves for 4–5 minutes until wilted. Drain thoroughly. When the spinach is cool enough to handle, squeeze out the excess liquid.

❀ Place the pine kernels on a baking tray and lightly toast under a preheated grill for 2–3 minutes or until golden brown.

❀ Place the ricotta, spinach and eggs in a bowl and mix together. Add the pine kernels, beat well, then stir in the ground almonds and Parmesan cheese.

❀ Roll out the puff pastry and make 2 x 20-cm/8-inch squares. Trim the edges, reserving the pastry trimmings.

❀ Place 1 pastry square on a baking tray. Spoon over the spinach mixture to within 1 cm/$\frac{1}{2}$ inch of the edge of the pastry. Brush the edges with beaten egg and place the second square over the top.

❀ Using a round-bladed knife, press the pastry edges together by tapping along the sealed edge. Use the pastry trimmings to make a few leaves to decorate the pie.

❀ Brush the pie with the beaten egg and bake in a preheated oven, 220°C/425°F/Gas Mark 8, for 10 minutes. Reduce the oven temperature to 190°C/375°F/Gas Mark 5 and bake for a further 25–30 minutes. Serve hot.

Ratatouille

1 large aubergine,
about 300 g/10½ oz
5 tbsp olive oil
2 large onions, thinly sliced
2 large garlic cloves, crushed
4 courgettes, sliced
800 g/1 lb 12 oz canned
chopped tomatoes
1 tsp sugar

1 bouquet garni of 2 sprigs
fresh thyme, 2 large sprigs
fresh parsley, 1 sprig fresh
basil and 1 bay leaf, tied in a
7.5-cm/3-inch piece of celery
salt and pepper
fresh basil leaves, to garnish

❊ Coarsely chop the aubergine, then place in a colander. Sprinkle with salt and set aside for 30 minutes to drain. Rinse well under cold running water to remove all traces of the salt and pat dry with kitchen paper.

❊ Heat the oil in a large, heavy-based flameproof casserole over a medium heat. Add the onions, lower the heat and cook, stirring occasionally, for 10 minutes until soft and light golden brown.

❊ Add the garlic and continue to fry for 2 minutes until the onions are tender.

❊ Add the aubergine, courgettes, tomatoes, with their can juices, sugar and bouquet garni. Season to taste with salt and pepper. Bring to the boil, then reduce the heat to very low, cover and simmer for 30 minutes.

❊ Taste and adjust the seasoning if necessary. Remove and discard the bouquet garni. Garnish with the basil leaves and serve immediately.

Hearty Bean Pot

4 tbsp butter or margarine
1 large onion, chopped
2 garlic cloves, crushed
2 carrots, sliced
2 celery sticks, sliced
1 tbsp paprika
2 tsp ground cumin
400 g/14 oz canned chopped
tomatoes

425 g/15 oz canned mixed
beans, rinsed and drained
150 ml/5 fl oz vegetable stock
1 tbsp muscovado sugar or
black treacle
350 g/12 oz tofu cubes
salt and pepper
crusty French bread, to serve

❊ Melt the butter in a large flameproof casserole and cook the onion and garlic over a medium heat, stirring occasionally, for about 5 minutes, until golden brown.

❊ Add the carrots and celery and cook, stirring occasionally, for a further 2 minutes, then stir in the paprika and ground cumin.

❊ Add the tomatoes and beans. Pour in the stock and add the sugar or treacle. Bring to the boil, then reduce the heat and simmer, uncovered, stirring occasionally, for 30 minutes.

❊ Add the tofu to the casserole, cover and cook, stirring occasionally, for a further 20 minutes.

❊ Season to taste with salt and pepper, then ladle on to plates and serve with the French bread.

Provençal Bean Stew

350 g/12 oz dried pinto
beans, soaked overnight
in water to cover
2 tbsp olive oil
2 onions, sliced
2 garlic cloves, finely chopped
1 red pepper, deseeded
and sliced
1 yellow pepper, deseeded
and sliced
400 g/14 oz canned chopped
tomatoes

2 tbsp tomato purée
1 tbsp torn fresh basil leaves
2 tsp chopped fresh thyme
2 tsp chopped fresh rosemary
1 bay leaf
salt and pepper
55 g/2 oz black olives, stoned
and halved
2 tbsp chopped fresh parsley,
to garnish

❋ Drain the beans and place in a large saucepan. Add cold water to cover and bring to the boil. Boil for 15 minutes, then cover and simmer for 1¼ hours, until almost tender. Drain, reserving 300 ml/10 fl oz of the cooking liquid.

❋ Heat the olive oil in a heavy-based saucepan. Add the onions and cook, stirring occasionally, for 5 minutes, until soft. Add the garlic and peppers and cook, stirring frequently, for 10 minutes.

❋ Add the tomatoes with their can juices, the tomato purée, basil, thyme, rosemary, bay leaf and beans and season to taste with salt and pepper. Cover and simmer for 40 minutes. Add the olives and simmer for 5 minutes more.

❋ Transfer the stew to a warmed serving dish, sprinkle with the parsley and serve immediately.

Lentil Roast

225 g/8 oz red lentils
450 ml/16 fl oz vegetable stock
1 bay leaf
15 g/½ oz butter or margarine,
softened
2 tbsp dried wholemeal
breadcrumbs
225 g/8 oz mature Cheddar
cheese, grated
1 leek, finely chopped
125 g/4½ oz button
mushrooms, finely chopped

85 g/3 oz fresh wholemeal
breadcrumbs
2 tbsp chopped fresh parsley
1 tbsp lemon juice
2 eggs, lightly beaten
salt and pepper
sprigs of fresh flat-leaf parsley,
to garnish
mixed roast vegetables,
to serve

❋ Put the lentils, stock and bay leaf in a saucepan. Bring to the boil, cover and simmer gently for 15–20 minutes, until all the liquid is absorbed and the lentils have softened. Discard the bay leaf.

❋ Base-line a 1-kg/2 lb 4-oz loaf tin with baking paper. Grease with the butter or margarine and sprinkle with the dried breadcrumbs.

❋ Stir the grated cheese, chopped leek and mushrooms, breadcrumbs and parsley into the lentils.

❋ Bind the mixture together with the lemon juice and eggs. Season with salt and pepper. Spoon into the prepared loaf tin and smooth the top.

❋ Bake in a preheated oven, 190°C/ 375°F/Gas Mark 5, for about 1 hour, until golden.

❋ Loosen the loaf with a palette knife and turn out on to a warmed serving plate. Garnish with the parsley and serve sliced, with the roast vegetables.

Potato & Lemon Casserole

❖ SERVES 4 ❖

100 ml/3¹/₂ fl oz olive oil
2 red onions, cut into 8 wedges
3 garlic cloves, crushed
2 tsp ground cumin
2 tsp ground coriander
pinch of cayenne pepper
1 carrot, thickly sliced
2 small turnips, quartered
1 courgette, sliced
500 g/1 lb 2 oz potatoes,
thickly sliced
juice and rind of 2 large lemons
300 ml/10 fl oz vegetable stock
2 tbsp chopped fresh coriander
salt and pepper

❖ Heat the olive oil in a flameproof casserole. Add the onions and sauté over a medium heat, stirring frequently, for 3 minutes.

❖ Add the garlic and cook for 30 seconds. Stir in the cumin, ground coriander and cayenne and cook, stirring constantly, for 1 minute.

❖ Add the carrot, turnips, courgette and potatoes and stir to coat in the oil.

❖ Add the lemon juice and rind and the vegetable stock. Season to taste with salt and pepper. Cover and cook over a medium heat, stirring occasionally, for 20–30 minutes until tender.

❖ Remove the lid, sprinkle in the chopped fresh coriander and stir well. Serve immediately.

Vegetable & Lentil Casserole

1 onion	2 potatoes, diced
4 cloves	2 carrots, chopped
225 g/8 oz Puy or	3 courgettes, sliced
green lentils	1 celery stick, chopped
1 bay leaf	1 red pepper, deseeded and
1.5 litres/2¾ pints vegetable	chopped
stock or water	1 tbsp lemon juice
2 leeks, sliced	salt and pepper

❄ Stick the onion with the cloves. Put the lentils in a large casserole, add the onion and bay leaf and pour in the stock. Cover and bake in a preheated oven, 180°C/350°F/Gas Mark 4, for 1 hour.

❄ Remove the casserole from the oven. Take out the onion and discard the cloves. Slice the onion and return it to the casserole with the leeks, potatoes, carrots, courgettes, celery and red pepper. Stir thoroughly and season to taste with salt and pepper. Cover and return to the oven for a further hour.

❄ Remove and discard the bay leaf. Stir the lemon juice into the casserole and serve immediately, straight from the dish.

Lentil & Rice Casserole

225 g/8 oz split red lentils	1 red pepper, deseeded and
55 g/2 oz long-grain rice	sliced
1.2 litres/2 pints vegetable stock	100 g/3½ oz small broccoli
1 leek, cut into chunks	florets
3 garlic cloves, crushed	8 baby sweetcorn cobs, halved
400 g/14 oz canned chopped	lengthways
tomatoes	55 g/2 oz French beans, halved
1 tsp ground cumin	1 tbsp shredded fresh basil
1 tsp chilli powder	salt and pepper
1 tsp garam masala	sprigs of fresh basil, to garnish

❄ Place the lentils, rice and stock in a large flameproof casserole and cook over a low heat, stirring occasionally, for 20 minutes.

❄ Add the leek, garlic, tomatoes and their can juices, ground cumin, chilli powder, garam masala, sliced pepper, broccoli, sweetcorn and French beans to the pan.

❄ Bring the mixture to the boil, reduce the heat, cover and simmer for a further 10–15 minutes or until the vegetables are tender.

❄ Add the shredded basil and season with salt and pepper to taste.

❄ Garnish with the sprigs of basil and serve immediately.

Mushroom & Cheese Risotto

❊ **SERVES 4** ❊

2 tbsp olive or vegetable oil
225 g/8 oz arborio rice
2 garlic cloves, crushed
1 onion, chopped
2 celery sticks, chopped
1 red or green pepper,
deseeded and chopped
225 g/8 oz mushrooms, sliced
1 tbsp chopped fresh oregano
or 1 tsp dried oregano
1 litre/1¾ pints vegetable stock

55 g/2 oz sun-dried tomatoes
in olive oil, drained and
chopped (optional)
55 g/2 oz Parmesan cheese,
finely grated
salt and pepper
sprigs of fresh flat-leaf parsley
and fresh bay leaves, to
garnish

❊ Heat the oil in a wok or large frying pan. Add the rice and cook, stirring constantly, for 5 minutes.

❊ Add the garlic, onion, celery and pepper and cook, stirring constantly, for 5 minutes. Add the mushrooms and cook for 3–4 minutes.

❊ Stir in the oregano and stock. Heat until just boiling, then reduce the heat, cover and simmer for 20 minutes or until the rice is tender and creamy.

❊ Add the sun-dried tomatoes, if using, and season the risotto to taste with salt and pepper. Stir in half of the grated Parmesan cheese.

❊ Top with the remaining cheese, garnish with the parsley and bay leaves and serve.

Green Risotto

❊ **SERVES 4** ❊

1 onion, chopped
2 tbsp olive oil
225 g/8 oz risotto rice
700 ml/1¼ pints hot vegetable
stock
350 g/12 oz mixed green
vegetables, such as
asparagus, thin French
beans, mangetout,
courgettes and frozen peas

2 tbsp chopped fresh parsley
55 g/2 oz fresh Parmesan
cheese, thinly shaved
salt and pepper

❊ Place the onion and oil in a large bowl. Cover and cook in a microwave oven on HIGH power for 2 minutes.

❊ Add the rice and stir until thoroughly coated in the oil. Pour in about 75 ml/3 fl oz of the hot stock. Cook, uncovered, for 2 minutes, until the liquid has been absorbed. Pour in another 75 ml/3 fl oz of the stock and cook, uncovered, on HIGH power for 2 minutes. Repeat once more.

❊ Chop or slice the vegetables into even-sized pieces. Stir into the rice with the remaining stock. Cover and cook on HIGH power for 8 minutes, stirring occasionally, until most of the liquid has been absorbed and the rice is just tender.

❊ Stir in the parsley and season generously. Leave to stand, covered, for almost 5 minutes. The rice should be tender and creamy.

❊ Scatter the Parmesan cheese over the risotto before serving.

Deep South Rice & Beans

175 g/6 oz long-grain rice
4 tbsp olive oil
1 small green pepper,
deseeded and chopped
1 small red pepper,
deseeded and chopped
1 onion, finely chopped
1 small red or green chilli,
deseeded and finely chopped
2 tomatoes, chopped
125 g/4^1/$_2$ oz canned red kidney
beans, rinsed and drained
1 tbsp chopped fresh basil
2 tsp chopped fresh thyme
1 tsp Cajun spice
salt and pepper
fresh basil leaves, to garnish

❊ Bring a large saucepan of lightly salted water to the boil and cook the rice for about 12 minutes until just tender. Rinse with cold water and drain well.

❊ Meanwhile, heat the olive oil in a frying pan and fry the peppers and onion gently for about 5 minutes until soft.

❊ Add the chilli and tomatoes and cook for a further 2 minutes.

❊ Add the vegetable mixture and the kidney beans to the rice. Stir well to combine thoroughly.

❊ Stir the chopped herbs and Cajun spice into the rice mixture. Season to taste with salt and pepper, and serve, garnished with the basil leaves.

Brown Rice Gratin

100 g/3¹/₂ oz brown rice
2 tbsp butter or margarine,
plus extra for greasing
1 red onion, chopped
2 garlic cloves, crushed
1 carrot, cut into thin batons
1 courgette, sliced
85 g/3 oz baby sweetcorn,
halved lengthways
2 tbsp sunflower seeds
3 tbsp chopped fresh
mixed herbs
100 g/3¹/₂ oz grated
mozzarella cheese
2 tbsp wholemeal
breadcrumbs
salt and pepper

❊ Bring a saucepan of lightly salted water to the boil and cook the rice for 20 minutes until tender. Drain well.

❊ Lightly grease an 850-ml/1¹/₂-pint ovenproof dish with butter.

❊ Melt the butter in a frying pan. Cook the onion over a low heat, stirring constantly, for 2 minutes or until soft.

❊ Add the garlic, carrot, courgette and sweetcorn and cook, stirring constantly, for a further 5 minutes until the vegetables are soft.

❊ Combine the drained rice with the sunflower seeds and mixed herbs and stir into the pan. Stir in half of the mozzarella cheese and season to taste with salt and pepper.

❊ Spoon the mixture into the prepared dish and top with the breadcrumbs and remaining cheese.

❊ Cook in a preheated oven, 180°C/350°F/Gas Mark 4, for about 25–30 minutes or until the cheese has begun to turn golden. Serve immediately.

Vegetable Fried Rice

125 g/4¹/₂ oz long-grain white rice
3 tbsp peanut oil
2 garlic cloves, crushed
¹/₂ tsp Chinese five-spice
powder
55 g/2 oz French beans
1 green pepper, deseeded and
chopped
4 baby sweetcorn cobs, sliced
25 g/1 oz bamboo shoots,
chopped
3 tomatoes, peeled, deseeded
and chopped
55 g/2 oz cooked peas
1 tsp sesame oil

❊ Bring a large saucepan of water to the boil.

❊ Add the rice to the pan and cook for about 15 minutes. Drain the rice well, rinse under cold running water and drain thoroughly again.

❊ Heat the peanut oil in a preheated wok or large frying pan. Add the garlic and Chinese five-spice and stir-fry for 30 seconds.

❊ Add the French beans, chopped pepper and sliced sweetcorn and stir-fry the ingredients in the wok for 2 minutes.

❊ Stir the bamboo shoots, tomatoes, peas and rice into the mixture in the wok and stir-fry for 1 further minute.

❊ Sprinkle with sesame oil and transfer to serving dishes. Serve immediately.

Vegetarian Paella

1/4 tsp saffron threads
3 tbsp hot water
6 tbsp olive oil
1 Spanish onion, sliced
3 garlic cloves, finely chopped
1 red pepper, deseeded and sliced
1 orange pepper, deseeded and sliced
1 large aubergine, cut into cubes
225 g/8 oz arborio rice
600 ml/1 pint vegetable stock
450 g/1 lb tomatoes, peeled and chopped
salt and pepper
115 g/4 oz mushrooms, sliced
115 g/4 oz French beans, halved
400 g/14 oz canned pinto beans or chickpeas

❖ Put the saffron and hot water in a small bowl and set aside. Meanwhile, heat the oil in a large heavy-based frying pan or a paella pan. Add the onion and cook, stirring occasionally, for 5 minutes until soft. Add the garlic, peppers and aubergine and cook, stirring occasionally, for 5 minutes more.

❖ Add the rice and stir for about 1 minute, until the grains are coated in oil. Add the stock, tomatoes, saffron and soaking water to the pan and season to taste with salt and pepper. Bring to the boil, reduce the heat and simmer, shaking the pan frequently and stirring the mixture occasionally, for 15 minutes.

❖ Stir in the mushrooms, French beans and pinto beans or chickpeas with their can juices. Cook for 10 minutes more, then serve.

Vegetable Couscous

2 tbsp vegetable oil
1 large onion, coarsely chopped
1 carrot, chopped
1 turnip, chopped
600 ml/1 pint vegetable stock
175 g/6 oz couscous
2 tomatoes, peeled and quartered
2 courgettes, chopped
1 red pepper, deseeded and chopped
125 g/4 1/2 oz French beans, chopped
grated rind of 1 lemon
pinch of ground turmeric (optional)
1 tbsp finely chopped fresh coriander or parsley
salt and pepper
sprigs of fresh flat-leaf parsley, to garnish

❖ Heat the oil in a large saucepan and fry the onion, carrot and turnip for 3–4 minutes. Add the stock, bring to the boil, cover and simmer for 20 minutes.

❖ Meanwhile, put the couscous in a bowl and moisten with a little boiling water, stirring, until the grains have swollen and separated.

❖ Add the tomatoes, courgettes, pepper and French beans to the pan.

❖ Stir the lemon rind into the couscous and add the turmeric, if using, and mix thoroughly. Put the couscous in a steamer and position it over the pan of vegetables. Simmer the vegetables so that the couscous steams for about 8–10 minutes.

❖ Pile the couscous on to warmed serving plates. Ladle the vegetables and some of the liquid over the top. Scatter with the coriander and serve at once, garnished with the sprigs of parsley.

Fragrant Curry

6 tbsp vegetable oil
2 onions, sliced
1 tsp finely chopped root ginger
1 tsp ground cumin
1 tsp ground coriander
1 tsp crushed garlic
1 tsp chilli powder
2 fresh green chillies, deseeded and chopped
fresh coriander leaves
150 ml/5 fl oz water
1 large potato
400 g/14 oz canned chickpeas, drained
1 tbsp lemon juice
warmed naan breads, to serve

❖ Heat the vegetable oil in a large saucepan. Add the onions and fry over a medium heat, stirring occasionally, for 5–8 minutes, until golden brown.

❖ Reduce the heat, add the ginger, cumin, ground coriander, garlic, chilli powder, chillies and coriander leaves to the pan and stir-fry for 2 minutes.

❖ Add the water to the mixture in the pan and stir well to mix.

❖ Using a sharp knife, cut the potato into small dice. Add the potato and the drained chickpeas to the mixture in the pan. Reduce the heat, cover and simmer, stirring occasionally, for 5–7 minutes.

❖ Sprinkle the lemon juice over the curry and stir again.

❖ Transter the curry to warmed individual serving dishes and serve immediately with the warmed naan breads.

Vegetable Stir-Fry

3 tbsp vegetable oil
8 baby onions, halved
1 aubergine, cubed
225 g/8 oz courgettes, sliced
225 g/8 oz open-cap
    mushrooms, halved
2 cloves garlic, crushed
400 g/14 oz canned chopped
    tomatoes

2 tbsp sun-dried tomato purée
2 tbsp soy sauce
1 tsp sesame oil
1 tbsp Chinese rice wine or
    dry sherry
pepper
fresh basil leaves, to garnish

❖ Heat the vegetable oil in a large preheated wok or frying pan.

❖ Add the baby onions and aubergine to the wok and stir-fry for 5 minutes or until the vegetables are golden and just beginning to soften.

❖ Add the courgettes, mushrooms, garlic, chopped tomatoes and tomato purée to the wok and stir-fry for about 5 minutes. Reduce the heat and leave to simmer for 10 minutes or until the vegetables are tender.

❖ Add the soy sauce, sesame oil and rice wine to the wok, bring back to the boil and cook for 1 minute.

❖ Season the vegetable stir-fry with pepper and scatter with the basil leaves. Serve immediately.

Eight Jewel Vegetables

2 tbsp groundnut oil
6 spring onions, sliced
3 garlic cloves, crushed
1 green pepper, deseeded
    and diced
1 red pepper, deseeded and
    diced
1 fresh red chilli, sliced
2 tbsp chopped water
    chestnuts
1 courgette, chopped

125 g/4^{1}/$_{2}$ oz oyster
    mushrooms
3 tbsp black bean sauce
2 tsp Chinese rice wine or
    dry sherry
4 tbsp dark soy sauce
1 tsp dark brown sugar
2 tbsp water
1 tsp sesame oil

❖ Heat the groundnut oil in a preheated wok or large frying pan until it is almost smoking.

❖ Reduce the heat slightly, add the spring onions and garlic and stir-fry for about 30 seconds.

❖ Add the peppers, chilli, water chestnuts and courgette to the wok and stir-fry for 2–3 minutes, or until the vegetables are just beginning to soften.

❖ Add the mushrooms, black bean sauce, rice wine, soy sauce, sugar and water to the wok and stir-fry for a further 4 minutes.

❖ Sprinkle the stir-fry with the sesame oil and serve immediately.

Sweet & Sour Vegetables

1 tbsp groundnut oil	50 g/1¾ oz canned bamboo
2 garlic cloves, crushed	shoots
1 tsp grated	225 g/8 oz marinated firm
root ginger	tofu, cubed
50 g/1¾ oz baby	2 tbsp dry sherry or Chinese
sweetcorn cobs	rice wine
50 g/1¾ oz mangetout	1 tbsp cornflour, blended
1 carrot, cut into	with 2 tbsp rice vinegar
matchsticks	2 tbsp clear honey
1 green pepper, deseeded	1 tbsp light soy sauce
and cut into matchsticks	150 ml/5 fl oz vegetable stock
8 spring onions	noodles or boiled rice, to serve

❊ Heat the oil in a preheated wok until it is almost smoking. Add the garlic and the ginger and cook over a medium heat, stirring frequently, for 30 seconds.

❊ Add the sweetcorn, mangetout, and the carrot and pepper matchsticks and stir-fry for about 5 minutes, or until the vegetables are tender, but still crisp.

❊ Add the spring onions, bamboo shoots and tofu and cook for 2 minutes.

❊ Stir in the sherry, the cornflour and vinegar, honey, soy sauce and stock and bring to the boil. Reduce the heat and simmer for 2 minutes until heated through.

❊ Transfer to warmed serving dishes and serve immediately.

Satay Noodles

275 g/9½ oz rice sticks	1 tsp chilli flakes
3 tbsp groundnut oil	4 tbsp crunchy peanut butter
2 cloves garlic, crushed	150 ml/5 fl oz coconut milk
2 shallots, sliced	1 tbsp tomato purée
225 g/8 oz French beans, sliced	sliced spring onions, to garnish
100 g/3½ oz cherry tomatoes,	
halved	

❊ Place the rice sticks in a large bowl and pour over enough boiling water to cover. Leave to stand for 10 minutes.

❊ Heat the groundnut oil in a large preheated wok or heavy-based frying pan.

❊ Add the crushed garlic and sliced shallots to the wok and stir-fry for 1 minute.

❊ Drain the rice sticks thoroughly. Add the French beans and drained noodles to the wok and stir-fry for about 5 minutes.

❊ Add the cherry tomatoes to the wok and mix well.

❊ Mix together the chilli flakes, peanut butter, coconut milk and tomato purée.

❊ Pour the chilli mixture over the noodles, toss well until all the ingredients are thoroughly combined and heat through.

❊ Transfer the satay noodles to warmed serving dishes, garnish with the spring onion slices and serve immediately.

Vegetable Chop Suey

2 tbsp groundnut oil
1 onion, chopped
3 garlic cloves, chopped
1 green pepper, deseeded
and diced
1 red pepper, deseeded
and diced
75 g/2¾ oz broccoli florets
1 courgette, sliced
25 g/1 oz French beans
1 carrot, cut into matchsticks
100 g/3½ oz beansprouts
2 tsp light brown sugar
2 tbsp light soy sauce
125 ml/4 fl oz vegetable stock
salt and pepper
noodles, to serve

❖ Heat the oil in a preheated wok until it is almost smoking. Add the chopped onion and garlic to the wok and stir-fry for 30 seconds.

❖ Add the peppers, broccoli, courgette, French beans and carrot to the wok and continue to stir-fry for a further 2–3 minutes.

❖ Stir in the beansprouts, sugar, soy sauce and stock and toss to combine thoroughly. Season the mixture to taste with salt and pepper and continue to cook for a further 2 minutes.

❖ Transfer the vegetables to warmed serving plates and serve immediately with the noodles.

Simple
vegetables & accompaniments

Carrots with Pineapple

1 tbsp sunflower oil
1 tbsp olive oil
1 small onion, finely sliced
2.5-cm/1-inch piece root
ginger,
peeled and grated
1–2 garlic cloves, crushed
500 g/1 lb 2 oz carrots,
thinly sliced

200 g/7 oz canned pineapple
in natural juice, chopped, or
250 g/9 oz fresh pineapple,
chopped
2–3 tbsp pineapple juice (from
the can or fresh)
salt and pepper
chopped fresh parsley or dill,
to garnish

❉ Heat the sunflower oil and the olive oil together in a wok. Add the onion, ginger and garlic to the wok and stir-fry briskly for 2–3 minutes.

❉ Add the carrots and continue to stir-fry, reducing the heat a little, for about 5 minutes.

❉ Add the pineapple and the pineapple juice to the wok with plenty of seasoning, and continue to stir-fry for about 5–6 minutes, or until the carrots are tender and the liquid has almost evaporated.

❉ Adjust the seasoning, adding plenty of pepper, and transfer the stir-fry to a warmed serving dish.

❉ Sprinkle the stir-fry with the chopped fresh parsley and serve as a vegetable accompaniment. Alternatively, you can allow the carrots to cool and serve them as a delicious salad, tossed in 2–4 tablespoons of French dressing to taste.

Carrot & Orange Stir-Fry

2 tbsp sunflower oil
450 g/1 lb carrots, grated
225 g/8 oz leeks, shredded
2 oranges, peeled and
segmented

2 tbsp tomato ketchup
1 tbsp demerara sugar
2 tbsp light soy sauce
100 g/3½ oz chopped peanuts

❉ Heat the sunflower oil in a large preheated wok.

❉ Add the grated carrot and leeks to the wok and stir-fry for 2–3 minutes, or until the vegetables have just softened.

❉ Add the orange segments to the wok and heat through gently, ensuring that you do not break up the orange segments as you stir the mixture.

❉ Mix the tomato ketchup, sugar and soy sauce together in a small bowl.

❉ Add the tomato and sugar mixture to the wok and stir-fry for a further 2 minutes.

❉ Transfer the stir-fry to warmed serving bowls and scatter with the chopped peanuts. Serve immediately.

Spiced Carrots with Orange

❊ **SERVES 4** ❊

675 g/1 lb 8 oz carrots, cut into thin strips
1 leek, sliced
300 ml/10 fl oz fresh orange juice
2 tbsp clear honey
1 garlic clove, crushed
1 tsp mixed spice
2 tsp chopped thyme
1 tbsp poppy seeds
salt and pepper
sprigs of fresh thyme and orange rind, to garnish

❊ Bring a saucepan of lightly salted water to the boil and cook the carrots and leek for 5–6 minutes. Drain well and transfer to a shallow ovenproof dish until required.

❊ Mix together the orange juice, honey, garlic, mixed spice and thyme and pour the mixture over the vegetables. Season to taste with salt and pepper.

❊ Cover the dish and cook in a preheated oven, 180°C/350°F/Gas Mark 4, for 30 minutes, or until the vegetables are tender.

❊ Remove the lid and sprinkle with poppy seeds. Transfer to a warmed serving dish, garnish with the sprigs of thyme and the orange rind and serve.

Peas with Baby Onions

❊ **SERVES 4** ❊

15 g/½ oz unsalted butter
175 g/6 oz baby onions
900 g/2 lb fresh peas, shelled
125 ml/4 fl oz water
2 tbsp plain flour
150 ml/5 fl oz double cream
1 tbsp chopped fresh parsley
1 tbsp lemon juice
salt and pepper

❊ Melt the butter in a large heavy-based saucepan. Add the whole baby onions and cook, stirring occasionally, for 5 minutes. Add the peas and cook, stirring constantly, for a further 3 minutes, then add the measured water and bring to the boil. Reduce the heat, partially cover and simmer for 10 minutes.

❊ Beat the flour into the cream. Remove the pan from the heat and stir in the cream mixture and parsley and season to taste with salt and pepper.

❊ Return the pan to the heat and cook, stirring gently but constantly, for about 3 minutes until thickened.

❊ Stir the lemon juice into the sauce and serve the peas immediately.

Glazed Baby Onions

500 g/1 lb 2 oz baby onions
2 tbsp olive oil
2 large garlic cloves, crushed
300 ml/10 fl oz vegetable stock
1 tbsp fresh thyme leaves
1 tbsp light brown sugar
2 tbsp red wine vinegar
about 1½ tsp balsamic vinegar
salt and pepper
sprigs of fresh thyme,
to garnish

❖ Put the baby onions in a large heatproof bowl, pour over enough boiling water to cover and set aside for 2 minutes. Drain well.

❖ Using a small knife and your fingers, peel off the skins, which should slip off easily.

❖ Heat the olive oil in a large frying pan over a medium heat. Add the onions and cook, stirring constantly, for about 8 minutes until they are golden all over.

❖ Add the crushed garlic and cook, stirring, for 2 minutes. Add the stock, thyme leaves, sugar and wine vinegar, stirring until the sugar has dissolved.

❖ Bring to the boil, then reduce the heat and simmer gently for 10 minutes or until the onions are tender when you pierce them with the tip of a sharp knife and the cooking liquid is reduced to a syrupy glaze.

❖ Stir in the balsamic vinegar. Season the glazed onions to taste with salt and pepper and add extra balsamic vinegar, if desired.

❖ Transfer to a serving dish and serve the onions either hot or cold, garnished with the sprigs of thyme.

Spicy Sweetcorn

200 g/7 oz frozen or canned sweetcorn
1 tsp ground cumin
1 tsp crushed garlic
1 tsp ground coriander
1 tsp salt
2 fresh green chillies
1 medium onion, finely chopped
3 tbsp unsalted butter
4 red chillies, crushed
½ tsp lemon juice
fresh coriander leaves, plus extra to garnish

❊ Thaw or drain the sweetcorn, if using canned, and set aside.

❊ Place the cumin, garlic, ground coriander, salt, 1 green chilli and the onion in a mortar or a food processor and grind to form a smooth paste.

❊ Heat the butter in a large frying pan. Add the onion and spice mixture to the pan and fry over a medium heat, stirring occasionally, for about 5–7 minutes.

❊ Add the crushed red chillies to the mixture in the pan and stir to combine.

❊ Add the sweetcorn to the pan and stir-fry for a further 2 minutes.

❊ Add the remaining green chilli, the lemon juice and the fresh coriander to the pan, stirring occasionally to combine.

❊ Transfer the spicy sweetcorn mixture to a warmed serving dish. Garnish with fresh coriander and serve hot.

Baked Celery with Cream

1 head of celery
½ tsp ground cumin
½ tsp ground coriander
1 garlic clove, crushed
1 red onion, thinly sliced
50 g/1¾ oz pecan nut halves
150 ml/5 fl oz vegetable stock
150 ml/ 5 fl oz single cream
50 g/1¾ oz fresh wholemeal breadcrumbs
25 g/1 oz grated Parmesan cheese
salt and pepper
celery leaves, to garnish

❊ Trim the celery and cut into matchsticks. Place the celery in an ovenproof dish, together with the ground cumin, coriander, garlic, red onion and pecan nuts.

❊ Mix the stock and cream together and pour over the vegetables. Season to taste with salt and pepper.

❊ Mix the breadcrumbs and cheese together and sprinkle over the top to cover the vegetables.

❊ Cook in a preheated oven, 200°C/400°F/Gas Mark 6, for 40 minutes or until the vegetables are tender and the top is crispy. Garnish with the celery leaves and serve at once.

Spicy Mushrooms

2 tbsp groundnut oil
2 garlic cloves, crushed
3 spring onions, chopped
300 g/10$\frac{1}{2}$ oz button
    mushrooms
2 large open-cup mushrooms,
    sliced
125 g/4$\frac{1}{2}$ oz oyster
    mushrooms

1 tsp chilli sauce
1 tbsp dark soy sauce
1 tbsp hoisin sauce
1 tbsp wine vinegar
$\frac{1}{2}$ tsp ground Szechuan
    pepper
1 tbsp dark brown sugar
1 tsp sesame oil
chopped parsley, to garnish

❈ Heat the groundnut oil in a preheated wok or large frying pan until almost smoking.

❈ Reduce the heat slightly, add the garlic and spring onions to the wok and stir-fry for 30 seconds.

❈ Add all the mushrooms to the wok, together with the chilli sauce, soy sauce, hoisin sauce, vinegar, Szechuan pepper and sugar and stir-fry for 4–5 minutes or until the mushrooms are cooked through. Stir constantly to prevent the mixture sticking to the base of the wok.

❈ Sprinkle the sesame oil on top of the mixture in the wok. Transfer to a warmed serving dish, garnish with the parsley and serve immediately.

Mushrooms & Spring Onions

2 garlic bulbs
2 tbsp olive oil
350 g/12 oz assorted
    mushrooms, such as
chestnut, open-cup and
chanterelles, halved
    if large

1 tbsp chopped fresh parsley
8 spring onions, cut into
    2.5-cm/1-inch lengths
salt and pepper

❈ Preheat the oven to 180°C/350°F/Gas Mark 4. Slice off the tops of the garlic bulbs and press down to loosen the cloves. Place them in an ovenproof dish and season to taste with salt and pepper. Drizzle 2 teaspoons of the oil over the bulbs and roast for 30 minutes. Remove from the oven and drizzle with 1 teaspoon of the remaining oil. Return to the oven and roast for a further 45 minutes. Remove from the oven and leave until cool enough to handle, then peel the cloves.

❈ Tip the oil from the dish into a heavy-based frying pan, add the remaining oil and heat. Add the mushrooms and cook over a medium heat, stirring frequently, for 4 minutes.

❈ Add the garlic cloves, parsley and spring onions and cook, stirring frequently, for 5 minutes. Season to taste with salt and pepper and serve immediately.

Spinach with Mushrooms

25 g/1 oz pine kernels
500 g/1 lb 2 oz fresh spinach
leaves
1 red onion
2 garlic cloves
3 tbsp vegetable oil
425 g/15 oz canned straw
mushrooms, drained
25 g/1 oz raisins
2 tbsp soy sauce
salt

❈ Heat a wok or large heavy-based frying pan.

❈ Dry-fry the pine kernels in the wok until lightly browned. Remove with a slotted spoon and set aside until required.

❈ Wash the spinach thoroughly, picking over the leaves and removing long stalks. Drain thoroughly and pat dry with absorbent kitchen paper.

❈ Heat the vegetable oil in the wok. Add the onion and garlic slices and stir-fry for 1 minute until slightly softened.

❈ Add the spinach and mushrooms, and continue to stir-fry until the leaves have wilted. Drain off any excess liquid.

❈ Stir in the raisins, reserved pine kernels and soy sauce. Stir-fry until thoroughly heated and all the ingredients are well combined.

❈ Season to taste with salt, transfer to a warmed serving dish and serve.

Garlic Spinach

2 garlic cloves
1 tsp lemon grass
900 g/2 lb fresh spinach
2 tbsp groundnut oil

1 tbsp dark soy sauce
2 tsp brown sugar
salt

❋ Peel the garlic cloves and crush them in a mortar with a pestle. Set aside until required.

❋ Using a sharp knife, finely chop the lemon grass. Set aside until required.

❋ Carefully remove the stems from the spinach. Rinse the spinach leaves and drain them thoroughly, patting them dry with absorbent kitchen paper.

❋ Heat the oil in a preheated wok or large frying pan until it is almost smoking.

❋ Reduce the heat slightly, add the garlic and lemon grass and stir-fry for 30 seconds.

❋ Add the spinach leaves and a pinch of salt to the wok and stir-fry for 2–3 minutes, or until the spinach leaves have just wilted.

❋ Stir the dark soy sauce and brown sugar into the mixture in the wok and cook for a further 3–4 minutes.

❋ Transfer the garlic spinach to a warmed serving dish and serve as an accompaniment to a main dish.

Kashmiri Spinach

❋ **SERVES 4** ❋

500 g/1 lb 2 oz spinach or
Swiss chard or baby leaf
spinach
2 tbsp mustard oil

¼ tsp garam masala
1 tsp yellow mustard seeds
2 spring onions, sliced

❋ Remove the tough stalks from the spinach.

❋ Heat the mustard oil in a preheated wok or large heavy-based frying pan until it smokes. Add the garam masala and mustard seeds. Cover the wok quickly – you will hear the mustard seeds popping inside.

❋ When the popping has ceased, remove the cover, add the spring onions and spinach. Cook, stirring constantly, until the spinach has wilted.

❋ Continue cooking the spinach, uncovered, over a medium heat for 10–15 minutes, until most of the water has evaporated. If using frozen spinach, it will not need to cook for so long – cook it until most of the water has evaporated.

❋ Remove the spinach and spring onions with a slotted spoon, draining off any remaining liquid. (This dish is best served as dry as possible.)

❋ Transfer to a warmed serving dish and serve immediately, while still piping hot.

Cauliflower & Spinach Curry

1 medium cauliflower	1 green chilli, sliced
6 tbsp vegetable oil	500 g/1 lb 2 oz spinach
1 tsp mustard seeds	5 tbsp vegetable stock
1 tsp ground cumin	1 tbsp chopped fresh coriander
1 tsp garam masala	salt and pepper
1 tsp turmeric	sprigs of fresh coriander, to
2 garlic cloves, crushed	garnish
1 onion, halved and sliced	

❊ Break the cauliflower into small florets.

❊ Heat the oil in a deep flameproof casserole. Add the mustard seeds and cook until they begin to pop.

❊ Stir in the remaining spices, the garlic, onion and chilli and cook, stirring constantly, for 2–3 minutes.

❊ Add the cauliflower, spinach, vegetable stock, chopped coriander and seasoning and cook over a gentle heat for 15 minutes, or until the cauliflower is tender. Uncover the dish and boil for 1 minute to thicken the juices.

❊ Transfer to a warmed serving dish, garnish with the sprigs of coriander and serve.

Cauliflower Fritters

1 large cauliflower,	150 ml/5 fl oz water
cut into florets	4 tbsp milk
115 g/4 oz plain flour	sunflower or corn oil,
pinch of dried thyme	for deep-frying
2 eggs, separated	salt

❊ Blanch the cauliflower in a large saucepan of boiling water for 5 minutes. Drain well and pat dry with kitchen paper.

❊ Sift the flour with a pinch of salt into a bowl and add the thyme, egg yolks and water. Beat well with a wooden spoon until smooth. Beat in the milk.

❊ In a separate, grease-free bowl, whisk the egg whites until stiff peaks form. Gently fold a little of the egg white into the batter, then fold in the rest.

❊ Heat the oil in a deep-fat fryer or pan to 180°C/350°F or until a cube of bread browns in 30 seconds. Dip the cauliflower florets in the batter to coat, then fry, in batches, until golden brown.

❊ Drain the cauliflower fritters on kitchen paper and serve immediately.

Spicy Cauliflower

500 g/1 lb 2 oz cauliflower, cut
into florets
1 tbsp sunflower oil
1 garlic clove
1/2 tsp turmeric
1 tsp cumin seeds, ground
1 tsp coriander seeds, ground
1 tsp yellow mustard seeds
12 spring onions, finely sliced
salt and pepper

❖ Blanch the cauliflower in boiling water, drain and set aside. Cauliflower holds a lot of water, which tends to make it over-soft, so turn the florets upside-down at this stage and you will end up with a crisper result.

❖ Heat the oil gently in a large heavy-based frying pan or wok. Add the garlic, turmeric, cumin, coriander and mustard seeds. Stir well and cover the pan.

❖ When you hear the mustard seeds popping, add the spring onions and stir. Cook for 2 minutes, stirring constantly, to soften them a little. Season to taste.

❖ Add the cauliflower and stir for 3–4 minutes until coated completely with the spices and thoroughly heated.

❖ Remove the garlic clove and serve immediately.

Cauliflower with Broccoli

2 baby cauliflowers
225 g/8 oz broccoli
8 tbsp olive oil
4 tbsp butter or margarine
2 tsp grated root ginger
juice and rind of 2 lemons
5 tbsp chopped coriander
5 tbsp grated Cheddar cheese
salt and pepper

❋ Using a sharp knife, cut the cauliflowers in half and the broccoli into very large florets.

❋ Bring a saucepan of lightly salted water to the boil and cook the cauliflower and broccoli for 10 minutes. Drain well, transfer to a shallow ovenproof dish and keep warm until required.

❋ Put the oil and butter in a saucepan and heat gently until the butter melts. Add the ginger, lemon juice and rind and coriander and simmer for 2–3 minutes, stirring occasionally.

❋ Season the sauce to taste with salt and pepper, then pour over the vegetables in the dish and sprinkle the cheese on top.

❋ Cook under a preheated hot grill for 2–3 minutes, or until the cheese is bubbling and golden. Leave to cool for 1–2 minutes and then serve.

Gingered Broccoli

5-cm/2-inch piece of root ginger
2 tbsp groundnut oil
1 garlic clove, crushed
675 g/1 lb 8 oz broccoli florets
1 leek, sliced
75 g/2¾ oz water chestnuts, halved
½ tsp caster sugar
125 ml/4 fl oz vegetable stock
1 tsp dark soy sauce
1 tsp cornflour
2 tsp water

❋ Using a sharp knife, finely chop the ginger. (Alternatively, cut the ginger into larger strips, to be discarded later, for a slightly milder ginger flavour.)

❋ Heat the oil in a preheated wok. Add the garlic and ginger and stir-fry for 30 seconds.

❋ Add the broccoli, leek and water chestnuts and stir-fry for a further 3–4 minutes.

❋ Add the sugar, stock and soy sauce to the wok, reduce the heat and simmer for 4–5 minutes, or until the broccoli is almost cooked.

❋ Blend the cornflour with the water to form a smooth paste and stir it into the wok. Bring to the boil and cook, stirring constantly, for 1 minute or until the mixture has thickened.

❋ If you are using the larger strips of ginger, remove them from the wok and discard.

❋ Transfer the vegetables to a serving dish and serve immediately.

French Bean Stir-Fry

❊ SERVES 4 ❊

450 g/1 lb French beans 1 garlic clove, crushed
2 fresh red chillies 2 tbsp light soy sauce
2 tbsp groundnut oil 2 tsp clear honey
$1/2$ tsp ground star anise $1/2$ tsp sesame oil

❊ Using a sharp knife, cut the French beans in half.

❊ Slice the fresh chillies, removing the seeds first if you prefer a milder dish.

❊ Heat the oil in a preheated wok or frying pan until it is almost smoking.

❊ Reduce the heat slightly, add the halved French beans to the wok and stir-fry for 1 minute.

❊ Add the chillies, star anise and garlic to the wok and stir-fry for a further 30 seconds.

❊ Mix together the soy sauce, honey and sesame oil in a small bowl.

❊ Stir the sauce mixture into the wok. Cook for a further 2 minutes, tossing the beans to ensure that they are thoroughly coated in the sauce.

❊ Transfer the mixture to a warmed serving dish and serve immediately.

French Beans with Tomatoes

❊ SERVES 6 ❊

500 g/1 lb 2 oz French beans, 1 tsp turmeric
cut into 5-cm/2-inch lengths $1/2$ tsp cayenne pepper
2 tbsp ghee 1 tsp ground coriander
2.5-cm/1-inch piece of 4 tomatoes, peeled, deseeded
root ginger, grated and diced
1 garlic clove, crushed 150 ml/5 fl oz vegetable stock

❊ Blanch the beans briefly in boiling water, drain, refresh under cold running water and drain again.

❊ Melt the ghee in a wok or a large frying pan over a medium heat. Add the ginger and garlic, stir and add the turmeric, cayenne pepper and coriander. Stir over a low heat for about 1 minute until fragrant.

❊ Add the tomatoes to the wok, tossing until they are thoroughly coated in the spice mix.

❊ Add the stock to the wok, bring to the boil and simmer over a medium–high heat, stirring occasionally, for about 10 minutes until the sauce has reduced and thickened.

❊ Add the beans, reduce the heat to moderate and heat through, stirring constantly, for 5 minutes.

❊ Transfer to a warmed serving dish and serve immediately.

Lemon Beans

900 g/2 lb mixed green beans, such as broad beans, French beans and runner beans
65 g/2¹/2 oz butter or margarine
4 tsp plain flour
300 ml/10 fl oz vegetable stock
5 tbsp dry white wine
90 ml/3 fl oz single cream
3 tbsp chopped mixed herbs
2 tbsp lemon juice
grated rind of 1 lemon
salt and pepper

❖ Bring a saucepan of lightly salted water to the boil and cook the beans for 10 minutes or until tender. Drain and place in a warmed serving dish.

❖ Meanwhile, melt the butter in a saucepan. Add the flour and cook, stirring constantly, for 1 minute. Remove the pan from the heat and gradually stir in the stock and wine. Return the pan to the heat and bring to the boil, stirring.

❖ Remove the pan from the heat once again and stir in the cream, mixed herbs, lemon juice and rind. Season to taste with salt and pepper. Pour the sauce over the beans, mixing well. Serve immediately.

Creamy Green Vegetables

❈ **SERVES 4** ❈

450 g/1 lb Chinese leaves, shredded
2 tbsp groundnut oil
2 leeks, shredded
4 garlic cloves, crushed
300 ml/10 fl oz vegetable stock
1 tbsp light soy sauce
2 tsp cornflour
4 tsp water
2 tbsp single cream or natural yogurt
1 tbsp chopped fresh coriander

❈ Blanch the Chinese leaves in boiling water for 30 seconds. Drain, rinse under cold running water, then drain thoroughly again.

❈ Heat the oil in a preheated wok and add the Chinese leaves, leeks and garlic. Stir-fry for 2–3 minutes.

❈ Add the stock and soy sauce to the wok, reduce the heat to low, cover and simmer for 10 minutes.

❈ Remove the vegetables from the wok with a slotted spoon and set aside. Bring the stock to the boil and boil vigorously until reduced by about half.

❈ Blend the cornflour with the water and stir into the wok. Bring to the boil, and cook, stirring constantly, until thickened and clear.

❈ Reduce the heat and stir in the vegetables and cream. Cook over a low heat for 1 minute.

❈ Transfer to a serving dish, sprinkle over the chopped coriander and serve.

Stir-Fried Greens

❈ **SERVES 4** ❈

8 spring onions
2 celery sticks
125 g/4 1/2 oz mooli
125 g/4 1/2 oz mangetout
175 g/6 oz Chinese leaves
175 g/6 oz pak choi or spinach
2 tbsp vegetable oil
2 garlic cloves, finely chopped
3 tbsp light soy sauce
1 tsp finely grated root ginger
pepper

❈ Finely slice the spring onions and celery. Cut the mooli into matchsticks. Top and tail the mangetout. Shred the Chinese leaves and the pak choi.

❈ Heat the vegetable oil and sesame oil together in a wok or large frying pan. Add the garlic and fry for about 1 minute.

❈ Add the spring onions, celery, mooli and mangetout to the wok and stir-fry for about 2 minutes.

❈ Add the shredded Chinese leaves and pak choi to the wok and continue to stir-fry for about 1 minute.

❈ Stir the soy sauce into the vegetables with the ginger. Cook for 1 minute. Season to taste with pepper, transfer to a warmed serving dish and serve at once.

Braised Red Cabbage

❖ **SERVES 6** ❖

2 tbsp sunflower oil
2 onions, thinly sliced
2 apples, peeled, cored and thinly sliced
900 g/2 lb red cabbage, cored and shredded
4 tbsp red wine vinegar
2 tbsp sugar
1/4 tsp ground cloves
55 g/2 oz raisins
125 ml/4 fl oz red wine
2 tbsp redcurrant jelly
salt and pepper

❖ Heat the oil in a large, heavy-based saucepan. Add the onions and cook, stirring occasionally, for 10 minutes, until softened and golden. Stir in the apples and cook for 3 minutes.

❖ Add the cabbage, vinegar, sugar, cloves, raisins and wine and season to taste with salt and pepper. Bring to the boil, stirring occasionally. Reduce the heat, cover and cook, stirring occasionally, for 40 minutes, until the cabbage is tender and most of the liquid has been absorbed.

❖ Stir in the redcurrant jelly, transfer the red cabbage to a warmed serving dish and serve immediately.

Cabbage & Walnut Stir-Fry

❖ **SERVES 4** ❖

350 g/12 oz white cabbage
350 g/12 oz red cabbage
4 tbsp groundnut oil
1 tbsp walnut oil
2 garlic cloves, crushed
8 spring onions
225 g/8 oz firm tofu, cubed
2 tbsp lemon juice
100 g/3 1/2 oz walnut halves
2 tsp Dijon mustard
2 tsp poppy seeds
salt and pepper

❖ Using a sharp knife, shred the white and red cabbages thinly and set aside until required.

❖ Heat the groundnut and walnut oils in a preheated wok or heavy-based frying pan. Add the garlic, cabbage, spring onions and tofu and cook, stirring constantly, for 5 minutes.

❖ Add the lemon juice, walnuts and Dijon mustard, season to taste with salt and pepper and cook for a further 5 minutes, or until the cabbage is tender.

❖ Transfer the stir-fry to a warmed serving bowl, sprinkle with poppy seeds and serve immediately.

Caraway Cabbage

500 g/1 lb 2 oz white cabbage
1 tbsp sunflower oil
4 spring onions, thinly sliced
diagonally
55 g/2 oz raisins
55 g/2 oz walnut pieces or
pecan nuts, roughly chopped
5 tbsp milk or vegetable stock
1 tbsp caraway seeds
1–2 tbsp freshly chopped mint
salt and pepper
sprigs of fresh mint, to garnish

❖ Remove any outer leaves from the cabbage and cut out the stem, then shred the leaves very finely, either by hand or using the fine slicing blade on a food processor.

❖ Heat the sunflower oil in a wok, swirling it around until it is really hot.

❖ Add the spring onions to the wok and stir-fry for a minute or so.

❖ Add the shredded cabbage and stir-fry for 3–4 minutes, keeping the cabbage moving all the time and stirring from the outside to the centre of the wok. Make sure the cabbage does not stick to the wok or go brown.

❖ Add the raisins, walnuts and milk and continue to stir-fry for 3–4 minutes until the cabbage begins to soften slightly but is still crisp.

❖ Season well with salt and pepper, add the caraway seeds and 1 tablespoon of the chopped mint and continue to stir-fry for a minute or so.

❖ Serve sprinkled with the remaining chopped mint and garnish with sprigs of fresh mint.

Baked Fennel

2 fennel bulbs
2 celery sticks, cut into
7.5-cm/3-inch sticks
6 sun-dried tomatoes, halved
200 g/7 oz passata
2 tsp dried oregano
50 g/1¾ oz Parmesan cheese, grated

❊ Using a sharp knife, trim the fennel, discarding any tough outer leaves, and cut the bulb into quarters.

❊ Bring a large saucepan of water to the boil, add the fennel and celery and cook for 8–10 minutes or until just tender. Remove with a slotted spoon and drain.

❊ Place the fennel pieces, celery and sun-dried tomatoes in a large ovenproof dish.

❊ Mix the tomato paste and oregano and pour the mixture over the fennel.

❊ Sprinkle with the Parmesan cheese and bake in a preheated oven, 375°F/190°C/Gas Mark 5, for 20 minutes or until hot. Serve as a starter with bread or as a vegetable side dish.

Fennel with Tomatoes

2 fennel bulbs
1 tbsp olive oil
1 onion, thinly sliced
2 tomatoes, peeled and chopped
55 g/2 oz black olives, stoned
2 tbsp torn fresh basil leaves
pepper

❊ Cut off and chop the fennel fronds. Cut the bulbs in half lengthways, then slice thinly.

❊ Heat the oil in a heavy-based frying pan. Add the onion to the pan and cook over a low heat, stirring occasionally, for 5 minutes until soft.

❊ Add the fennel slices and cook, stirring occasionally, for a further 10 minutes.

❊ Increase the heat and add the tomatoes and olives. Cook, stirring frequently, for 10 minutes, then stir in the basil and season to taste with pepper.

❊ Transfer the vegetables to a warmed serving dish, garnish with the fennel fronds and serve immediately.

Sweet & Sour Courgettes

500 g/1 lb 2 oz courgettes
3 tbsp olive oil
1 large garlic clove, finely chopped
3 tbsp white wine vinegar
3 tbsp water

6–8 anchovy fillets, canned or salted
3 tbsp pine kernels
3 tbsp raisins
salt and pepper
sprigs of fresh flat-leaf parsley, to garnish

❈ Cut the courgettes into long, thin strips. Heat the olive oil in a large heavy-based frying pan over a medium heat. Add the garlic and fry, stirring constantly, for about 2 minutes.

❈ Add the courgettes and cook, stirring frequently, until they just start to turn brown. Add the vinegar and water. Reduce the heat and simmer, stirring frequently, for 10 minutes.

❈ Meanwhile, drain the anchovies, if canned, or rinse if they are salted. Coarsely chop, then use the back of a wooden spoon to mash them to a paste.

❈ Stir the anchovies, pine kernels and raisins into the pan. Increase the heat and stir until the courgettes are coated in a thin sauce and are tender. Taste and adjust the seasoning, remembering that the anchovies are very salty.

❈ Either serve immediately or set aside to cool completely and then serve at room temperature. To serve, garnish with the parsley.

Italian Courgettes

2 tbsp olive oil
1 large onion, chopped
1 garlic clove, finely chopped
5 courgettes, sliced
150 ml/5 fl oz vegetable stock

1 tsp chopped fresh marjoram
salt and pepper
1 tbsp chopped fresh flat-leaf parsley, to garnish

❈ Heat the olive oil in a large heavy-based frying pan. Add the onion and garlic and cook, stirring occasionally, for 5 minutes until soft.

❈ Add the courgettes and cook, stirring frequently, for 3–4 minutes until they are just beginning to brown.

❈ Add the stock and marjoram and season to taste with salt and pepper. Simmer for about 10 minutes, until almost all the liquid has evaporated. Transfer to a warmed serving dish, sprinkle with the parsley and serve immediately.

Peperonata

4 tbsp olive oil
1 onion, halved and finely sliced
2 red peppers, deseeded and
cut into strips
2 green peppers, deseeded and
cut into strips
2 yellow peppers, deseeded and
cut into strips
2 garlic cloves, crushed
800 g/1 lb 12 oz canned
chopped tomatoes, drained
2 tbsp chopped coriander
2 tbsp chopped stoned
black olives
salt and pepper

❈ Heat the olive oil in a large frying pan. Add the sliced onion and sauté for 5 minutes, stirring constantly, until just beginning to colour.

❈ Add the pepper strips and the garlic to the pan and cook for a further 3–4 minutes.

❈ Stir in the tomatoes and chopped coriander and season to taste with salt and pepper. Cover the pan and cook the vegetables gently for about 30 minutes or until the mixture is dry.

❈ Stir in the black olives and serve the peperonata immediately.

Roasted Peppers

2 each red, yellow and orange peppers
4 tomatoes, halved
1 tbsp olive oil
3 garlic cloves, chopped
1 onion, sliced in rings
2 tbsp fresh thyme
salt and pepper

❄ Halve and deseed the peppers. Place them, cut side down, on a baking tray and cook under a preheated grill for 10 minutes.

❄ Add the tomatoes to the baking tray and grill for 5 minutes, until the skins of the peppers and tomatoes are charred.

❄ Put the peppers into a polythene bag for 10 minutes to sweat, which will make the skin easier to peel.

❄ Remove the tomato skins and chop the flesh. Peel the skins from the peppers and slice the flesh into strips.

❄ Heat the oil in a large frying pan and fry the garlic and onion, stirring occasionally, for 3–4 minutes or until soft.

❄ Add the peppers and tomatoes to the frying pan and cook for 5 minutes. Stir in the thyme and season to taste with salt and pepper.

❄ Transfer to serving bowls and serve warm or chilled.

Peppers with Rosemary

4 tbsp olive oil
finely grated rind of 1 lemon
4 tbsp lemon juice
1 tbsp balsamic vinegar
1 tbsp crushed fresh rosemary, or 1 tsp dried rosemary
2 red peppers, halved, cored and deseeded
2 yellow peppers, halved, cored and deseeded
2 tbsp pine kernels
salt and pepper
sprigs of fresh rosemary, to garnish

❄ Mix together the olive oil, lemon rind, lemon juice, vinegar and rosemary. Season with salt and pepper.

❄ Place the peppers, skin side upwards, on the rack of a foil-lined grill pan. Brush the olive oil mixture over them.

❄ Grill the peppers for 3–4 minutes or until the skin begins to char, basting frequently with the lemon juice mixture. Remove from the heat, cover with foil to trap the steam and leave for 5 minutes.

❄ Meanwhile, scatter the pine kernels on the grill rack and toast them lightly for 2–3 minutes. Keep a close eye on the pine kernels as they tend to burn very quickly.

❄ Peel the peppers, slice them into strips and place them in a warmed serving dish. Sprinkle with the pine kernels and drizzle any remaining lemon juice mixture over them. Garnish with the sprigs of rosemary and serve at once.

Grilled Aubergines

1 large aubergine
3 tbsp olive oil
1 tsp sesame oil
salt and pepper

CUCUMBER SAUCE
150 ml/5 fl oz natural yogurt
5-cm/2¹/₂-inch piece of
   cucumber
¹/₂ tsp mint sauce

PESTO
1 clove garlic
25 g/1 oz pine kernels
15 g/¹/₂ oz fresh basil leaves
2 tbsp grated Parmesan
   cheese
6 tbsp olive oil

❋ Remove the stalk from the aubergine, then cut it lengthways into 8 thin slices.

❋ Lay the slices on a plate or board and sprinkle them liberally with salt to remove the bitter juices. Leave to stand.

❋ Meanwhile, prepare the baste. Combine the olive and sesame oils, season with pepper and set aside.

❋ To make the cucumber sauce, place the yogurt in a mixing bowl. Remove the seeds from the cucumber and finely dice the flesh. Stir into the yogurt with the mint sauce.

❋ To make the pesto, put the garlic, pine kernels, basil and cheese in a food processor until finely chopped. With the machine running, gradually add the oil in a thin stream. Season to taste.

❋ Rinse the aubergine slices and pat them dry on absorbent kitchen paper. Baste with the oil mixture and grill under a preheated medium grill for 10 minutes, turning once. The aubergine should be golden and just tender.

❋ Transfer the aubergine slices to serving plates and serve with either the pesto or the cucumber sauce.

Roast Tomatoes & Vegetables

6 plum tomatoes, halved
1 red onion, cut into wedges
1 white onion, cut into wedges
2 small courgettes,
   cut into chunks
1 aubergine, cut into chunks
1 red pepper, deseeded and
   thickly sliced

5 tbsp olive oil
few sprigs fresh rosemary
few sprigs fresh thyme
1 tbsp rock salt
2 large tomatoes, roughly
   chopped
pepper

❋ Preheat the oven to 200°C/400°F/Gas Mark 6. Place all the tomatoes and vegetables on a large baking tray and drizzle with oil.

❋ Arrange the herbs on top, reserving one sprig of thyme for a garnish, and cook in the oven for 20–30 minutes. Toss the vegetables halfway through to coat with the oil. Season to taste with salt and pepper and cook for a further 15–20 minutes until the vegetables are tender and browned.

❋ Remove the baking tray from the oven, stir in the chopped tomatoes, garnish with the remaining thyme and serve immediately.

Sauté of Summer Vegetables

225 g/8 oz baby carrots,
scrubbed
125 g/4¹/2 oz runner beans
2 courgettes, trimmed
1 bunch of large spring onions
1 bunch of radishes
4 tbsp butter
2 tbsp light olive oil
2 tbsp white wine vinegar
4 tbsp dry white wine
1 tsp caster sugar
1 tbsp chopped fresh tarragon
salt and pepper
sprigs of fresh tarragon,
to garnish

❃ Cut the carrots in half lengthways, slice the runner beans and courgettes, and halve the spring onions and radishes, so that all the vegetables are cut into even-sized pieces.

❃ Melt the butter in a large heavy-based frying pan or wok. Add all the vegetables and fry them over a medium heat, stirring frequently, until they are tender, but still crisp and firm to the bite.

❃ Meanwhile, pour the olive oil, vinegar and wine into a small saucepan and add the sugar. Place over a low heat, stirring constantly until the sugar has dissolved. Remove the pan from the heat and add the chopped tarragon.

❃ When the vegetables are just cooked, pour over the dressing. Stir through, tossing the vegetables well to coat. Season to taste with salt and pepper and then transfer to a warmed serving dish.

❃ Garnish with the sprigs of tarragon and serve immediately.

Steamed Vegetable Parcels

115 g/4 oz French beans
55 g/2 oz mangetout
12 baby carrots
8 baby onions or shallots
12 baby turnips
8 radishes
4 thin strips of lemon rind
55 g/2 oz unsalted butter
4 tsp finely chopped fresh chervil
4 tbsp dry white wine
salt and pepper

❉ Cut out 4 double thickness rounds of greaseproof paper about 30 cm/12 inches in diameter.

❉ Divide the French beans, mangetout, carrots, onions, turnips and radishes between the rounds, placing them on one half. Season to taste with salt and pepper and dot with the butter. Add a strip of lemon rind to each. Sprinkle with the chervil and drizzle with the wine. Fold over the double layer of paper, twisting the edges together to seal.

❉ Bring a large saucepan of water to the boil and place a steamer on top. Put the parcels in the steamer, cover tightly and steam for 8–10 minutes. Serve the parcels immediately, to be unwrapped at table.

Layered Vegetable Bake

1 tbsp olive oil, for brushing
675 g/1 lb 8 oz potatoes
2 leeks
2 beef tomatoes
8 fresh basil leaves
1 garlic clove, finely chopped
300 ml/10 fl oz vegetable stock
salt and pepper

❉ Preheat the oven to 180°C/350°F/Gas Mark 4. Brush a large ovenproof dish with a little of the olive oil. Prepare all the vegetables. Peel and thinly slice the potatoes, trim and slice the leeks and slice the tomatoes.

❉ Place a layer of potato slices in the base of the dish, sprinkle with half the basil leaves and cover with a layer of leeks. Top with a layer of tomato slices. Repeat these layers until all the vegetables are used up, ending with a layer of potatoes.

❉ Stir the garlic into the stock and season to taste with salt and pepper. Pour the stock over the vegetables and brush the top with the remaining olive oil.

❉ Bake in the preheated oven for 1½ hours, or until the vegetables are tender and the topping is golden brown. Serve immediately.

Seasonal Stir-Fry

1 medium red pepper, deseeded
115 g/4 oz courgettes
115 g/4 oz cauliflower
115 g/4 oz French beans
3 tbsp vegetable oil
a few small slices of fresh root ginger
$\frac{1}{2}$ tsp salt
$\frac{1}{2}$ tsp sugar
1–2 tbsp vegetable stock or water (optional)
1 tbsp light soy sauce
a few drops of sesame oil (optional)

❉ Using a sharp knife, cut the red pepper into small squares. Thinly slice the courgettes. Trim the cauliflower and divide into small florets, discarding any thick stems. Make sure the vegetables are cut into roughly similar shapes and sizes to ensure that they cook evenly. Trim the French beans, then cut them in half.

❉ Heat the vegetable oil in a preheated wok or large heavy-based frying pan. Add the prepared vegetables with the ginger and stir-fry for about 2 minutes.

❉ Add the salt and sugar to the wok and continue to stir-fry for 1–2 minutes, adding a little vegetable stock if the mixture appears to be too dry. Do not add any liquid unless necessary.

❉ Add the soy sauce and the sesame oil, if using, and stir well to coat the vegetables lightly.

❉ Transfer the stir-fried vegetables to a warmed serving dish or bowl and serve immediately.

Vegetable Medley

150 g/5$\frac{1}{2}$ oz young, tender French beans
8 baby carrots
6 baby turnips
$\frac{1}{2}$ small cauliflower
2 tbsp vegetable oil
2 large onions, sliced
2 garlic cloves, finely chopped
300 ml/10 fl oz low-fat natural yogurt
1 tbsp cornflour
2 tbsp tomato purée
large pinch of chilli powder
salt

❉ Top and tail the beans and snap them in half. Cut the carrots in half and the turnips in quarters. Divide the cauliflower into florets, discarding the thickest part of the stalk. Steam the vegetables over boiling salted water for 3 minutes, then tip them into a colander and plunge them at once into a large bowl of cold water to prevent further cooking.

❉ Heat the vegetable oil in a frying pan and fry the onions until they are translucent. Stir in the garlic and cook for a further minute.

❉ Mix together the yogurt, cornflour and tomato purée to form a smooth paste. Stir this paste into the onions in the pan and cook for 1–2 minutes until the sauce is well blended.

❉ Drain the vegetables well, then gradually stir them into the sauce, taking care not to break them up. Season to taste with salt and chilli powder, cover and simmer gently for 5 minutes until the vegetables are just tender. Taste and adjust the seasoning if necessary. Serve immediately.

Vegetable Galette

2 large aubergines, sliced
4 courgettes, sliced
800 g/1 lb 12 oz canned
chopped tomatoes, drained
2 tbsp tomato purée
2 garlic cloves, crushed
4 tbsp olive oil
1 tsp caster sugar
2 tbsp chopped basil
olive oil, for frying
225 g/8 oz mozzarella cheese,
sliced
salt and pepper
basil leaves, to garnish

❖ Put the aubergine slices in a colander and sprinkle with salt. Leave to stand for 30 minutes, then rinse well under cold water and drain. Thinly slice the courgettes.

❖ Meanwhile, put the tomatoes, tomato purée, garlic, olive oil, sugar and chopped basil into a saucepan and simmer for 20 minutes or until reduced by half. Season to taste with salt and pepper.

❖ Heat 2 tablespoons of the oil in a large frying pan and cook the aubergine slices for 2–3 minutes until just beginning to brown. Remove from the pan.

❖ Add the remaining oil to the pan and fry the courgette slices until browned.

❖ Lay half the aubergine slices in the base of an ovenproof dish. Top with half of the tomato sauce and the courgettes and then half of the mozzarella.

❖ Repeat the layers and bake in a preheated oven, 180°C/350°F/Gas Mark 4, for 45–50 minutes, or until the vegetables are tender. Garnish with basil leaves and serve.

Boston Beans

500 g/1 lb 2 oz dried haricot
beans, soaked overnight in
cold water to cover
2 onions, chopped

2 large tomatoes, peeled
and chopped
2 tsp American mustard
2 tbsp treacle
salt and pepper

❖ Drain the beans and place in a large saucepan. Add enough cold water to cover, bring to the boil and boil for 15 minutes. Drain, reserving 300 ml/10 fl oz of the cooking liquid. Transfer the beans to a large casserole and add the onions.

❖ Return the reserved cooking liquid to the pan and add the tomatoes. Bring to the boil and simmer for 10 minutes. Remove the pan from the heat, stir in the mustard and treacle and season to taste with salt and pepper.

❖ Pour the tomato mixture into the casserole and bake in a preheated oven, 140°C/275°F/Gas Mark 1, for 5 hours. Serve immediately.

Chilli Beans

350 g/12 oz dried black haricot
or red kidney beans, soaked
for 3–4 hours
1 bay leaf
2 onions, chopped
2 garlic cloves, finely chopped
2–3 fresh green chillies
2 tbsp corn oil
salt

3 tomatoes, peeled, deseeded
and chopped, to garnish

TO SERVE
mozzarella cheese, grated
baby tomatoes
spring onion
flour tortillas

❖ Drain the beans, rinse well and place in a large heavy-based saucepan. Cover the beans with cold water, then add the bay leaf, half the onion, half the garlic and the chillies. Bring to the boil and boil rapidly for 15 minutes. Reduce the heat, cover and simmer for 1 hour, adding more boiling water if necessary. Add 1 tablespoon of the oil and simmer for 30–45 minutes until tender. Season with salt and reserve.

❖ Heat the remaining oil in a frying pan. Add the remaining onion and garlic and cook, stirring occasionally, for 5 minutes, until soft. Add the tomatoes and cook for a further 5 minutes.

❖ Add 3 tablespoons of the cooked beans to the frying pan and mash the mixture thoroughly. Stir the mixture into the remaining beans and re-heat gently. Taste and adjust the seasoning, if necessary. Serve with the grated cheese, baby tomatoes, spring onions and flour tortillas.

Beans in Tomato Sauce

❖ **SERVES 4** ❖

400 g/14 oz canned cannellini beans	1 celery stick, thinly sliced
	2 garlic cloves, chopped
400 g/14 oz canned borlotti beans	175 g/6 oz baby onions, halved
	450 g/1 lb tomatoes
2 tbsp olive oil	85 g/3 oz rocket

❖ Drain both cans of beans and reserve 6 tablespoons of the liquid.

❖ Heat the oil in a large saucepan. Add the celery, garlic and onions and sauté for 5 minutes or until the onions are golden.

❖ Cut a cross in the base of each tomato and plunge them into boiling water for 30 seconds until the skins split. Remove them with a slotted spoon and set aside until cool enough to handle. Peel off the skins and chop the flesh. Add the tomatoes and the reserved bean liquid to the pan and cook for 5 minutes.

❖ Add the beans to the pan and cook for a further 3–4 minutes or until the beans are hot.

❖ Stir in the rocket and allow to wilt slightly before serving.

Garlic Mash

❖ **SERVES 4** ❖

900 g/2 lb floury potatoes, cut into chunks	85 g/3 oz butter
	pinch of freshly grated nutmeg
8 garlic cloves, crushed	salt and pepper
150 ml/5 fl oz milk	

❖ Put the potatoes in a large saucepan. Add enough cold water to cover and a pinch of salt. Bring to the boil and cook for 10 minutes. Add the garlic and cook for a further 10 minutes, until the potatoes are tender.

❖ Drain the potatoes and garlic thoroughly, reserving 3 tablespoons of the cooking liquid.

❖ Return the reserved liquid to the pan, add the milk and bring to simmering point. Add the butter and return the potatoes and garlic to the pan. Mash thoroughly with a potato masher.

❖ Season to taste with nutmeg and salt and pepper and beat the potato mixture with a wooden spoon until light and fluffy. Serve immediately.

Garlic Potato Wedges

3 large baking potatoes,
scrubbed
4 tbsp olive oil
25 g/1 oz butter
2 garlic cloves, chopped
1 tbsp chopped fresh rosemary
1 tbsp chopped fresh parsley
1 tbsp chopped fresh thyme
salt and pepper

❖ Bring a large saucepan of water to the boil and par-boil the potatoes for 10 minutes. Drain the potatoes, refresh under cold water and drain them again thoroughly.

❖ Transfer the potatoes to a chopping board. When the potatoes are cold enough to handle, cut them into thick wedges but do not remove the skins.

❖ Heat the oil and butter in a small saucepan together with the garlic. Cook gently until the garlic begins to brown, then remove the pan from the heat.

❖ Stir the herbs and salt and pepper to taste into the mixture in the pan.

❖ Brush the herb mixture all over the potatoes.

❖ Grill the potatoes under a preheated medium grill, brushing liberally with any of the remaining herb and butter mixture, for 10–15 minutes or until the potatoes are just tender.

❖ Transfer the potatoes to a warmed serving plate and serve.

Candied Sweet Potatoes

675 g/1 lb 8 oz sweet potatoes, sliced
40 g/1½ oz butter
1 tbsp lime juice
75 g/2¾ oz soft dark brown sugar
1 tbsp brandy
grated rind of 1 lime
lime wedges, to garnish

❄ Bring a saucepan of lightly salted water to the boil and cook the sweet potatoes for about 5 minutes. Test that the potatoes have softened by pricking with a fork. Remove the sweet potatoes with a slotted spoon and drain thoroughly.

❄ Melt the butter in a large frying pan. Add the lime juice and sugar and heat gently, stirring, to dissolve the sugar.

❄ Stir the sweet potatoes and the brandy into the sugar and lime juice mixture. Cook over a low heat for about 10 minutes or until the potato slices are cooked through.

❄ Sprinkle the lime rind over the top of the sweet potatoes and mix well.

❄ Transfer the candied sweet potatoes to a serving plate. Garnish with the lime wedges and serve at once.

Parmesan Potatoes

6 potatoes
50 g/1¾ oz Parmesan cheese, grated
pinch of grated nutmeg
1 tbsp chopped fresh parsley
4 rashers smoked bacon, cut into strips
oil, for roasting
salt

❄ Cut the potatoes in half lengthways and cook them in a saucepan of boiling salted water for 10 minutes. Drain thoroughly.

❄ Mix together the cheese, nutmeg and parsley in a shallow bowl.

❄ Roll the potato pieces in the cheese mixture to coat them completely. Shake off any excess.

❄ Pour a little oil into a roasting tin and heat it in a preheated oven, 200°C/400°F/Gas Mark 6, for 10 minutes. Remove from the oven and place the potatoes in the tin. Return the tin to the oven and cook for 30 minutes, turning once.

❄ Remove from the oven and sprinkle the bacon strips on top of the potatoes. Return to the oven for 15 minutes or until the potatoes and bacon are cooked. Drain off any excess fat and serve.

Curried Roast Potatoes

2 tsp cumin seeds	2 garlic cloves, crushed
2 tsp coriander seeds	2 dried red chillies
85 g/3 oz butter	750 g/1 lb 10 oz baby new
1 tsp ground turmeric	potatoes
1 tsp black mustard seeds	

❄ Grind the cumin and coriander seeds together in a mortar with a pestle or spice grinder. Grinding them fresh like this captures all of the flavour before it has a chance to dry out.

❄ Melt the butter gently in a roasting tin and add the turmeric, mustard seeds, garlic and chillies and the ground cumin and coriander seeds. Stir well to combine evenly. Place in a preheated oven, 200°C/400°F/Gas Mark 6, for 5 minutes.

❄ Remove the tin from the oven – the spices should be very fragrant at this stage – and add the potatoes. Stir well so that the butter and spice mix coats the potatoes completely.

❄ Return to the oven and bake for 20–25 minutes. Stir occasionally to ensure that the potatoes are coated evenly. Test the potatoes with a skewer – if they drop off the end of the skewer when lifted, they are done. Transfer to a serving dish and serve immediately.

Chilli Roast Potatoes

500 g/1 lb 2 oz small new potatoes, scrubbed	1/2 tsp caraway seeds
150 ml/5 fl oz vegetable oil	1 tsp salt
1 tsp chilli powder	1 tbsp chopped basil

❄ Cook the potatoes in a saucepan of boiling water for 10 minutes, then drain thoroughly.

❄ Pour a little of the oil into a shallow roasting tin to coat the base. Heat the oil in a preheated oven, 200°C/400°F/Gas Mark 6, for 10 minutes. Add the potatoes to the tin and brush them with the hot oil.

❄ In a small bowl, mix together the chilli powder, caraway seeds and salt. Sprinkle the mixture over the potatoes, turning to coat them all over.

❄ Add the remaining oil to the tin and roast in the oven for about 15 minutes, or until the potatoes are cooked through.

❄ Using a slotted spoon, remove the potatoes from the oil, draining them well, and transfer them to a warmed serving dish. Sprinkle the chopped basil over the top and serve immediately.

Potatoes with Almonds

2 large potatoes, unpeeled
and sliced
1 tbsp vegetable oil
1 red onion, halved and sliced
1 garlic clove, crushed
50 g/1¾ oz almond flakes
½ tsp turmeric
300 ml/10 fl oz double cream
125 g/4½ oz rocket
salt and pepper

❉ Bring a saucepan of lightly salted water to the boil and cook the sliced potatoes for 10 minutes. Drain thoroughly.

❉ Heat the vegetable oil in a heavy-based frying pan. Add the onion and garlic and fry over a medium heat, stirring frequently, for 3–4 minutes.

❉ Add the almonds, turmeric and potato slices to the frying pan and cook, stirring constantly, for 2–3 minutes. Stir in the rocket.

❉ Transfer the potato and almond mixture to a shallow ovenproof dish. Pour the double cream over the top and season with salt and pepper.

❉ Cook in a preheated oven, 190°C/375°F/Gas Mark 5, for 20 minutes, or until the potatoes are cooked through. Transfer to a warmed serving dish and serve immediately.

Souffléd Cheesy Potatoes

900 g/2 lb potatoes, cut into chunks
150 ml/5 fl oz double cream
75 g/2¾ oz Gruyère cheese, grated
pinch of cayenne pepper
2 egg whites
oil, for deep-frying
salt and pepper
chopped flat-leaf parsley and grated cheese, to garnish

❊ Bring a saucepan of lightly salted water to the boil and cook the potatoes for about 10 minutes. Drain thoroughly and pat dry with absorbent kitchen paper. Set aside until required.

❊ Mix the cream and the Gruyère cheese in a large bowl. Stir in the cayenne pepper and season to taste with salt and pepper.

❊ Whisk the egg whites until stiff peaks form. Gently fold into the cheese mixture until fully incorporated.

❊ Add the cooked potatoes, turning to coat thoroughly in the mixture.

❊ Heat the oil for deep-frying to 180°C/350°F or until a cube of bread browns in 30 seconds. Remove the potatoes from the cheese mixture with a slotted spoon and cook in the oil, in batches, if necessary, for 3–4 minutes or until golden.

❊ Transfer the potatoes to a warmed serving dish and garnish with the parsley and grated cheese. Serve immediately.

Cheesy Garlic Potatoes

1 tbsp butter
675 g/1 lb 8 oz waxy potatoes, sliced
2 garlic cloves, crushed
1 red onion, sliced
85 g/3 oz Gruyère cheese, grated
300 ml/10 fl oz double cream
salt and pepper

❊ Lightly grease a 1-litre/1¾-pint shallow ovenproof dish with butter.

❊ Arrange a single layer of potato slices in the base of the prepared dish.

❊ Top the potato slices with half the garlic, half the onion and one-third of the grated cheese. Season to taste with a little salt and some pepper.

❊ Repeat the layers in exactly the same order, finishing with a layer of potatoes topped with grated cheese.

❊ Pour the cream over the top of the potatoes and cook in a preheated oven, 180°C/350°F/Gas Mark 4, for 1½ hours, or until the potatoes are cooked through and the top is browned and crispy. Serve the potatoes at once, straight from the dish.

Potatoes Fried with Onions

1.25 kg/2 lb 12 oz potatoes
4 tbsp olive oil
25 g/1 oz butter
2 onions, sliced

2–3 garlic cloves, crushed
(optional)
salt and pepper
chopped parsley, to garnish

❖ Slice the potatoes into 5-mm/$\frac{1}{4}$-inch slices. Put in a large saucepan of lightly salted water and bring to the boil. Cover and simmer gently for about 10–12 minutes until just tender. Avoid boiling too rapidly or the potatoes will break up and lose their shape. When cooked, drain well.

❖ While the potatoes are cooking, heat the oil and butter in a very large frying pan. Add the onions and garlic, if using, and fry over a medium heat, stirring frequently, until the onions are soft.

❖ Add the cooked potato slices to the frying pan and cook with the onions, carefully stirring occasionally, for about 5–8 minutes until the potatoes are well browned.

❖ Season to taste with salt and pepper. Sprinkle over the chopped parsley to serve. If liked, transfer the potatoes and onions to a large ovenproof dish and keep warm in a low oven until ready to serve.

Cheese & Potato Layer

500 g/1 lb 2 oz potatoes
1 leek, sliced
3 garlic cloves, crushed
50 g/1$\frac{3}{4}$ oz grated Cheddar
cheese
50 g/1$\frac{3}{4}$ oz grated
mozzarella cheese

25 g/1 oz Parmesan cheese,
grated
2 tbsp chopped parsley
150 ml/5 fl oz single cream
150 ml/5 fl oz milk
salt and pepper
chopped flat-leaf parsley,
to garnish

❖ Bring a saucepan of lightly salted water to the boil and cook the potatoes for 10 minutes. Drain well.

❖ Cut the potatoes into thin slices. Arrange a layer of potatoes in the base of an ovenproof dish. Layer with a little of the leek, garlic, cheeses and parsley. Season to taste.

❖ Repeat the layers until all of the ingredients have been used, finishing with a layer of cheese. Mix the cream and milk together, season with salt and pepper to taste and pour over the potato layers.

❖ Cook in a preheated oven, 160°C/325°F/Gas Mark 3, for 1–1$\frac{1}{4}$ hours or until the cheese is golden brown and bubbling and the potatoes are cooked through and tender.

❖ Garnish with the flat-leaf parsley and serve immediately.

Potatoes Anna

55 g/2 oz butter, melted
675 g/1 lb 8 oz waxy potatoes
4 tbsp chopped mixed herbs
salt and pepper
chopped fresh herbs, to garnish

❄ Brush a shallow 1-litre/1¾-pint ovenproof dish with a little of the melted butter.

❄ Thinly slice the potatoes and pat dry with kitchen paper.

❄ Arrange a layer of potato slices in the prepared dish until the base is covered. Brush with a little butter and sprinkle with a quarter of the chopped mixed herbs. Season to taste.

❄ Continue layering the potato slices, brushing each layer with melted butter and sprinkling with herbs, until they are all used up.

❄ Brush the top layer of potato slices with butter, cover the dish and cook in a preheated oven, 190°C/375°F/Gas Mark 5, for 1½ hours.

❄ Turn out on to a warmed ovenproof platter and return to the oven for a further 25–30 minutes, until golden brown. Serve at once, garnished with fresh herbs.

268

Herby Potatoes with Onion

900 g/2 lb waxy potatoes, cut into cubes
125 g/4½ oz butter
1 red onion, cut into eighths
2 garlic cloves, crushed
1 tsp lemon juice
2 tbsp chopped thyme
salt and pepper

❊ Cook the cubed potatoes in a saucepan of boiling water for 10 minutes. Drain thoroughly.

❊ Melt the butter in a large heavy-based frying pan and add the onion wedges, garlic and lemon juice. Cook, stirring constantly, for 2–3 minutes.

❊ Add the potatoes to the pan and mix well to coat in the butter mixture.

❊ Reduce the heat, cover and cook for 25–30 minutes or until the potatoes are golden brown and tender.

❊ Sprinkle the chopped thyme over the top of the potatoes and season.

❊ Transfer to a warmed serving dish and serve immediately.

Spicy Indian Potatoes

½ tsp coriander seeds
1 tsp cumin seeds
4 tbsp vegetable oil
2 cardamom pods
1-cm/½-inch piece of root ginger, grated
1 red chilli, chopped
1 onion, chopped
2 garlic cloves, crushed
500 g/1 lb 2 oz new potatoes, quartered
150 ml/5 fl oz vegetable stock
675 g/1 lb 8 oz spinach, chopped
4 tbsp natural (unsweetened) yogurt
salt and pepper

❊ Grind the coriander and cumin seeds using a pestle and mortar.

❊ Heat the oil in a frying pan. Add the coriander and the cumin seeds to the pan, together with the cardamom pods and ginger and cook for about 2 minutes.

❊ Add the chilli, onion and garlic to the pan. Cook, stirring frequently, for a further 2 minutes.

❊ Add the potatoes to the pan, together with the stock. Cook gently, stirring occasionally, for 30 minutes or until the potatoes are cooked through.

❊ Add the spinach to the pan and cook for a further 5 minutes.

❊ Remove the pan from the heat and stir in the yogurt. Season to taste with salt and pepper. Transfer the potatoes and spinach to a warmed serving dish and serve immediately.

Spanish Potatoes

2 tbsp olive oil
500 g/1 lb 2 oz small new
    potatoes, halved
1 onion, halved and sliced
1 green pepper,
    seeded and cut into strips

1 tsp chilli powder
1 tsp prepared mustard
300 ml/10 fl oz passata
300 ml/10 fl oz vegetable stock
chopped parsley, to garnish

❊ Heat the olive oil in a large heavy-based frying pan. Add the potatoes and the onion and cook, stirring frequently, for 4–5 minutes, until the onion slices are soft and translucent.

❊ Add the pepper strips, chilli powder and mustard to the pan and cook for a further 2–3 minutes.

❊ Stir the passata and the stock into the pan and bring to the boil. Reduce the heat and simmer for about 25 minutes or until the potatoes are tender.

❊ Transfer the potatoes to a warmed serving dish. Sprinkle the parsley over the top and serve immediately. Alternatively, leave to cool completely and serve cold, at room temperature.

Potatoes, Olives & Anchovies

450 g/1 lb baby new potatoes,
    scrubbed
85 g/3 oz mixed olives
8 canned anchovy fillets,
    drained and chopped
2 tbsp olive oil

2 fennel bulbs, trimmed
    and sliced
2 sprigs fresh rosemary,
    stalks removed
salt

❊ Bring a large saucepan of lightly salted water to the boil. Add the potatoes, bring back to the boil and simmer over a medium heat for 8–10 minutes or until tender. Remove the potatoes from the pan using a slotted spoon and set aside to cool slightly.

❊ Once the potatoes are cool enough to handle, cut them into wedges, using a sharp knife.

❊ Stone the mixed olives and cut them in half.

❊ Using a sharp knife, chop the anchovy fillets into thinner strips.

❊ Heat the olive oil in a large heavy-based frying pan. Add the potato wedges, fennel and rosemary. Cook over a medium heat, gently stirring occasionally, for 7–8 minutes or until the potatoes are golden.

❊ Stir in the olives and anchovies and cook for 1 minute or until completely warmed through.

❊ Transfer the potato mixture to warmed individual serving plates and serve immediately.

Potatoes with Peas

150 ml/5 fl oz oil
3 medium onions, sliced
1 tsp crushed garlic
1 tsp finely chopped root ginger
1 tsp chilli powder
$1/2$ tsp turmeric
1 tsp salt
2 fresh green chillies,
finely chopped
300 ml/10 fl oz water
3 potatoes
100 g/$3^1/2$ oz peas
fresh coriander leaves and
chopped red chillies,
to garnish

❖ Heat the oil in a large heavy-based frying pan.

❖ Add the onions to the frying pan and fry, stirring occasionally, until the onions are golden brown.

❖ Mix together the garlic, ginger, chilli powder, turmeric, salt and chillies. Add the spice mixture to the onions in the pan.

❖ Stir in 150 ml/5 fl oz of the water, cover and cook until the onions are cooked through.

❖ Meanwhile, cut the potatoes into six slices each, using a sharp knife.

❖ Add the potato slices to the mixture in the pan and stir-fry for 5 minutes.

❖ Add the peas and the remaining 150 ml/5 fl oz of the water to the pan, cover and cook for 7–10 minutes.

❖ Transfer the potatoes and peas to serving plates and serve, garnished with the coriander.

Potato Hash

2 tbsp butter
1 red onion, halved and sliced
1 carrot, diced
25 g/1 oz French beans, halved
900 g/2 lb waxy potatoes, diced
2 tbsp plain flour
600 ml/1 pint vegetable stock
225 g/8 oz firm tofu, diced
salt and pepper
chopped fresh parsley,
    to garnish

❊ Melt the butter in a large heavy-based frying pan. Add the onion, carrot, French beans and potatoes and fry over a fairly low heat, stirring constantly, for about 5–7 minutes or until the vegetables begin to turn golden brown.

❊ Add the flour to the pan and cook, stirring constantly, for 1 minute. Gradually pour in the stock, still stirring constantly.

❊ Reduce the heat to low and simmer for 15 minutes or until the potatoes are tender.

❊ Add the tofu to the pan and cook for a further 5 minutes. Season to taste with salt and pepper.

❊ Sprinkle the parsley over the top of the potato hash to garnish and then serve hot, straight from the frying pan.

Crispy Potato Cakes

900 g/2 lb potatoes
25–55 g/1–2 oz unsalted butter
    or margarine
1–2 tbsp olive oil
salt and pepper

❊ Cook the unpeeled potatoes in a large saucepan of water for 10 minutes. Drain and leave to cool. Transfer he potatoes to a plate and chill in the refrigerator for 30 minutes or longer.

❊ Peel and coarsely grate the potatoes. Melt 25 g/1 oz of the butter with 1 tablespoon of the olive oil in a heavy-based 23-cm/9-inch frying pan over a medium heat. Spread out the grated potato evenly in the pan, reduce the heat and cook for 10 minutes.

❊ Cover the pan with a plate and invert the pan and the plate. Slide the potato back into the pan to cook the second side. Cook for 10 minutes more, adding more butter and olive oil if necessary. Season to taste with salt and pepper and serve immediately.

Singapore Noodles

225 g/8 oz rice noodles
25 g/1 oz dried Chinese
mushrooms, soaked in hot
water for 30 minutes
4 tbsp groundnut or
sunflower oil
4 shallots, chopped
2 garlic cloves, finely chopped
2 fresh green chillies,
deseeded and finely chopped

2 tsp curry powder
115 g/4 oz baby sweetcorn,
halved
115 g/4 oz mangetout
1 green pepper, deseeded
and sliced
115 g/4 oz Chinese leaves,
shredded
2 tbsp soy sauce
salt

❈ Soak the noodles in a bowl of boiling water for 10 minutes, or according to the packet instructions. Meanwhile, drain the mushrooms, discard the stalks and slice the caps. Drain the noodles and pat dry with kitchen paper.

❈ Heat half the oil in a preheated wok or frying pan. Add the noodles and a pinch of salt and stir-fry for 2 minutes. Transfer to a dish and keep warm.

❈ Heat the remaining oil in the wok. Add the shallots, garlic and chillies and stir-fry for 2–3 minutes. Stir in the curry powder and cook, stirring, for 1 minute. Add the sweetcorn, mangetout, green pepper and Chinese leaves and stir-fry for 5 minutes or until the vegetables are tender but still have some bite.

❈ Stir in the mushrooms and return the noodles to the wok. Stir-fry for 2 minutes, then add the soy sauce. Serve immediately.

Thai-Style Stir-Fried Noodles

225 g/8 oz dried rice noodles
2 red chillies, deseeded and
finely chopped
2 shallots, finely chopped
2 tbsp sugar
2 tbsp tamarind water
1 tbsp lime juice

2 tbsp light soy sauce
1 tbsp sunflower oil
1 tsp sesame oil
175 g/6 oz diced smoked tofu
pepper
2 tbsp chopped roasted
peanuts, to garnish

❈ Cook the noodles as directed on the packet, or soak them in boiling water for 5 minutes.

❈ Grind together the chillies, shallots, sugar, tamarind water, lime juice, soy sauce and pepper to taste.

❈ Heat both the oils together in a preheated wok or large, heavy frying pan over a high heat. Add the tofu and stir for 1 minute.

❈ Add the chilli mixture, bring to the boil, and cook, stirring constantly, for about 2 minutes, until thickened.

❈ Drain the rice noodles and add them to the chilli mixture. Use 2 spoons to lift and stir them until they are no longer steaming. Serve immediately, garnished with the peanuts.

Sesame Hot Noodles

500 g/1 lb 2 oz dried medium
egg noodles
3 tbsp sunflower oil
2 tbsp sesame oil
1 garlic clove, crushed
1 tbsp smooth peanut butter
1 small green chilli, deseeded
and very finely chopped
3 tbsp toasted sesame seeds
4 tbsp light soy sauce
$\frac{1}{2}$ tbsp lime juice
4 tbsp chopped fresh coriander
salt and pepper

❖   Place the noodles in a large saucepan of boiling water, then immediately remove from the heat. Cover and leave to stand for 6 minutes, stirring once halfway through the time. At the end of 6 minutes the noodles will be perfectly cooked. Alternatively, cook the noodles following the packet instructions.

❖   Meanwhile, make the dressing. Mix together the sunflower oil, sesame oil, crushed garlic and peanut butter in a mixing bowl until smooth.

❖   Add the chilli, sesame seeds and soy sauce to the bowl. Add the lime juice, according to taste, and mix well. Season to taste with salt and pepper.

❖   Drain the noodles thoroughly then place in a heated serving bowl.

❖   Add the dressing and the coriander to the noodles and toss well to mix. Serve hot as a main meal or as an accompaniment.

Fried Noodles

275 g/9½ oz egg noodles
3–4 tbsp vegetable oil
1 small onion, finely shredded
125 g/4½ oz fresh beansprouts

1 spring onion, finely shredded
2 tbsp light soy sauce
a few drops of sesame oil
salt

❋ Bring a wok or saucepan of lightly salted water to the boil, add the egg noodles and cook according to the instructions on the packet (usually no more than 4–5 minutes).

❋ Drain the noodles well and rinse in cold water; drain thoroughly again, then transfer to a large mixing bowl and toss with a little vegetable oil.

❋ Heat the remaining vegetable oil in a preheated wok or large frying pan until really hot.

❋ Add the onion to the wok and stir-fry for about 30–40 seconds.

❋ Add the beansprouts and drained noodles to the wok, stir and toss for 1 more minute.

❋ Add the spring onion and soy sauce and blend well.

❋ Transfer the noodles to a warmed serving dish, sprinkle with the sesame oil and serve immediately.

Fried Vegetable Noodles

350 g/12 oz dried egg noodles
2 tbsp groundnut oil
2 garlic cloves, crushed
½ tsp ground star anise
1 carrot, cut into matchsticks
1 green pepper, cut into matchsticks
1 onion, quartered and sliced

125 g/4½ oz broccoli florets
75 g/2¾ oz bamboo shoots
1 celery stick, sliced
1 tbsp light soy sauce
150 ml/5 fl oz vegetable stock
oil, for deep-frying
1 tsp cornflour
2 tsp water

❋ Bring a saucepan of lightly salted water to the boil and cook the noodles for 1–2 minutes. Drain well and rinse under cold running water. Leave the noodles to drain thoroughly in a colander until required.

❋ Heat the groundnut oil in a preheated wok until smoking. Reduce the heat, add the garlic and star anise and stir-fry for 30 seconds. Add the remaining vegetables and stir-fry for 1–2 minutes.

❋ Add the soy sauce and stock to the wok and cook over a low heat for 5 minutes.

❋ Heat the oil for deep-frying to 180°C/350°F or until a cube of bread browns in 30 seconds.

❋ Using a fork, twist the drained noodles and form them into rounds. Deep-fry them in batches until crisp, turning once. Leave to drain on kitchen paper.

❋ Blend the cornflour with the water to form a paste and stir into the wok. Bring to the boil, stirring until the sauce is thickened and clear.

❋ Arrange the noodles on a warmed serving plate, spoon the vegetables on top and serve immediately.

Pilau Rice

❖ **SERVES 4** ❖

200 g/7 oz basmati rice	3 peppercorns
2 tbsp ghee	1/2 tsp salt
3 green cardamoms	1/2 tsp saffron
2 cloves	400 ml/14 fl oz boiling water

❖ Rinse the rice twice under running water and set aside until required.

❖ Heat the ghee in a saucepan. Add the cardamoms, cloves and peppercorns to the pan and fry, stirring constantly, for about 1 minute.

❖ Add the rice and stir-fry over a medium heat for a further 2 minutes.

❖ Add the salt, saffron and water to the rice mixture and reduce the heat. Cover the pan and simmer over a low heat until the water has been absorbed.

❖ Transfer to a serving dish and serve hot.

Special Fried Rice

❖ **SERVES 4** ❖

175 g/6 oz long-grain rice	1 garlic clove, crushed
55 g/2 oz cashew nuts	125 g/41/2 oz frozen peas,
1 carrot	thawed
1/2 cucumber	1 tbsp soy sauce
1 yellow pepper	1 tsp salt
2 spring onions	fresh coriander leaves,
2 tbsp vegetable oil	to garnish

❖ Bring a large saucepan of water to the boil. Add the rice to the pan and simmer for 15 minutes. Tip the rice into a sieve and rinse; drain thoroughly.

❖ Heat a wok or large heavy-based frying pan, add the cashew nuts and dry-fry until lightly browned. Remove and set aside.

❖ Cut the carrot in half along the length, then slice thinly into semi-circles. Halve the cucumber lengthways and remove the seeds, using a teaspoon, then dice the flesh. Deseed and slice the pepper and chop the spring onions.

❖ Heat the oil in a wok or large frying pan. Add the prepared vegetables and the garlic. Stir-fry for 3 minutes. Add the rice, peas, soy sauce and salt. Continue to stir-fry until the vegetables are just cooked and the rice is thoroughly heated.

❖ Stir in the reserved cashew nuts. Transfer to a warmed serving dish, garnish with the coriander leaves and serve immediately.

Egg-Fried Rice

150 g/5^1/$_2$ oz long-grain rice
3 eggs, beaten
2 tbsp vegetable oil
2 garlic cloves, crushed
4 spring onions, chopped
125 g/4^1/$_2$ oz cooked peas
1 tbsp light soy sauce
pinch of salt
shredded spring onion,
to garnish

❖ Bring a large saucepan of lightly salted water to the boil and cook the rice for 10–12 minutes until it is almost cooked but not soft. Drain well, rinse under cold water and drain again.

❖ Place the beaten eggs in a saucepan and cook over a gentle heat, stirring until softly scrambled.

❖ Heat the vegetable oil in a preheated wok or large frying pan, swirling the oil around the base of the wok until it is really hot.

❖ Add the crushed garlic, spring onions and cooked peas and sauté, stirring occasionally, for 1–2 minutes. Stir the rice into the wok, mixing to combine.

❖ Add the scrambled eggs, the soy sauce and a pinch of salt to the wok and stir until the eggs are thoroughly mixed in.

❖ When the eggs are cooked, transfer the egg-fried rice to warmed serving dishes and serve, garnished with the shredded spring onion.

Chinese Fried Rice

700 ml/1¼ pints water
½ tsp salt
300 g/10½ oz long-grain rice
2 eggs
4 tsp cold water
3 tbsp sunflower oil
4 spring onions, sliced
diagonally

1 red, green or yellow pepper,
deseeded and thinly sliced
3–4 rashers lean bacon, rinded
and cut into strips
200 g/7 oz fresh beansprouts
115 g/4 oz frozen peas, thawed
2 tbsp soy sauce (optional)
salt and pepper

❄ Pour the water into a wok with the salt and bring to the boil. Rinse the rice in a sieve under cold running water until the water runs clear, drain well and add to the boiling water. Stir well, then cover the wok tightly with the lid, and simmer gently for 12–13 minutes. (Don't remove the lid during cooking or the steam will escape and the rice will not be cooked.)

❄ Remove the lid, stir the rice and spread out on a large plate or baking tray to cool and dry.

❄ Beat each egg separately with salt and pepper and 2 teaspoons of cold water. Heat 1 tablespoon of the oil in the wok, pour in the first egg, swirl it around and cook, undisturbed, until set. Remove to a board and cook the second egg. Cut the omelettes into thin strips.

❄ Add the remaining oil to the wok, add the spring onions and pepper and stir-fry for 1–2 minutes. Add the bacon and continue to stir-fry for a further 1–2 minutes. Add the beansprouts and peas and toss together thoroughly. Stir in the soy sauce, if using.

❄ Add the rice and seasoning and stir-fry for about 1 minute, then add the strips of omelette and continue to stir for about 2 minutes or until the rice is piping hot. Transfer to a warmed serving dish and serve immediately. Remove the lid, stir the rice and spread out on a large plate or baking tray to cool and dry.

Cumin Rice

2 tbsp butter
1 tbsp vegetable oil
1 green pepper, deseeded and
sliced
1 red pepper, deseeded and
sliced
3 spring onions, thinly sliced

3–4 garlic cloves, finely
chopped
175 g/6 oz long-grain rice
1½ tsp cumin seeds
½ tsp dried oregano or
marjoram, crushed
450 ml/16 fl oz vegetable stock

❄ Heat the butter and oil in a heavy-based saucepan or flameproof casserole. Add the sliced peppers and cook, stirring occasionally, until soft.

❄ Add the spring onions, garlic, rice and cumin seeds. Cook, stirring constantly, for about 5 minutes or until the rice turns slightly golden.

❄ Add the oregano and the stock to the pan, bring to the boil, then reduce the heat and simmer gently for 5–10 minutes until the rice is tender.

❄ Cover with a clean tea towel and remove from the heat. Set aside for about 10 minutes to cool slightly. Fluff up the rice with a fork, transfer to a large serving dish and serve.

Fragrant Coconut Rice

275 g/9½ oz long-grain rice
600 ml/1 pint water
½ tsp salt
100 ml/3½ fl oz coconut milk
25 g/1 oz desiccated coconut

❊ Rinse the rice under cold running water until the water runs completely clear.

❊ Drain the rice thoroughly in a sieve set over a large bowl. This is to remove some of the starch and to prevent the grains sticking together.

❊ Place the rice in a wok with the water. Add the salt and coconut milk to the wok and bring to the boil.

❊ Cover the wok with its lid or a lid made of foil, curved into a domed shape and resting on the sides of the wok. Reduce the heat and leave to simmer for 10 minutes.

❊ Remove the lid from the wok and fluff up the rice with a fork – all of the liquid should be absorbed and the rice grains should be tender. If the rice is not quite cooked, add a little more water, replace the lid and continue to simmer for a few more minutes until all the liquid has been absorbed.

❊ Spoon the rice into a warmed serving bowl and scatter with the desiccated coconut. Serve immediately.

Saffron Rice

12 saffron threads, lightly crushed
2 tbsp warm water
400 ml/14 fl oz water
225 g/8 oz basmati rice
1 tbsp toasted, flaked almonds

❊ Put the saffron threads into a bowl with the warm water and leave for 10 minutes. They need to be crushed before soaking to ensure that the maximum flavour and colour is extracted at this stage.

❊ Put the water and rice into a medium-sized saucepan and set it over the heat to boil. Add the saffron and saffron water and stir.

❊ Bring back to a gentle boil, stir again and let the rice simmer, uncovered, for about 10 minutes, until all the water has been absorbed.

❊ Cover tightly, reduce the heat as much as possible and leave for 10 minutes. Do not remove the lid. This ensures that the grains separate and that the rice is not soggy.

❊ Alternatively, you can soak the rice overnight and drain before cooking. Cook as before but reduce the cooking time by 3–4 minutes to compensate for the presoaking.

❊ Remove the rice from the heat and transfer to a serving dish. Fork through the rice gently and sprinkle over the toasted almonds before serving.

Rice with Lime

2 tbsp vegetable oil
1 small onion, finely chopped
3 garlic cloves, finely chopped
175 g/6 oz long-grain rice
450 ml/16 fl oz vegetable stock
juice of 1 lime
1 tbsp chopped fresh coriander

❖ Heat the oil in a heavy-based saucepan or flameproof casserole. Add the onion and garlic and cook gently, stirring occasionally, for 2 minutes.

❖ Add the rice and cook for a further minute, stirring constantly. Pour in the stock, increase the heat and bring the rice to the boil. Reduce the heat to a very low simmer.

❖ Cover and cook the rice for about 10 minutes or until it is just tender and the liquid is absorbed.

❖ Sprinkle in the lime juice and fork the rice to fluff up and to mix the juice in. Sprinkle with the chopped coriander and serve immediately.

Fruity Coconut Rice

85 g/3 oz creamed coconut
700 ml/1¼ pints boiling water
1 tbsp sunflower oil (or olive oil
    for a stronger flavour)
1 onion, thinly sliced
    or chopped
250 g/9 oz long-grain rice
¼ tsp turmeric
6 whole cloves

1 cinnamon stick
½ tsp salt
55–85 g/2–3 oz raisins or
    sultanas
55 g/2 oz walnut or pecan nut
    halves, roughly chopped
2 tbsp pumpkin seeds
    (optional)

❉ Blend the creamed coconut with half the boiling water until smooth, then stir in the remainder until well blended.

❉ Heat the oil in a preheated wok, add the onion and stir-fry gently for 3–4 minutes until the onion begins to soften.

❉ Rinse the rice thoroughly under cold running water, drain well and add to the wok with the turmeric. Cook for 1–2 minutes, stirring all the time.

❉ Add the coconut milk, cloves, cinnamon stick and salt to the wok and bring to the boil. Cover and cook very gently for 10 minutes.

❉ Add the raisins, nuts and pumpkin seeds, if using, and mix well. Cover the wok again and continue to cook for a further 5–8 minutes or until all the liquid has been absorbed and the rice is tender. Remove from the heat and leave to stand, still tightly covered, for 5 minutes. Remove the cinnamon stick and serve.

Tomato Rice

150 ml/5 fl oz vegetable oil
2 medium onions, sliced
1 tsp onion seeds
1 tsp finely chopped
    root ginger
1 tsp crushed garlic
½ tsp ground turmeric
1 tsp chilli powder
1½ tsp salt

400 g/14 oz canned tomatoes
500 g/1 lb 2 oz basmati rice
600 ml/1 pint water

TO GARNISH
3 fresh green chillies, finely
    chopped
chopped fresh coriander
3 hard-boiled eggs

❉ Heat the oil in a heavy-based saucepan. Add the onions and fry over a moderate heat, stirring frequently, for 5 minutes until golden brown.

❉ Add the onion seeds, ginger, garlic, turmeric, chilli powder and salt, stirring to combine.

❉ Reduce the heat, add the tomatoes and stir-fry for 10 minutes, breaking them up.

❉ Add the rice to the tomato mixture, stirring gently to coat the rice completely. Stir in the water. Cover the pan and cook over a low heat until the water has been absorbed and the rice is tender, but still has some bite.

❉ Transfer the tomato rice to a warmed serving dish. Garnish with the finely chopped green chillies, coriander leaves and hard-boiled eggs. Serve the tomato rice immediately.

Lemon-Scented Rice

❊ **SERVES 6–8** ❊

2 tbsp olive oil or butter
2–4 spring onions, finely chopped
3–4 tbsp chopped fresh mint
300 g/10$^{1}/_{2}$ oz long-grain rice
500 ml/18 fl oz chicken stock

1 lemon
salt and pepper

TO GARNISH
2–3 sprigs fresh mint
thin slices of lemon
thin slices of lime

❊ Heat the oil in a medium-sized heavy-based saucepan over a medium heat. Add the spring onions and mint and cook, stirring constantly, for about 1 minute until brightly coloured and giving off their aroma.

❊ Add the rice and cook, stirring frequently, for about 2 minutes until well coated with the oil and just translucent. Add the stock and bring to the boil, stirring once or twice. Season to taste with salt and pepper.

❊ Pare 3–4 strips of lemon rind and add to the pan. Squeeze the juice from the lemon and stir into the rice and stock.

❊ When the stock comes to the boil, reduce the heat to low and simmer gently, tightly covered, for about 20 minutes until the rice is tender and the stock absorbed. Remove the pan from the heat and set aside for 5–10 minutes.

❊ Fork the rice into a warmed serving bowl, garnish with the mint and slices of lemon and lime. Serve hot.

Green Rice

❊ **SERVES 4** ❊

1–2 onions, halved and unpeeled
6–8 large garlic cloves, unpeeled
1 large mild chilli, or 1 green pepper and 1 small green chilli
1 bunch of fresh coriander leaves, chopped

225 ml/8 fl oz chicken or vegetable stock
6 tbsp vegetable or olive oil
175 g/6 oz long-grain rice
salt and pepper
sprig of fresh coriander, to garnish

❊ Heat a heavy-based ungreased frying pan and cook the onion, garlic, chilli and green pepper, if using, until lightly charred on all sides, including the cut sides of the onions. Cover and then set aside to cool.

❊ When the vegetables are cool enough to handle, remove the seeds and skins from the chilli and green pepper, if using. Chop the flesh.

❊ Remove the skins from the onions and garlic and chop the flesh finely.

❊ Place the chilli, green pepper, if using, onions and garlic in a food processor with the coriander leaves and stock, then process to a smooth thin purée.

❊ Heat the oil in a heavy-based saucepan and fry the rice until it is glistening and lightly browned in places, stirring to prevent it burning. Add the vegetable purée, cover and cook over a low heat for 10–15 minutes until the rice is just tender.

❊ Fluff up the rice with a fork, then cover and set for about 5 minutes. Adjust the seasoning, garnish with the sprig of coriander and serve.

Spiced Rice with Lentils

200 g/7 oz basmati rice
175 g/6 oz masoor dhal
2 tbsp ghee
1 small onion, sliced
1 tsp finely chopped
root ginger
1 tsp crushed garlic
1/2 tsp turmeric
600 ml/1 pint water
1 tsp salt

❖ Combine the rice and dhal and rinse thoroughly in cold running water. Set aside until required.

❖ Heat the ghee in a large saucepan. Add the onion and fry, stirring occasionally, for about 2 minutes.

❖ Reduce the heat, add the ginger, garlic and turmeric to the pan and stir-fry for 1 minute.

❖ Add the rice and dhal to the mixture in the pan and blend together, mixing gently, but thoroughly.

❖ Add the water to the mixture in the pan and bring it to the boil over a medium heat. Reduce the heat, cover and cook for 20–25 minutes until the rice is tender and the liquid is absorbed.

❖ Just before serving, add the salt and mix to combine.

❖ Transfer the spiced rice and lentils to a warmed serving dish and serve immediately.

Oriental–Style Millet Pilau

300 g/10^1/$_2$ oz millet grains
1 tbsp vegetable oil
1 bunch of spring onions, white
and green parts, chopped
1 garlic clove, crushed
1 tsp grated root ginger
1 orange pepper, deseeded
and diced
600 ml/1 pint water

1 orange
115 g/4 oz chopped stoned
dates
2 tsp sesame oil
115 g/4 oz roasted cashew nuts
2 tbsp pumpkin seeds
salt and pepper
salad vegetables,
to serve

❊ Place the millet in a large saucepan and toast over a medium heat, shaking the pan occasionally, for 4–5 minutes until the grains begin to crack and pop.

❊ Heat the oil in another saucepan. Add the spring onions, garlic, ginger and pepper and cook over a medium heat, stirring frequently, for 2–3 minutes until just soft but not brown. Add the millet and pour in the water.

❊ Using a vegetable peeler, pare the rind from the orange and add the rind to the pan. Squeeze the juice from the orange into the pan. Season to taste with salt and pepper.

❊ Bring to the boil, reduce the heat, cover and cook gently for 20 minutes until all the liquid has been absorbed. Remove the pan from the heat, stir in the dates and sesame oil and set aside to stand for 10 minutes.

❊ Remove and discard the orange rind and stir in the cashew nuts. Pile into a warmed serving dish, sprinkle with the pumpkin seeds and serve immediately with the salad vegetables.

Soda Bread

❊ SERVES 4 ❊

butter, for greasing
300 g/10^1/$_2$ oz plain white flour,
plus extra for dusting
300 g/10^1/$_2$ oz plain wholemeal
flour
2 tsp baking powder

1 tsp bicarbonate of soda
25 g/1 oz caster sugar
1 tsp salt
1 egg, beaten
425 ml/15 fl oz natural yogurt

❊ Grease a baking tray with butter and dust with flour.

❊ Sift the flours, baking powder, bicarbonate of soda, sugar and salt into a large bowl and add any bran remaining in the sieve.

❊ In a jug, beat together the egg and yogurt and pour the mixture into the dry ingredients. Mix everything together to make a soft and sticky dough.

❊ On a lightly floured surface, knead the dough for a few minutes until it is smooth, then shape the dough into a round about 5 cm/2 inches deep.

❊ Transfer the dough to the baking tray. Mark a cross shape in the top of the loaf.

❊ Bake in a preheated oven, 190°C/375°F/Gas Mark 5, for about 40 minutes or until the bread is golden brown all over.

❊ Transfer the loaf to a wire rack and leave to cool completely. Cut into slices to serve.

Nutty Soda Bread

450 g/1 lb plain flour, plus extra for dusting
1 tsp bicarbonate of soda
1 tsp cream of tartar
1 tsp salt
1 tsp sugar
50 g/1¾ oz chopped walnuts
50 g/1¾ oz chopped pecan nuts
300 ml/10 fl oz buttermilk

❖ Preheat the oven to 180°/350°F/Gas Mark 4. Dust a baking tray with flour.

❖ Sift the flour, bicarbonate of soda, cream of tartar and salt into a large mixing bowl. Stir in the sugar and nuts. Pour in the buttermilk and mix to a soft dough.

❖ With floured hands, knead the dough briefly on a lightly floured work surface, then shape into a 20–25-cm/8–10-inch round and transfer to the prepared baking tray. Cut a cross in the top of the dough.

❖ Bake in the preheated oven for 30 minutes, then cover with foil and bake for a further 15 minutes.

❖ Remove from the oven and allow to cool slightly. Serve warm, in slices.

Garlic Bread Rolls

butter, for greasing
12 garlic cloves, peeled
350 ml/12 fl oz milk
450 g/1 lb strong white flour
1 tsp salt
1 sachet easy-blend dried yeast
1 tbsp dried mixed herbs
2 tbsp sunflower oil
1 egg, beaten
milk, for brushing
rock salt, for sprinkling

❖ Lightly grease a baking tray with a little butter.

❖ Place the garlic cloves and milk in a saucepan, bring to the boil and simmer gently for 15 minutes. Leave to cool slightly, then process in a blender or food processor to purée the garlic.

❖ Sift the flour and salt into a large mixing bowl and stir in the dried yeast and mixed herbs.

❖ Add the garlic-flavoured milk, sunflower oil and beaten egg to the dry ingredients and mix everything thoroughly to form a dough.

❖ Place the dough on a lightly floured work surface and knead lightly for a few minutes until smooth and soft.

❖ Place the dough in a lightly greased bowl, cover and set aside to rise in a warm place for about 1 hour or until doubled in size.

❖ Knock back the dough by kneading it for 2 minutes. Shape into 8 rolls and place on the baking tray. Score the top of each roll with a knife, cover and set aside for 15 minutes.

❖ Brush the rolls with milk and sprinkle rock salt over the top. Bake in a preheated oven, 220°C/425°F/Gas Mark 7, for 15–20 minutes. Transfer the rolls to a wire rack and leave to cool before serving.

Sesame Breadsticks

225 g/8 oz unbleached strong white flour, plus extra for dusting
225 g/8 oz strong wholemeal flour
1 sachet easy-blend dried yeast
2 tsp salt
½ tsp sugar
450 ml/16 fl oz lukewarm water
4 tbsp olive oil, plus extra for greasing
1 egg white, lightly beaten
sesame seeds, for sprinkling

❖ Combine the flours, yeast, salt and sugar in a bowl and make a well in the centre. Gradually stir in most of the water and the olive oil to make a dough. Gradually add the remaining water, if necessary, drawing in all the flour.

❖ Turn out on to a lightly floured surface and knead for about 10 minutes until smooth and elastic. Wash the bowl and lightly coat with olive oil.

❖ Shape the dough into a ball, put it in the bowl and turn over so it is coated. Cover tightly with a tea towel or lightly oiled clingfilm and set aside in a warm place until the dough has doubled in volume. Meanwhile, line a baking tray with baking paper.

❖ Turn out the dough on to a lightly floured surface and knead lightly. Divide the dough into 2 equal pieces. Roll each piece into a 40-cm/16-inch rope and then cut each rope into 8 equal pieces. Cut each piece in half again to make a total of 32 pieces.

❖ Cover the dough you are not working with a tea towel or clingfilm to prevent it from drying out. Roll each piece of dough into a thin 25-cm/10-inch rope on a very lightly floured surface. Carefully transfer to the baking tray.

❖ Cover and set aside to rise for 10 minutes. Brush with the egg white, then sprinkle evenly and thickly with sesame seeds. Bake in a preheated oven, 230°C/450°F/ Gas Mark 8, for 10 minutes.

❖ Brush again with egg white, and bake for a further 5 minutes or until golden brown and crisp. Transfer the breadsticks to wire racks to cool.

Sweet Potato Bread

5 tbsp butter, plus extra
for greasing
225 g/8 oz sweet potatoes,
diced
150 ml/5 fl oz hand-hot water
2 tbsp clear honey
2 tbsp vegetable oil

3 tbsp orange juice
75 g/2¾ oz semolina
225 g/8 oz strong white flour
1 sachet easy-blend dried yeast
1 tsp ground cinnamon
grated rind of 1 orange

❖ Lightly grease a 675-g/1½-lb loaf tin. Bring a saucepan of lightly salted water to the boil and cook the sweet potatoes for about 10 minutes or until soft. Drain well and mash until smooth.

❖ Meanwhile, mix together the water, honey, vegetable oil and orange juice in a large mixing bowl.

❖ Add the mashed sweet potatoes, semolina, three-quarters of the flour, the yeast, ground cinnamon and grated orange rind and mix thoroughly to form a dough. Set aside for about 10 minutes.

❖ Dice the butter and knead it into the dough with the remaining flour. Knead for about 5 minutes until smooth.

❖ Place the dough in the prepared loaf tin. Cover and set aside in a warm place for 1 hour or until doubled in size.

❖ Bake the loaf in a preheated oven, 190°C/375°F/Gas Mark 5, for 45–60 minutes, or until the base sounds hollow when tapped.

❖ Serve the bread while it is still warm, cut into slices.

Mexican Cornbread

125 g/4½ oz plain flour
125 g/4½ oz polenta
1 tbsp baking powder
½ tsp salt
1 green chilli, deseeded and
finely chopped

5 spring onions, finely chopped
2 eggs
140 ml/4½ fl oz soured cream
125 ml/4 fl oz sunflower oil

❖ Grease a 20-cm/8-inch square cake tin and line the base with baking paper.

❖ In a large bowl, mix together the flour, polenta, baking powder and salt.

❖ Add the chilli and the spring onions to the dry ingredients and mix well.

❖ In a mixing jug, beat the eggs together with the soured cream and sunflower oil. Pour the mixture into the bowl of dry ingredients. Mix everything together quickly and thoroughly.

❖ Pour the mixture into the prepared cake tin.

❖ Bake in a preheated oven, 200°C/ 400°F/ Gas Mark 6, for about 20–25 minutes or until the loaf has risen and is lightly browned.

❖ Leave the bread to cool slightly before turning out of the tin. Cut into bars or squares to serve.

Red Pepper Cornbread

1 large red pepper, deseeded and sliced	1 tsp salt
	2 tsp sugar
175 g/6 oz fine polenta	250 ml/9 fl oz milk
115 g/4 oz strong white flour	2 eggs, lightly beaten
	3 tbsp olive oil, plus extra
1 tbsp baking powder	for oiling

❊ Preheat the oven to 200°C/400°F/Gas Mark 6. Lightly oil a 450-g/1-lb loaf tin. Arrange the pepper slices on a baking tray and roast in the preheated oven for 35 minutes until tender and the skin begins to blister. Set aside to cool slightly, then peel away the skin.

❊ Meanwhile, mix together the polenta, flour, baking powder, salt and sugar in a large mixing bowl. Beat together the milk, eggs and oil in a separate bowl or jug and gradually add to the flour mixture. Beat with a wooden spoon to make a thick, smooth, batter-like consistency.

❊ Finely chop the red pepper and fold into the polenta mixture, then spoon into the prepared tin. Bake in the preheated oven for 30 minutes until lightly golden. Leave in the tin for 10 minutes, then run a knife around the edge of the tin and turn out the loaf on to a wire rack to cool. To keep fresh, wrap the loaf in foil or seal in a polythene bag.

Spiced Pumpkin Bread

450 g/1 lb pumpkin flesh	225 g/8 oz plain flour, sifted
125 g/4½ oz butter, softened	1½ tsp baking powder
175 g/6 oz caster sugar	½ tsp salt
2 eggs, beaten	1 tsp mixed spice

❊ Grease a 900-g/2-lb loaf tin with oil.

❊ Chop the pumpkin into large pieces and wrap in buttered foil. Cook in a preheated oven, 200°C/400°F/Gas Mark 6, for 30–40 minutes or until tender.

❊ Leave the pumpkin to cool completely before mashing well to make a thick purée.

❊ In a bowl, cream together the butter and sugar until light and fluffy. Add the eggs a little at a time.

❊ Stir in the pumpkin purée. Fold in the flour, baking powder, salt and mixed spice.

❊ Fold the pumpkin seeds gently through the mixture. Spoon the mixture into the loaf tin.

❊ Bake in a preheated oven, 160°C/325°F/Gas Mark 3, for 1¼–1½ hours, or until a skewer inserted into the centre of the loaf comes out clean.

❊ Leave the loaf to cool and serve buttered, if wished.

Sun-Dried Tomato Loaf

1^1/$_2$ tsp dried yeast
1 tsp granulated sugar
300 ml/10 fl oz hand-hot water
450 g/1 lb strong white flour
1 tsp salt
2 tsp dried basil
2 tbsp sun-dried tomato purée
12 sun-dried tomatoes in oil,
drained and cut into strips
oil, for oiling
margarine, for greasing

❖ Place the yeast and sugar in a bowl and mix with 100 ml/3^1/$_2$ fl oz of the water. Leave to ferment in a warm place for 15 minutes.

❖ Place the flour in a bowl and stir in the salt. Make a well in the dry ingredients and add the basil, yeast mixture, tomato purée and half the remaining water. Using a wooden spoon, draw the flour into the liquid and mix to form a dough, adding the rest of the water a little at a time.

❖ Turn out the dough on to a floured surface and knead for 5 minutes or until smooth. Cover with oiled clingfilm and leave in a warm place to rise for about 30 minutes or until doubled in size.

❖ Lightly grease a 900-g/2-lb loaf tin with a little margarine.

❖ Remove the dough from the bowl and knead in the sun-dried tomatoes. Knead again for 2–3 minutes.

❖ Place the dough in the prepared tin and leave to rise for 30–40 minutes or until it has doubled in size again. Bake in a preheated oven, 190°C/375°F/Gas Mark 5, for 30–35 minutes or until golden and the base sounds hollow when tapped. Cool on a wire rack.

Olive Rolls

115 g/4 oz black or green olives in brine or oil, drained
750 g/1 lb 10 oz unbleached strong white flour, plus extra for dusting
1½ tsp salt
1 sachet easy-blend dried yeast
450 ml/16 fl oz tepid water
2 tbsp extra virgin olive oil, plus extra for brushing
4 tbsp finely chopped fresh oregano, parsley or thyme leaves, or 1 tbsp dried mixed herbs

❉ Stone the olives and chop finely. Pat off the excess brine or oil with kitchen paper. Set aside.

❉ Combine the flour, salt and yeast in a bowl and make a well in the centre. Gradually stir in most of the water and the olive oil to make a dough. Gradually add the remaining water, if necessary, drawing in all the flour. Lightly knead in the chopped olives and herbs. Turn out the dough on to a lightly floured surface and knead for 10 minutes until smooth and elastic. Wash the bowl and lightly coat with oil.

❉ Shape the dough into a ball, put it in the bowl and turn over so it is coated. Cover tightly with a tea towel or lightly oiled clingfilm and set aside to rise until it has doubled in volume. Dust a baking tray with flour.

❉ Turn out the dough on to a lightly floured surface and knead lightly. Roll the dough into 20-cm/8-inch ropes on a very lightly floured surface.

❉ Cut the dough into 16 even-sized pieces. Shape each piece into a ball and place on the prepared baking tray. Cover and set aside to rise for 15 minutes.

❉ Lightly brush the top of each roll with olive oil. Bake in a preheated oven, 220°C/425°F/Gas Mark 7, for about 25–30 minutes or until the rolls are golden brown. Transfer to a wire rack and set aside to cool completely.

Mediterranean Bread

400 g/14 oz plain flour, plus extra for dusting
1 sachet easy-blend dried yeast
1 tsp salt
1 tbsp coriander seeds, lightly crushed
2 tsp dried oregano
200 ml/7 fl oz tepid water
3 tbsp olive oil, plus extra for greasing
150 g/5½ oz sun-dried tomatoes in oil, drained, patted dry and chopped
85 g/3 oz feta cheese (drained weight), patted dry and cubed
115 g/4 oz black olives, patted dry, stoned and sliced

❉ Combine the flour, yeast, salt, coriander seeds and oregano and make a well in the centre. Gradually add most of the water and the oil to make a dough. Gradually add the remaining water, if needed, drawing in all the flour.

❉ Turn out on to a lightly floured surface and knead for 10 minutes. Knead in the tomatoes, cheese and olives. Wash the bowl and lightly coat it with oil.

❉ Shape the dough into a ball, put it in the bowl and turn the dough over. Cover tightly and set aside the dough until it doubles in volume.

❉ Turn out the dough on to a lightly floured surface. Knead lightly, then shape into a ball. Place on a lightly floured baking tray. Cover and set aside to rise until it doubles in volume again.

❉ Lightly sprinkle the top of the loaf with flour. Using a sharp knife, cut 3 shallow slashes in the top. Bake in a preheated oven, 230°C/450°F/Gas Mark 8, for 20 minutes. Reduce the temperature to 200°C/400°F/Gas Mark 6 and bake for a further 20 minutes or until the loaf sounds hollow when you tap it on the base. Transfer to a wire rack to cool completely. This loaf keeps well for up to 3 days in an airtight container.

Olive Oil Bread with Cheese

15 g/$\frac{1}{2}$ oz dried yeast
1 tsp sugar
250 ml/9 fl oz tepid water
350 g/12 oz strong white flour
1 tsp salt

3 tbsp olive oil
200 g/7 oz pecorino cheese, cubed
$\frac{1}{2}$ tbsp fennel seeds, lightly crushed

❖ Mix the yeast with the sugar and 100 ml/3$\frac{1}{2}$ fl oz of the water. Leave to ferment in a warm place for about 15 minutes.

❖ Mix the flour with the salt. Add 1 tablespoon of the oil, the yeast mixture and the remaining water to form a smooth dough. Knead the dough for 4 minutes.

❖ Divide the dough into 2 equal portions. Roll out each portion to a form a round 6 mm/$\frac{1}{4}$ inch thick. Place 1 round on a baking tray.

❖ Scatter the cheese and half the fennel seeds evenly over the round.

❖ Place the second round on top and squeeze the edges together to seal so that the filling does not leak during the cooking time.

❖ Using a sharp knife, make a few slashes in the top of the dough and brush with the remaining olive oil.

❖ Sprinkle with the remaining fennel seeds and leave the dough to rise for 20–30 minutes.

❖ Bake in a preheated oven, 200°C/400°F/Gas Mark 6, for 30 minutes or until golden brown. Serve immediately.

Herb Focaccia

400 g/14 oz unbleached strong white flour, plus extra for dusting
1 sachet easy-blend dried yeast
1$\frac{1}{2}$ tsp salt
$\frac{1}{2}$ tsp sugar
300 ml/10 fl oz tepid water

3 tbsp extra virgin olive oil, plus extra for greasing
4 tbsp finely chopped fresh herbs
sea salt, for sprinkling

❖ Combine the flour, yeast, salt and sugar in a bowl and make a well in the centre. Gradually stir in most of the water and 2 tablespoons of the olive oil to make a dough. Gradually add the remaining water, if necessary, drawing in all the flour.

❖ Turn out on to a lightly floured surface and knead. Transfer to a bowl and lightly knead in the herbs for 10 minutes until soft but not sticky. Wash the bowl and lightly coat with olive oil. Shape the dough into a ball, put it in the bowl and turn the dough over. Cover tightly with a tea towel or lightly greased clingfilm and set aside in a warm place to rise until the dough has doubled in volume. Meanwhile, sprinkle flour over a baking tray.

❖ Turn out the dough on to a lightly floured surface and knead lightly. Cover with the upturned bowl and leave for 10 minutes.

❖ Roll out and pat the dough into a 25-cm/10-inch circle, about 1 cm/$\frac{1}{2}$ inch thick, and carefully transfer it to the floured baking tray. Cover the dough with a tea towel and leave to rise again for 15 minutes.

❖ Using a lightly oiled finger, poke indentations all over the surface of the loaf. Drizzle over the remaining olive oil and sprinkle lightly with the sea salt. Bake in a preheated oven, 230°C/450°F/Gas Mark 8, for 15 minutes or until golden and the loaf sounds hollow when tapped on the bottom. Transfer the loaf to a wire rack to cool completely.

Roman Focaccia

1 sachet easy-blend dried yeast
1 tsp sugar
300 ml/10 fl oz tepid water
450 g/1 lb strong white flour
2 tsp salt
3 tbsp rosemary, chopped
2 tbsp olive oil
450 g/1 lb mixed red and white onions, sliced into rings
4 garlic cloves, sliced

❖ Place the yeast and the sugar in a small bowl and mix with 100 ml/3^1/$_2$ fl oz of the water. Leave to ferment in a warm place for 15 minutes.

❖ Mix the flour with the salt in a large bowl. Add the yeast mixture, half of the rosemary and the remaining water and mix to form a smooth dough. Knead the dough for 4 minutes.

❖ Cover the dough with oiled clingfilm and leave to rise for 30 minutes or until doubled in size.

❖ Meanwhile, heat the oil in a large frying pan. Add the onions and garlic and fry for 5 minutes or until soft. Cover the pan and continue to cook for 7–8 minutes or until the onions are lightly caramelized.

❖ Remove the dough from the bowl and knead it again for 1–2 minutes.

❖ Roll out the dough to form a square shape. The dough should be no more than 6 mm/ ^{1}/$_4$ inch thick because it will rise during cooking. Place the dough on a large baking tray, pushing out the edges until even.

❖ Spread the onions over the dough and sprinkle with the remaining rosemary.

❖ Bake in a preheated oven, 200°C/400°F/Gas Mark 6, for 25–30 minutes or until golden brown. Cut the focaccia into 16 squares and serve immediately.

Garlic Bread

1 French stick
115 g/4 oz butter, softened
6–8 garlic cloves, finely chopped
2 tsp finely grated lemon rind (optional)
2 tbsp chopped fresh herbs, such as parsley, thyme or chives, or a mixture

❖ Preheat the oven to 200°C/400°F/Gas Mark 6. Slice the bread diagonally without cutting all the way through.

❖ Beat the butter in a bowl until creamy, then beat in the garlic, lemon rind, if using, and herbs. Alternatively, melt the butter in a small saucepan, then stir in the remaining ingredients.

❖ Spread or brush the butter on to both sides of the bread slices. Place the bread on a large sheet of foil. If there is any butter mixture remaining, dot or pour it over the top of the bread. Bring up the long sides of the foil and fold together to enclose the bread. Place on a baking tray and bake for 15 minutes. Unwrap, cut into separate slices and serve immediately.

Cheese & Mustard Bread

butter, for greasing
225 g/8 oz plain flour
1 tsp salt
1/2 tsp mustard powder
2 tsp baking powder
125 g/41/2 oz Red Leicester cheese, grated
175 g/6 oz potatoes, cooked and mashed
200 ml/7 fl oz water
1 tbsp oil

❖ Lightly grease a baking tray with butter.

❖ Sift the flour, salt, mustard powder and baking powder into a mixing bowl.

❖ Reserve 2 tablespoons of the grated cheese and stir the rest into the bowl with the potatoes.

❖ Pour in the water and the oil, and stir all the ingredients together (the mixture will be wet at this stage). Mix them all to make a soft dough.

❖ Turn out the dough on to a floured surface and shape it into a 20-cm/8-inch round.

❖ Place the round on the baking tray and mark it into 4 portions with a knife, without cutting through. Sprinkle with the reserved cheese.

❖ Bake the bread in a preheated oven, 220°C/425°F/Gas Mark 7, for about 25–30 minutes.

❖ Transfer the bread to a wire rack and leave to cool. Serve the bread as fresh as possible.

Cheese & Potato Strudel

❋ **SERVES 8** ❋

butter, for greasing
675 g/1 lb 8 oz strong white
flour, plus extra for dusting
175 g/6 oz floury
potatoes, diced
2 sachets easy-blend dried
yeast

450 ml/16 fl oz vegetable stock
2 garlic cloves, crushed
2 tbsp chopped fresh rosemary
115 g/4 oz Gruyère cheese,
grated
1 tbsp vegetable oil

❋ Lightly grease a baking tray with butter and dust it with flour. Bring a saucepan of lightly salted water to the boil and cook the potatoes for 10 minutes or until soft. Drain well and mash.

❋ Transfer the mashed potatoes to a large mixing bowl, stir in the yeast, flour and stock and mix to form a smooth dough. Add the garlic, chopped rosemary and 85 g/3 oz of the cheese and knead for 5 minutes. Make a hollow in the dough, pour in the oil and knead the dough again.

❋ Cover the dough and set it aside in a warm place for about 1½ hours or until doubled in size.

❋ Knead the dough again and divide it into 3 equal portions. Roll each portion into a sausage shape about 35 cm/14 inches long.

❋ Press one end of each of the sausage shapes firmly together, then carefully plait the dough, without breaking it, and fold the remaining ends under, sealing them together firmly.

❋ Place the plait on the baking tray, cover and set aside to rise for a further 30 minutes.

❋ Sprinkle the remaining cheese over the top of the plait and bake in a preheated oven, 190°C/375°F/Gas Mark 5, for 40 minutes or until the base of the loaf sounds hollow when tapped. Serve while it is still warm.

Cheese & Chive Scones

❋ **MAKES 10** ❋

225 g/8 oz self-raising flour
1 tsp powdered mustard
½ tsp cayenne pepper
½ tsp salt
100 g/3½ oz soft cheese with
added herbs
2 tbsp fresh snipped chives,
plus extra to garnish

100 ml/3½ fl oz milk, plus
extra for brushing
55 g/2 oz mature Cheddar
cheese, grated
soft cheese, to serve

❋ Sift the flour, mustard, cayenne pepper and salt into a large mixing bowl.

❋ Add the soft cheese to the mixture and mix together until well incorporated. Stir in the snipped chives.

❋ Make a well in the centre of the ingredients and gradually pour in the milk, stirring as you pour, until the mixture forms a soft dough.

❋ Turn out the dough on to a floured surface and knead lightly. Roll out until 2 cm/¾ inch thick and use a 5-cm/2-inch plain pastry cutter to stamp out as many rounds as you can. Transfer the rounds to a baking tray.

❋ Re-knead the dough trimmings together and roll out again. Stamp out more rounds – you should be able to make 10 scones in total.

❋ Brush the scones with milk and sprinkle with the grated cheese. Bake in a preheated oven, 200°C/400°F/Gas Mark 6, for 15–20 minutes until risen and golden. Transfer to a wire rack to cool.

❋ Serve the scones warm with the soft cheese, garnished with chives.

Thyme Puffs

100 g/3¹/₂ oz butter, softened,
plus extra for greasing
250 g/9 oz fresh ready-made
puff pastry
1 garlic clove, crushed
1 tsp lemon juice
1 tsp dried thyme

❈ Lightly grease a baking tray with butter.

❈ On a lightly floured surface, roll out the pastry to form a 25-cm/10-inch round and cut into 8 wedges.

❈ In a small bowl, mix the butter, garlic, lemon juice and thyme together until soft. Season to taste with salt and pepper.

❈ Spread a little of the butter and thyme mixture on to each wedge of pastry, dividing it equally between them.

❈ Carefully roll up each wedge, starting from the wide end.

❈ Arrange the crescents on the prepared baking tray and chill for 30 minutes.

❈ Dampen the baking tray with cold water. This will create a steamy atmosphere in the oven while the crescents are baking and help the pastries to rise.

❈ Bake in a preheated oven, 200°C/400°F/Gas Mark 6, for 10–15 minutes, or until the crescents are well risen and golden.

Chapatis

225 g/8 oz wholemeal flour (ata or chapati flour)

½ tsp salt

200 ml/7 fl oz water

❊ Place the flour in a large mixing bowl. Add the salt and mix to combine.

❊ Make a well in the middle of the flour and gradually pour in the water, mixing well with your fingers to form a supple dough.

❊ Knead the dough for about 7–10 minutes. Ideally, set the dough aside and leave to rise for about 15–20 minutes, but if time is short roll out the dough immediately. Divide the dough into 10–12 equal portions. Roll out each piece to form a round on a well-floured surface.

❊ Place a heavy-based frying-pan over a high heat. When steam starts to rise from the pan, reduce the heat to medium.

❊ Place a chapati in the frying pan and when the chapati starts to bubble turn it over. Carefully press down on the chapati with a clean tea towel or a flat spoon and turn the chapati over once again. Remove the chapati from the pan, set aside and keep warm while you make the others.

❊ Repeat the process until all of the chapatis are cooked.

Parathas

85 g/3 oz plain wholemeal flour

85 g/3 oz plain flour

pinch of salt

1 tbsp vegetable oil, plus extra for greasing

75 ml/3 fl oz tepid water

❊ Place the flours and the salt in a bowl. Drizzle 1 tablespoon of oil over the flour, add the tepid water and mix to form a soft dough, adding a little more water, if necessary. Knead on a lightly floured surface until smooth, then cover and leave for 30 minutes.

❊ Knead the dough on a floured surface and divide into 6 equal pieces. Shape each one into a ball. Roll out on a floured surface to a 15-cm/6-inch round and brush very lightly with oil.

❊ Fold in half, and then in half again to form a triangle. Roll out to form an 18-cm/7-inch triangle (when measured from point to centre top), dusting with extra flour as necessary.

❊ Brush a large heavy-based frying pan with a little oil and heat until hot, then add one or two parathas and cook for about 1–1½ minutes. Brush the surfaces very lightly with oil, then turn and cook the other sides for 1½ minutes until completely cooked through.

❊ Place the cooked parathas on a plate and cover with foil, or place between the folds of a clean tea towel to keep warm, while you are cooking the remainder in the same way, greasing the pan between cooking each batch.

Naan Bread

1 tsp sugar
1 tsp fresh yeast
150 ml/5 fl oz warm water
200 g/7 oz plain flour
1 tbsp ghee
1 tsp salt
50 g/1¾ oz unsalted butter
1 tsp poppy seeds

❈ Put the sugar and yeast in a small bowl or jug together with the warm water and mix thoroughly until the yeast has completely dissolved. Set aside for about 10 minutes or until the mixture is frothy.

❈ Place the flour in a large mixing bowl. Make a well in the centre of the flour, add the ghee and salt and pour in the yeast mixture. Mix thoroughly to form a dough, using your hands and adding more water if required.

❈ Turn out the dough on to a floured work surface and knead for about 5 minutes or until smooth.

❈ Return the dough to the bowl, cover and set aside to rise in a warm place for 1½ hours or until doubled in size.

❈ Turn out the dough on to a floured surface and knead for a further 2 minutes. Break off small balls with your hand and pat them into rounds about 12 cm/5 inches in diameter and 1 cm/½ inch thick.

❈ Place the dough rounds on a greased sheet of foil and grill under a very hot preheated grill for 7–10 minutes, turning twice and brushing with the butter and sprinkling with the poppy seeds.

❈ Serve warm immediately, or keep wrapped in foil until required.

Gram Flour Bread

100 g/3½ oz wholemeal flour (ata or chapati flour), plus extra for dusting
85 g/3 oz gram flour
½ tsp salt
1 small onion
fresh coriander leaves, very finely chopped
2 fresh green chillies, deseeded and very finely chopped
150 ml/5 fl oz water
2 tsp ghee

❈ Sift the wholemeal and gram flours together into a large mixing bowl. Add the salt to the flours and mix together thoroughly.

❈ Chop the onion very finely. Stir the onion, coriander and chillies into the flour mixture and stir to blend.

❈ Add the water and mix to form a soft dough. Cover the dough with a clean tea towel or clingfilm and set aside for about 15 minutes.

❈ Turn out the dough and knead thoroughly for 5–7 minutes. Divide the dough into 8 equal portions.

❈ Roll out the dough portions to 18-cm/7-inch rounds on a lightly floured surface.

❈ Place the dough rounds individually in a frying pan and cook over a medium heat, turning them over three times and lightly greasing each side with the ghee each time.

❈ Transfer the bread to serving plates and serve hot.

Poori

225 g/8 oz wholemeal flour (ata or chapatti flour)
$^{1}/_{2}$ tsp salt
150 ml/5 fl oz water
600 ml/1 pint vegetable oil

❄ Place the flour and salt in a large mixing bowl and stir to combine.

❄ Make a well in the centre of the flour. Gradually pour in the water and mix together to form a dough, adding more water if necessary.

❄ Knead the dough until it is smooth and elastic and set aside in a warm place to rise for about 15 minutes.

❄ Divide the dough into about 10 equal portions and with lightly oiled or floured hands pat each into a smooth ball.

❄ On a lightly oiled or floured work surface, roll out each ball to form a thin round.

❄ Heat the vegetable oil in a deep frying pan. Deep-fry the rounds, in batches, turning once, until they are golden brown in colour.

❄ Remove from the pan and drain. Serve hot.

Buttered Nut & Lentil Dip

55 g/2 oz butter	1/2 tsp grated root ginger
1 small onion, chopped	1 tsp chopped fresh coriander
85 g/3 oz red lentils	salt and pepper
300 ml/10 fl oz vegetable stock	sprigs of fresh coriander,
55 g/2 oz blanched almonds	to garnish
55 g/2 oz pine kernels	fresh vegetable crudités and
1/2 tsp ground coriander	breadsticks, to serve
1/2 tsp ground cumin	

❖ Melt half the butter in a saucepan and fry the onion over a medium heat, stirring frequently, until golden brown.

❖ Add the lentils and stock. Bring to the boil, then reduce the heat and simmer gently, uncovered, for about 25–30 minutes until the lentils are tender. Drain well.

❖ Melt the remaining butter in a small frying pan. Add the almonds and pine kernels and fry them over a low heat, stirring frequently, until golden brown. Remove from the heat.

❖ Put the lentils, almonds and pine kernels, with any remaining butter, into a food processor or blender. Add the ground coriander, cumin, ginger and fresh coriander. Process for about 15–20 seconds until the mixture is smooth. Alternatively, press the lentils through a sieve to purée them and then mix with the finely chopped nuts, spices and herbs.

❖ Season the dip with salt and pepper and garnish with the sprigs of coriander. Serve with the fresh vegetable crudités and breadsticks.

Heavenly Garlic Dip

2 garlic bulbs	2 tbsp chopped fresh parsley
6 tbsp olive oil	salt and pepper
1 small onion, finely chopped	fresh vegetable crudités,
2 tbsp lemon juice	French bread or warmed
3 tbsp tahini	pitta breads, to serve

❖ Separate the bulbs of garlic into individual cloves. Place them on a baking tray and roast in a preheated oven, 200°C/400°F/Gas Mark 6, for about 8–10 minutes. Set them aside to cool for a few minutes.

❖ When they are cool enough to handle, peel the garlic cloves and then chop them finely.

❖ Heat the olive oil in a saucepan or frying pan and add the garlic and onion. Fry over a low heat, stirring occasionally, for 8–10 minutes until soft. Remove the pan from the heat.

❖ Mix in the lemon juice, tahini and parsley. Season to taste with salt and pepper. Transfer the dip to a small heatproof bowl and keep warm.

❖ Serve with the fresh vegetable crudités.

Mint & Cannellini Bean Dip

❖ **SERVES 4** ❖

PASTRY CASES
450 g/1 lb puff pastry
1 egg, beaten

FILLING
225 g/8 oz sweet potatoes, diced
100 g/3½ oz baby asparagus spears

2 tbsp butter or margarine
1 leek, sliced
2 small open-cup mushrooms, sliced
1 tsp lime juice
1 tsp chopped fresh thyme
pinch of mustard powder
salt and pepper

❖ Cut the pastry into 4 equal pieces. Roll out each piece on a lightly floured work surface to form a 13-cm/5-inch square. Place on a dampened baking tray and score a smaller 6-cm/2½-inch square inside.

❖ Brush with the beaten egg and cook in a preheated oven, 200°C/400°F/Gas Mark 6, for 20 minutes or until risen and golden brown.

❖ While the pastry is cooking, start the filling. Cook the sweet potato in boiling water for 15 minutes, then drain. Blanch the asparagus in boiling water for 10 minutes or until tender. Drain and reserve.

❖ Remove the pastry squares from the oven. Carefully cut out the central square of pastry, lift out and reserve.

❖ Melt the butter in a saucepan and sauté the leek and mushrooms for 2–3 minutes. Add the lime juice, thyme and mustard, season well and stir in the sweet potatoes and asparagus. Spoon into the pastry cases, top with the reserved pastry squares and serve immediately.

Hummus & Garlic Toasts

❖ **SERVES 4** ❖

HUMMUS
400 g/14 oz canned chickpeas
juice of 1 large lemon
6 tbsp tahini
2 tbsp olive oil
2 garlic cloves, crushed
salt and pepper
chopped fresh coriander and black olives, to garnish

TOASTS
1 ciabatta loaf, sliced
2 garlic cloves, crushed
1 tbsp chopped coriander
4 tbsp olive oil

❖ To make the hummus, first drain the chickpeas, reserving a little of the liquid. Put the chickpeas and liquid in a food processor and process, gradually adding the reserved liquid and lemon juice. Blend well after each addition until smooth.

❖ Stir in the tahini and all but 1 teaspoon of the olive oil. Add the garlic, season to taste and blend again until smooth.

❖ Spoon the hummus into a serving dish and smooth the top. Drizzle the remaining olive oil over the top and garnish with the chopped coriander and olives. Set aside in the refrigerator to chill while you are preparing the toasts.

❖ Place the slices of ciabatta on a grill rack in a single layer.

❖ Mix the garlic, coriander and olive oil together and drizzle over the bread slices. Cook under a hot grill, turning once, for about 2–3 minutes, until golden brown. Serve the toasts immediately with the hummus.

Vegetables with Tahini Dip

225 g/8 oz small broccoli florets
225 g/8 oz small cauliflower
florets
225 g/8 oz asparagus, sliced
into 5-cm/2-inch lengths
2 small red onions, quartered
1 tbsp lime juice
2 tsp toasted sesame seeds
1 tbsp chopped fresh chives,
to garnish

TAHINI DIP
1 tsp sunflower oil
2 garlic cloves, crushed
1/2–1 tsp chilli powder
salt and pepper
2 tsp tahini
150 ml/5 fl oz low-fat natural
fromage frais
2 tbsp chopped fresh chives

❊ Line the base of a steamer with baking paper and arrange the broccoli florets, cauliflower florets, asparagus and onion pieces on top.

❊ Bring a wok or a large saucepan of water to the boil, and place the steamer on the top. Sprinkle the vegetables with lime juice for extra flavour and steam for 10 minutes until they are just tender.

❊ Meanwhile, make the dip. Heat the oil in a small non-stick saucepan, add the garlic, chilli powder and seasoning to taste and fry gently for 2–3 minutes until the garlic is soft.

❊ Remove the saucepan from the heat and stir in the tahini and fromage frais. Return the pan to the heat and cook gently for 1–2 minutes without boiling. Stir in the chopped chives.

❊ Remove the vegetables from the steamer and arrange them on a warmed serving platter.

❊ Sprinkle the vegetables with the sesame seeds and garnish with the chopped chives. Serve with the hot dip.

Aubergine Dipping Platter

❄ **SERVES 4** ❄

1 aubergine, peeled and cut into 2.5-cm/1-inch cubes
3 tbsp sesame seeds, roasted in a dry saucepan over a low heat
1 tsp sesame oil
grated rind and juice of $1/2$ lime
1 small shallot, diced
1 tsp sugar
1 fresh red chilli, deseeded and sliced
115 g/4 oz broccoli florets
2 carrots, cut into batons
8 baby sweetcorn cobs, cut in half lengthways
2 celery sticks, cut into batons
1 baby red cabbage, cut into 8 wedges, the leaves of each wedge held together by the core
salt and pepper

❄ Cook the diced aubergine in a saucepan of boiling water for 7–8 minutes. Drain well and set aside to cool slightly.

❄ Meanwhile, grind the sesame seeds with the oil in a food processor or in a mortar with a pestle.

❄ Add the aubergine, lime rind and juice, shallot, sugar and chilli to the sesame seeds. Season to taste with salt and pepper, then process or chop and mash by hand, until smooth.

❄ Adjust the seasoning to taste, then spoon the dip into a bowl.

❄ Serve the aubergine dipping platter surrounded by the broccoli, carrots, sweetcorn, celery and cabbage.

Tzatziki

❄ **SERVES 12** ❄

2 large cucumbers
600 ml/1 pint Greek-style yogurt or natural thick yogurt
3 garlic cloves, crushed
1 tbsp finely chopped fresh dill
1 tbsp extra virgin olive oil
1 tbsp sesame seeds
salt and pepper
cayenne pepper, for dusting
sprigs of fresh dill (optional), to garnish

❄ Using the coarse side of a grater, grate the cucumbers into a bowl lined with an absorbent, perforated kitchen cloth. Pull up the corners of the cloth to make a tight bundle and squeeze very hard to extract all the moisture.

❄ Put the cucumbers in a bowl and stir in the yogurt, garlic, dill and olive oil and season to taste with salt and pepper. Cover with clingfilm and chill for at least 3 hours for the flavours to blend.

❄ When ready to serve, remove the dip from the refrigerator and stir. Taste and adjust the seasoning if necessary.

❄ Put the sesame seeds into a small ungreased frying pan and dry-fry them over a medium heat until they turn golden and start to give off their aroma. Immediately pour them out of the pan on to the tzatziki – they will sizzle.

❄ Sprinkle some cayenne pepper on to a plate. Lightly dip the tip of a dry pastry brush into the cayenne, then tap a light sprinkling of cayenne all over the tzatziki. Garnish with the dill, if wished, and serve. (Ungarnished tzatziki will keep for up to 3 days in the refrigerator.)

Aïoli

4 large garlic cloves or to taste
2 large egg yolks
300 ml/10 fl oz extra virgin
olive oil
1–2 tbsp lemon juice
1 tbsp fresh white
breadcrumbs
sea salt and pepper

TO SERVE
a selection of raw vegetables,
such as sliced red peppers,
courgette slices, whole
spring onions and tomato
wedges
a selection of blanched and
cooled vegetables, such
as baby artichoke hearts,
cauliflower or broccoli florets
or French beans

❈ Finely chop the garlic on a chopping board. Add a pinch of sea salt to the garlic and use the tip and broad side of a knife to work the garlic and salt into a smooth paste.

❈ Transfer the garlic paste to a food processor. Add the egg yolks and process until well blended, scraping down the sides of the bowl with a rubber spatula, if necessary.

❈ With the motor running, slowly pour in the olive oil in a steady stream through the feeder tube, processing until a thick mayonnaise forms.

❈ Add 1 tablespoon of the lemon juice and the breadcrumbs and process again. Taste and add more lemon juice if necessary. Season to taste with sea salt and pepper.

❈ Place the aïoli in a bowl, cover and chill until ready to serve. To serve, place the bowl of aïoli on a large platter and surround with a selection of raw and lightly blanched vegetables.

Skordalia

55 g/2 oz day-old bread
150 g/5½ oz almonds
4–6 large garlic cloves,
coarsely chopped
150 ml/5 fl oz extra virgin
olive oil

2 tbsp white wine vinegar
salt and pepper
sprigs of fresh coriander or
flat-leaf parsley, to garnish
sesame breadsticks, to serve

❈ Cut the crusts off the bread and tear the bread into small pieces. Put into a bowl, pour over enough water to cover and set aside to soak for 10–15 minutes. Squeeze the bread dry, then set aside.

❈ To blanch the almonds, put them into a heatproof bowl and pour over just enough boiling water to cover. Leave for 30 seconds, then drain. The skins should slide off easily.

❈ Transfer the almonds and garlic to a food processor and process until finely chopped. Add the squeezed bread and process again until well blended.

❈ With the motor running, gradually add the olive oil through the feeder tube in a thin, steady stream until a thick paste forms. Add the vinegar and process again. Season to taste with salt and pepper.

❈ Scrape the mixture into a bowl, cover and chill until required. It will keep in the refrigerator for up to 4 days. Garnish with the coriander and serve with the breadsticks.

Caponata

4 tbsp olive oil
1 onion, sliced
2 celery sticks, sliced
1 aubergine, diced
5 plum tomatoes, chopped
1 garlic clove, finely chopped
3 tbsp red wine vinegar
1 tbsp sugar
12 black olives, stoned
2 tbsp capers, drained
and rinsed
salt
3 tbsp chopped fresh flat-leaf
parsley, to garnish

❉ Heat 2 tablespoons of the oil in a large, heavy-based saucepan. Add the onion and celery and cook over a low heat, stirring frequently, for 5 minutes until soft. Add the remaining oil with the aubergine and cook, stirring constantly, for 10 minutes.

❉ Stir in the tomatoes, garlic, vinegar and sugar. Cover the surface with a circle of greaseproof paper and simmer for 10 minutes.

❉ Stir the olives and capers into the mixture and season to taste with salt.

❉ Transfer the mixture to a serving dish and leave to cool to room temperature. Sprinkle with the chopped parsley and serve.

Frijoles

❈ **SERVES 6** ❈

350 g/12 oz dried red kidney
beans, soaked in cold water
for 3 hours
2 onions, chopped
2 garlic cloves, chopped
2 fresh green chillies,
deseeded and chopped

1 bay leaf
2 tbsp corn oil
2 tomatoes, peeled and
chopped
salt

❈ Drain the beans and place in a large heavy-based saucepan. Add sufficient cold water to cover by about 2.5 cm/1 inch. Add half the onion, half the garlic, the chillies and bay leaf. Bring to the boil and boil vigorously for 15 minutes, then reduce the heat and simmer for 30 minutes, adding more boiling water if the mixture begins to dry out.

❈ Add 1 tablespoon of the oil and simmer for a further 30 minutes, adding more boiling water if necessary. Season to taste with salt and simmer for a further 30 minutes, but do not add any more water.

❈ Meanwhile, heat the remaining oil in a frying pan. Add the remaining onion and garlic and cook, stirring occasionally, for 5 minutes, until softened. Stir in the tomatoes and cook for 5 minutes more. Add 3 tablespoons of the cooked beans to the tomato mixture, mash thoroughly to a paste and then stir the paste into the beans. Heat through gently, then serve.

Fiery Salsa

❈ **SERVES 4** ❈

2 small fresh red chillies
1 tbsp lime or lemon juice
2 large ripe avocados
5-cm/2-inch piece of cucumber
2 tomatoes, peeled
1 small garlic clove, crushed

few drops of Tabasco sauce
salt and pepper
lime or lemon slices,
to garnish
tortilla chips, to serve

❈ Remove and discard the stem and seeds from 1 chilli. Chop the flesh very finely and place in a large mixing bowl.

❈ To make a chilli flower for garnish, using a small, sharp knife, slice the remaining chilli from the stem to the tip several times without removing the stem. Place in a bowl of iced water, so that the 'petals' open out.

❈ Add the lime juice to the mixing bowl. Halve, stone and peel the avocados. Add the flesh to the mixing bowl and mash thoroughly with a fork. The salsa should be slightly chunky. (The lime juice prevents the avocado discolouring.)

❈ Finely chop the cucumber and tomatoes and add to the avocado mixture with the garlic.

❈ Stir in the Tabasco sauce and season to taste with salt and pepper. Transfer the dip to a serving bowl. Garnish with the slices of lime and the chilli flower.

❈ Put the bowl on a large plate, surround with tortilla chips and serve. Do not keep this dip standing for long or it will discolour.

Tomato & Mango Salsa

6 medium ripe tomatoes
1 tbsp oil
1 onion, finely chopped
1 large mango, halved, stoned, peeled and diced
2 tbsp chopped fresh coriander
salt and pepper
tortilla chips, to serve

❖ Place the tomatoes in a large bowl. Cover with boiling water, leave to stand for 1 minute, then lift out. Using a knife, pierce the skin and peel it off. Cut the tomato into quarters, then cut out the central core and seeds. Chop the remaining flesh and place in a large bowl.

❖ Heat the oil in a frying pan. Add the onion and gently fry until soft. Add to the bowl of tomatoes together with the mango and coriander. Season to taste with salt and pepper.

❖ Serve cold with tortilla chips.

Speedy Tomato Relish

2 large cooking apples, peeled, quartered, cored and chopped
2 tbsp caster sugar
1/2 tsp mixed spice
4–5 cloves
2 tbsp water
1 tbsp oil
1 large red onion, roughly chopped
6 tomatoes, peeled and chopped

❖ Place the apples, sugar, mixed spice and cloves in a large saucepan. Add the water and cook gently until soft but not puréed.

❖ Heat the oil in a large frying pan. Add the onion and fry until soft. Add the tomatoes and stir together for 30 seconds. Add to the apples, mix well and leave the mixture to cool.

❖ Transfer the relish to a clean jar, cover and store in the refrigerator for 3–4 days.

Tomato & Red Onion Relish

8 ripe tomatoes
1–2 tbsp virgin olive oil
salt and pepper

SAUCE
1 tbsp virgin olive oil
2 large red onions, thinly sliced
55 g/2 oz rocket or baby
spinach leaves

❖ Preheat the oven to 150°C/300°F/Gas Mark 2. Cut the tomatoes in half, cut out the cores and arrange all the halves, skin side down, in a large roasting tin. Drizzle with the oil and season well with salt and pepper. Cook in the oven for $1^{1}/_{4}$–$1^{1}/_{2}$ hours, or until roasted but still moist.

❖ For the sauce, heat the oil in a large frying pan. Add the onions and fry over a gentle heat until soft and golden brown. Place 8 of the oven-dried tomatoes in a food processor and process until puréed. Add to the onions in the pan.

❖ Slice the remaining 8 tomato halves and add to the pan with the rocket. Season to taste with salt and pepper and cook until the leaves have just wilted. Serve immediately.

Simple
baking & desserts

Rich Chocolate Cake

225 g/8 oz butter, plus extra for greasing
100 g/3$\frac{1}{2}$ oz plain chocolate, chopped
150 ml/5 fl oz water
300 g/10$\frac{1}{2}$ oz plain flour
2 tsp baking powder
275 g/9$\frac{1}{2}$ oz soft brown sugar

150 ml/5 fl oz soured cream
2 eggs, beaten

ICING
200 g/7 oz plain chocolate
6 tbsp water
3 tbsp single cream
1 tbsp butter, chilled

❖ Grease a 33 x 20-cm/13 x 8-inch cake tin and line the base with baking paper. In a saucepan, melt the butter and chocolate with the water over a low heat, stirring frequently.

❖ Sift the flour and baking powder into a mixing bowl and stir in the sugar.

❖ Pour the hot chocolate liquid into the bowl and then beat well until all of the ingredients are evenly mixed. Stir in the soured cream, followed by the eggs.

❖ Pour the mixture into the prepared tin and bake in a preheated oven, 190°C/375°F/Gas Mark 5, for 40–45 minutes.

❖ Leave the cake to cool in the tin before turning out on to a wire rack. Leave it to cool completely.

❖ To make the icing, melt the chocolate with the water in a saucepan over a very low heat, stir in the cream and remove from the heat. Stir in the chilled butter, then pour the icing over the cooled cake, using a spatula to spread it evenly over the top of the cake.

Marbled Chocolate Loaf

175 g/6 oz soft margarine, plus extra for greasing
175 g/6 oz caster sugar
$\frac{1}{2}$ tsp vanilla essence
3 eggs

225 g/8 oz self-raising flour, sifted
50 g/1$\frac{3}{4}$ oz plain chocolate
icing sugar, for dusting

❖ Lightly grease a 450-g/1-lb loaf tin.

❖ Beat together the sugar and margarine in a bowl until light and fluffy.

❖ Beat in the vanilla essence. Gradually add the eggs, beating well after each addition. Carefully fold in the flour.

❖ Divide the mixture in half. Melt the chocolate and stir into one half of the mixture until well combined.

❖ Place the vanilla mixture in the tin and level the top. Spread the chocolate layer over the vanilla layer.

❖ Bake in a preheated oven, 190°C/ 375°F/Gas Mark 5, for 30 minutes or until springy to the touch.

❖ Leave to cool in the tin for a few minutes before transferring the loaf to a wire rack to cool completely.

❖ Serve the cake dusted with icing sugar.

Chocolate Brownies

butter, for greasing
55 g/2 oz unsweetened stoned dates, chopped
55 g/2 oz prunes, chopped
6 tbsp unsweetened apple juice
4 eggs, beaten
300 g/10½ oz dark muscovado sugar
1 tsp vanilla essence
4 tbsp low-fat drinking chocolate powder, plus extra for dusting

2 tbsp cocoa powder
175 g/6 oz plain flour
55 g/2 oz plain chocolate chips

ICING
125 g/4½ oz icing sugar
1–2 tsp water
1 tsp vanilla essence

❊ Preheat the oven to 180°C/350°F/Gas Mark 4. Grease an 18 x 28-cm/7 x 11-inch cake tin with butter and line with baking paper. Place the dates and prunes in a small saucepan and add the apple juice. Bring to the boil, cover and simmer for 10 minutes until soft. Beat to form a smooth paste, then set aside to cool.

❊ Place the cooled fruit in a mixing bowl and stir in the eggs, sugar and vanilla essence. Sift in the drinking chocolate, the cocoa and the flour, and fold in along with the chocolate chips until well incorporated.

❊ Spoon the mixture into the prepared tin and smooth over the top. Bake for 25–30 minutes until firm to the touch or until a skewer inserted into the centre comes out clean. Cut into 12 bars and leave to cool in the tin for 10 minutes. Transfer to a wire rack to cool completely.

❊ Sift the icing sugar into a bowl and mix with water and vanilla essence to form a soft, but not too runny, icing.

❊ Drizzle the icing over the chocolate brownies and allow to set. Dust with chocolate powder before serving.

Pistachio Nut Brownies

225 g/8 oz butter, softened, plus extra for greasing
150 g/5½ oz plain chocolate, broken into pieces
225 g/8 oz self-raising flour
125 g/4½ oz caster sugar

4 eggs, beaten
75 g/2¾ oz pistachio nuts, chopped
100 g/3½ oz white chocolate, roughly chopped
icing sugar, for dusting

❊ Lightly grease a 23-cm/9-inch baking tin with a little butter and line with baking paper.

❊ Melt the plain chocolate and butter in a heatproof bowl set over a saucepan of simmering water. Leave to cool slightly.

❊ Sift the flour into a separate mixing bowl and stir in the caster sugar.

❊ Stir the eggs into the melted chocolate mixture, then pour this mixture into the flour and sugar mixture, beating well. Stir in the pistachio nuts and the white chocolate, then pour the mixture into the tin, spreading it evenly into the corners.

❊ Bake in a preheated oven, 180°C/ 350°/Gas Mark 4, for 30–35 minutes, or until firm to the touch. Leave to cool in the tin for 20 minutes, then turn out on to a wire rack.

❊ Dust the brownie with icing sugar and cut into 12 pieces when cold.

Chocolate Chip & Sultana Flapjacks

125 g/4^1/$_2$ oz butter, plus extra
for greasing
75 g/2^3/$_4$ oz caster sugar
1 tbsp golden syrup
350 g/12 oz rolled oats
75 g/2^3/$_4$ oz plain
chocolate chips
50 g/1^3/$_4$ oz sultanas

❊ Lightly grease a shallow 20-cm/8-inch square cake tin with a little butter.

❊ Place the butter, sugar and golden syrup in a saucepan and cook over a low heat, stirring until the butter and sugar melt and the mixture is well combined.

❊ Remove the pan from the heat and stir in the rolled oats until they are well coated. Add the chocolate chips and the sultanas and mix well to combine everything.

❊ Turn into the prepared tin and press down well.

❊ Bake in a preheated oven, 180°C/350°F/Gas Mark 4, for 30 minutes. Cool slightly, then mark into fingers. When almost cold, cut into bars or squares and transfer to a wire rack until cold.

Chewy Cherry Flapjacks

❄ MAKES 16 ❄

200 g/7 oz butter, plus extra for greasing
200 g/7 oz demerara sugar
2 tbsp golden syrup
275 g/9^1/$_2$ oz porridge oats
100 g/3^1/$_2$ oz desiccated coconut
75 g/2^3/$_4$ oz glacé cherries, chopped

❄ Lightly grease a 30 x 23-cm/12 x 9-inch shallow cake tin with a little butter.

❄ Heat the butter, sugar and golden syrup in a large saucepan until just melted.

❄ Stir in the oats, coconut and cherries and mix well until evenly combined.

❄ Spread the mixture in the base of the cake tin and press down with the back of a palette knife to make a smooth surface.

❄ Bake in a preheated oven, 190°C/325°F/Gas Mark 3, for about 30 minutes.

❄ Remove from the oven and leave to cool on the baking tray for about 10 minutes.

❄ Cut the mixture into squares using a sharp knife.

❄ Carefully transfer the flapjack squares to a wire rack and leave to cool completely.

Apricot Slices

❄ MAKES 12 ❄

PASTRY
100 g/3^1/$_2$ oz margarine, cut into small pieces, plus extra for greasing
225 g/8 oz wholemeal flour
55 g/2 oz finely ground mixed nuts
4 tbsp water
milk, to glaze

FILLING
225 g/8 oz dried apricots
grated rind of 1 orange
300 ml/10 fl oz apple juice
1 tsp ground cinnamon
55 g/2 oz raisins

❄ Lightly grease a 23-cm/9-inch square cake tin with a little margarine. To make the pastry, place the flour and nuts in a mixing bowl and rub in the margarine with your fingers until the mixture resembles breadcrumbs. Stir in the water and bring together to form a dough. Wrap and set aside to chill in the refrigerator for 30 minutes.

❄ To make the filling, place the apricots, orange rind and apple juice in a saucepan and bring to the boil. Simmer for 30 minutes until the apricots are mushy. Cool slightly, then process in a food processor or blender to a purée. Alternatively, press the mixture through a fine sieve. Stir in the cinnamon and raisins.

❄ Divide the pastry in half, roll out 1 half and use to line the base of the tin. Spread the apricot purée over the top, leaving a margin around the edge, and brush the edges of the pastry with water. Roll out the rest of the dough to fit over the top of the apricot purée. Press down and seal the edges.

❄ Prick the top of the pastry with a fork and brush with the milk. Bake in a preheated oven, 200°C/400°F/Gas Mark 6, for 20–25 minutes until the pastry is golden. Set aside to cool slightly before cutting into 12 bars. Serve either warm or cold.

Vanilla Coconut Squares

75 g/2¾ oz butter, plus extra for greasing
225 g/8 oz plain chocolate digestive biscuits
175 g/6 oz canned evaporated milk
1 egg, beaten
1 tsp vanilla essence
25 g/1 oz caster sugar
50 g/1¾ oz self-raising flour, sifted
125 g/4½ oz desiccated coconut
50 g/1¾ oz plain chocolate (optional)

❄ Grease a shallow 20-cm/8-inch square cake tin with a little butter and base-line with baking paper.

❄ Crush the biscuits in a polythene bag with a rolling pin or process them in a food processor.

❄ Melt the butter in a saucepan and stir in the crushed biscuits until well combined.

❄ Press the mixture into the base of the cake tin.

❄ Beat together the evaporated milk, egg, vanilla and sugar until smooth. Stir in the flour and desiccated coconut. Pour over the biscuit base and level the top.

❄ Bake in a preheated oven, 190°C/ 375°F/Gas Mark 5, for 30 minutes, or until the coconut topping is firm and just golden.

❄ Leave to cool in the cake tin for about 5 minutes, then cut into squares. Leave to cool completely in the tin.

❄ Carefully remove the squares from the tin and place them on a board. Melt the plain chocolate, if using, and drizzle it over the squares to decorate them. Leave the chocolate to set before serving.

Nutty Muesli Squares

115 g/4 oz unsalted butter, plus extra for greasing
4 tbsp clear honey
25 g/1 oz unrefined caster sugar
250 g/9 oz porridge oats
25 g/1 oz dried cranberries
25 g/1 oz stoned dates, chopped
25 g/1 oz hazelnuts, chopped
70 g/2½ oz flaked almonds

❄ Preheat the oven to 190°C/375°F/Gas Mark 5. Grease a 20-cm/8-inch square baking tin with a little butter.

❄ Melt the butter with the honey and sugar in a saucepan and stir together. Add the remaining ingredients and mix thoroughly.

❄ Turn the mixture into the prepared tin and press down well. Bake in the preheated oven for 20–30 minutes.

❄ Remove from the oven and leave to cool in the tin. Cut into 16 squares.

Sunflower Seed Cakes

250 g/9 oz butter, softened,
plus extra for greasing
250 g/9 oz caster sugar
3 eggs, beaten
250 g/9 oz self-raising flour
$^1/_2$ tsp bicarbonate of soda
1 tbsp ground cinnamon
150 ml/5 fl oz soured cream
100 g/3$^1/_2$ oz sunflower seeds

❖ Lightly grease a 23-cm/9-inch square cake tin with a little butter and base-line with baking paper.

❖ In a large mixing bowl, cream together the butter and sugar until the mixture is light and fluffy.

❖ Gradually add the beaten eggs to the mixture, beating well after each addition.

❖ Sift the flour, bicarbonate of soda and ground cinnamon into the creamed mixture and fold in gently, using a metal spoon.

❖ Spoon in the soured cream and sunflower seeds and gently mix until well combined.

❖ Spoon the mixture into the prepared cake tin and level the surface with the back of a spoon or a knife.

❖ Bake in a preheated oven, 180°C/ 350°F/Gas Mark 4, for about 45 minutes until the mixture is firm to the touch when pressed with a finger.

❖ Loosen the edges with a round-bladed knife, then turn out on to a wire rack to cool completely. Slice into 12 squares.

Almond Slices

3 eggs	½ tsp saffron strands
75 g/2¾ oz ground almonds	100 g/3½ oz unsalted butter
200 g/7 oz milk powder	25 g/1 oz flaked almonds
200 g/7 oz sugar	

❈ Beat the eggs together in a bowl and set aside.

❈ Place the ground almonds, milk powder, sugar and saffron in a large mixing bowl and stir to mix well.

❈ Melt the butter in a small saucepan. Pour the melted butter over the dry ingredients and mix well until thoroughly combined.

❈ Add the reserved beaten eggs to the mixture and stir to blend well.

❈ Spread the mixture in a shallow 15–20-cm/7–9-inch ovenproof dish and bake in a preheated oven, 160°C/ 325°F/ Gas Mark 3, for 45 minutes. Test whether the cake is cooked through by piercing with the tip of a sharp knife or a skewer – it will come out clean if it is cooked thoroughly.

❈ Cut the almond cake into slices. Decorate the almond slices with the flaked almonds and transfer to serving plates. Serve hot or cold.

Caramel Oat Squares

100 g/3½ oz soft margarine	**CARAMEL FILLING**
50 g/1¾ oz light muscovado sugar	25 g/1 oz butter
	25 g/1 oz light muscovado sugar
125 g/4½ oz plain flour	200 g/7 oz condensed milk
40 g/1½ oz rolled oats	

TOPPING
100 g/3½ oz plain chocolate
25 g/1 oz white chocolate
(optional)

❈ Beat together the margarine and muscovado sugar in a bowl until light and fluffy. Beat in the flour and the rolled oats. Use your fingertips to bring the mixture together, if necessary.

❈ Press the mixture into the base of a shallow 20-cm/ 8-inch square cake tin.

❈ Bake in a preheated oven, 180°C/350°F/Gas Mark 4, for 25 minutes, or until just golden and firm. Cool in the tin.

❈ Place the ingredients for the caramel filling in a saucepan and heat gently, stirring, until the sugar has dissolved and the ingredients combine. Bring to the boil over a very low heat, then boil gently, stirring constantly, for 3–4 minutes until thickened.

❈ Pour the caramel filling over the biscuit base in the tin and leave to set.

❈ Melt the plain chocolate and spread it over the caramel. If using the white chocolate, melt it and pipe lines of white chocolate over the plain chocolate. Using a cocktail stick or a skewer, feather the white chocolate into the plain chocolate. Leave to set. Cut into squares to serve.

Refrigerator Squares

❊ **MAKES 16** ❊

275 g/9^1/$_2$ oz plain chocolate
175 g/6 oz butter
4 tbsp golden syrup
2 tbsp dark rum (optional)
175 g/6 oz plain biscuits,
such as Rich Tea
25 g/1 oz toasted rice cereal

50 g/1^3/$_4$ oz chopped walnuts
or pecan nuts
100 g/3^1/$_2$ oz glacé cherries,
chopped roughly
25 g/1 oz white chocolate,
to decorate

❊ Place the plain chocolate in a large mixing bowl with the butter, syrup and rum, if using, and set over a saucepan of gently simmering water until melted, stirring until blended.

❊ Break the biscuits into small pieces and stir into the chocolate mixture along with the rice cereal, nuts and cherries.

❊ Line an 18-cm/7-inch square cake tin with baking paper. Pour the mixture into the tin and level the top, pressing down well with the back of a spoon. Chill for 2 hours.

❊ To decorate, melt the white chocolate and drizzle it over the top of the cake in a random pattern. Leave to set. To serve, carefully turn out of the tin and remove the baking paper. Cut into 16 squares.

Rich Chocolate Loaf

❊ **MAKES 16 SLICES** ❊

75 g/2^3/$_4$ oz almonds
150 g/5^1/$_2$ oz plain chocolate
6 tbsp unsalted butter
200 ml/7 fl oz condensed milk
2 tsp cinnamon

75 g/2^3/$_4$ oz amaretti biscuits,
broken
50 g/1^3/$_4$ oz dried apricots,
roughly chopped

❊ Line a 675-g/1^1/$_2$-lb loaf tin with a sheet of kitchen foil.

❊ Using a sharp knife, roughly chop the almonds.

❊ Place the chocolate, butter, condensed milk and cinnamon in a heavy-based saucepan.

❊ Heat the chocolate mixture over a low heat for about 3–4 minutes, stirring constantly with a wooden spoon, until the chocolate has melted. Beat the mixture well.

❊ Stir the chopped almonds, broken biscuits and chopped apricots into the chocolate mixture, stirring with a wooden spoon, until well mixed.

❊ Pour the mixture into the prepared tin and leave to chill in the refrigerator for about 1 hour or until set. Cut the rich chocolate loaf into slices to serve.

Chocolate Rice Squares

❖ MAKES 16 ❖

butter, for greasing

WHITE LAYER
50 g/1¾ oz butter
1 tbsp golden syrup
150 g/5½ oz white chocolate
50 g/1¾ oz toasted rice cereal

DARK LAYER
50 g/1¾ oz butter
2 tbsp golden syrup
125 g/4½ oz plain chocolate,
broken into small pieces
75 g/2¾ oz toasted rice cereal

❖ Grease a 20-cm/8-inch square cake tin with a little butter and line with baking paper.

❖ To make the white layer, melt the butter, golden syrup and white chocolate in a bowl set over a saucepan of gently simmering water.

❖ Remove from the heat and stir in the rice cereal until it is well combined .

❖ Press into the prepared tin and level the surface.

❖ To make the dark layer, melt the butter, golden syrup and plain chocolate in a bowl set over a saucepan of gently simmering water.

❖ Remove from the heat and stir in the rice cereal until it is well coated. Pour the dark layer over the hardened white layer and chill until the top layer has hardened.

❖ Turn out of the cake tin and cut into small squares, using a sharp knife.

Spiced Apple Gingerbread

150 g/5¹/2 oz butter, plus extra for greasing
175 g/6 oz soft brown sugar
2 tbsp black treacle
225 g/8 oz plain flour
1 tsp baking powder
2 tsp bicarbonate of soda
2 tsp ground ginger
150 ml/5 fl oz milk
1 egg, beaten
2 dessert apples, peeled, chopped and coated with 1 tbsp lemon juice

❊ Grease a 23-cm/9-inch square cake tin with a little butter and line with baking paper.

❊ Melt the butter, sugar and treacle in a saucepan over a low heat and leave the mixture to cool.

❊ Sift the flour, baking powder, bicarbonate of soda and ginger into a mixing bowl.

❊ Stir in the milk, beaten egg and cooled buttery liquid, followed by the chopped apples coated with the lemon juice.

❊ Mix everything together gently, then pour the mixture into the prepared tin.

❊ Bake in a preheated oven, 160°C/325°F/Gas Mark 3, for 30–35 minutes, or until the cake has risen and a fine skewer inserted into the centre comes out clean.

❊ Leave the cake to cool in the tin before turning out and cutting into 12 bars.

Classic Carrot Cake

butter, for greasing
125 g/4¹/2 oz self-raising flour
pinch of salt
1 tsp ground cinnamon
125 g/4¹/2 oz soft brown sugar
2 eggs
100 ml/3¹/2 fl oz sunflower oil
125 g/4¹/2 oz carrot, peeled and finely grated
25 g/1 oz desiccated coconut
25 g/1 oz walnuts, chopped
walnut pieces, to decorate

ICING
50 g/1³/4 oz butter, softened
50 g/1³/4 oz full-fat soft cheese
225 g/8 oz icing sugar, sifted
1 tsp lemon juice

❊ Lightly grease a 20-cm/8-inch square cake tin with a little butter and line with baking paper.

❊ Sift the flour, salt and ground cinnamon into a large bowl and stir in the brown sugar. Add the eggs and oil to the dry ingredients and mix well.

❊ Stir in the carrot, coconut and walnuts.

❊ Pour the mixture into the prepared tin and bake in a preheated oven, 180°C/350°F/Gas Mark 4, for 20–25 minutes, or until just firm to the touch. Leave to cool in the tin.

❊ Meanwhile, make the icing. In a bowl, beat together the butter, soft cheese, icing sugar and lemon juice until the mixture is fluffy and creamy.

❊ Turn the cake out of the tin and cut into 12 bars or slices. Spread with the icing and then decorate with walnut pieces.

Chocolate Orange Cake

175 g/6 oz butter, plus extra for greasing
175 g/6 oz caster sugar
3 eggs, beaten
175 g/6 oz self-raising flour, sifted
2 tbsp cocoa powder, sifted

2 tbsp milk
3 tbsp orange juice
grated rind of ½ orange

ICING
175 g/6 oz icing sugar
2 tbsp orange juice

❈ Lightly grease a 20-cm/8-inch deep round cake tin with a little butter.

❈ Beat together the sugar and butter or margarine in a bowl until light and fluffy. Gradually add the eggs, beating well after each addition. Carefully fold in the flour.

❈ Divide the mixture in half. Add the cocoa powder and milk to one half, stirring until well combined. Flavour the other half with the orange juice and rind.

❈ Place spoonfuls of each mixture in the prepared tin and swirl together with a skewer to create a marbled effect. Bake in a preheated oven, 190°C/375°F/Gas Mark 5, for 25 minutes or until springy to the touch.

❈ Leave the cake to cool in the tin for a few minutes before transferring to a wire rack to cool completely.

❈ To make the icing, sift the icing sugar into a mixing bowl and mix in enough of the orange juice to form a smooth icing. Spread the icing over the top of the cake and leave to set before serving.

Glazed Honey & Almond Cake

100 g/3½ oz margarine, softened, plus extra for greasing
50 g/1¾ oz soft brown sugar
2 eggs
175 g/6 oz self-raising flour
1 tsp baking powder

4 tbsp milk
2 tbsp clear honey
50 g/1¾ oz flaked almonds

SYRUP
150 ml/5 fl oz clear honey
2 tbsp lemon juice

❈ Grease an 18-cm/7-inch round cake tin with margarine and line with baking paper.

❈ Place the margarine, sugar, eggs, flour, baking powder, milk and honey in a large mixing bowl and beat well with a wooden spoon for about 1 minute, or until all of the ingredients are thoroughly mixed together.

❈ Spoon into the prepared tin, level the surface with the back of a spoon or a knife and sprinkle with the almonds.

❈ Bake in a preheated oven, 180°C/350°F/Gas Mark 4, for about 50 minutes or until the cake is well risen.

❈ Meanwhile, make the syrup. Combine the honey and lemon juice in a small saucepan and simmer for about 5 minutes, or until the syrup starts to coat the back of a spoon.

❈ As soon as the cake comes out of the oven, pour over the syrup, allowing it to seep into the middle of the cake.

❈ Leave the cake to cool for at least 2 hours before slicing.

Rich Pecan Nut Ring

FUDGE SAUCE
40 g/1½ oz butter
40 g/1½ oz light muscovado
sugar
4 tbsp golden syrup
2 tbsp milk
1 tbsp cocoa powder
40 g/1½ oz plain chocolate
50 g/1¾ oz pecan nuts,
finely chopped

CAKE
100 g/3½ oz soft margarine,
plus extra for greasing
100 g/3½ oz light muscovado
sugar
125 g/4½ oz self-raising flour
2 eggs
2 tbsp milk
1 tbsp golden syrup

❖ Lightly grease a 20-cm/8-inch ring tin with margarine.

❖ To make the fudge sauce, place the butter, sugar, syrup, milk and cocoa powder in a small saucepan and heat gently, stirring until combined.

❖ Break the chocolate into pieces, add to the mixture and stir until melted. Stir in the chopped nuts. Pour into the base of the tin and leave to cool.

❖ To make the cake, place all of the ingredients in a mixing bowl and beat until smooth. Carefully spoon the cake mixture over the chocolate fudge sauce.

❖ Bake in a preheated oven, 180°C/ 350°F/Gas Mark 4, for 35 minutes, or until the cake is springy to the touch.

❖ Leave to cool in the tin for 5 minutes, then turn out on to a serving dish and serve.

Banana & Lime Cake

butter, for greasing
300 g/10½ oz plain flour
1 tsp salt
1½ tsp baking powder
175 g/6 oz light muscovado
sugar
1 tsp lime rind, grated
1 egg, beaten
1 banana, mashed with 1 tbsp
lime juice
150 ml/5 fl oz low-fat natural
fromage frais
115 g/4 oz sultanas
banana chips and finely grated
lime rind, to decorate

TOPPING
115 g/4 oz icing sugar
1–2 tsp lime juice
½ tsp finely grated lime rind

❈ Grease a deep 18-cm/7-inch round cake tin with a little butter and line with baking paper.

❈ Sift the flour, salt and baking powder into a mixing bowl and stir in the sugar and lime rind.

❈ Make a well in the centre of the dry ingredients and add the egg, banana, fromage frais and sultanas. Mix well until thoroughly incorporated.

❈ Spoon the mixture into the tin and smooth the surface. Bake in a preheated oven, 180°C/350°F/Gas Mark 4, for 40–45 minutes until firm to the touch or until a skewer inserted in the centre comes out clean. Leave the cake to cool for 10 minutes, then turn out on to a wire rack.

❈ To make the topping, sift the icing sugar into a small bowl and mix with the lime juice to form a soft, but not too runny icing. Stir in the grated lime rind. Drizzle the icing over the cake, letting it run down the sides.

❈ Decorate the cake with the banana chips and lime rind. Let the cake stand for 15 minutes so that the icing sets.

Pear Cake

margarine, for greasing
4 pears, peeled and cored
2 tbsp water
200 g/7 oz plain flour
2 tsp baking powder
100 g/3½ oz soft light brown
sugar
4 tbsp milk
2 tbsp clear honey, plus extra
for drizzling
2 tsp ground cinnamon
2 egg whites

❈ Grease a 20-cm/8-inch cake tin with margarine and base-line with baking paper.

❈ Put 1 pear in a food processor with the water and process until almost smooth. Transfer to a mixing bowl.

❈ Sift in the flour and baking powder. Beat in the sugar, milk, honey and cinnamon and mix well.

❈ Chop all but 1 of the remaining pears and add to the mixture.

❈ Whisk the egg whites until peaks form and gently fold into the mixture until fully blended.

❈ Slice the remaining pear and arrange it in a fan pattern on the base of the prepared tin.

❈ Spoon the cake mixture into the tin and cook in a preheated oven, 150°C/300°F/Gas Mark 2, for 1¼ –1½ hours or until cooked through.

❈ Remove the cake from the oven and set aside to cool in the tin for 10 minutes. Turn out the cake on to a wire cooling rack and drizzle with the honey. Set aside to cool completely, then cut into slices to serve.

Apple Cake with Cider

❊ SERVES 8 ❊

85 g/3 oz butter, cut into small pieces, plus extra for greasing
225 g/8 oz self-raising flour
1 tsp baking powder
85 g/3 oz caster sugar
55 g/2 oz dried apple, chopped
85 g/3 oz raisins
150 ml/5 fl oz sweet cider
1 egg, beaten
175 g/6 oz raspberries

❊ Grease a 20-cm/8-inch cake tin with a little butter and line with baking paper.

❊ Sift the flour and baking powder into a mixing bowl and rub in the butter with your fingertips until the mixture resembles fine breadcrumbs.

❊ Stir in the caster sugar, chopped dried apple and raisins.

❊ Pour in the sweet cider and egg and mix together until thoroughly blended. Stir in the raspberries very gently so they do not break up.

❊ Pour the mixture into the prepared cake tin.

❊ Bake in a preheated oven, 190°C/375°F/Gas Mark 5, for about 40 minutes until risen and lightly golden.

❊ Leave the cake to cool in the tin, then turn out on to a wire rack. Leave until completely cold before serving.

Crunchy Coffee Sponge Cake

❊ SERVES 8 ❊

100 g/3½ oz butter, melted and cooled, plus extra for greasing
275 g/9½ oz plain flour
1 tbsp baking powder
75 g/2¾ oz caster sugar
150 ml/5 fl oz milk
2 eggs
2 tbsp instant coffee mixed with 1 tbsp boiling water
50 g/1¾ oz almonds, chopped
icing sugar, for dusting

TOPPING
75 g/2¾ oz self-raising flour
75 g/2¾ oz demerara sugar
25 g/1 oz butter, cut into small pieces
1 tsp ground mixed spice
1 tbsp water

❊ Grease a 23-cm/9-inch loose-based round cake tin with a little butter and line with baking paper. Sift together the flour and baking powder into a mixing bowl, then stir in the caster sugar.

❊ Whisk the milk, eggs, butter and coffee mixture together and pour on to the dry ingredients. Add the chopped almonds and mix lightly together. Spoon the mixture into the tin.

❊ To make the topping, mix the flour and demerara sugar together in a separate bowl.

❊ Rub in the butter with your fingers until the mixture is crumbly. Sprinkle in the mixed spice and the water and bring the mixture together in loose crumbs. Sprinkle the topping over the cake mixture.

❊ Bake in a preheated oven, 190°C/375°F/Gas Mark 5, for 50 minutes–1 hour. Cover loosely with foil if the topping starts to brown too quickly. Leave to cool in the tin, then turn out. Dust with the icing sugar just before serving.

Lemon Sponge Cake

butter, for greasing
200 g/7 oz plain flour
2 tsp baking powder
200 g/7 oz caster sugar
4 eggs
150 ml/5 fl oz soured cream
grated rind 1 large lemon
4 tbsp lemon juice
150 ml/5 fl oz sunflower oil

SYRUP
4 tbsp icing sugar
3 tbsp lemon juice

❖ Lightly grease a 20-cm/8-inch loose-based round cake tin with a little butter and base-line with baking paper.

❖ Sift the flour and baking powder into a mixing bowl and stir in the caster sugar.

❖ In a separate bowl, whisk the eggs, soured cream, lemon rind, lemon juice and oil together.

❖ Pour the egg mixture into the dry ingredients and mix well until evenly combined.

❖ Pour the mixture into the prepared tin and bake in a preheated oven, 180°C/350°F/ Gas Mark 4, for 45–60 minutes until risen and golden brown.

❖ Meanwhile, to make the syrup, mix together the icing sugar and lemon juice in a small saucepan. Stir over a low heat until just beginning to bubble and turn syrupy.

❖ As soon as the cake comes out of the oven, prick the surface with a fine skewer, then brush the syrup over the top. Leave the cake to cool completely in the tin before turning out and serving.

Jewelled Sponge Cake

175 g/6 oz butter, softened,
plus extra for greasing
175 g/6 oz caster sugar
3 eggs, beaten
175 g/6 oz self-raising flour,
sifted

25 g/1 oz ground rice
finely grated rind of 1 lemon
4 tbsp lemon juice
125 g/4½ oz glacé fruits,
chopped
icing sugar, to dust (optional)

❖ Lightly grease an 18-cm/7-inch cake tin with a little butter and line with baking paper.

❖ In a bowl, whisk together the softened butter and caster sugar until light and fluffy.

❖ Add the beaten eggs a little at a time. Using a metal spoon, fold in the flour and ground rice.

❖ Add the grated lemon rind and juice, followed by the chopped glacé fruits. Lightly mix all the ingredients together.

❖ Spoon the mixture into the prepared tin and level the surface with the back of a spoon or a knife.

❖ Bake in a preheated oven, 180°C/350°F/Gas Mark 4, for 1 hour–1 hour 10 minutes until well risen or until a fine skewer inserted into the centre of the cake comes out clean.

❖ Leave the cake to cool in the tin for 5 minutes, before turning it out on to a wire rack to cool completely.

❖ Dust well with the icing sugar, if using, before serving.

Crunchy Fruit Cake

100 g/3½ oz butter, softened,
plus extra for greasing
100 g/3½ oz caster sugar
2 eggs, beaten
50 g/1¾ oz self-raising flour,
sifted
1 tsp baking powder

100 g/3½ oz polenta
225 g/8 oz mixed dried fruit
25 g/1 oz pine kernels
grated rind of 1 lemon
4 tbsp lemon juice
2 tbsp milk

❖ Grease an 18-cm/7-inch cake tin with a little butter and base-line with baking paper.

❖ In a bowl, whisk together the butter and sugar until light and fluffy.

❖ Whisk in the beaten eggs, a little at a time, whisking thoroughly after each addition.

❖ Gently fold the flour, baking powder and polenta into the mixture until totally incorporated.

❖ Stir in the mixed dried fruit, pine kernels, grated lemon rind, lemon juice and milk.

❖ Spoon the mixture into the prepared tin and level the surface.

❖ Bake in a preheated oven, 180°C/350°F/Gas Mark 4, for about 1 hour or until a fine skewer inserted into the centre of the cake comes out clean.

❖ Leave the cake to cool in the tin before turning out.

Olive Oil, Fruit & Nut Cake

butter, for greasing	4 tbsp orange juice
225 g/8 oz self-raising flour	150 ml/5 fl oz olive oil
55 g/2 oz caster sugar	100 g/3½ oz mixed dried fruit
125 ml/4 fl oz milk	25 g/1 oz pine kernels

❖ Grease an 18-cm/7-inch cake tin with a little butter and line with baking paper.

❖ Sift the flour into a mixing bowl and stir in the caster sugar.

❖ Make a well in the centre of the dry ingredients and pour in the milk and orange juice. Stir the mixture with a wooden spoon, gradually beating in the flour and sugar.

❖ Pour in the olive oil, stirring well so that all of the ingredients are thoroughly mixed.

❖ Stir the mixed dried fruit and pine kernels into the mixture and spoon into the prepared tin. Smooth the top with a palette knife.

❖ Bake in a preheated oven, 180°C/350°F/Gas Mark 4, for about 45 minutes, until the cake is golden and firm to the touch.

❖ Leave the cake to cool in the tin for a few minutes before transferring to a wire rack to cool completely.

❖ Serve the cake warm or cold and cut into slices.

Banana & Cranberry Loaf

butter, for greasing	55 g/2 oz dried cranberries
175 g/6 oz self-raising flour	5–6 tbsp orange juice
½ tsp baking powder	2 eggs, beaten
150 g/5½ oz soft brown sugar	150 ml/5 fl oz sunflower oil
2 bananas, mashed	85 g/3 oz icing sugar, sifted
55 g/2 oz chopped mixed peel	grated rind of 1 orange
25 g/1 oz chopped mixed nuts	

❖ Grease a 900-g/2-lb loaf tin with a little butter and base-line with baking paper.

❖ Sift the flour and baking powder into a mixing bowl. Stir in the brown sugar, bananas, chopped mixed peel, nuts and dried cranberries.

❖ Stir the orange juice, eggs and sunflower oil together until well combined. Add the mixture to the dry ingredients and mix until thoroughly blended. Spoon the mixture into the prepared loaf tin and use a palette knife to smooth the top.

❖ Bake in a preheated oven, 180°C/350°F/Gas Mark 4, for about 1 hour until firm to the touch or until a fine skewer inserted into the centre of the loaf comes out clean.

❖ Turn out the loaf and leave to cool on a wire rack.

❖ Mix the icing sugar with a little water and drizzle the icing over the loaf. Sprinkle the orange rind over the top. Leave the icing to set before serving the loaf in slices.

Spicy Fruit Loaf

150 g/5½ oz butter, cut into
small pieces, plus extra
for greasing
350 g/12 oz plain flour
pinch of salt
1 tbsp baking powder
1 tbsp ground cinnamon
125 g/4½ oz soft brown sugar
175 g/6 oz currants
finely grated rind of 1 orange
5–6 tbsp orange juice
6 tbsp milk
2 eggs, beaten lightly

❖ Grease a 900-g/2-lb loaf tin with a little butter and base-line smoothly with baking paper.

❖ Sift the flour, salt, baking powder and ground cinnamon into a bowl. Then rub in the pieces of butter with your fingers, until the mixture resembles coarse breadcrumbs.

❖ Stir in the sugar, currants and orange rind. Beat the orange juice, milk and eggs together and add to the dry ingredients. Mix well together.

❖ Spoon the mixture into the prepared tin. Make a slight dip in the middle of the mixture to help it rise evenly.

❖ Bake in a preheated oven, 180°C/350°F/Gas Mark 4, for about 1 hour–1 hour 10 minutes, or until a fine metal skewer inserted into the centre of the loaf comes out clean.

❖ Leave the loaf to cool before turning out of the tin. Transfer to a wire rack and allow to cool completely before slicing.

Tropical Fruit Bread

❄ **MAKES 1 LOAF** ❄

2 tbsp butter, cut into small
pieces, plus extra
for greasing
350 g/12 oz strong white flour
55 g/2 oz bran
1/2 tsp salt
1/2 tsp ground ginger
1 sachet easy-blend dried yeast
25 g/1 oz soft brown sugar

250 ml/9 fl oz lukewarm water
85 g/3 oz glacé pineapple,
finely chopped
25 g/1 oz dried mango, finely
chopped
55 g/2 oz desiccated coconut,
toasted
1 egg, lightly beaten
2 tbsp coconut shreds

❄ Lightly grease a baking tray with a little butter. Sift the flour into a large mixing bowl. Stir in the bran, salt, ginger, dried yeast and sugar. Rub in the butter with your fingers, then add the water and mix to form a dough.

❄ On a lightly floured surface, knead the dough for 5–8 minutes until smooth. Alternatively, use an electric mixer with a dough hook. Place the dough in a greased bowl, cover and leave to rise in a warm place for 30 minutes until doubled in size.

❄ Knead the pineapple, mango and desiccated coconut into the dough. Shape into a round and place on the baking tray. Score the top with the back of a knife. Cover and leave for a further 30 minutes in a warm place.

❄ Brush the loaf with the beaten egg and sprinkle with the coconut shreds. Bake in a preheated oven, 220°C/425°F/Gas Mark 7, for about 30 minutes or until golden brown.

❄ Leave the bread to cool on a wire rack before serving.

Honeyed Fruit Bread

❄ **MAKES 1 LOAF** ❄

100 g/3 1/2 oz butter, cut into
small pieces, plus extra for
greasing
225 g/8 oz self-raising flour
75 g/2 3/4 oz caster sugar

125 g/4 1/2 oz stoned dates,
chopped
2 bananas, roughly mashed
2 eggs, lightly beaten
2 tbsp honey

❄ Grease a 900-g/2-lb loaf tin with a little butter and base-line with baking paper.

❄ Sift the flour into a mixing bowl.

❄ Rub the butter into the flour with your fingertips until the mixture resembles fine breadcrumbs.

❄ Stir the sugar, chopped dates, bananas, beaten eggs and honey into the dry ingredients. Mix together to form a soft dropping consistency.

❄ Spoon the mixture into the prepared tin and level the surface with the back of a knife.

❄ Bake in a preheated oven, 160°C/325°F/Gas Mark 3, for about 1 hour, or until golden and a fine metal skewer inserted into the centre comes out clean.

❄ Leave the loaf to cool in the tin before turning out and transferring to a wire rack.

❄ Serve the loaf warm or cold, cut into thick slices.

Fruit & Nut Loaf

225 g/8 oz strong white flour, plus extra for dusting
1/2 tsp salt
1 tbsp margarine, plus extra for greasing
2 tbsp soft light brown sugar
100 g/31/2 oz sultanas
55 g/2 oz dried apricots, chopped
55 g/2 oz chopped hazelnuts
2 tsp easy-blend dried yeast
6 tbsp orange juice
6 tbsp low-fat natural yogurt
2 tbsp sieved apricot jam

❖ Sift the flour and salt into a bowl. Rub in the margarine and stir in the sugar, sultanas, apricots, nuts and yeast.

❖ Warm the orange juice in a saucepan but do not allow it to boil.

❖ Stir the warmed orange juice into the flour mixture with the yogurt and then bring the mixture together to form a dough.

❖ Lightly grease a baking tray with a little margarine. Knead the dough on a lightly floured surface for 5 minutes until smooth and elastic. Shape into a round and place on the baking tray. Cover with a clean tea towel and set aside to rise in a warm place until doubled in size.

❖ Cook the loaf in a preheated oven, 220°C/425°F/Gas Mark 7, for about 35–40 minutes until cooked through. Transfer to a cooling rack and brush the cake with the apricot jam. Let the cake cool before serving.

Potato & Nutmeg Scones

margarine, for greasing
225 g/8 oz floury potatoes, diced
125 g/41/2 oz plain flour
11/2 tsp baking powder
1/2 tsp freshly grated nutmeg
50 g/13/4 oz sultanas
1 egg, beaten
3 tbsp double cream
2 tsp soft light brown sugar
butter, to serve

❖ Grease a flat baking tray or Swiss roll tin with a little margarine and line with baking paper.

❖ Bring a saucepan of unsalted water to the boil and cook the diced potatoes for 10 minutes or until soft. Drain well and mash the potatoes.

❖ Transfer to a large mixing bowl and stir in the flour, baking powder and nutmeg, mixing well to combine the ingredients thoroughly.

❖ Stir in the sultanas, egg and double cream and beat the mixture with a wooden spoon until smooth.

❖ Shape the mixture into 8 rounds, approximately 2 cm/ 3/4 inches thick, and place on the baking tray.

❖ Cook in a preheated oven, 200°C/ 400°F/Gas Mark 6, for 15 minutes or until the scones have risen and are golden. Sprinkle the scones with the sugar and serve warm, spread with butter.

Sultana & Cherry Scones

❖ **MAKES 8** ❖

75 g/2¾ oz butter, cut into small pieces, plus extra for greasing
225 g/8 oz self-raising flour
1 tbsp caster sugar
pinch of salt
40 g/1½ oz glacé cherries, chopped
40 g/1½ oz sultanas
1 egg, beaten
50 ml/2 fl oz milk
butter, to serve

❊ Lightly grease a baking tray with a little butter.

❊ Sift the flour, sugar and salt into a mixing bowl and rub in the butter with your fingers until the scone mixture resembles breadcrumbs.

❊ Stir in the glacé cherries and sultanas. Add the egg.

❊ Reserve 1 tablespoon of the milk for glazing, then add the remainder to the mixture. Mix together to form a soft dough.

❊ On a lightly floured surface, roll out the dough to a thickness of 2 cm/¾ inch and cut out 8 scones, using a 5-cm/2-inch cutter.

❊ Place the scones on the baking tray and brush with the reserved milk.

❊ Bake in a preheated oven, 220°C/425°F/Gas Mark 7, for 8–10 minutes, or until the scones are golden brown.

❊ Leave to cool on a wire rack, then serve split and buttered.

Rich Chocolate Chip Scones

❊ **MAKES 9** ❊

55 g/2 oz butter, plus extra for greasing
225 g/8 oz self-raising flour, sifted
1 tbsp caster sugar
50 g/1¾ oz chocolate chips
about 150 ml/5 fl oz milk

❊ Lightly grease a baking tray with a little butter. Place the flour in a mixing bowl. Cut the butter into small pieces and rub it into the flour with your fingertips; do this until the scone mixture resembles fine breadcrumbs.

❊ Stir in the caster sugar and chocolate chips.

❊ Mix in enough milk to form a soft dough.

❊ On a lightly floured surface, roll out the dough to form a rectangle 10 x 15 cm/4 x 6 inches, about 2.5 cm/1 inch thick. Cut the dough into 9 squares.

❊ Place the scones, spaced well apart, on the prepared baking tray.

❊ Brush with a little milk and bake in a preheated oven, 220°C/425°F/Gas Mark 7, for 10–12 minutes, or until the scones are risen and golden.

Fruity Buns

❊ **MAKES 10** ❊

225 g/8 oz self-raising wholemeal flour
2 tsp baking powder
25 g/1 oz light muscovado sugar
100 g/3½ oz dried apricots, finely chopped
1 banana, mashed with 1 tbsp orange juice
1 tsp finely grated orange rind
300 ml/10 fl oz skimmed milk
1 egg, beaten
3 tbsp corn oil
2 tbsp rolled oats
fruit spread, honey or maple syrup, to serve

❊ Place 10 paper bun cases in a deep bun tin. Sift the flour and baking powder into a mixing bowl, adding any bran that remains in the sieve. Stir in the sugar and chopped apricots.

❊ Make a well in the centre and add the banana, orange rind, milk, beaten egg and oil. Mix together well to form a thick batter. Divide the batter evenly between the 10 paper cases.

❊ Sprinkle a few rolled oats on top of the buns and bake in a preheated oven, 200°C/400°F/Gas Mark 6, for about 25–30 minutes until well risen and firm to the touch or until a skewer inserted into the centre comes out clean.

❊ Transfer the buns to a wire rack and leave them to cool slightly. Serve while still warm with a little fruit spread.

Chocolate Yogurt Muffins

100 g/3½ oz soft margarine
225 g/8 oz caster sugar
2 large eggs
150 ml/5 fl oz full-fat natural yogurt
5 tbsp milk
275 g/9½ oz plain flour
1 tsp bicarbonate of soda
175 g/6 oz plain chocolate chips

❊ Line 12-cup muffin tin with paper cases.

❊ Place the margarine and sugar in a large mixing bowl and beat with a wooden spoon until light and fluffy. Beat in the eggs, yogurt and milk until combined.

❊ Sift the flour and bicarbonate of soda together and add to the mixture. Stir until just blended.

❊ Stir in the chocolate chips, then spoon the mixture into the paper cases and bake in a preheated oven, 190°C/375°F/ Gas Mark 5, for 25 minutes or until a fine skewer inserted into the centre comes out clean. Leave to cool in the tin for 5 minutes, then turn out on to a wire rack to cool completely.

Oat & Raisin Biscuits

4 tbsp butter, plus extra for greasing
125 g/4½ oz caster sugar
1 egg, beaten
50 g/1¾ oz plain flour
½ tsp salt
½ tsp baking powder
175 g/6 oz rolled oats
125 g/4½ oz raisins
2 tbsp sesame seeds

❊ Lightly grease 2 baking trays with a little butter.

❊ In a large mixing bowl, cream together the butter and sugar until light and fluffy.

❊ Gradually add the beaten egg, beating well after each addition, until thoroughly combined.

❊ Sift the flour, salt and baking powder into the creamed mixture. Mix gently to combine. Add the rolled oats, raisins and sesame seeds and mix together until thoroughly combined.

❊ Place spoonfuls of the mixture, spaced well apart on the prepared baking trays to allow room to expand during cooking, and flatten them slightly with the back of a spoon.

❊ Bake the biscuits in a preheated oven, 180°C/350°F/ Gas Mark 4, for 15 minutes.

❊ Leave the biscuits to cool slightly on the baking trays.

❊ Carefully transfer the biscuits to a wire rack and leave to cool completely before serving.

Shortbread

175 g/6 oz unsalted butter, at room temperature, plus extra for greasing
225 g/8 oz plain flour
55 g/2 oz rice flour
¼ tsp salt
60 g/2 oz caster sugar
25 g/1 oz icing sugar, sifted
¼ tsp vanilla essence (optional)
sugar, for sprinkling

❉ Use a little butter to lightly grease 2 x 20–23-cm/8–9-inch cake or tart tins with removable bases. Sift the plain flour, rice flour and salt into a bowl; set aside.

❉ Using an electric mixer, beat the butter for about 1 minute in a large bowl until creamy. Add the sugars and continue beating for 1–2 minutes until very light and fluffy. If using, beat in the vanilla essence.

❉ Using a wooden spoon, stir the flour mixture into the butter and sugar mixture until well blended. Turn out on to a lightly floured surface and knead lightly to blend completely.

❉ Divide the dough evenly between the 2 tins, smoothing the surface. Using a fork, press 2-cm/³⁄₄-inch radiating lines around the edge of the dough. Lightly sprinkle the surfaces with a little sugar, then prick the surface lightly with the fork.

❉ Using a sharp knife, mark each dough round into 8 wedges. Bake in a preheated oven, 120°C/250°F/Gas Mark ½, for 50–60 minutes until pale golden and crisp. Cool in the tins on a wire rack for about 5 minutes.

❉ Carefully remove the side of each tin and slide the bases on to a heatproof surface. Using the knife marks as a guide, cut each shortbread into 8 wedges while still warm. Cool completely on the wire rack, then store in an airtight container.

Orange Gingernuts

125 g/4^1/$_2$ oz butter, plus extra for greasing
350 g/12 oz self-raising flour
pinch of salt
200 g/7 oz caster sugar

1 tbsp ground ginger
1 tsp bicarbonate of soda
75 g/2^3/$_4$ oz golden syrup
1 egg, beaten
1 tsp grated orange rind

✣ Lightly grease several baking trays with a little butter.

✣ Sift the flour, salt, sugar, ginger and bicarbonate of soda into a large mixing bowl.

✣ Heat the butter and golden syrup together in a saucepan over a very low heat until the butter has melted.

✣ Leave the butter mixture to cool slightly, then pour it on to the dry ingredients.

✣ Add the egg and orange rind and mix thoroughly.

✣ Using your hands, carefully shape the dough into 30 even-sized balls.

✣ Place the balls well apart on the prepared baking trays, then flatten them slightly with your fingers.

✣ Bake in a preheated oven, 160°C/325°F/Gas Mark 3, for 15–20 minutes, then transfer them to a wire rack to cool.

Chocolate & Vanilla Biscuits

125 g/4^1/$_2$ oz soft margarine, plus extra for greasing
175 g/6 oz plain flour
1 tsp baking powder
85 g/3 oz light muscovado sugar

55 g/2 oz caster sugar
^{1}/$_2$ tsp vanilla essence
1 egg
125 g/4^1/$_2$ oz plain chocolate chips

✣ Lightly grease 2 baking trays with a little margarine.

✣ Place all of the ingredients in a large mixing bowl and beat until well combined.

✣ Place tablespoonfuls of the mixture on the baking trays, spacing them well apart to allow for spreading during cooking.

✣ Bake in a preheated oven, 190°C/375°F/Gas Mark 5, for 10–12 minutes, or until the biscuits are golden brown.

✣ Using a palette knife, transfer the biscuits to a wire rack to cool completely.

Crunchy Peanut Biscuits

125 g/4$\frac{1}{2}$ oz butter, softened, plus extra for greasing
150 g/5$\frac{1}{2}$ oz chunky peanut butter
225 g/8 oz granulated sugar
1 egg, lightly beaten

150 g/5$\frac{1}{2}$ oz plain flour
$\frac{1}{2}$ tsp baking powder
pinch of salt
75 g/2$\frac{3}{4}$ oz unsalted peanuts, chopped

❊ Lightly grease 2 baking trays with a little butter.

❊ In a large mixing bowl, beat together the butter and peanut butter.

❊ Gradually add the sugar and beat well.

❊ Add the beaten egg to the mixture, a little at a time, until it is thoroughly combined.

❊ Sift the flour, baking powder and salt into the peanut butter mixture.

❊ Add the peanuts and bring all of the ingredients together to form a soft dough. Wrap and leave to chill for about 30 minutes.

❊ Form the dough into 20 balls and place them on the prepared baking trays, about 5 cm/2 inches apart to allow for spreading. Flatten them slightly with your hand.

❊ Bake in a preheated oven, 190°C/375°F/Gas Mark 5, for 15 minutes until golden brown. Transfer the biscuits to a wire rack and leave to cool.

Traditional Apple Pie

750 g–1 kg/1 lb 10 oz–2 lb 4 oz cooking apples, peeled, cored and sliced
about 125 g/4$\frac{1}{2}$ oz brown or white sugar, plus extra for sprinkling
$\frac{1}{2}$–1 tsp ground cinnamon, mixed spice or ground ginger
1–2 tbsp water

SHORTCRUST PASTRY
350 g/12 oz plain flour
pinch of salt
85 g/3 oz butter or margarine
85 g/3 oz white vegetable fat
about 6 tbsp cold water
beaten egg or milk, for glazing

❊ To make the pastry, sift the flour and salt into a mixing bowl. Add the butter and vegetable fat and rub in with your fingertips until the mixture resembles fine breadcrumbs. Add the water and gather the mixture together into a dough. Wrap the dough and chill for 30 minutes.

❊ Roll out almost two-thirds of the pastry thinly and use to line a 20–23-cm/8–9-inch deep pie plate or shallow pie tin.

❊ Mix the apples with the sugar and spice and pack into the pastry case; the filling can come up above the rim. Add the water if liked, particularly if the apples are a dry variety.

❊ Roll out the remaining pastry to form a lid. Dampen the edges of the pie rim with water and position the lid, pressing the edges firmly together. Trim and crimp the edges.

❊ Use the trimmings to cut out leaves or other shapes to decorate the top of the pie, dampen and attach. Glaze the top of the pie with the beaten egg, make 1–2 slits in the top and put the pie on a baking tray.

❊ Bake in a preheated oven, 220°C/425°F/Gas Mark 7, for 20 minutes, then reduce the temperature to 180°C/350°F Gas Mark 4 and cook for about 30 minutes, until the pastry is a light golden brown. Serve hot or cold, sprinkled with sugar.

Sweet Pumpkin Pie

1.8 kg/4 lb sweet pumpkin
55 g/2 oz cold unsalted butter, in small pieces, plus extra for greasing
140 g/5 oz plain flour, plus extra for dusting
$1/4$ tsp baking powder
$1^1/2$ tsp ground cinnamon
$3/4$ tsp ground nutmeg
$3/4$ tsp ground cloves
1 tsp salt
50 g/1$3/4$ oz caster sugar
3 eggs
400 ml/14 fl oz condensed milk
$1/2$ tsp vanilla essence
1 tbsp demerara sugar

STREUSEL TOPPING
2 tbsp plain flour
4 tbsp demerara sugar
1 tsp ground cinnamon
2 tbsp cold unsalted butter, in small pieces
75 g/2$3/4$ oz shelled pecan nuts, chopped
75 g/2$3/4$ oz shelled walnuts, chopped

❖ Preheat the oven to 190°C/375°F/Gas Mark 5. Halve the pumpkin and remove the seeds. Remove and discard the stem and stringy insides. Put the pumpkin halves, face down, in a shallow baking tin and cover with foil. Bake in the preheated oven for 1$1/2$ hours, then remove from the oven and leave to cool. Scoop out the flesh and mash with a potato masher or purée it in a food processor. Drain away any excess liquid. Cover with clingfilm and chill until ready to use. It will keep for 3 days (or several months in a freezer).

❖ To make the pastry, first grease a 23-cm/9-inch round pie dish with butter. Sift the flour and baking powder into a large bowl. Stir in $1/2$ teaspoon of the cinnamon, $1/4$ teaspoon of the nutmeg, $1/4$ tsp of the cloves, $1/2$ tsp of the salt and all the caster sugar. Rub in the butter with your fingertips until the mixture resembles fine breadcrumbs, then make a well in the centre. Lightly beat 1 egg and pour it into the well. Mix together with a wooden spoon, then use your hands to shape the dough into a ball. Place it on a clean work surface lightly dusted with flour, and roll out to a round large enough to line the pie dish. Use it to line the dish, then trim the edge. Cover with clingfilm and chill in the refrigerator for 30 minutes.

❖ Preheat the oven to 220°C/425°F/Gas Mark 7. To make the filling, put the pumpkin purée in a large bowl, then stir in the condensed milk and remaining eggs. Add the remaining spices and salt, then stir in the vanilla essence and demerara sugar. Pour into the pastry case and bake for 15 minutes.

❖ Meanwhile, make the topping. Combine the flour, sugar and cinnamon in a bowl, rub in the butter until crumbly, then stir in the nuts. Remove the pie from the oven and reduce the heat to 180°C/350°F/Gas Mark 4. Sprinkle the topping over the pie, then bake for a further 35 minutes. Remove from the oven and serve hot or cold.

Banana & Mango Tart

PASTRY
20-cm/8-inch baked pastry case

FILLING
2 small ripe bananas
1 mango, sliced

3^1/2 tbsp cornflour
50 g/1^3/4 oz demerara sugar
300 ml/10 fl oz milk
150 ml/5 fl oz coconut milk
1 tsp vanilla essence
toasted coconut chips, to decorate

❊ Slice the bananas and arrange half in the baked pastry case with half of the mango pieces.

❊ Put the cornflour and sugar in a saucepan and mix together. Gradually, stir in the milk and coconut milk until combined and cook over a low heat, beating until the mixture thickens.

❊ Stir in the vanilla essence then pour the mixture over the fruit.

❊ Top with the remaining fruit and toasted coconut chips. Chill in the refrigerator for 1 hour before serving.

Lemon Tart

grated rind of 2–3 large lemons
150 ml/5 fl oz lemon juice
100 g/3^1/2 oz caster sugar
125 ml/4 fl oz double cream or crème fraîche
3 large eggs
3 large egg yolks
icing sugar, for dusting

PASTRY
175 g/6 oz plain flour
^{1}/2 tsp salt
115 g/4 oz cold unsalted butter, diced
1 egg yolk, beaten with 2 tbsp ice-cold water

❊ To make the pastry, sift the flour and salt into a bowl. Using your fingertips, rub the butter into the flour until the mixture resembles fine breadcrumbs. Add the egg yolk and water to the flour and stir to make a dough.

❊ Gather the dough into a ball, wrap in clingfilm and refrigerate for at least 1 hour. Roll out on a lightly floured work surface and use to line a 23–25-cm/9–10-inch loose-based fluted tart tin. Prick the base all over with a fork and line with a sheet of baking paper. Cover the base with baking beans.

❊ Bake in a preheated oven, 200°C/400°F/Gas Mark 6, for 15 minutes until the pastry looks set. Remove the paper and beans. Reduce the oven temperature to 190°C/375°F/Gas Mark 5.

❊ Beat the lemon rind, lemon juice and sugar together until blended. Slowly beat in the cream, then beat in the eggs and yolks, one by one.

❊ Set the pastry case on a baking sheet and pour in the filling. Transfer to the preheated oven and bake for 20 minutes until the filling is set.

❊ Leave to cool completely on a wire rack. Dust the tart with icing sugar. Serve garnished with candied citrus peel.

Boston Chocolate Pie

❋ SERVES 6 ❋

225 g/8 oz shortcrust pastry

CHOCOLATE CARAQUE
225 g/8 oz plain chocolate, broken into squares

FILLING
3 eggs
125 g/4½ oz caster sugar
55 g/2 oz flour, plus extra for dusting

1 tbsp icing sugar
pinch of salt
1 tsp vanilla essence
400 ml/14 fl oz milk
150 ml/5 fl oz natural yogurt
150 g/5½ oz plain chocolate, broken into pieces
2 tbsp kirsch

TOPPING
150 ml/5 fl oz crème fraîche

❋ Roll out the pastry and use to line a 23-cm/9-inch loose-based flan tin. Prick the base with a fork, line with baking paper and fill with baking beans. Bake blind for 20 minutes. Remove the beans and paper and return to the oven for 5 minutes. Remove from the oven and place the tin on a wire rack to cool.

❋ To make the chocolate caraque, put squares of plain chocolate on a heatproof plate over a saucepan of simmering water until melted. Spread on a cool surface with a palette knife. When cool, scrape it into curls with a sharp knife.

❋ To make the filling, whisk the eggs and caster sugar until fluffy. Sift in the flour, icing sugar and salt. Stir in the vanilla essence. Bring the milk and yogurt to the boil in a small saucepan and strain on to the egg mixture. Pour into a double boiler or set over a saucepan of simmering water. Stir until it coats the back of a spoon.

❋ Gently heat the chocolate and kirsch in a small saucepan until melted. Stir into the custard. Remove from the heat and stand the double boiler or bowl in cold water. Leave it to cool. Pour the chocolate mixture into the pastry case. Spread the crème fraîche over the chocolate and arrange the caraque rolls on top.

Baklava

❋ MAKES 25 PIECES ❋

300 g/10 oz walnut halves
200 g/7 oz pistachio nuts
100 g/3½ oz blanched almonds
4 tbsp pine kernels, finely chopped
finely grated rind of 2 large oranges
6 tbsp sesame seeds
1 tbsp sugar
½ tsp ground cinnamon
½ tsp mixed spice

about 300 g/10½ oz butter, melted
23 sheets filo pastry, each 25 cm/10 inches square, thawed, if frozen

SYRUP
600 g/1 lb 5 oz caster sugar
500 ml/18 fl oz water
5 tbsp honey
3 cloves
2 large strips lemon rind

❋ Put the nuts in a food processor and pulse until finely chopped but not ground. Transfer to a bowl and stir in the orange rind, sesame seeds, sugar, cinnamon and mixed spice.

❋ Butter a 25-cm/10-inch square, 5-cm/2-inch deep ovenproof dish. Cut the stacked sheets of filo pastry to size, using a ruler. Keep them covered with a damp tea towel. Place a sheet of filo on the bottom of the dish and brush with melted butter. Top with 7 more sheets, brushing with butter between each layer. Sprinkle with 125 g/4½ oz of the filling. Top with 3 more sheets of filo, brushing each one with butter. Continue until all the filo and filling are used, ending with a top layer of 3 sheets of filo. Brush with butter.

❋ Using a very sharp knife cut the baklava into 25 5-cm/2-inch squares. Brush again with butter. Bake in a preheated oven, 160°C/325°F/Gas Mark 3, for 1 hour.

❋ Meanwhile, place all of the syrup ingredients in a saucepan, stirring to dissolve the sugar. Bring to the boil, then simmer for 15 minutes, without stirring, until a thin syrup forms. Leave to cool.

❋ Remove the baklava from the oven and pour the syrup over the top. Leave to set in the dish.

Pecan Pie

PASTRY
225 g/8 oz plain flour
pinch of salt
115 g/4 oz butter, cut into small
pieces
1 tbsp lard or white vegetable
fat, cut into small pieces
55 g/2 oz golden caster sugar
6 tbsp cold milk

FILLING
3 eggs
225 g/8 oz dark muscovado
sugar
1 tsp vanilla essence
pinch of salt
85 g/3 oz butter, melted
3 tbsp golden syrup
3 tbsp black treacle
225 g/8 oz shelled pecan nuts,
roughly chopped
pecan nut halves, to decorate
whipped cream or vanilla ice
cream, to serve

❖ To make the pastry, sift the flour and salt into a mixing bowl and rub in the butter and lard with your fingertips until the mixture resembles breadcrumbs. Work in the caster sugar and add the milk. Work the mixture together until a soft dough has formed. Wrap the dough and chill in the refrigerator for 30 minutes.

❖ Preheat the oven to 200°C/400°F/Gas Mark 6. Roll out the pastry and use it to line a 23–25-cm/9–10-inch flan tin. Trim off the excess by running the rolling pin over the top of the flan tin. Line with baking paper, then fill with baking beans. Bake blind in the preheated oven for about 20 minutes. Take out of the oven and remove the paper and beans. Reduce the oven temperature to 180°C/350°F/Gas Mark 4. Place a baking tray in the oven.

❖ To make the filling, put the eggs in a bowl and beat lightly. Beat in the sugar, vanilla essence and salt. Stir in the butter, syrup, treacle and chopped nuts. Pour into the pastry case and decorate with the pecan nut halves.

❖ Place on the heated baking tray and bake in the oven for 35–40 minutes until the filling is set. Serve warm or at room temperature with the whipped cream.

Sweet Pear & Ginger Pastries

250 g/9 oz ready-made puff pastry
25 g/1 oz soft brown sugar
25 g/1 oz butter, plus extra for brushing
1 tbsp stem ginger, finely chopped
3 pears, peeled, halved and cored
cream, to serve

❉ On a lightly floured surface, roll out the pastry and cut out 6 x 10-cm/4-inch rounds.

❉ Place the rounds on a large baking tray and leave to chill for 30 minutes.

❉ Cream together the sugar and butter in a small bowl, then stir in the ginger.

❉ Prick the pastry rounds with a fork and spread a little of the ginger mixture on to each one.

❉ Slice the pear halves lengthways, keeping them intact at the tip. Fan out the slices slightly.

❉ Place a fanned-out pear half on top of each pastry round. Make small flutes around the edge of the pastry rounds and brush each pear half with melted butter.

❉ Bake in a preheated oven, 200°C/400°F/Gas Mark 6, for 15–20 minutes or until the pastry is well risen and golden. Serve warm with a little cream.

Plum Cobbler

butter, for greasing
1 kg/2 lb 4 oz plums, stoned and sliced
100 g/3½ oz caster sugar
1 tbsp lemon juice
250 g/9 oz plain flour
2 tsp baking powder
85 g/3 oz granulated sugar
1 egg, beaten
150 ml/5 fl oz buttermilk
85 g/3 oz butter, melted and cooled
double cream, to serve

❉ Lightly grease a 2-litre/3½-pint ovenproof dish with butter.

❉ In a large bowl, mix together the plums, caster sugar, lemon juice and 25 g/1 oz of the flour.

❉ Spoon the coated plums into the bottom of the prepared ovenproof dish, spreading them out evenly.

❉ Sift the remaining flour, together with the baking powder into a large bowl and add the granulated sugar. Stir well to combine.

❉ Add the beaten egg, buttermilk and cooled melted butter. Mix everything gently together to form a soft dough.

❉ Place spoonfuls of the dough on top of the fruit mixture until it is almost completely covered.

❉ Bake the cobbler in a preheated oven, 190°C/375°F/Gas Mark 5, for about 35–40 minutes until the topping is golden brown and the plums are bubbling.

❉ Serve the cobbler piping hot, with the cream.

Mixed Fruit Crumble

2 mangoes, sliced	100 g/3$\frac{1}{2}$ oz margarine
1 paw-paw, seeded and sliced	100 g/3$\frac{1}{2}$ oz light brown sugar
225 g/8 oz fresh pineapple,	175 g/6 oz plain flour
cubed	55 g/2 oz desiccated coconut,
1$\frac{1}{2}$ tsp ground ginger	plus extra to decorate

❋ Place the fruit in a saucepan with $\frac{1}{2}$ teaspoon of the ginger, 2 tablespoons of the margarine and 4 tablespoons of the sugar. Cook over a low heat for 10 minutes until the fruit softens. Spoon the fruit into the base of a shallow ovenproof dish.

❋ Combine the flour and remaining ginger. Rub in the remaining margarine until the mixture resembles fine breadcrumbs. Stir in the remaining sugar and the coconut and spoon over the fruit to cover completely.

❋ Cook the crumble in a preheated oven, 180°C/350°F/ Gas Mark 4, for about 40 minutes or until the top is crisp. Decorate with a sprinkling of desiccated coconut and serve.

Rhubarb & Orange Crumble

500 g/1 lb 2 oz rhubarb	**CRUMBLE**
500 g/1 lb 2 oz Bramley apples	225 g/8 oz plain flour
grated rind and juice of	125 g/4$\frac{1}{2}$ oz butter or
1 orange	margarine
$\frac{1}{2}$–1 tsp ground cinnamon	125 g/4$\frac{1}{2}$ oz light brown sugar
about 85 g/3 oz light soft brown	40–55 g/1$\frac{1}{2}$–2 oz toasted
sugar	chopped hazelnuts
	2 tbsp demerara sugar
	(optional)

❋ Cut the rhubarb into 2.5-cm/1-inch lengths and place in a large saucepan.

❋ Peel, core and slice the apples and add to the rhubarb, together with the orange rind and juice.

❋ Bring to the boil, reduce the heat and simmer for 2–3 minutes, until the fruit begins to soften.

❋ Add the cinnamon and sugar to taste and turn the mixture into an ovenproof dish. Make sure that the dish is not more than two-thirds full.

❋ Sift the flour into a bowl and rub in the butter or margarine until the mixture resembles fine breadcrumbs (this can be done by hand or in a food processor). Stir in the sugar, followed by the nuts.

❋ Spoon the crumble mixture evenly over the fruit in the dish and level the top. Sprinkle with the demerara sugar, if liked.

❋ Cook in a preheated oven, 200°C/400°F/Gas Mark 6, for 30–40 minutes, until the topping is browned. Serve the crumble hot or cold.

Eve's Pudding

6 tbsp butter, plus extra
for greasing
450 g/1 lb cooking apples,
peeled, cored and sliced
85 g/3 oz granulated sugar
1 tbsp lemon juice
55 g/2 oz sultanas
85 g/3 oz caster sugar
1 egg, beaten
150 g/5½ oz self-raising flour
3 tbsp milk
25 g/1 oz flaked almonds
custard or double cream,
to serve

❄ Grease a 900-ml/1½-pint ovenproof dish with butter.

❄ Mix the apples with the granulated sugar, lemon juice and sultanas. Spoon the mixture into the prepared dish.

❄ In a bowl, cream the butter and caster sugar together until pale. Add the beaten egg, a little at a time.

❄ Carefully fold in the self-raising flour and stir in the milk to give a soft, dropping consistency.

❄ Spread the mixture over the apples and sprinkle with the flaked almonds.

❄ Bake in a preheated oven, 180°C/350°F/Gas Mark 4, for 40–45 minutes until the sponge is golden brown.

❄ Serve the pudding piping hot, accompanied by the custard.

Cherry Clafoutis

125 g/4½ oz plain flour
4 eggs, lightly beaten
2 tbsp caster sugar
pinch of salt
600 ml/1 pint milk

butter, for greasing
500 g/1 lb 2 oz black cherries,
  fresh or canned, stoned
3 tbsp brandy
1 tbsp sugar, to decorate

❄ Sift the flour into a large mixing bowl. Make a well in the centre and add the eggs, sugar and salt. Gradually draw in the flour from around the edges and whisk.

❄ Pour in the milk and whisk the batter thoroughly until very smooth.

❄ Thoroughly grease a 1.75-litre/3-pint ovenproof serving dish with butter and pour in about half the batter.

❄ Spoon over the cherries and pour the remaining batter over the top. Sprinkle the brandy over the batter.

❄ Bake in a preheated oven, 180°C/ 350°F/Gas Mark 4, for 40 minutes until risen and golden.

❄ Remove from the oven and sprinkle over the sugar just before serving. Serve warm.

Summer Fruit Clafoutis

500 g/1 lb 2 oz prepared fresh
  assorted soft fruits, such as
  blackberries, raspberries,
  strawberries, blueberries,
  gooseberries, redcurrants
  and blackcurrants
4 tbsp soft fruit liqueur such
  as crème de cassis, kirsch or
  framboise
4 tbsp skimmed milk powder
115 g/4 oz plain flour

pinch of salt
55 g/2 oz caster sugar
2 eggs, beaten
300 ml/10 fl oz skimmed milk
1 tsp vanilla essence
2 tsp caster sugar, for dusting

TO SERVE
assorted soft fruits
low-fat yogurt or natural
  fromage frais

❄ Place the assorted soft fruits in a mixing bowl and spoon over the fruit liqueur. Cover and leave to chill for 1 hour to allow the fruit to macerate.

❄ In a large bowl, combine the skimmed milk powder, flour, salt and sugar. Make a well in the centre and gradually whisk in the eggs, milk and vanilla essence, using a balloon whisk, until smooth. Transfer to a jug and set aside for 30 minutes.

❄ Base-line a 23-cm/9-inch round ovenproof dish with baking paper, and spoon in the fruits and juices.

❄ Whisk the batter again and pour it over the fruits, stand the dish on a baking tray and bake in a preheated oven, 200°C/400°F/Gas Mark 6, for 50 minutes until firm, risen and golden brown.

❄ Dust with the caster sugar. Serve immediately with the extra fruits and yogurt.

Cherry Pancakes

FILLING	PANCAKES
400 g/14 oz canned stoned cherries	100 g/3½ oz plain flour
½ tsp almond essence	pinch of salt
½ tsp mixed spice	2 tbsp chopped mint
2 tbsp cornflour	1 egg
	300 ml/10 fl oz milk
	vegetable oil, for frying
	icing sugar and toasted flaked almonds, to decorate

❄ Put the cherries and 300 ml/10 fl oz of the can juices in a saucepan with the almond essence and mixed spice. Stir in the cornflour and bring to the boil, stirring until thickened and clear. Set aside.

❄ To make the pancakes, sift the flour into a bowl with the salt. Add the chopped mint and make a well in the centre. Gradually beat in the egg and milk to make a smooth batter.

❄ Heat 1 tablespoon of the oil in an 18-cm/7-inch frying pan; pour off the oil when hot. Add just enough batter to coat the base of the pan and cook for 1–2 minutes or until the underside is cooked. Flip the pancake over and cook for 1 minute. Remove from the pan and keep warm. Heat 1 tablespoon of the oil in the pan again and repeat to use up all the batter.

❄ Spoon a quarter of the cherry filling on to a quarter of each pancake and fold the pancake into a cone shape. Dust with the icing sugar and sprinkle the flaked almonds over the top. Serve immediately.

Coconut Crêpes

115 g/4 oz rice flour	4 tbsp desiccated coconut
3 tbsp caster sugar	vegetable oil, for frying
pinch of salt	2 tbsp palm sugar, to decorate
2 eggs	fresh mango or banana,
600 ml/1 pint coconut milk	to serve

❄ Place the rice flour, sugar and salt in a bowl and add the eggs and coconut milk, whisking until a smooth batter forms. Alternatively, place all the ingredients in a blender and process to a smooth batter. Beat in half the coconut.

❄ Heat a small amount of oil in a wide heavy-based frying pan. Pour in a little batter, swirling the pan to cover the surface thinly and evenly. Cook until pale golden underneath.

❄ Turn or toss the crêpe and cook the other side until light golden brown.

❄ Turn out the crêpes and keep hot while using the remaining batter to make a total of 8 crêpes.

❄ Serve the crêpes folded or loosely rolled, with slices of mango and sprinkled with the palm sugar and the remaining coconut, toasted.

Exotic Fruit Crêpes

❄ SERVES 4 ❄

BATTER
125 g/4¹/₂ oz plain flour
pinch of salt
1 egg
1 egg yolk
300 ml/10 fl oz coconut milk
4 tsp vegetable oil, plus extra
for frying

FILLING
1 banana
1 paw-paw
juice of 1 lime
2 passion fruit
1 mango, peeled, stoned and
sliced
4 lychees, stoned and halved
1–2 tbsp clear honey
flowers or sprigs of fresh mint,
to decorate

❄ Sift the flour and salt into a bowl. Make a well in the centre and add the egg, egg yolk and a little of the coconut milk. Gradually draw the flour into the egg mixture, beating well and gradually adding the remaining coconut milk to make a smooth batter. Stir in the oil. Cover and chill for 30 minutes.

❄ Peel and slice the banana and place in a bowl. Peel and slice the paw-paw, discarding the seeds. Add to the banana with the lime juice and mix well. Cut the passion fruit in half and scoop out the flesh and seeds into the fruit bowl. Stir in the mango, lychees and honey.

❄ Heat a little oil in a 15-cm/6-inch frying pan. Pour in just enough of the crêpe batter to cover the base of the pan and tilt so that it spreads thinly and evenly. Cook until the crêpe is just set and the underside is lightly browned, then turn and briefly cook the other side. Remove from the pan and keep warm. Repeat with the remaining batter to make a total of 8 crêpes.

❄ To serve, place a little of the prepared fruit filling along the centre of each crêpe and then roll it into a cone shape. Lay seam side down on warmed serving plates, decorate with the flowers and serve.

Lace Crêpes with Fruit

3 egg whites
4 tbsp cornflour
3 tbsp cold water
1 tsp vegetable oil

FRUIT FILLING
350 g/12 oz fresh lychees
¼ Galia melon

175 g/6 oz seedless green
 grapes
1-cm/½-inch piece of fresh
 root ginger
2 pieces of stem ginger in
 syrup
2 tbsp ginger wine or dry
 sherry.

❄ To make the fruit filling, peel the lychees and remove the stones. Place the lychees in a bowl. Scoop out the seeds from the melon and remove the skin. Cut the melon flesh into small pieces and place in the bowl.

❄ Wash and dry the grapes, remove the stalks and add to the bowl. Peel the root ginger and cut into thin shreds or grate finely. Drain the stem ginger pieces, reserving the syrup, and chop the ginger pieces finely.

❄ Stir the root and stem ginger into the bowl with the ginger wine or sherry and the stem ginger syrup. Cover with clingfilm and set aside.

❄ Meanwhile, prepare the crêpes. In a small jug, combine the egg whites, cornflour and cold water, stirring until very smooth.

❄ Brush a small non-stick crêpe pan with oil and heat until hot. Drizzle the surface of the pan with a quarter of the cornflour mixture to give a lacy effect. Cook for a few seconds until set, then carefully lift out and transfer to absorbent kitchen paper to drain. Set aside and keep warm. Repeat with the remaining mixture to make 4 crêpes in total.

❄ To serve, place a crêpe on each of 4 serving plates and top with the fruit filling. Fold over the crêpes and serve hot.

Raspberry Shortcake

100 g/3½ oz butter, cut into
 cubes, plus extra for greasing
175 g/6 oz self-raising flour
85 g/3 oz caster sugar
1 egg yolk
1 tbsp rosewater
600 ml/1 pint whipping cream,
 lightly whipped

225 g/8 oz raspberries, plus a
 few extra for decoration

TO DECORATE
icing sugar
fresh mint leaves

❄ Lightly grease 2 baking trays with a little butter.

❄ To make the shortcake, sift the self-raising flour into a bowl. Add the butter and rub it into the flour with your fingertips until the mixture resembles fine breadcrumbs.

❄ Stir the caster sugar, egg yolk and rose water into the mixture and bring together with your fingers to form a soft dough. Divide the dough in half.

❄ Roll out each piece of dough to a 20-cm/8-inch round on a lightly floured surface. Carefully lift each one with the rolling pin on to the prepared baking trays. Gently crimp the edges of the dough with your finger.

❄ Bake in a preheated oven, 190°C/375°F/Gas Mark 5, for 15 minutes until lightly golden brown. Transfer the shortcakes to a wire rack and leave them to cool completely.

❄ Mix the lightly whipped cream with the raspberries and spoon the mixture on top of one of the shortcakes, spreading it out evenly to cover completely. Place the other shortcake round on top. Dust the raspberry shortcake with a little icing sugar and decorate with the extra raspberries and mint leaves.

Chocolate Fudge Pudding

50 g/1³/4 oz margarine, plus extra for greasing
75 g/2³/4 oz light brown sugar
2 eggs, beaten
350 ml/12 fl oz milk
50 g/1³/4 oz chopped walnuts
40 g/1¹/2 oz plain flour
2 tbsp cocoa powder
icing sugar and cocoa powder, to dust

❉ Lightly grease a 1-litre/1³/4-pint ovenproof dish with margarine.

❉ Cream together the margarine and sugar in a large mixing bowl until fluffy. Beat in the eggs.

❉ Gradually stir in the milk and add the walnuts, stirring to mix.

❉ Sift the flour and cocoa powder into the mixture and fold in gently with a metal spoon until well mixed.

❉ Spoon the mixture into the dish and cook in a preheated oven, 180°C/350°F/Gas Mark 4, for 35–40 minutes, or until the sponge is cooked.

❉ Dust with sugar and cocoa powder and serve.

Strawberry Roulade

3 large eggs
125 g/4¹/2 oz caster sugar
125 g/4¹/2 oz plain flour
1 tbsp hot water

FILLING
200 ml/7 fl oz natural fromage frais
1 tsp almond essence
225 g/8 oz small strawberries
15 g/¹/2 oz toasted almonds, flaked
1 tsp icing sugar

❉ Preheat the oven to 220°C/425°F/Gas Mark 7. Line a 35 x 25-cm/14 x 10-inch Swiss roll tin with baking paper. Place the eggs in a mixing bowl with the caster sugar. Place the bowl over a saucepan of hot water and whisk until pale and thick.

❉ Remove the bowl from the pan. Sift in the flour and fold into the eggs with the hot water. Pour the mixture into the tin and bake for 8–10 minutes, until golden and set.

❉ Transfer the mixture to a sheet of baking paper. Peel off the lining paper and roll up the sponge tightly along with the baking paper. Wrap in a tea towel and let cool.

❉ Mix together the fromage frais and the almond essence. Reserving a few strawberries for decoration, wash, hull and slice the rest. Leave the mixture to chill in the refrigerator until required.

❉ Unroll the sponge, spread the fromage frais mixture over the sponge and sprinkle with strawberries. Roll the sponge up again and transfer to a serving plate. Sprinkle with almonds and lightly dust with icing sugar. Decorate with the reserved strawberries.

Mascarpone Cheesecake

50 g/1¾ oz unsalted butter, plus extra for greasing
150 g/5½ oz ginger biscuits, crushed
25 g/1 oz stem ginger, chopped
500 g/1 lb 2 oz mascarpone cheese
finely grated rind and juice of 2 lemons
100 g/3½ oz caster sugar
2 large eggs, separated
fruit coulis, to serve

❊ Grease a 25-cm/10-inch springform or loose-based cake tin with a little butter and base-line with baking paper.

❊ Melt the butter in a saucepan and stir in the crushed biscuits and chopped ginger. Use the mixture to line the tin, pressing the mixture about 6 mm/¼ inch up the sides.

❊ Beat together the cheese, lemon rind and juice, sugar and egg yolks until quite smooth.

❊ Whisk the egg whites until they are stiff and fold into the cheese and lemon mixture.

❊ Pour the mixture into the tin and bake in a preheated oven, 180°C/350°F/Gas Mark 4, for 35–45 minutes until just set. Don't worry if it cracks or sinks – this is quite normal.

❊ Leave the cheesecake in the tin to cool. Serve with the fruit coulis.

Berry Cheesecake

❉ **SERVES 8** ❉

BASE	125 ml/4 fl oz evaporated milk
6 tbsp margarine	1 egg
175 g/6 oz oatmeal biscuits	6 tbsp light brown sugar
55 g/2 oz desiccated coconut	450 g/1 lb soft cream cheese
	350 g/12 oz mixed berries
TOPPING	2 tbsp clear honey
1$\frac{1}{2}$ tsp gelatine	
9 tbsp cold water	

❉ Melt the margarine in a saucepan. Put the biscuits in a food processor and process until crushed or crush finely with a rolling pin. Stir the crumbs into the margarine with the coconut.

❉ Press the mixture evenly into a base-lined 20-cm/8-inch springform tin and set aside to chill in the refrigerator.

❉ To make the topping, sprinkle the gelatine over the water and stir to dissolve. Bring to the boil and boil for 2 minutes. Set aside to cool slightly.

❉ Beat the milk with the egg, sugar and cream cheese until smooth. Stir in 55 g/2 oz of the berries. Add the gelatine in a thin stream, stirring constantly.

❉ Spoon the mixture on to the biscuit base and return to the refrigerator to chill for 2 hours or until set.

❉ Remove the cheesecake from the tin and transfer to a serving plate. Arrange the remaining berries on top of the cheesecake and drizzle the honey over the top. Serve.

Tiramisù Layers

❉ **SERVES 4** ❉

300 g/10$\frac{1}{2}$ oz plain chocolate	6 tbsp dark rum or brandy
400 g/14 oz mascarpone cheese	36 sponge fingers,
150 ml/5 fl oz double cream,	about 40 g/1$\frac{1}{2}$ oz cocoa
whipped until it just holds	powder, for dusting
its shape	
400 ml/14 fl oz black coffee	
with 50 g/1$\frac{3}{4}$ oz caster	
sugar, cooled	

❉ Melt the chocolate in a bowl set over a saucepan of simmering water, stirring occasionally. Leave the chocolate to cool slightly, then stir it into the mascarpone and cream.

❉ Mix the coffee and rum together in a bowl. Dip the sponge fingers into the mixture briefly so that they absorb the coffee and rum liquid but do not become soggy.

❉ Place 3 sponge fingers on 4 serving plates.

❉ Spoon a layer of the mascarpone and chocolate mixture over the sponge fingers.

❉ Place 3 more sponge fingers on top of the mascarpone layer. Spread another layer of mascarpone and chocolate mixture and place 3 more sponge fingers on top.

❉ Leave the tiramisù to chill in the refrigerator for at least 1 hour. Dust all over with a little cocoa powder just before serving.

Chocolate Meringues

4–5 egg whites, at room temperature
pinch of salt
1/4 tsp cream of tartar
1/4–1/2 tsp vanilla essence
175–200 g/6–7 oz caster sugar
1/8–1/4 tsp ground cinnamon

115 g/4 oz bitter or plain chocolate, grated

TO SERVE
ground cinnamon
115 g/4 oz strawberries
chocolate-flavoured cream

❄ Whisk the egg whites until they are foamy, then add the salt and cream of tartar and whisk until very stiff. Whisk in the vanilla, then slowly whisk in the sugar, a small amount at a time, until the meringue is shiny and stiff. This should take about 3 minutes by hand, and less than a minute with an electric whisk.

❄ Whisk in the cinnamon and grated chocolate. Spoon or pipe mounds of about 2 tablespoons, spaced well apart, on to an ungreased non-stick baking tray.

❄ Place in a preheated oven, 150°C/300°F/Gas Mark 2, and cook for 2 hours until set and dry.

❄ Carefully remove the meringues from the baking tray with a palette knife. If the meringues are still too moist and soft, return them to the oven to firm up and dry out a little more. Allow to cool completely on a wire rack.

❄ Serve the meringues, dusted with a sprinkling of cinnamon and accompanied by strawberries and chocolate-flavoured cream.

Pavlova

6 egg whites
1/2 tsp cream of tartar
225 g/8 oz caster sugar
1 tsp vanilla flavouring
300 ml/10 fl oz whipping cream

400 g/14 oz strawberries, hulled and halved
3 tbsp orange-flavoured liqueur
fruit of your choice, to decorate

❄ Line a baking tray with baking paper and mark out a circle to fit your serving plate. The recipe makes enough meringue for a 30-cm/12-inch circle.

❄ Whisk the egg whites and cream of tartar together until stiff. Gradually beat in the caster sugar and vanilla flavouring. Whisk well until glossy and stiff.

❄ Either spoon or pipe the meringue mixture into the marked circle, in an even layer, slightly raised at the edges, to form a dip in the centre.

❄ Baking the meringue depends on your preference. If you like a soft chewy meringue, bake at 140°C/275°F/ Gas Mark 1 for about 1 1/2 hours until dry but slightly soft in the centre. If you prefer a drier meringue, bake in the oven at 110°C/225°F/Gas Mark 1/4 for 3 hours until dry.

❄ Before serving, whip the cream to a piping consistency, and either spoon or pipe on to the meringue base, leaving a border of meringue all around the edge.

❄ Stir the strawberries and liqueur together and spoon on to the cream. Decorate with fruit of your choice.

Brown Sugar Pavlovas

2 large egg whites
1 tsp cornflour
1 tsp raspberry vinegar
100 g/3 1/2 oz light muscovado sugar, crushed free of lumps
2 tbsp redcurrant jelly
2 tbsp unsweetened orange juice
150 ml/5 fl oz low-fat natural fromage frais
175 g/6 oz raspberries, thawed, if frozen
rose-scented geranium leaves, to decorate (optional)

❖ Preheat the oven to 150°C/300°F/Gas Mark 2. Line a large baking tray with baking paper. Whisk the egg whites until very stiff and dry. Fold in the cornflour and vinegar.

❖ Gradually whisk in the sugar, a spoonful at a time, until the mixture is thick and glossy.

❖ Divide the mixture in 4 and spoon on to the baking tray, spacing well apart. Smooth into rounds, about 10 cm/4 inches across, and bake in the oven for 40–45 minutes until lightly browned and crisp. Leave to cool on the baking tray.

❖ Place the redcurrant jelly and orange juice in a small pan and heat, stirring, until melted. Leave to cool for 10 minutes.

❖ Using a palette knife, carefully remove each pavlova from the baking paper and transfer to a serving plate. Top with the fromage frais and the raspberries. Brush the fruit with the redcurrant jelly mixture, and decorate with the geranium leaves, if using.

Satsuma & Pecan Pavlova

❄ **SERVES 8** ❄

4 egg whites	55 g/2 oz pecan nuts
225 g/8 oz light muscovado sugar	4 satsumas, peeled
300 ml/10 fl oz double or whipping cream	1 passion fruit or pomegranate

❄ Line 2 baking trays with non-stick baking paper or greaseproof paper. Draw a 23-cm/9-inch circle on one of the trays.

❄ Whisk the egg whites in a large grease-free bowl until stiff. Add the sugar gradually, continuing to whisk until the mixture is very glossy.

❄ Pipe or spoon a layer of meringue mixture on to the circle marked on the baking paper; then pipe large rosettes or place spoonfuls on top of the meringue's outer edge. Pipe any remaining meringue mixture in tiny rosettes on to the second baking tray.

❄ Bake in a preheated oven, 140°C/275°F/Gas Mark 1, for 2–3 hours, making sure that the oven is well-ventilated by using a folded tea towel to keep the door slightly open. Remove from the oven and leave to cool completely. When cold, peel off the baking paper carefully.

❄ Whip the cream in a large chilled bowl until thick. Spoon about one-third into a piping bag, fitted with a star nozzle. Reserve a few pecan nuts and 1 satsuma for decoration. Chop the remaining nuts and fruit, and fold into the remaining cream.

❄ Pile on top of the meringue base and decorate with the tiny meringue rosettes, piped cream, satsuma segments and pecan nuts. Scoop the seeds from the passion fruit or pomegranate with a teaspoon and sprinkle them on top.

Ginger & Apricot Alaskas

❄ **SERVES 2** ❄

2 slices rich, dark ginger cake, about 2 cm/¾ inch thick	4 tbsp orange juice or water
1–2 tbsp ginger wine or rum	15 g/½ oz flaked almonds
1 eating apple	2 small egg whites
6 dried apricots, chopped	100 g/3½ oz caster sugar

❄ Place each slice of ginger cake on an ovenproof plate and sprinkle with the ginger wine or rum.

❄ Quarter, core and slice the apple into a small saucepan. Add the chopped apricots and orange juice or water, and simmer over a low heat for about 5 minutes or until tender.

❄ Stir the almonds into the fruit and spoon the mixture equally over the slices of soaked cake, piling it up in the centre.

❄ Whisk the egg whites until very stiff and dry, then whisk in the sugar, a little at a time, making sure the meringue has become stiff again before adding any more sugar.

❄ Either pipe or spread the meringue over the fruit and cake, making sure that both are completely covered.

❄ Place in a preheated oven, 200°C/400°F/Gas Mark 6, for 4–5 minutes until golden brown. Serve hot.

Baked Coconut Rice Pudding

85 g/3 oz short or round-grain pudding rice
600 ml/1 pint coconut milk
300 ml/10 fl oz milk
1 large strip lime rind

55 g/2 oz caster sugar
knob of butter
pinch of ground star anise (optional)
fresh or stewed fruit, to serve

❀ Lightly grease a 1.4-litre/2½-pint shallow ovenproof dish.

❀ Mix the pudding rice with the coconut milk, milk, lime rind and caster sugar until all the ingredients are well blended.

❀ Pour the rice mixture into the greased ovenproof dish and dot the surface with a little butter. Bake in the oven for about 30 minutes.

❀ Remove the dish from the oven. Remove and discard the strip of lime from the rice pudding.

❀ Stir the pudding well, add the pinch of ground star anise, if using, return to the oven and cook for a further 1–2 hours or until almost all the milk has been absorbed and a golden brown skin has baked on the top of the pudding.

❀ Cover the top of the pudding with foil if it starts to brown too much towards the end of the cooking time.

❀ Serve warm, or chilled if you prefer, with the fruit.

Passion Fruit Rice

175 g/6 oz jasmine fragrant rice
600 ml/1 pint milk
125 g/4½ oz caster sugar
6 cardamom pods, split open
1 dried bay leaf

1 cinnamon stick
150 ml/5 fl oz double cream, whipped
4 passion fruit
soft berry fruits, to decorate

❀ Place the rice in a large bowl with the milk, sugar, cardamom pods, bay leaf and cinnamon stick. Cover and cook in a microwave oven on MEDIUM power for 25–30 minutes, stirring occasionally. The rice should be just tender and have absorbed most of the milk. Add a little extra milk, if necessary.

❀ Leave the rice to cool, still covered. Remove the bay leaf, cardamom husks and cinnamon stick.

❀ Gently fold the cream into the cooled rice mixture.

❀ Halve the each passion fruit and scoop out the centres into a bowl.

❀ Layer the rice with the passion fruit in 4 tall glasses, finishing with a layer of passion fruit. Leave to chill in the refrigerator for 30 minutes.

❀ Decorate the rice with the soft berry fruits and serve immediately.

Orange-Scented Rice

140 g/5 oz round-grain rice
225 ml/8 fl oz freshly squeezed
orange juice
pinch of salt
500 ml/18 fl oz milk
1 vanilla pod, split
5-cm/2-inch piece of root
ginger, gently bruised
200 g/7 oz sugar
50 ml/2 fl oz double cream
4 tbsp orange-flavoured liqueur
2 tbsp butter
4–6 seedless oranges
2 pieces of stem ginger, sliced
thinly, plus 2 tbsp ginger
syrup from the jar
ground ginger, for dusting

❋ Put the rice in a pan with the orange juice and salt. Bring to the boil, skimming off any foam. Reduce the heat and simmer for about 10 minutes, stirring occasionally, until the juice is absorbed.

❋ Gradually stir in the milk, add the vanilla pod and root ginger and simmer for 30 minutes, stirring frequently, until the milk is absorbed and the rice is very tender. Remove from the heat. Remove the vanilla pod and ginger.

❋ Stir in half the sugar, half the cream, the orange liqueur and butter until the sugar is dissolved and the butter is melted. Set aside to cool, then stir in the remaining cream and pour into a bowl. Cover and set aside at room temperature.

❋ Pare the rind from the oranges and reserve. Working over a bowl to catch the juices, remove the pith from all the oranges. Cut out the segments and drop into the bowl. Stir in the stem ginger and syrup. Chill in the refrigerator.

❋ Cut the pared orange rind into thin strips and blanch for 1 minute. Drain and rinse. Bring 225 ml/8 fl oz water to the boil with the remaining sugar. Add the rind strips and simmer gently until the syrup is reduced by half. Set aside to cool.

❋ Serve the rice with the chilled oranges and top with the caramelized orange rind strips.

Rice & Banana Brûlée

❊ **SERVES 2** ❊

400 g/14 oz canned creamed rice pudding	2 tsp ginger syrup from the jar
grated rind of 1/2 orange	40 g/1 1/2 oz raisins
2 pieces of stem ginger, finely chopped	1–2 bananas
	1–2 tsp lemon juice
	4–5 tbsp demerara sugar

❊ Empty the can of rice pudding into a bowl and stir in the grated orange rind, ginger, ginger syrup and raisins.

❊ Cut the bananas diagonally into slices, toss them in the lemon juice to prevent them discolouring, then drain and divide the slices between 2 individual flameproof dishes.

❊ Spoon the rice mixture in an even layer over the bananas so that the dishes are almost full.

❊ Sprinkle an even layer of sugar over the rice in each dish.

❊ Place the dishes under a preheated moderate grill and heat until the sugar melts, watching carefully that the sugar does not burn.

❊ Set aside to cool until the caramel sets, then chill in the refrigerator until ready to serve. Tap the caramel with the back of a spoon to break it.

Mixed Fruit Brûlées

❊ **SERVES 4** ❊

450 g/1 lb prepared assorted summer fruits (such as strawberries, raspberries, blackcurrants, redcurrants and cherries), thawed , if frozen	150 ml/5 fl oz double cream
	150 ml/5 fl oz natural fromage frais
	1 tsp vanilla essence
	4 tbsp demerara sugar

❊ Divide the prepared summer fruits evenly between 4 small heatproof ramekin dishes.

❊ Mix together the cream, fromage frais and vanilla essence until well combined.

❊ Generously spoon the mixture over the fruit in the ramekin dishes, to cover the fruit completely.

❊ Preheat the grill to hot.

❊ Top each serving with 1 teaspoon of the demerara sugar and grill the desserts for 2–3 minutes, until the sugar melts and begins to caramelize. Leave to stand for a couple of minutes before serving.

Apricot Brûlée

125 g/4¹/₂ oz unsulphured
dried apricots
150 ml/5 fl oz orange juice
4 egg yolks
2 tbsp caster sugar

150 ml/5 fl oz natural yogurt
150 ml/5 fl oz double cream
1 tsp vanilla essence
85 g/3 oz demerara sugar
meringues, to serve (optional)

❉ Place the apricots and orange juice in a bowl and set aside to soak for at least 1 hour. Pour into a small saucepan, bring slowly to the boil and simmer for 20 minutes. Process in a blender or food processor or chop very finely and push through a sieve.

❉ Beat together the egg yolks and sugar until the mixture is light and fluffy. Place the yogurt in a small saucepan, add the cream and vanilla and bring to the boil over a low heat.

❉ Pour the yogurt mixture over the eggs, beating all the time, then transfer to the top of a double boiler or place the bowl over a saucepan of simmering water. Stir until the custard thickens. Divide the apricot mixture between 6 ramekins and carefully pour on the custard. Cool, then chill in the refrigerator for at least 1 hour.

❉ Sprinkle the demerara sugar evenly over the custard and place under a preheated grill until the sugar caramelizes. Set aside to cool. To serve the brûlée, crack the hard caramel topping with the back of a tablespoon.

Creamy Fruit Parfait

225 g/8 oz cherries
2 large peaches
2 large apricots
700 ml/1¹/₄ pints Greek-style
yogurt, or natural thick
yogurt

55 g/2 oz walnut halves
2 tbsp flower-scented honey
fresh redcurrants or berries,
to decorate (optional)

❉ To prepare the fruit, use a cherry stoner to remove the cherry stones. Cut each cherry in half. Cut the peaches and apricots in half lengthways and remove the stones, then finely chop the flesh of all the fruit.

❉ Place the fruit in a bowl and gently stir together.

❉ Spoon one-third of the yogurt into an attractive glass serving bowl. Top with half the fruit mixture.

❉ Repeat with another layer of yogurt and fruit and, finally, top with the remaining yogurt.

❉ Place the walnuts in a small food processor and pulse until chopped, but not finely ground. Sprinkle the walnuts over the top layer of the yogurt.

❉ Drizzle the honey over the nuts and yogurt. Cover the bowl with clingfilm and chill in the refrigerator for at least 1 hour. Decorate the bowl with a small bunch of redcurrants, if using, just before serving.

Coconut Cream Moulds

CARAMEL

125 g/4¹/₂ oz granulated sugar
150 ml/5 fl oz water

CUSTARD

300 ml/10 fl oz water
85 g/3 oz creamed coconut,
chopped
2 eggs
2 egg yolks
1¹/₂ tbsp caster sugar
300 ml/10 fl oz single cream
sliced banana or slivers of
fresh pineapple, to serve
1–2 tbsp freshly grated or
desiccated coconut, to
sprinkle

❖ Have ready 8 x 150-ml/¹/₄-pint ovenproof dishes. To make the caramel, place the granulated sugar and water in a saucepan and heat gently to dissolve the sugar, then boil rapidly, without stirring, until the mixture turns a rich golden brown.

❖ Immediately remove the pan from the heat and dip the base into a bowl of cold water in order to stop it cooking further. Quickly, but carefully, pour the caramel into the ovenproof dishes to coat the bases.

❖ To make the custard, place the water in the same pan, add the coconut and heat, stirring constantly, until the coconut dissolves. Place the eggs, egg yolks and caster sugar in a bowl and beat well with a fork. Add the hot coconut milk and stir well to dissolve the sugar. Stir in the cream and strain the mixture into a jug.

❖ Arrange the ovenproof dishes in a roasting tin and fill it with enough cold water to come halfway up the sides of the dishes. Pour the custard mixture into the caramel-lined dishes, cover with greaseproof paper or foil and cook in a preheated oven, 150°C/300°F/Gas Mark 2, for about 40 minutes, or until set.

❖ Remove the dishes, set aside to cool and then chill overnight. To serve, run a knife around the edge of each dish and turn out on to a serving plate. Serve with the slices of banana, sprinkled with coconut.

Mocha Swirl Mousse

1 tbsp coffee and chicory essence
2 tsp cocoa powder, plus extra for dusting
1 tsp drinking chocolate powder
150 ml/5 fl oz crème fraîche, plus 4 tsp to serve

2 tsp powdered gelatine
2 tbsp boiling water
2 large egg whites
2 tbsp caster sugar
4 chocolate coffee beans, to serve

❄ Place the coffee and chicory essence in one bowl, and the cocoa powder and drinking chocolate in another bowl. Divide the crème fraîche between the 2 bowls and mix both well.

❄ Dissolve the gelatine in the boiling water and set aside. In a grease-free bowl, whisk the egg whites and sugar until stiff and divide this evenly between the two mixtures.

❄ Divide the dissolved gelatine between the 2 mixtures and, using a large metal spoon, gently fold until well mixed.

❄ Spoon small amounts of the 2 mousses alternately into 4 serving glasses and swirl together gently. Chill for 1 hour or until set.

❄ To serve, top each mousse with a teaspoonful of crème fraîche, a chocolate coffee bean and a light dusting of cocoa powder. Serve immediately.

Chocolate Mousse

100 g/3^1/$_2$ oz plain chocolate, melted
300 ml/10 fl oz natural yogurt
150 ml/5 fl oz Quark
4 tbsp caster sugar
1 tbsp orange juice
1 tbsp brandy
1^1/$_2$ tsp gelatine

9 tbsp cold water
2 large egg whites

TO DECORATE
roughly grated plain and white chocolate
orange rind

❄ Put the melted chocolate, yogurt, Quark, sugar, orange juice and brandy in a food processor or blender and process for 30 seconds. Transfer the mixture to a large bowl.

❄ Sprinkle the gelatine over the water and stir until dissolved.

❄ In a saucepan, bring the gelatine and water to the boil for 2 minutes. Cool slightly, then stir into the chocolate mixture.

❄ Whisk the egg whites until stiff peaks form and fold into the chocolate mixture using a metal spoon.

❄ Line a 500-g/1 lb 2-oz loaf tin with clingfilm. Spoon the mousse into the tin. Chill in the refrigerator for 2 hours until set. Turn out the mousse on to a serving plate, decorate with the grated chocolate and orange rind and serve.

Sweet Mascarpone Mousse

450 g/1 lb mascarpone cheese
4 egg yolks
100 g/3 1/2 oz caster sugar
400 g/14 oz frozen summer
fruits, such as raspberries
and redcurrants

redcurrants, to garnish
amaretti biscuits, to serve

❄ Place the mascarpone cheese in a large mixing bowl. Using a wooden spoon, beat the mascarpone cheese until quite smooth.

❄ Stir the egg yolks and sugar into the mascarpone cheese, mixing well. Leave the mixture to chill in the refrigerator for about 1 hour.

❄ Spoon a layer of the mascarpone mixture into the base of 4 individual serving dishes. Spoon a layer of the summer fruits on top. Repeat the layers in the same order, reserving some of the mascarpone mixture for the top.

❄ Leave the mousses to chill in the refrigerator for about 20 minutes. The fruits should still be slightly frozen.

❄ Serve the mousses with amaretti biscuits.

Chocolate Cheese Pots

300 ml/10 fl oz natural
fromage frais
150 ml/5 fl oz natural yogurt
2 tbsp icing sugar
4 tsp drinking chocolate
powder
4 tsp cocoa powder
1 tsp vanilla essence

2 tbsp dark rum (optional)
2 egg whites
4 chocolate cake decorations

TO SERVE
pieces of kiwi fruit, orange and
banana
strawberries and raspberries

❄ Combine the fromage frais and yogurt in a bowl. Sift in the icing sugar, drinking chocolate and cocoa powder and mix well. Add the vanilla essence and rum, if using.

❄ In a clean bowl, whisk the egg whites until stiff. Using a metal spoon, gently fold the egg whites into the chocolate mixture.

❄ Spoon the fromage frais and chocolate mixture into 4 small china dessert pots and set aside in the refrigerator to chill for about 30 minutes.

❄ Decorate each chocolate cheese pot with a chocolate cake decoration and serve with an assortment of fresh fruit.

Raspberry Fool

300 g/10½ oz fresh raspberries
50 g/1¾ oz icing sugar
300 ml/10 fl oz crème fraîche
½ tsp vanilla essence
2 egg whites
raspberries and lemon balm
leaves, to decorate

❄ Put the raspberries and icing sugar in a food processor or blender and process until smooth. Alternatively, press through a sieve with the back of a spoon.

❄ Reserve 4 tablespoons of crème fraîche to decorate.

❄ Put the vanilla essence and remaining crème fraîche in a bowl and stir in the raspberry mixture.

❄ Whisk the egg whites in a separate mixing bowl until stiff peaks form. Gently fold the egg whites into the raspberry mixture, using a metal spoon, until fully incorporated.

❄ Spoon the raspberry fool into individual serving dishes and chill for at least 1 hour. Decorate with the reserved crème fraîche, raspberries and lemon balm leaves and serve.

Tropical Fruit Fool

1 medium ripe mango
2 kiwi fruit
1 medium banana
2 tbsp lime juice
1/2 tsp finely grated lime rind,
  plus extra to decorate

2 medium egg whites
425 g/15 oz canned custard
1/2 tsp vanilla essence
2 passion fruit

❊ Peel the mango and slice either side of the central stone. Blend the flesh in a food processor or blender until smooth. Alternatively, mash with a fork.

❊ Peel the kiwi fruit, chop the flesh into small pieces and place in a bowl. Peel and chop the banana and add to the bowl. Toss all of the fruit in the lime juice and rind and mix well.

❊ In a grease-free bowl, whisk the egg whites until stiff and then gently fold in the custard and vanilla essence until thoroughly mixed.

❊ In 4 tall glasses, alternately layer the chopped fruit, mango purée and custard mixture, finishing with the custard on top. Leave to chill in the refrigerator for 20 minutes.

❊ Halve the passion fruits, scoop out the seeds and spoon the passion fruit over the fruit fools. Decorate each serving with the extra lime rind and serve.

Peach & Ginger Fool

400 g/14 oz ripe peaches
1 tsp chopped stem ginger
  in syrup
500 ml/18 fl oz natural yogurt

3 tbsp ginger syrup from the
  stem ginger
4 amaretti biscuits, crushed

❊ Put the peaches into a large, heatproof bowl and cover with boiling water. Leave for 1 minute. Using a slotted spoon, lift out the fruit. When cool enough to handle, peel away the skins, remove and discard the stones and roughly chop the flesh. Transfer to a food processor or blender, add the ginger and process to a purée.

❊ Stir the yogurt and ginger syrup together in a bowl.

❊ Spoon a little of the yogurt mixture into 4 serving glasses, then top with a spoonful of the fruit purée. Repeat until the mixtures are used up. Chill in the refrigerator for 3 hours.

❊ Scatter over the crushed amaretti biscuits before serving.

Sticky Sesame Bananas

4 ripe bananas
3 tbsp lemon juice
125 g/4 1/2 oz caster sugar
4 tbsp cold water
2 tbsp sesame seeds
150 ml/5 fl oz low-fat natural fromage frais

1 tbsp icing sugar
1 tsp vanilla essence
lemon and lime rind, shredded, to decorate

❊ Peel the bananas and cut into 5-cm/2-inch pieces. Place the banana pieces in a bowl, spoon over the lemon juice and stir well to coat – this will help prevent the bananas discolouring.

❊ Place the sugar and water in a small saucepan and heat gently, stirring, until the sugar dissolves. Bring to the boil and cook for 5–6 minutes until the mixture turns golden brown.

❊ Meanwhile, drain the bananas and blot with kitchen paper to dry. Line a baking tray or board with baking paper and arrange the bananas, well spaced out, on top.

❊ When the caramel is ready, drizzle it over the bananas, working quickly because the caramel sets almost instantly. Sprinkle the sesame seeds over the caramelized bananas and leave to cool for 10 minutes.

❊ Mix the fromage frais together with the icing sugar and vanilla essence.

❊ Peel the bananas away from the paper and arrange on serving plates.

❊ Serve the fromage frais as a dip, decorated with the shredded lemon and lime rind.

Baked Bananas

4 bananas
2 passion fruit
4 tbsp orange juice
4 tbsp orange-flavoured liqueur

ORANGE-FLAVOURED CREAM
150 ml/5 fl oz double cream
3 tbsp icing sugar
2 tbsp orange-flavoured liqueur

❊ To make the orange-flavoured cream, pour the double cream into a mixing bowl and sprinkle over the icing sugar. Whisk the mixture until it is standing in soft peaks. Carefully fold in the orange-flavoured liqueur and chill in the refrigerator until required.

❊ Peel the bananas and place each one on a sheet of kitchen foil.

❊ Cut the passion fruit in half and squeeze the juice of one half over each banana. Spoon over the orange juice and liqueur.

❊ Fold the kitchen foil over the top of the bananas so that they are completely enclosed.

❊ Place the parcels on a baking sheet and bake the bananas in a preheated oven, 180°C/350°F/Gas Mark 4, for about 10 minutes or until they are just tender (test by inserting a cocktail stick).

❊ Transfer the foil parcels to warmed individual serving plates. Open out the foil parcels at the table and then serve immediately with the chilled orange-flavoured cream.

Apple Fritters

100 g/3¹/₂ oz plain flour
pinch of salt
¹/₂ tsp ground cinnamon
175 ml/6 fl oz warm water
4 tsp vegetable oil
2 egg whites
2 dessert apples, peeled
vegetable or sunflower oil,
for deep-frying
caster sugar and cinnamon,
to decorate

SAUCE
150 ml/5 fl oz natural yogurt
¹/₂ tsp almond essence
2 tsp clear honey

❖ Sift the flour and salt together into a large mixing bowl.

❖ Add the cinnamon and mix well. Stir in the warm water and vegetable oil to make a smooth batter.

❖ Whisk the egg whites until stiff peaks form and fold into the batter.

❖ Using a sharp knife, cut the apples into chunks and dip the pieces of apple into the batter to coat.

❖ Heat the oil for deep-frying to 180°C/350°F or until a cube of bread browns in 30 seconds. Fry the apple pieces, in batches if necessary, for about 3–4 minutes until they are light golden brown and puffy.

❖ Remove the apple fritters from the oil with a slotted spoon and drain on absorbent kitchen paper.

❖ Mix together the caster sugar and the cinnamon and sprinkle over the warm fritters.

❖ Mix the sauce ingredients in a serving bowl and serve with the fritters.

Baked Apples with Berries

4 cooking apples
1 tbsp lemon juice
100 g/3½ oz prepared
blackberries, thawed, if
frozen
15 g/½ oz flaked almonds
½ tsp mixed spice

½ tsp finely grated lemon rind
2 tbsp demerara sugar
300 ml/10 fl oz ruby port
1 cinnamon stick, broken
2 tsp cornflour blended with
2 tbsp cold water
custard, to serve

❉ Preheat the oven to 200°C/400°F/Gas Mark 6. Wash and dry the apples. Using a small sharp knife, make a shallow cut through the skin around the middle of each apple – this will help the apples to cook through.

❉ Core the apples, brush the centres with the lemon juice to prevent discoloration and stand in an ovenproof dish.

❉ In a bowl, mix together the blackberries, almonds, mixed spice, lemon rind and sugar. Using a teaspoon, spoon the mixture into the centre of each apple.

❉ Pour the port into the dish, add the cinnamon stick and bake the apples in the oven for 35–40 minutes or until tender and soft. Drain the cooking juices into a saucepan and keep the apples warm.

❉ Discard the cinnamon and add the cornflour mixture to the cooking juices. Heat, stirring, until thickened.

❉ Heat the custard until piping hot. Pour the sauce over the apples and serve with the custard.

Fresh Fruit Compôte

1 lemon
55 g/2 oz caster sugar
4 tbsp elderflower cordial
300 ml/10 fl oz water
4 dessert apples

225 g/8 oz blackberries
2 fresh figs
150 g/5½ oz Greek-style yogurt
and 2 tbsp clear honey, to
serve

❉ Thinly pare the rind from the lemon using a swivel vegetable peeler. Squeeze the juice. Put the lemon rind and juice into a saucepan, together with the sugar, elderflower cordial and water. Set over a low heat and simmer, uncovered, for 10 minutes.

❉ Core and slice the apples. Add the apples to the saucepan. Simmer gently for about 4–5 minutes, until just tender. Remove the pan from the heat and set aside to cool.

❉ When cold, transfer the apples and syrup to a serving bowl and add the blackberries. Slice and add the figs. Stir gently to mix. Cover and chill in the refrigerator until ready to serve.

❉ Spoon the yogurt into a small serving bowl and drizzle the honey over the top. Cover and chill before serving.

Poached Spiced Pears

4 large, ripe pears	55 g/2 oz raisins
300 ml/10 fl oz orange juice	2 tbsp light brown sugar
2 tsp ground mixed spice	grated orange rind, to decorate

❖ Using an apple corer, core the pears.

❖ Using a sharp knife, peel the pears and cut them in half.

❖ Place the pear halves in a large saucepan.

❖ Add the orange juice, mixed spice, raisins and sugar to the saucepan and heat gently, stirring, until the sugar has dissolved.

❖ Bring the mixture in the pan to the boil and continue to boil for 1 minute.

❖ Reduce the heat to low and leave to simmer for about 10 minutes, or until the pears are cooked, but still fairly firm. Test whether the pears are cooked by inserting the tip of a sharp knife.

❖ Remove the pears from the pan with a slotted spoon and transfer to serving plates.

❖ Decorate with the grated orange rind and serve hot with the syrup.

Pears with Maple Cream

❖ **SERVES 4** ❖

	MAPLE CREAM
1 lemon	115 g/4 oz ricotta cheese
4 firm pears	115 g/4 oz natural fromage
300 ml/10 fl oz dry cider or	frais
unsweetened apple juice	1/2 tsp ground cinnamon
1 cinnamon stick, broken	1/2 tsp grated lemon rind
in half	1 tbsp maple syrup
fresh mint leaves, to decorate	lemon rind, to decorate

❖ Using a vegetable peeler, remove the rind from the lemon and place in a non-stick frying pan. Squeeze the lemon and pour into a shallow bowl.

❖ Peel the pears, then halve and core them. Toss them in the lemon juice to prevent discoloration. Place in the frying pan and pour over the remaining lemon juice.

❖ Add the cider or apple juice and cinnamon stick halves. Gently bring to the boil, reduce the heat so the liquid just simmers and cook the pears for 10 minutes. Remove the pears using a slotted spoon. Reserve the cooking liquid. Place the pears in a warmed heatproof serving dish, cover with foil and put in a warming drawer or low oven.

❖ Return the pan to the heat, bring to the boil, then simmer for 8–10 minutes until reduced by half. Spoon over the pears.

❖ To make the maple cream, combine all the ingredients. Decorate the cream with lemon rind and the pears with mint leaves and serve together.

Spun Sugar Pears

❖ SERVES 4 ❖

150 ml/5 fl oz water
150 ml/5 fl oz sweet Madeira wine
115 g/4 oz caster sugar
2 tbsp lime juice
4 ripe pears, peeled, stalks left on
sprigs of fresh mint, to decorate

SPUN SUGAR
115 g/4 oz caster sugar
3 tbsp water

❖ Combine the water, Madeira, sugar and lime juice in a large bowl. Cover and cook in a microwave oven on HIGH power for 3 minutes. Stir well until the sugar dissolves.

❖ Peel the pears and cut a thin slice from the base of each, so that they stand upright.

❖ Add the pears to the bowl, spooning the wine syrup over them. Cover and cook on HIGH power for about 10 minutes, turning the pears over every few minutes, until they are tender. The cooking time may vary slightly depending on the ripeness of the pears. Set aside to cool, covered, in the syrup.

❖ Remove the cooled pears from the syrup and set aside on serving plates. Cook the syrup, uncovered, on HIGH power for about 15 minutes until reduced by half and thickened slightly. Set aside for 5 minutes. Spoon the syrup over the pears.

❖ To make the spun sugar, combine the sugar and water in a bowl. Cook, uncovered, on HIGH power for $1^{1}/_{2}$ minutes. Stir until the sugar has dissolved completely. Continue to cook on HIGH power for about 5–6 minutes more until the sugar has caramelized.

❖ Wait for the caramel bubbles to subside and set aside for 2 minutes. Dip a teaspoon in the caramel and spin sugar around each pear in a circular motion. Serve decorated with the mint.

Caramelized Oranges

❖ **SERVES 6** ❖

6 large oranges
225 g/8 oz sugar
250 ml/9 fl oz water
6 whole cloves (optional)
2–4 tbsp orange-flavoured
liqueur or brandy

❖ Using a citrus zester or vegetable peeler, pare the rind from 2 of the oranges in narrow strips without any white pith attached. If using a potato peeler, cut the peel into very thin julienne strips.

❖ Put the strips into a small saucepan and barely cover with water. Bring to the boil and simmer for 5 minutes. Drain the strips and reserve the water.

❖ Cut away all the white pith and peel from the remaining oranges using a very sharp knife, then cut horizontally into 4 slices. Reassemble the oranges and hold in place with wooden cocktail sticks. Stand in a heatproof dish.

❖ Put the sugar and water into a heavy-based saucepan with the cloves, if using. Bring to the boil and simmer gently until the sugar has dissolved, then boil hard without stirring until the syrup thickens and begins to colour. Continue to cook until a light golden brown, then quickly remove from the heat and carefully pour in the reserved orange rind liquid.

❖ Place over a gentle heat until the caramel has fully dissolved again, then remove from the heat and add the liqueur or brandy. Pour over the oranges.

❖ Sprinkle the orange strips over the oranges, cover with clingfilm and leave until cold. Chill for at least 3 hours and preferably for 24–48 hours before serving. If time allows, spoon the syrup over the oranges several times while they are marinating. Discard the cocktail stick before serving.

Grilled Cinnamon Oranges

❖ **SERVES 4** ❖

4 large oranges
1 tsp ground cinnamon
1 tbsp demerara sugar

❖ Preheat the grill to high. Cut the oranges in half crossways and discard any pips. Using a sharp or curved grapefruit knife, carefully cut the flesh away from the skin by cutting around the edge of the fruit. Cut across the segments to loosen the flesh into bite-sized pieces that will spoon out easily.

❖ Place the orange halves, cut side up, in a shallow, heatproof dish. Mix the cinnamon with the sugar in a small bowl and sprinkle evenly over the orange halves. Cook under the preheated grill for 3–5 minutes, or until the sugar has caramelized and is golden and bubbling. Serve immediately.

Oranges & Strawberries

3 sweet oranges
225 g/8 oz strawberries
grated rind and juice of 1 lime

1–2 tbsp caster sugar
sprigs of fresh mint, to
decorate

❋ Using a sharp knife, cut a slice off the top and bottom of the oranges, then remove the peel and all the pith, cutting downwards and taking care to retain the shape of the oranges.

❋ Using a small sharp knife, cut down between the membranes of the oranges to remove the segments. Discard the membranes.

❋ Hull the strawberries, pulling the leaves off with a pinching action. Cut into slices, along the length of the strawberries.

❋ Put the oranges and strawberries in a bowl, then sprinkle with the lime rind and juice and sugar. Chill in the refrigerator until ready to serve.

❋ To serve, transfer to a serving bowl and decorate the dish with a sprig of mint.

Poached Peaches

❋ SERVES 4–6 ❋

8–12 ripe peaches
1 large lime
450 ml/16 fl oz fruity, dry white wine
1 tbsp black peppercorns, lightly crushed
7.5-cm/3-inch cinnamon stick, halved

finely pared rind of 1 lemon
100 g/3½ oz caster sugar
sprigs of fresh mint, to decorate

AMARETTO-MASCARPONE CREAM
2 tbsp Amaretto liqueur
250 g/9 oz mascarpone cheese

❋ Fill a large bowl with iced water. Bring a large saucepan of water to the boil. Add the peaches and cook for 1 minute. Using a slotted spoon, immediately transfer the peaches to the iced water to stop the cooking process.

❋ Squeeze the juice from the lime into a bowl of water. Peel the peaches, then quarter each and remove the stone. Drop the fruit into the lime water as it is prepared. Cover and chill in the refrigerator for 24 hours.

❋ Meanwhile, make the Amaretto-mascarpone cream. Stir the amaretto into the mascarpone cheese until thoroughly incorporated, cover and chill.

❋ Place the wine, peppercorns, cinnamon, lemon rind and sugar in a saucepan over a medium–high heat and stir until the sugar dissolves. Boil the syrup for 2 minutes. Reduce to a simmer. Remove the peaches from the refrigerator, add them to the syrup and poach for 2 minutes or until tender – they should not be falling apart.

❋ Using a slotted spoon, transfer the peaches to a bowl. Bring the syrup to the boil and continue boiling until thickened and reduced to about 125 ml/4 fl oz. Pour the syrup into a heatproof bowl and set aside to cool. When cool, pour over the peaches. Cover and chill until required. To serve, decorate with the mint.

Pineapple with Lime

1 pineapple
2 cardamom pods
1 strip of lime rind, thinly pared
4 tbsp water
1 tbsp soft light brown sugar
3 tbsp lime juice
sprigs of fresh mint and
whipped cream, to decorate

❄ Using a sharp knife, cut the top and base from the pineapple, then cut away the peel and remove all the 'eyes' from the flesh. Cut into quarters lengthways and remove the core. Slice the pineapple flesh lengthways.

❄ Crush the cardamom pods in a mortar with a pestle and place in a small saucepan with the lime rind and water. Heat gently until the mixture is boiling, then simmer for 30 seconds.

❄ Remove the pan from the heat and stir in the sugar until it has dissolved, then cover and set aside to infuse for 5 minutes.

❄ Add the lime juice, stir well to mix, then strain the syrup over the pineapple. Chill for 30 minutes.

❄ Arrange the pineapple on a serving dish, spoon the syrup over it and serve, decorated with the mint and the whipped cream.

Mangoes in Syrup

2 large, ripe mangoes   1 lemon grass stalk, chopped
1 lime   3 tbsp caster sugar

❄ Peel the mangoes, then cut away the flesh from either side of the large stones. Slice the flesh into long, thin slices and arrange in a large, chilled serving dish.

❄ Remove a few strips of the rind from the lime and reserve for decoration, then cut the lime in half and squeeze out the juice.

❄ Place the lime juice in a small saucepan with the lemon grass and sugar. Heat gently, without boiling, until the sugar is completely dissolved. Remove from the heat and set aside to cool completely.

❄ Strain the cooled syrup into a jug and pour evenly over the mango slices. Sprinkle with the lime rind strips, cover and chill before serving.

Tropical Salad

1 paw-paw   1 small pineapple or 2 baby
2 tbsp fresh orange juice   pineapples
3 tbsp rum   2 passion fruit
2 bananas   pineapple leaves, to decorate
2 guavas

❄ Cut the paw-paw in half and remove the seeds. Peel and slice the flesh into a bowl.

❄ Pour over the orange juice together with the rum.

❄ Peel and slice the bananas and the guavas, and add both to the bowl.

❄ Cut the top and base from the pineapple, then cut off the skin.

❄ Slice the pineapple flesh, discard the core, cut into pieces and add to the bowl.

❄ Halve the passion fruit, scoop out the flesh with a teaspoon, add to the bowl and stir well to mix.

❄ Spoon the salad into glass bowls and decorate with pineapple leaves.

Green Fruit Salad

1 small Charentais or
honeydew melon
2 green apples
2 kiwi fruit
125 g/4¹/2 oz seedless white
grapes
sprigs of fresh mint, to
decorate

SYRUP
1 lemon
150 ml/5 fl oz white wine
150 ml/5 fl oz water
4 tbsp clear honey
few sprigs of fresh mint

❄ To make the syrup, pare the rind from the lemon using a vegetable peeler.

❄ Put the lemon rind in a saucepan with the white wine, water and clear honey. Bring to the boil, then simmer gently for 10 minutes.

❄ Remove the syrup from the heat. Add the sprigs of mint and leave to cool.

❄ To prepare the fruit, first slice the melon in half and scoop out the seeds. Use a melon baller or a teaspoon to make melon balls.

❄ Core and chop the apples. Peel and slice the kiwi fruit.

❄ Strain the cooled syrup into a serving bowl, removing and reserving the lemon rind and discarding the mint sprigs.

❄ Add the apple, grapes, kiwi fruit and melon to the serving bowl. Stir through gently to mix.

❄ Serve the fruit salad, decorated with sprigs of fresh mint and some of the reserved lemon rind.

Melon & Kiwi Fruit Salad

¹/2 Galia melon
2 kiwi fruit
125 g/4¹/2 oz white seedless
grapes
1 paw-paw, halved
3 tbsp orange-flavoured
liqueur, such as Cointreau

1 tbsp chopped fresh lemon
verbena, lemon balm or mint
sprigs of fresh lemon verbena
or Cape gooseberries,
to decorate

❄ Remove the seeds from the melon, cut it into 4 slices and carefully cut away the skin. Cut the flesh into cubes and put into a bowl.

❄ Peel the kiwi fruit and cut across into slices. Add to the melon with the white grapes.

❄ Remove the seeds from the paw-paw and cut off the skin. Slice the flesh thickly and cut into diagonal pieces. Add to the fruit bowl and mix well.

❄ Mix together the liqueur and the chopped lemon verbena, pour over the fruit and leave to macerate for 1 hour, stirring occasionally.

❄ Spoon the fruit salad into glasses, pour over the juices and decorate with lemon verbena sprigs or Cape gooseberries.

Summary Fruit Salad

85 g/3 oz caster sugar
5 tbsp water
grated rind and juice of
1 small orange
250 g/9 oz redcurrants, stripped
from their stalks
2 tsp arrowroot
2 tbsp port
115 g/4 oz blackberries
115 g/4 oz blueberries
115 g/4 oz strawberries
225 g/8 oz raspberries
fromage frais, to serve

❉ Put the sugar, water and grated orange rind into a heavy-based saucepan and heat gently, stirring until the sugar has dissolved.

❉ Add the redcurrants and orange juice, bring to the boil and simmer gently for 2–3 minutes.

❉ Strain the fruit, reserving the syrup, and put into a bowl.

❉ Blend the arrowroot with a little water. Return the syrup to the pan, add the arrowroot and bring to the boil, stirring constantly, until thickened.

❉ Add the port and mix together well. Then pour the syrup over the redcurrants in the bowl.

❉ Add the blackberries, blueberries, strawberries and raspberries. Mix the fruit together and set aside to cool until required. Serve in individual glass dishes with the fromage frais.

Red Fruits with Frothy Sauce

225 g/8 oz redcurrants, topped
and tailed, thawed, if frozen
225 g/8 oz cranberries
85 g/3 oz light muscovado
sugar
200 ml/7 fl oz unsweetened
apple juice
1 cinnamon stick, broken
300 g/10$\frac{1}{2}$ oz small
strawberries, hulled and
halved

SAUCE
225 g/8 oz raspberries, thawed,
if frozen
2 tbsp fruit cordial
100 g/3$\frac{1}{2}$ oz marshmallows

❖ Place the redcurrants, cranberries and sugar in a pan. Pour in the apple juice and add the cinnamon stick. Bring the mixture to the boil and simmer gently for 10 minutes until the fruit is soft.

❖ Stir the strawberries into the fruit mixture and mix well. Transfer the mixture to a bowl, cover with clingfilm and set aside to chill in the refrigerator for about 1 hour. Remove and discard the cinnamon stick.

❖ Just before serving, make the sauce. Place the raspberries and fruit cordial in a small saucepan, bring to the boil and simmer for 2–3 minutes until the fruit is just beginning to soften. Stir the marshmallows into the raspberry mixture and heat through, stirring, until the marshmallows begin to melt.

❖ Transfer the fruit mixture to serving bowls. Spoon over the raspberry and marshmallow sauce and serve.

Balsamic Strawberries

450 g/1 lb fresh strawberries
2–3 tbsp balsamic vinegar
fresh mint leaves, torn
115–175 g/4–6 oz mascarpone
cheese

pepper
fresh mint leaves, to decorate
(optional)

❖ Wipe the strawberries with a damp cloth, rather than rinsing them, so they do not become soggy. Using a paring knife, cut off the green stalks at the top and then use the tip of the knife to remove the core.

❖ Cut each strawberry in half lengthways or into quarters if large. Transfer to a bowl.

❖ Add the balsamic vinegar, allowing $\frac{1}{2}$ tablespoon per person. Add several twists of pepper, then gently stir together. Cover with clingfilm and chill for up to 4 hours.

❖ Just before serving, stir in the torn mint leaves to taste. Spoon the mascarpone into bowls and spoon the berries on top. Decorate with a few mint leaves, if using. Sprinkle with extra pepper to taste.

Summer Puddings

vegetable oil or butter, for greasing
6–8 thin slices white bread, crusts removed
175 g/6 oz caster sugar
300 ml/10 fl oz water
225 g/8 oz strawberries
500 g/1 lb 2 oz raspberries
175 g/6 oz black- and/or redcurrants
175 g/6 oz blackberries
sprigs of fresh mint, to decorate
pouring cream, to serve

❊ Grease 6 x 150-ml/¼-pint moulds with the oil.

❊ Line the moulds with the most of the bread, cutting it so it fits snugly.

❊ Place the sugar in a saucepan with the water and heat gently, stirring frequently until dissolved, then bring to the boil and boil for 2 minutes.

❊ Reserve 6 large strawberries for decoration. Add half the raspberries and the rest of the fruits to the syrup, cutting the strawberries in half if large, and simmer gently for a few minutes, until beginning to soften but still retaining their shape.

❊ Spoon the fruits and some of the liquid into moulds. Cover with more slices of bread. Spoon a little juice around the sides of the moulds so the bread is well soaked. Cover with a saucer and a heavy weight, leave to cool, then chill thoroughly, preferably overnight.

❊ Process the remaining raspberries in a food processor or blender, or press through a non-metallic strainer. Add enough of the liquid from the fruits to give a coating consistency.

❊ Turn on to serving plates and spoon over the raspberry sauce. Decorate with the mint and the reserved strawberries and serve with the cream.

Winter Puddings

325 g/11½ oz fruit malt loaf
150 g/5½ oz dried apricots, coarsely chopped
85 g/3 oz dried apple, coarsely chopped
425 ml/15 fl oz orange juice
1 tsp grated orange rind, plus extra to decorate
2 tbsp orange liqueur
crème fraîche or natural fromage frais, to serve

❊ Cut the malt loaf into 5-mm/½-inch slices.

❊ Place the apricots, apple and orange juice in a saucepan. Bring to the boil, then simmer for 10 minutes. Remove the fruit using a slotted spoon and reserve the liquid. Place the fruit in a dish and set aside to cool. Stir in the orange rind and orange liqueur.

❊ Line 4 x 175-ml/6-fl oz pudding basins or ramekin dishes with baking paper. Cut 4 circles from the malt loaf slices to fit the tops of the moulds and cut the remaining slices to line them.

❊ Soak the malt loaf slices in the reserved fruit syrup, then arrange around the base and sides of the moulds. Trim away any crusts that overhang the edges. Fill the centres with the chopped fruit, pressing down well, and place the malt loaf circles on top.

❊ Cover with baking paper and weigh down each basin with a 225-g/8-oz weight or a food can. Chill in the refrigerator overnight.

❊ Remove the weight and baking paper. Carefully turn out the puddings on to 4 serving plates. Remove the lining paper.

❊ Decorate with the orange rind and serve the winter puddings with the crème fraîche.

Lemon Granita

rind from 3 lemons
200 ml/7 fl oz lemon juice
100 g/3^1/$_2$ oz caster sugar
500 ml/18 fl oz cold water

❖ Finely grate the lemon rind. Place the lemon rind, lemon juice and caster sugar in a saucepan. Bring the mixture to the boil and leave to simmer for 5–6 minutes or until thick and syrupy. Leave to cool.

❖ Once cooled, stir in the cold water and pour into a shallow freezer container with a lid.

❖ Freeze the granita for 4–5 hours, stirring occasionally to break up the ice. Serve as a palate cleanser between dinner courses.

Citrus Meringue Crush

❈ **SERVES 4** ❈

8 ready-made meringue nests
300 ml/10 fl oz natural yogurt
1/2 tsp finely grated orange rind
1/2 tsp finely grated lemon rind
1/2 tsp finely grated lime rind
2 tbsp orange liqueur or
orange juice

TO DECORATE
sliced kumquat
grated lime rind

SAUCE
55 g/2 oz kumquats
8 tbsp orange juice
2 tbsp lemon juice
2 tbsp lime juice
2 tbsp water
2–3 tsp caster sugar
1 tsp cornflour mixed with
1 tbsp water

❈ Place the meringues in a plastic bag and, with a rolling pin, crush into small pieces. Place in a mixing bowl. Stir in the yogurt, grated citrus rinds and the liqueur or juice. Spoon the mixture into 4 mini-basins and freeze for 1 1/2– 2 hours until firm.

❈ Thinly slice the kumquats for the sauce and place them in a small saucepan with the fruit juices and water. Bring the water gently to the boil and then simmer over a low heat for 3–4 minutes until the kumquats are soft.

❈ Sweeten with sugar to taste, stir in the cornflour mixture and cook, stirring, until thickened.

❈ Pour into a small bowl, cover the surface with clingfilm and set aside to cool – the film will help prevent a skin forming. Chill in the refrigerator until required.

❈ To serve, dip the meringue basins in hot water for 5 seconds, or until they loosen, and turn on to serving plates. Spoon over a little sauce, decorate with the slices of kumquat and lime rind and serve.

Berry Yogurt Ice

❈ **SERVES 4** ❈

125 g/4 1/2 oz raspberries
125 g/4 1/2 oz blackberries
125 g/4 1/2 oz strawberries
1 large egg

175 ml/6 fl oz Greek-style
yogurt
125 ml/4 fl oz red wine
2 1/4 tsp powdered gelatine
fresh berries, to decorate

❈ Place the raspberries, blackberries and strawberries in a blender or food processor and process until a smooth purée forms. Rub the purée through a sieve into a bowl to remove the seeds.

❈ Break the egg and separate the yolk and white into separate bowls. Stir the egg yolk and yogurt into the berry purée and set the egg white aside.

❈ Pour the wine into a heatproof bowl and sprinkle the gelatine on the surface. Leave to stand for 5 minutes to soften, then set the bowl over a saucepan of simmering water until the gelatine has dissolved. Pour the mixture into the berry purée in a steady stream, whisking constantly. Transfer the mixture to a freezerproof container and freeze for 2 hours, or until slushy.

❈ Whisk the egg white in a spotlessly clean, grease-free bowl until very stiff. Remove the berry mixture from the freezer and fold in the egg white. Return to the freezer and freeze for 2 hours, or until firm. To serve, scoop the berry yogurt ice into glass dishes and decorate with fresh berries of your choice.

Icy Fruit Blizzard

❄ **SERVES 4** ❄

1 pineapple, peeled and cut into chunks
1 large piece of deseeded watermelon, peeled and cut into small pieces
225 g/8 oz strawberries or other berries, hulled and whole or sliced
1 mango, peach or nectarine, peeled and sliced
1 banana, peeled and sliced
orange juice
caster sugar

❄ Cover 2 baking trays with a sheet of clingfilm. Arrange the fruit on top and freeze for at least 2 hours or until firm and icy.

❄ Place 1 type of fruit in a food processor and process until it is broken up into small pieces.

❄ Add a little orange juice and sugar, to taste, and continue to process until it forms a granular mixture. Repeat with the remaining fruit. Arrange in chilled bowls and serve immediately.

Rose Ice

❄ **SERVES 4** ❄

400 ml/14 fl oz water
2 tbsp coconut cream
4 tbsp condensed milk
2 tsp rosewater
a few drops pink food colouring (optional)
pink rose petals, to decorate

❄ Place the water in a small saucepan and add the coconut cream. Heat the mixture gently without boiling, stirring.

❄ Remove from the heat and allow to cool. Stir in the condensed milk, rosewater and food colouring, if using.

❄ Pour into a freezer container and freeze for 1–1$\frac{1}{2}$ hours until slushy.

❄ Remove from the freezer and break up the ice crystals with a fork. Return to the freezer and freeze until firm.

❄ Spoon the ice roughly into a pile on a serving dish and scatter with rose petals to serve.

Mango & Lime Sorbet

❖ SERVES 4 ❖

6 tbsp caster sugar
100 ml/3¹/₂ fl oz water
rind of 3 limes, finely grated
2 tbsp coconut cream
2 large, ripe mangoes
135 ml/4¹/₂ fl oz lime juice
curls of fresh coconut, toasted,
to decorate

❖ Place the sugar, water and lime rind in a small saucepan and heat gently, stirring constantly, until the sugar dissolves. Boil rapidly for 2 minutes to reduce slightly, then remove from the heat and strain into a bowl or jug. Stir in the coconut cream and set aside to cool.

❖ Halve the mangoes, remove the stones and peel thinly. Chop the flesh roughly and place in a food processor with the lime juice. Process to a smooth purée and transfer to a small bowl.

❖ Pour the cooled syrup into the mango purée, mixing evenly. Tip into a freezer container and freeze for 1 hour, or until slushy in texture.

❖ Remove the container from the freezer and beat with an electric mixer to break up the ice crystals. Refreeze for a further hour, then remove from the freezer and beat the contents again until smooth.

❖ Cover the container, return to the freezer and freeze until firm. To serve, remove from the freezer and leave at room temperature for about 15 minutes to soften slightly before scooping. Sprinkle with toasted coconut to serve.

377

Lychee & Ginger Sorbet

❖ SERVES 4 ❖

800 g/1 lb 12 oz canned
lychees in syrup
rind of 1 lime, finely grated
2 tbsp lime juice
3 tbsp stem ginger syrup
2 egg whites

TO DECORATE
slices of star fruit
flakes of stem ginger

❖ Drain the lychees, reserving the syrup. Place the fruits in a blender or food processor with the lime rind, juice and stem ginger syrup and process until completely smooth. Transfer to a mixing bowl.

❖ Mix the purée thoroughly with the reserved syrup, then pour into a freezerproof container and freeze for about 1–1¹⁄₂ hours until slushy in texture.

❖ Remove from the freezer and whisk to break up the ice crystals. Whisk the egg whites in a clean, dry bowl until stiff, then quickly and lightly fold them into the iced lychee mixture.

❖ Return to the freezer and freeze until firm. Remove from the freezer 15 minutes before serving to soften slightly. Serve the sorbet in scoops, with the slices of starfruit and the flakes of ginger to decorate.

Blueberry Frozen Yogurt

❖ SERVES 4 ❖

175 g/6 oz fresh blueberries
finely grated rind and juice of
1 orange

3 tbsp maple syrup
500 g/1 lb 2 oz natural yogurt

❖ Put the blueberries and orange juice into a food processor or blender and process to a purée. Strain through a nylon sieve into a bowl or jug.

❖ Stir the maple syrup and yogurt together in a large mixing bowl, then fold in the fruit purée.

❖ Churn the mixture in an ice-cream maker, following the manufacturer's instructions, then freeze for 5–6 hours. If you don't have an ice-cream maker, transfer the mixture to a freezerproof container and freeze for 2 hours. Remove from the freezer, turn out into a bowl and beat until smooth. Return to the freezer and freeze until firm.

Rich Vanilla Ice Cream

600 ml/1 pint double cream   4 eggs, beaten
1 vanilla pod   2 egg yolks
pared rind of 1 lemon   175 g/6 oz caster sugar

❖ Place the cream in a heavy-based saucepan and heat gently, whisking. Add the vanilla pod, lemon rind, eggs and egg yolks and heat until the mixture reaches just below boiling point.

❖ Reduce the heat and cook for 8–10 minutes, whisking the mixture constantly, until thickened.

❖ Stir the sugar into the cream mixture, set aside and leave to cool.

❖ Strain the cream mixture into a bowl through a sieve.

❖ Slit open the vanilla pod, scoop out the tiny black seeds and stir them into the cream.

❖ Pour the ice cream mixture into a shallow freezing container with a lid and freeze overnight until set. The ice cream can be stored in the freezer until required, but transfer it to the refrigerator just before serving to soften slightly.

Chocolate Chip Ice Cream

❖ **SERVES 4** ❖

300 ml/10 fl oz milk   300 ml/10 fl oz natural yogurt
1 vanilla pod   125 g/4½ oz chocolate chip
2 eggs   biscuits, broken into small
2 egg yolks   pieces
55 g/2 oz caster sugar

❖ Pour the milk into a small saucepan, add the vanilla pod and bring to the boil over a low heat. Remove from the heat, cover the pan and set aside to cool.

❖ Beat the eggs and egg yolks in a double boiler or in a bowl set over a saucepan of simmering water. Add the sugar and continue beating until the mixture is pale and creamy.

❖ Reheat the milk to simmering point and strain it over the egg mixture. Stir constantly until the custard is thick enough to coat the back of a spoon. Remove the custard from the heat and stand the pan or bowl in cold water to prevent any further cooking. Wash and dry the vanilla pod for future use.

❖ Stir the yogurt into the cooled custard and beat until it is well blended. When the mixture is thoroughly cold, stir in the broken biscuits.

❖ Transfer the mixture to a chilled metal cake tin or plastic container, cover and freeze for 4 hours. Remove from the freezer every hour, transfer to a chilled bowl and beat vigorously to prevent ice crystals from forming, then return to the freezer. Alternatively, freeze the mixture in an ice-cream maker, following the manufacturer's instructions.

❖ An hour before you are ready to serve the ice cream, transfer it to the main part of the refrigerator to soften slightly. Serve scoops of the ice cream in individual glass bowls.

Brown Bread Ice Cream

175 g/6 oz fresh wholemeal
breadcrumbs
25 g/1 oz finely chopped
walnuts
55 g/2 oz caster sugar
1/2 tsp ground nutmeg
1 tsp finely grated orange rind
450 ml/16 fl oz natural yogurt
2 large egg whites

TO DECORATE
walnut halves
orange slices
fresh mint

❉ Preheat the grill to medium. Mix the breadcrumbs, walnuts and sugar and spread over a sheet of foil in the grill pan.

❉ Grill, stirring frequently, for 5 minutes until crisp and evenly browned (take care that the sugar does not burn). Remove from the heat and leave to cool.

❉ When cool, transfer to a mixing bowl and mix in the nutmeg, orange rind and yogurt. In another bowl, whisk the egg whites until stiff. Gently fold into the breadcrumb mixture, using a metal spoon.

❉ Spoon the mixture into 4 mini basins, smooth over the tops and freeze for 1 1/2–2 hours until firm.

❉ To serve, hold the bases of the moulds in hot water for a few seconds, then immediately turn out the ice cream on to serving plates.

❉ Serve at once, decorated with the walnuts, oranges and fresh mint.

Index

382